Wildlife Photography
On A Budget

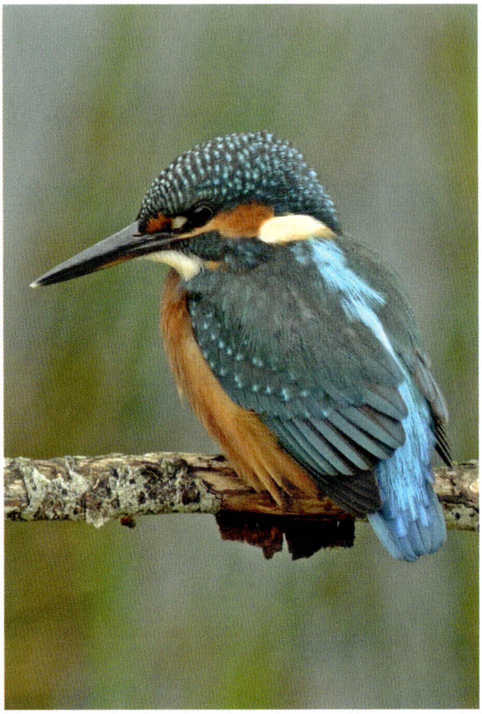

European Kingfisher

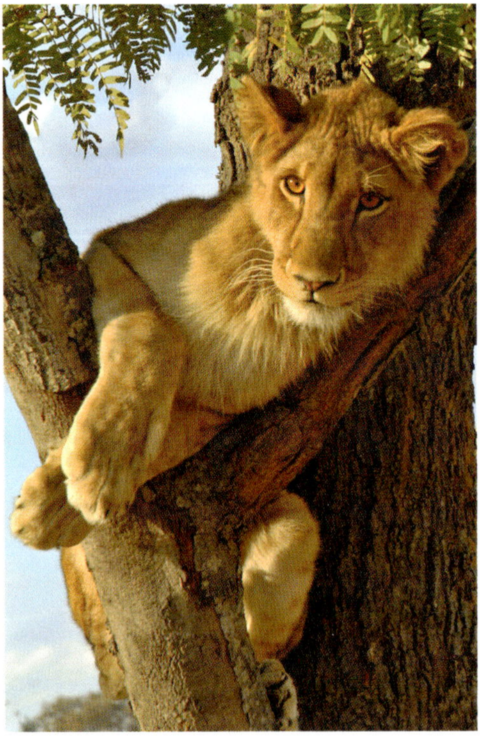

Young Male Lion - Zimbabwe

Wildlife Photography

On A Budget

Second edition
www.naturepicturesworldwide.com

Brian Pettit

First Published in 2012 by Brian Pettit, c/o 18 Okeford Road,
Broadstone, Poole, Dorset BH18 8PA
www.naturepicturesworldwide.com

Second edition published 2014

ISBN 978-0-9572825-1-3

Revised edition April 2014

Produced by Shore Books and Design,
Blackborough End, Norfolk PE32 1SF

Contents

Chapter 1

By Way Of Introduction

This book has been a long time in the coming!

It suffered badly from a fragmented childhood and entered its adult life in the form of diary entries, trip reports, random thoughts of the moment and mini articles written in the evenings to pass the time when travelling. Its development parallels the stages in my own lifecycle from the period when the area behind my ears was still wet and only a light fluff that blew in the wind adorned my upper lip, up to the most recent metamorphic stage from which I have emerged bearded, hirsute and (but you have to look closely) beginning to show the ravages of time.

All these, and other articles written with more studied and deliberate intent, have now undergone a great coming together and have resulted in this book. Its title manifests one of my long held beliefs that too many people are put off Wildlife Photography as a serious pursuit because of fears that its undertaking would either stretch their various capabilities beyond tolerable levels or that it may be academically beyond them.

This book is aimed at all those who would love to become Wildlife Photographers, to some extent or other, but who feel that restricting influences in their own circumstances would turn their aspirations into self delusions with little, or no, chance of success. Too often it is felt that to take up Wildlife Photography requires obsessional dedication coupled with a bottomless pocket for equipment.

I would sincerely hope that the contents of this book go at least some way – I would like to think "all the way"- towards dispelling these beliefs and that readers may subsequently go forth into the great unknown, armed with whatever camera gear they can aspire to and with the firm belief that the world of Wildlife Photography is their oyster and they are about to pluck it from its shell.

At first glance the title may seem to imply that finance is the primary concern. Not so! There are many forms of budget that control the way we live our lives, some voluntarily adopted and others forced upon us. Most of us are subject to at least one, and often several. In addition to the obvious budget of financial constraints there are many other factors that limit our potential input to Wildlife Photography and which need to be borne in mind if we are to successfully overcome them. There are budgets of "available time", "physical capability", "mental aptitude" and, very importantly, "purpose". To achieve consistently high standards you must establish and accept the parameters and restrictions that your various personal budgets force upon you and then learn to work within them. By all means stretch those parameters to their limits, or until their pips squeak, but at the end of the day you do have to accept that those parameters exist.

It is, for example, asking for never ending disappointment to launch forth, full of good intent, as a Bird Photographer armed only with a compact or an SLR fitted with a 50mm lens. Certainly there are many possibilities in the birdworld with this level of equipment, as will be seen later in this book particularly under the "Photographing Waterfowl" section, but shots of raptors in flight or small passerines in bushes will be beyond the scope of the equipment.

Where physical capability is concerned it is courting disaster to decide to specialise in montane species if you are suffering from heart, respiratory or ambulatory problems. If you do have the misfortune to suffer from any of these, or any other of a host of physical impairments that limit your mobility, then do not despair but rather try to take on a sector of Wildlife Photography that you can reasonably expect to have easy, or even vehicular, access to, and the number of these opportunities are countless. Beware, nevertheless, because the early days in the pursuit of this hobby can be misleading in that you will probably be working with a minimum amount of equipment that seems to weigh hardly anything, and which you can probably stick in your pockets, leading you to believe that you can get yourself and your gear almost anywhere on your own two feet. However as time, and your aspirations, increase you will find that the pile of "must have with me and daren't leave at home" items will grow not only taller but also heavier. Even for the more hale and hearty amongst us it is no fun scaling, albeit what at first glance from below seemed but a gentle slope, on a hot day laden with cameras, tripod, lenses, water bottle, lunch and a myriad other supposed essentials, in pursuit of a quarry far more mobile than ourselves. There are many fairly sedentary forms of Wildlife that can be just as spectacular in close-up, and often even more so, than many of the species more commonly thought of as archetypal Wildlife Photography subjects.

For those whose time is limited some aspects of Wildlife Photography would drive a time and motion man to drink. This is particularly so in the case of bird or mammal photography involving the use of a hide. Human nature is such that we normally require at least a modicum of continuously ongoing and successful results to maintain and develop our interests. Unfortunately it is not unknown for a whole succession of hide outings to produce not a single shot. OK I grant that, on the odd successful occasion, there can be times when you may feel that the end result was worth the wait but, in a day and age when time and money frequently equate to the same thing, it can often represent a very poor return on your investment.

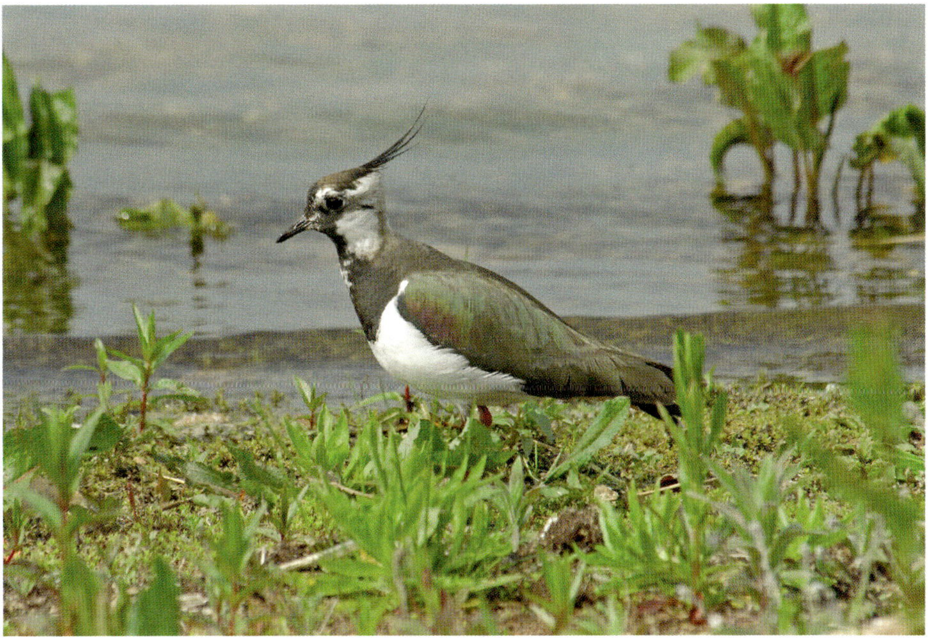

Lapwing taken from hide

On the aptitude front there are two areas of consideration – subject knowledge and equipment knowledge and the level of your desire to become proficient in either or both. Where the former is concerned you need have no worries. Firstly there are a great number of Clubs and Societies concerned with Wildlife Conservation and study. Many of them are inexpensive, easy to join and hold monthly meetings which normally include an illustrated lecture or talk. Speakers are usually drawn from the ranks of Professional Photographers or Specialists in various Wildlife matters, or even from within the ranks of their own membership. You can use these talks as a source of knowledge and information and benefit from the experiences of others. They are also, of course, invaluable venues for meeting other like minded souls. Additionally there are an enormous number of well illustrated field guides now available covering many aspects of Wildlife, its conservation and its life cycles.

Regarding the second of the aptitude testers – that of equipment knowledge – modern times, with their plethora of photographic gadgetry, have never been so good, or so bad, depending on your point of view. There is now such a range of equipment available that, for the uninitiated, it can seem like a minefield. It is not the purpose of this book to delve too deeply into the specifics and finer points of pure photography and its myriad ramifications, especially on the equipment front, as this is better covered by publications designed specifically for that purpose. Apart from a wealth of books dedicated solely to the taking and subsequent handling of images, many of which can be obtained through the local library to avoid the chance of paying out good money for expensive literature that may subsequently prove not to be what you really wanted, there are several weekly and monthly magazines stocked by most periodical retailers. Suffice to say that the purpose of this book is to convince its readers that, whatever form of picture taking gadget they opt for, there will be ample opportunity to indulge in some form of Wildlife Photography to a degree that will provide them with decent images, satisfactory for the purpose, bearing always in mind the "parameters" mentioned above. My own personal advice to those who are in a position to expend a certain amount of "kickoff capital" is to go for an SLR digital camera on which you can change the lenses. Also, if funds will run to it, invest in a flash unit with a "fill flash" facility. Having said this if you already have some other form of camera, and can't afford to change it, don't worry as there are still many opportunities out there for you.

The control systems of many modern cameras can seem like the flight deck of Concorde. We are all born with various aptitudes but if none of yours are electronic then, however wide your purse, stay away from all singing all dancing cameras initially, unless you are going to use them in basic automatic mode, which really negates the object of that level of equipment. Rather start with more straightforward gear until you have achieved a reasonable level of proficiency that allows you to ultimately upgrade relatively painlessly and already knowing exactly what you want.

I qualified the last of my above mentioned "budgets" as "very importantly, purpose". You need to determine exactly what your purpose is with this hobby and make your mind up as to what you want from it since this can determine your entire "modus operandi" and choice of suitable equipment. If you are looking merely for an excuse to pay regular visits to the countryside and take the odd shot or two for your own benefit, or to show your friends, then you can afford to adopt a fairly casual approach. If, however, you wish to "bag" each one of a group of species, or to acquire saleable photographs, or to provide material for the giving of slideshows, then a more in depth approach and degree of dedication will be called for. If you are not able, given the circumstances of your life, to devote this amount of input then you are looking outside your budgets and would be advised to back off and lower your sights a little.

Taking all the above of life's limitations into account the one form of Wildlife Photography that fulfils virtually all requirements and allows for all normal "budgets" is that of "macro" or close-up photography. If you aim towards this, and particularly if you can adopt a non specialist approach regarding your chosen species, then you will never be short of subject matter, wherever you may live, within minutes of your backdoor. The whole object of this book is to highlight the various groups of Wildlife that lend themselves to this form of Photography and are freely available on a daily basis, and to provide background information and photographic tips to help you on your way.

One of the first difficulties to be overcome is to be able to recognize suitable subjects. Some of them will have been so taken for granted throughout life that you may not realise their potential. Macro photography allows you to work at distances so close that many living things, so small as to have been virtually invisible during the hustle and bustle of your erstwhile "other life", suddenly become viable photographic subjects. I say "other life" in parenthesis since, once you start down this route, life will never be the same again. Macro photography enables you to turn a subject just over an inch long, such as a Grasshopper, into an image that completely fills the frame of your picture. This allows you to unmask and highlight features in the subject, be it plant or animal, which would hitherto have been unnoticed by the naked eye. Suddenly creatures which you may have previously dismissed, trodden on or not even been aware of, will become highly desirable subject matter and you will come to see the world of Wildlife from a completely different point of view. Not only that but their number is legion and, once you acquire a practised eye at discerning potential subjects, you will often find that, after a hard day's photography, you have got no further than a few metres from the spot where you parked earlier on that morning.

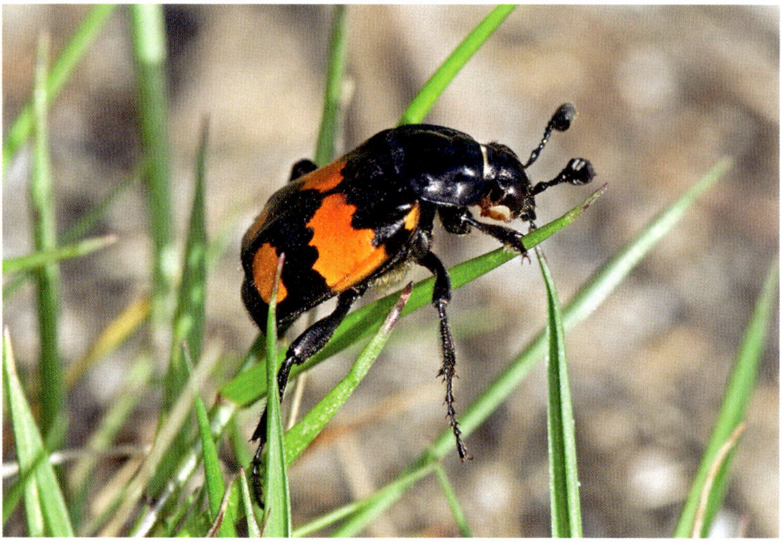

Burying Beetle - Macro

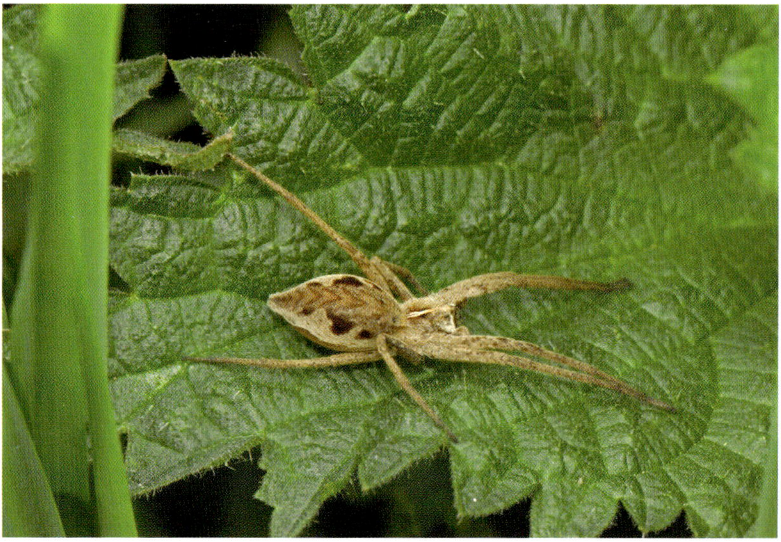

Wolf Spider - Macro

Remember that the physical size of your subject bears little relationship to the size of the image you portray. Thus your insect shot can be even larger that someone else's lion or elephant. Furthermore, in view of the fact that many people have never had the opportunity to study many of the often under recorded "macro suitable" subjects close-up, you will often find that you can get more acclaim from your images than the bulk of the other, run of the mill, photographers. Generally speaking, these days, a lion would need to be doing the can-can in fishnet tights and a red fez and a grizzly bear would need to be juggling with three salmon whilst holding a fisherman between his knees, to evoke much more than a casual glance. However a Grasshopper, Dragonfly, Butterfly or Orchid has but to smile, wink or wave at you, or even just look kindly in your direction, to give you a world beating shot!

Because of the diversity of camera equipment now on the market I have deliberately avoided going into too much detail on this subject. There are many sources of information available to assist prospective purchasers such as books, periodicals, the internet and even word of mouth, specifically devoted to the equipment side of life and to these I would refer my readers. My purpose is to highlight the groups of Wildlife that can sensibly be included under the "macro" banner and offer advice as to how and when to approach and photograph them. I feel safe in my claim that "macro photography" satisfies all "budgets" including the financial one of maybe not being able to invest in new equipment. In this day and age most people, and especially those with even only a latent Wildlife Photography desire, will already have some form of image taking hardware and virtually all those gadgets feature a close-up facility. I will here repeat my earlier advice to either those who currently have no equipment, and so will be forced into buying some anyway, or those who, despite having cameras that have served them well thus far would, nevertheless, like to invest in something that offers a more diverse range of image taking possibilities, and that is to invest in a digital SLR and, at least for starters, a short range zoom lens. Because of the speed at which digital hardware becomes superseded these days, and because so many people feel the inherent need to have the absolute latest model, there is a wealth of perfectly usable second-hand equipment on the market at prices far removed from those of the latest new offerings. Additionally, if you feel the need to buy new, then camera "kits" comprising a body and short range zoom of anything from or between 18 to 100 mm can usually be obtained at a price much lower than buying the separates. The advantage of this equipment is that you can then buy either screw in close-up filters or extension tubes for a very few pounds and these will give you up to, and even exceeding, life-size images. My advice is to go for the screw ins as you don't need to remove the lens to fit them. Also to add or to take away extra filters is a relatively quick process. Extension tubes involve removing the lens, since they fit between the lens and the body and, quite frankly, adding or taking away a tube in the heat of the moment can be a right pain in the backside, not to mention the danger of dust getting onto your sensor each time you take the lens off.

Some may query the need to be able to record images from a very close distance when, in this digital age in which we find ourselves, you could take a smaller subject image from further away with far less hassle and then crop it up to the desired size in your computer. Whilst this cropping facility is an undoubted boon, and I use it myself to a certain extent on many occasions, I do not depend on it to provide me with decent sized images. This is mainly because, for detail, a decent shot taken close-up will always beat a distant shot cropped up no matter how good is the latter. I realise that many will disagree with this and no doubt allege that with powerful lenses you often cannot tell the difference. This I would concede, but only to a certain extent. My point here is that I am basing my advice on budget equipment and this does not include long length lenses costing 100's and sometimes 1000's of pounds. The ultimate longterm objective would be to acquire specialist "macro" lenses but these are somewhat expensive and, in the meantime, I maintain my above assertions.

To illustrate my point I would pose the following example, bearing in mind that the lens on your camera operates much as the eye in your head. If the markings on my nose were freckles (and not the result of a dissolute past) and I asked you to count them from a distance of some 18 inches I would expect most people to manage a reasonable count. From 6 feet away you would begin to miss quite a few and from 10 feet and upwards you would progressively be unable to differentiate between them, and my nose would eventually become just a blob of colour (albeit redder than I would, by choice, have opted for). And so it is with photographic images. I have had the great good fortune to work with various species of big cats on many occasions in my life – some obviously more approachable than others. In particular I have some images of young lions taken from less than a metre away on a fairly basic digital SLR (Nikon D70s), with a standard short lens, and you can count each individual hair, even when blown up and printed to A3+ size. I have other more distant shots of lions taken on a better camera (Nikon D200) with an excellent quality Nikon 80/400 mm lens and the shots are perfectly sharp and, I feel sure, as good as could be obtained with the equipment at that distance – but you cannot count the hairs when you blow them up! Some may say that this is nit picking but once you embark on "macro" photography you will develop an eye for detail that you never thought yourself capable of. Hence my advice to get in as close as you safely can without endangering yourself or stressing the object of your desires. On that subject I would say that should you, too, ever have the chance to photograph big cats from a very close distance it is not too bright an idea to place your flash unit too close to the bit that bites! In those circumstances best to settle for ambient light!

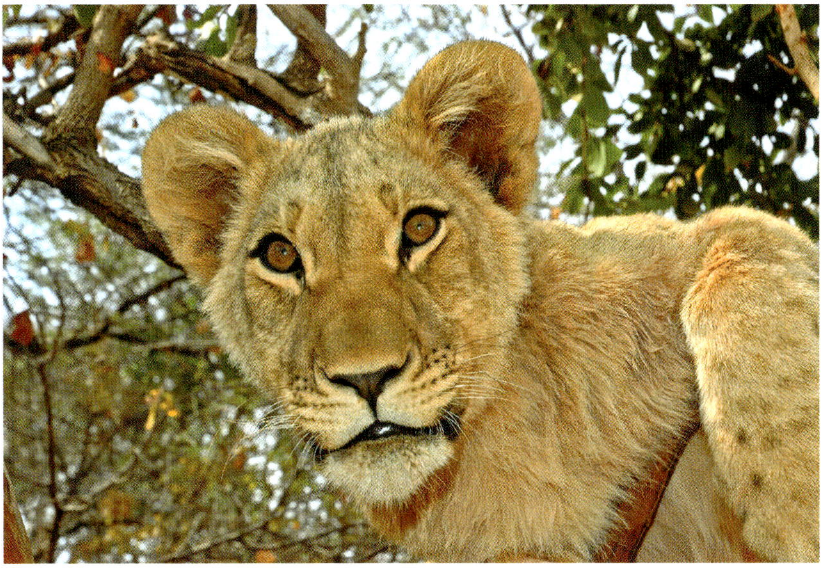

Lion Cub - "Showing every hair"

I often wonder what quirk of genetic inheritance pointed me in the direction the paths of my life have taken and wonder what has prompted others to follow a similar route. For many the "thrill of the hunt will be in the chase" but I suspect that, whilst this may be an integral and necessary part of it, the real thrill will be in the "capture" when you finally press your shutter release. Often the hunt will demand the same tracking skills and research that our more primitive forbears would have had to employ. Normally the longer and harder the hunt then the greater will be the satisfaction when you finally get your shot.

Some people become actively involved in Wildlife Photography as a furtherance of a specific interest but many others almost "drift" into it as an extension of a more generalised interest in Wildlife. This latter group often start by taking pictures on a haphazard basis during Nature Walks or Rambles. This is fine up to a point and frequently equates, ultimately, to a limbering up process. I can well remember the time when I could regularly spend the whole day photographing without getting further that the lay-by I had pulled into at the outset. In those days I would photograph anything and everything that wasn't bolted down. Whilst this doesn't necessarily begin to pall, nevertheless, after a while, you normally begin to feel the need for a little more purpose in your photographic aspirations.

Most people these days have a built-in "Collector" instinct in them that manifests itself in many, often strange and varied, ways. One of the more appealing aspects of collecting whatever it is that takes your fancy, is if there is a chance of building up to "a full set". For those of us whose Collectors' Instinct takes the form of acquiring photographic images this "full set" appeal is no less inspirational.

In the U.K., as opposed to mainland Europe where the diversity of species is often much greater, there are a number of groups of Wildlife with a fairly limited species count and distribution. For many of them this can be so sparse and fragmented that the chance of simply "bumping into" all the species concerned, on a random wander, is remote. With diligence, research and varying degrees of difficulty, however, most of them can be located and photographed making the achievement of a "full set" an ongoing and inspiring possibility.

Some of the groups which I refer to are:- Dragon and Damselflies, Grasshoppers and Bush Crickets, Butterflies and possibly day flying Moths, Reptiles and Amphibians, and, in the plant kingdom, either Bulbous Plants in general or Orchids in particular. There are many other groups that could no doubt be included but I have tried to highlight those that seem to attract the widest, initially non-specialist, appeal. It may seem strange that I have not included Birds or Mammals in the list but these groups, more often than not, seem to appeal to those with an inclination to specialise. I am more interested here in offering help and advice to those with a more casual and non-specialist approach but a by no means diminished enthusiasm. Though more generalised in its scope this enthusiasm, by its very nature, often covers a far broader sphere of interest than that expressed by "specialists".

The advantage of becoming involved with the above groups is that, in the UK, they all consist of a finite number of species that, with some effort and research, can all be located and photographed. The Bulbous Plants are a mixed group of Genera and so pose possibly a greater challenge by virtue of the extent of the range involved but, specifically, both Orchids and Butterflies contain only between 50 and 60 species each in the U.K. and the other groups even less. You will appreciate, therefore, that with these limited numbers obtaining a "full set" is a not unattainable aspiration.

In practice you will probably find that you can locate, identify and photograph the bulk of the species in any one group without too much trouble. The last few, however, can demand more effort, research and, often, travel than the rest put together. It is in conducting the necessary research into the rarer species that you will learn the most. This research can be quite involved and will no doubt mean poring through various tomes on the subject. You will find that although you are maybe focussing on just one species you will, nevertheless, "bump into" a myriad other facts, figures and species as you flick through the pages. Some of these will catch your eye and, with luck, some may even imprint themselves onto your memory banks, to some extent or other, for future reference.

I have not specifically included sections relevant to film photography since I feel that, whether we like it or not, that technology is about to join the ranks of the Dinosaurs and Dodo's. Whether it does or not will, of course, be the subject of conjecture but to all intents and purposes it looks as though it will be left behind in the image taking race by all but a few of its staunch supporters. Suffice to say that much of the advice offered on the various subject species will be applicable whatever form of image taking instrument you opt for.

I have also taken the liberty of using this book to express some of my own opinions on a variety of matters photographically associated. In this I would stress that I am voicing my personal opinions and, whilst intending no slight, can appreciate that there will be those who strongly disagree or who may find some of my views controversial. That, I am afraid, I cannot help but would hope that they do not find me unbearably so. Whether you agree or not you have to start somewhere and so I would suggest that you read, mark, learn and inwardly digest as much as you can and then gird up your loins and get out there amongst it and formulate your own techniques and opinions. The secret to photographic happiness is to find out what suits and pleases you best, and then stick with it and leave the Joneses to keep up with themselves.

So there we have it! If all that has held you back from becoming a Wildlife Photographer of worldwide renown is one or more of the budgets mentioned above, and you would wish to overcome them, then read on and see what potential subjects are out there for you. If not, and you wish to go no further, then may I say what a pleasure it has been to have your company thus far - and could you kindly dispose of this book in such a way that others may have the opportunity to read it!

Chapter 2

My Metamorphosis

I am often asked whether, at heart, I am a Wildlife Specialist with an interest in Photography or a Photographer with an interest in Wildlife? In truth I do not really know the answer but suspect that it is a blending of the two.

Certainly my involvement with Wildlife began many years before I picked up a camera with serious intent. Much of my life had been spent working with, and surrounded by, Wildlife in a myriad of forms and settings before ever I started to photograph it seriously.

My father was an ardent photographer and bought me a small bellows camera, which I remember well from when I was but a boy just trying to keep up with Dad. I had no strong propensity to Photography in those days but it did, nevertheless, give me an early introduction to the mysteries of taking pictures. No doubt I also probably picked up some basic techniques though, at the time, I was not aware of having embarked on a career that would catch up with me later in my life.

We all come into this vocation for different reasons. Some drift in by accident and some come in by intent. Personally my entire life, both as boy and man, has been dominated, and its course dictated, by an almost obsessive interest in Wildlife. Whilst that interest has manifested itself in various ways over the years I must say that, for all its ups and downs, I find my current expression of that interest ie: Wildlife Photography, the most gratifying of them all.

My own introduction to Wildlife came at an early age. I had the great good fortune to be a boy in the days when you could build a den in the woods and scrump apples with only the threat of a thick ear if you were caught. I spent most of my formative years overseas and must confess that, as a young boy, my contribution to Wildlife Conservation manifested itself in collecting and pinning butterflies on a board and emptying birds' eggs, preferably at the pre-incubation stage, by a process known as "blowing", in order to build up collections of as many local species as possible. Both the above trophies eventually became highly tradable commodities when I finally graduated to boarding school where bartering anything and everything became the order of the day and formed a large part of extra curricular activities. To this day I can remember agonizing between my love of Heinz "Sandwich Spread", of which I was the proud possessor of a nearly full jar, and the desire to add a Griffon Vulture's egg, owned by one of my friends, to my collection. That collector's instinct that lurks within us all beat my sweet tooth by a narrow margin and won the day, and my precious jar changed ownership. I do seem, though, to recall managing to remove a hefty finger full from the middle of the jar, where it's absence would escape casual scrutiny, before handing it over.

I make no excuses for these early depredations on the world's wildlife since, like all of us, I was a product of the time and, in that time, that was the sort of thing that little boys did. The long term benefits of these, and associated pastimes, was that it inadvertently forced me to develop a sense of "Wildlife Awareness" without which most of the activities concerned would have been doomed to failure. For many of my compatriots, as in my own case, their indulgence in those childhood pursuits acted as a springboard for later life and they have become guiding lights and specialists in all manner of Wildlife and Conservation matters.

Throughout these early exploits I was forced to study habits, habitats and animal psychology to be successful in my pursuits and, over a period, gradual though it may have been, I found that I was more interested in studying Wildlife than I was in its capture or extermination. After all Wildlife Photography is, in itself, a form of hunting with the advantage that nothing needs to die or become stressed in the process. It is because of the "hunting" aspect of photography that so many animals are "camera shy". You will often find that you can approach many subjects quite closely while ever you maintain a casual attitude. However, the second that you start to concentrate, raise the camera, and start circling to get better light or position, then they disappear into the distance. This is because, at that moment of ceasing to be casual, your entire body language becomes that of a hunter and most wild things will sense it. Indeed however politically incorrect and antisocial it may appear to be in the modern sanitised world in which we live, the concept of "Man the Hunter" is not so much a joke but rather an expression of our fundamental origins. I feel sure that Wildlife Photography is a form of exercising, albeit in what we have come to regard as a more civilised fashion, of that primeval hunting instinct that is present in many more of us than would care to admit it.

Most of us live in a structured society where our food is mainly grown, bred or gathered by someone else and supplied in a tin, packet or plastic bag without us, as individuals, having to contend with the messy, and often bloody, processes that are involved. In that kind of background and devoid of any intimate contact with, or true understanding of, nature, it is easy for some idealists to form and express misconceived and unrealistic conservation ideals that, whilst sometimes seeming credible on the surface, are only able to do so because of the immediate society in which we live. Marooned on a desert island with no chance of rescue I suspect we would all adopt a somewhat different set of priorities!

There is no doubt that, as Wildlife Photographers, we are privileged to observe "wild life (and death)" as it really is and you will often find that the consequently more informed outlook on the realities of life that you enjoy is at odds with those "lesser mortals" who do not share your interests. In some circles you may find your views considered as controversial and, in some circles, they well may be so. In addition, however, yours will certainly be more practical and realistic than those of many others. You can draw great satisfaction from the fact that, in pursuit of your interests, your objective is to observe and record and you do not, yourself, have to kill or injure. At the same time, however, do not deny your Wildlife subjects the right to do so or think any the less of them because of it.

As Wildlife Photographers you will frequently be confronted by, and have to come to terms with, a more realistic view of life and death than is afforded the man in the street. Most of your subjects will live in environments where "kill or be killed" is the order of the day. Whatever direction your interest takes you, be it either the plant or the animal kingdom, the struggles in the hunt for food, to eliminate competition or to win a mate, are often to the death. From an observer's point of view the animal kingdom usually provides the messier and more gory spectacles but the struggles in the plant world are no less intense. On a personal level it is, of course, difficult to become emotionally overwrought just from watching one plant shading out all its neighbours, or a strangler fig gradually killing off its supporting victim. However, watching a Big Cat killing some other animal's newborn offspring, or seeing Wolves or Wild Dogs start eating often still living prey, can mount a heck of an assault on your own sentiments and sensitivities. It is often very difficult to adopt a dispassionate view of the whole wide spectrum of wild life and death but it is really just a question of degree. Most people could happily watch a Spider catch and kill a Fly, or see a Thrush battering a Slug or Snail to death, and not bat an eyelid, and that is the kind of attitude to which you will often find you need to aspire in order to avoid constant heartache.

Try not to be selective in your sentiments. Easier said than done, it is true, but necessary nevertheless. Generally speaking the non-photographing public take against the "bloodletter" in favour of the "victim" without stopping to think that the Big Cat, in killing the "Fawn" is only, after all, being a Big Cat and no doubt trying to feed its own young. Very few wild animals kill just for the hell of it. Most anyone will agree that Big Cat cubs are cute, cuddly and loveable and then promptly put blinkers on when it comes to the feeding of them.

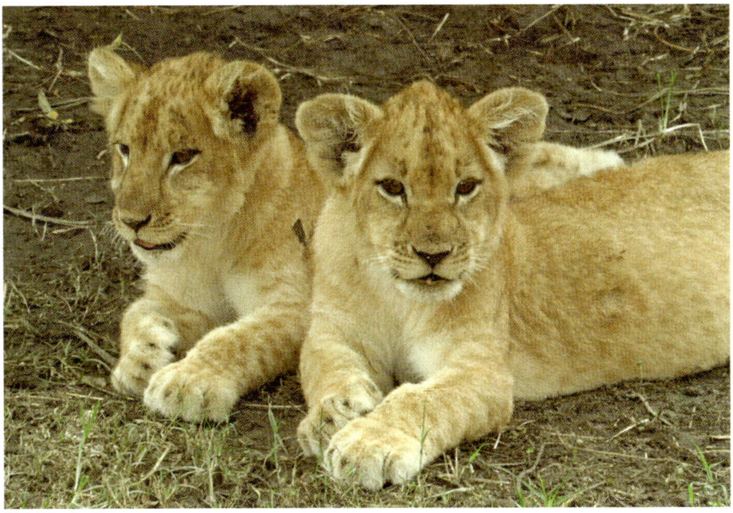

Lion Cubs - "Cute and cuddlies"

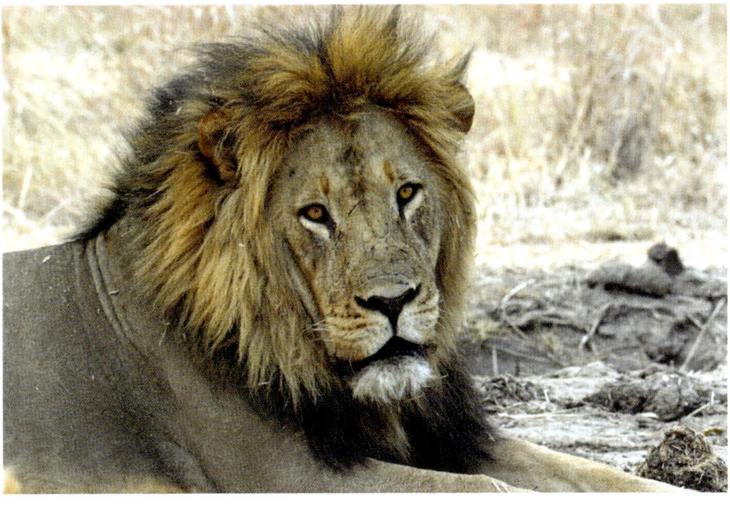

Big Daddy

I well remember an instance, when I had my Zoo, involving the Otters. These were diurnal by nature and so had to be fed during daylight. In summer this was normally done after closing time since there were often some hours of daylight left, especially in high summer. In winter, however, it was necessary to feed during opening hours. The Otters needed a varied diet and I was, one day, confronted by an irate parent absolutely incensed that dead chicks formed part of that diet and he felt that they shouldn't be allowed to be seen. That those chicks were the humanely killed male by- product of a hatchery producing laying hens to provide his family's breakfast eggs and that, on prompting, he admitted to often stopping off at a Kentucky Fried Chicken with his family on the way home, didn't seem to enter the equation. You would think (or future generations will) that chickens hatch out "oven ready", and wearing the plastic bags they are normally sold in, rather than feathers!

There could probably be a never ending debate on the degree of sanitising that should be carried out in showing the Wildlife World to the general public. Many T.V. programmes edit out the "gooey" bits before screening. I agree that there should be no need for gratuitous gore but I often feel a more realistic presentation could only be but educational.

In this day and age modern concepts dictate that many Zoo animals, particularly Reptiles, have to be specially trained to eat dead food. This is not always easy and can sometimes lead to the death of the animal concerned. Again it seems to be a question of degree. Even in this day and age it would appear to be O.K. to feed a pet Gecko with live crickets but not so O.K. to feed a Python with a live rat or mouse. I well remember several years ago visiting a Reptile House in a Zoo in the days when live feeding was not only the norm but was announced on a notice board of feeding times. A crowd had gathered in front of a Boa Constrictor's pen where it was being presented with a live rat. In front of me were a couple and I can hear his words to this day – "Ugh, that's really disgusting. It should never be allowed. For Pete's sake, dear, move your head out of the way, I can't see!" I am neither condoning nor advocating a return to the practices of those days, since time and perceptions have moved on, but on the hypocrisy front – I rest my case! Well not quite - because a picture of live crabs and lobsters on a fishmonger's slab, with their claws elastic band bound and awaiting their "higher intellect" purchasers whose "perceptions have moved on", comes to mind. Still I expect they'll be bought for release out to sea don't you?

Coming back to my life-cycle, in my early 20's I returned to the UK to seek my fortune. Not for want of trying, said fortune successfully eluded me and, after casting my net on several different, but obviously over fished waters, I returned to my great love of wildlife. Force of circumstance, however, dictated that this time it would be in the sphere of captive livestock and so followed a number of years that were totally absorbing, emotionally fulfilling and completely unrewarding from a financial point of view, as I graduated through ownership of various enterprises from a Pet Shop, to a Zoo, to a Bird Garden, to a number of years as a Wildlife Consultant for a large International Corporation to, finally, a large Wildlife breeding and study centre.

Several further fulfilling years ensued which terminated in a particularly troublesome and wearying period in life's rich tapestry. This depleted my immune system to the extent that I contracted a chronic case of "Early Onset Middle-aged Male Menopausal Madness". As a result of this I severed all ties with the UK and moved to a Utopian setting in Spain way up in the mountains of the Costa Blanca.

(I thought that I was retiring to the sun - something that I have now done on more than one occasion - each time completely overlooking potential increases in the cost of living and my innate ability to fritter away that which I have periodically accumulated, on whims and flights of fancy!)

(My article entitled "Castell de Castells" in the Site Guide section of this book gives a little insight into this period).

For the first time in many years I was without the tie of livestock maintenance and found myself looking round in complete wonder at the beauty of nature on my own doorstep. As for so many people, my "not really thought about it, back of the mind feeling" was that natural beauty was something that generally occurred in far off exotic places and not just outside your own backyard. I was, therefore, amazed to see what were obviously the wild forbears of many garden plants, which I had erstwhile taken for granted, growing in profusion on every hill and roadside in the area. One could not but notice the plethora of insect life and other associated species that co-existed with this floral pageant and, within two flicks of a grasshopper's hind leg, I became the proud owner of a brand new, state of the art, Video Camera. (I should have learnt my lesson then because, even back in those distant days, I think that it had been superseded before I got it home from the shop!) However, armed with this, I set forth to become the world's leading maker of Wildlife Documentaries. Attenborough was going to be forced into early retirement and the BBC would surely give me my own full time channel! Oh the dreams of mice and men!

8mm Video Cameras and, indeed, the TV sets used for playback in those dim and distant pre home-computer days were, of course, far less sophisticated than they are now and I quickly became disillusioned with the reproductive qualities that could be obtained, particularly in the field of Wildlife video close-ups. Then, like manna from heaven, I inadvertently made one of those rare, unintentional but nevertheless earth moving, life changing decisions that means that things will never be the same again --- I decided to take all my close-ups on slide so that I could subsequently transfer them onto the Video and hopefully get a better colour reproduction. Case done and dusted! Very quickly I became so enamoured with the qualities of slide photography that Attenborough was allowed to continue with his career without further interruptions from me, the BBC was left to sink or swim of its own accord without my help and I was off and running on what has become the love of my life – Macro or Close-up Wildlife Photography.

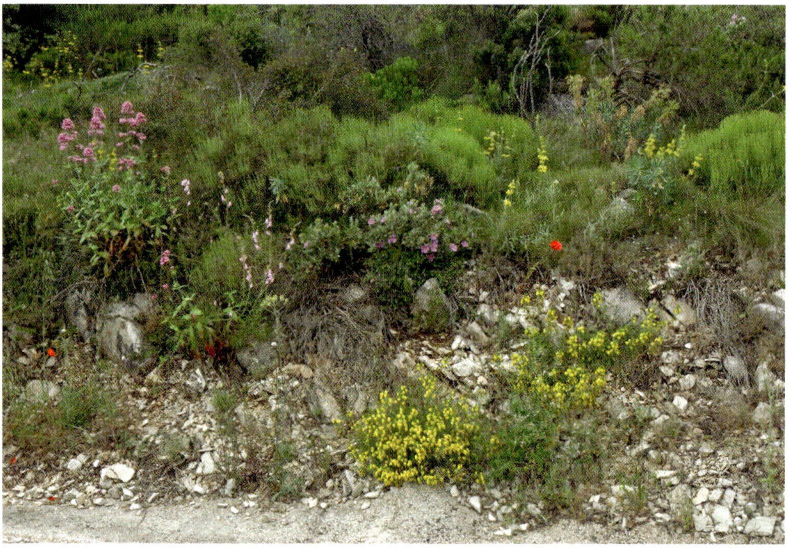

Roadside verge - Spain

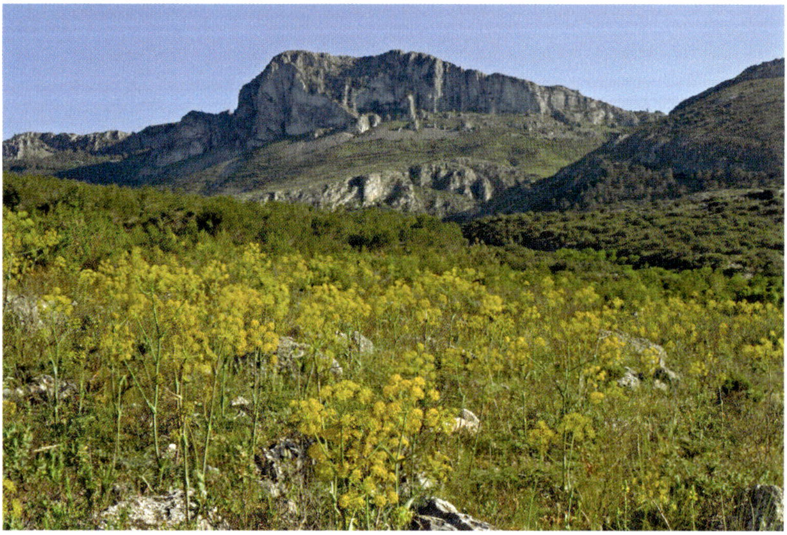

Abandoned Terraces - Spain

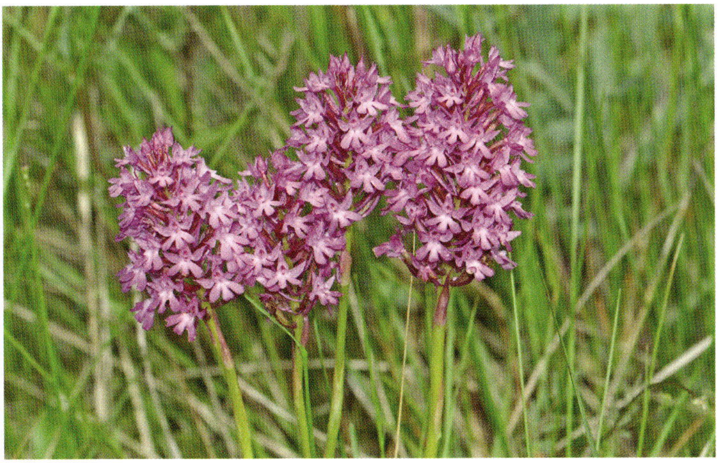

Pyramidal Orchids - Costa Blanca

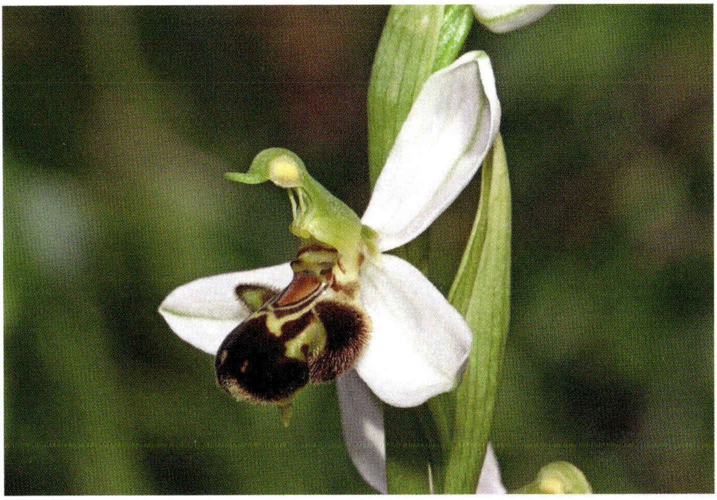

Bee Orchid - Costa Blanca

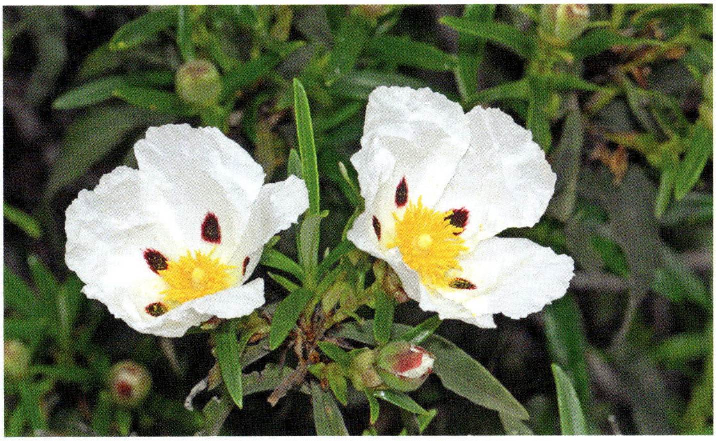

Cistus ladanifer - Central Spain

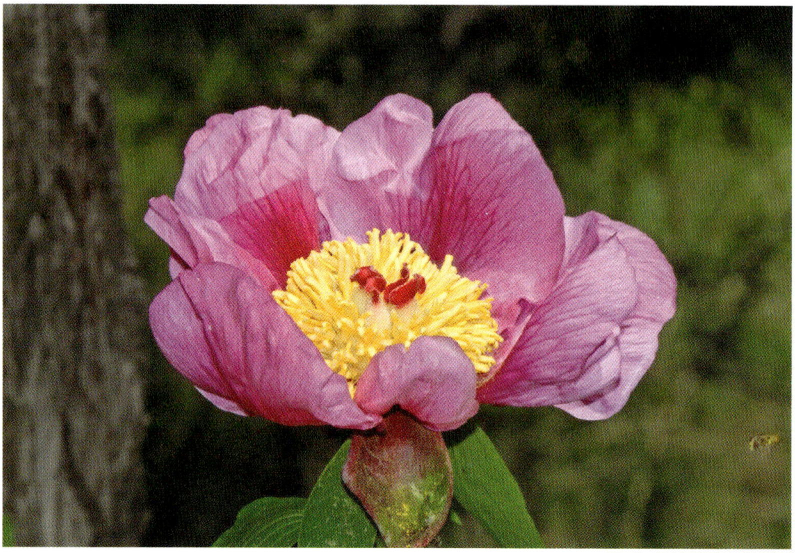

Wild Peony - Spain

Whilst, in its early stages, my career scarcely qualified under the heading of "illustrious" it was, nevertheless, very fulfilling and marked the beginning of a learning curve that persists to this day and to which I can, thankfully, see no end. By dint of great good fortune my sphere of wildlife interests has always been extremely wide and so I have tended not to specialise photographically save only that I try to concentrate on species that lend themselves to macro photography. Of course, as one's fieldcraft improves, more and more hitherto distant species come to qualify under your personal "macro" banner.

The photographic opportunities offered by my situation in Spain were many and varied but the devious and frequent twists and turns of Dame Fortune are such that, some years later, I found myself back in the UK on an almost fulltime basis. My photography, however, continued unabated. In fact, with my newfound knowledge, I was amazed to see what a veritable cornucopia of Wildlife I had left behind in what were my old stamping grounds, and which I had always been too pre-occupied with the rigours of modern-day life to notice.

There are a substantial number of Clubs, Societies and Trusts with the interests of Wildlife as their sole preoccupation and I quickly became a professional "goer" to other peoples' talks and on other peoples' field trips both at home and abroad. I learnt many things from these forays. One was that too many Professional Photographers, and other Specialists in wildlife matters, unintentionally give the impression that the achievement of success in their particular field is outside the scope of the common man, be it for financial or academic reasons. It is all too easy for a speaker, no doubt master of his particular craft, but maybe more used to addressing specifically qualified audiences, to leave a group of aspiring "Wildlifers", who may not have benefited from a scientific education, feeling somewhat like second class citizens with little or no hope of achieving their ambitions. Another of the lessons learnt was that on a mixed Field Trip a serious, or even semi-serious, photographer can definitely be "persona non grata". Invariably the "others" (this being a euphemism for a lower life form that doesn't take pictures) are sat in the minibus having "been there and done that" and patently ready to go just when you, as a photographer, are about to capture the front cover of the next National Geographic, and lifelong acclaim from the Royal Photographic – if only the wind would drop long enough to get off a couple of shots!

These and other experiences prompted my decisions for two things. I had, at various times in my life been an enthusiastic giver of talks on whatever was my "in vogue" interest at the time. For many years it was the mutations that occur in captive livestock and how to "fix" them genetically. These talks were more along the lines of lectures really and, whilst they did feature certain visual aids, they were never illustrated in the conventional way by means of a projector and slides. However, I now found myself as a fledgling Wildlife Photographer with a steadily increasing "slidepile" and a new battle cry of "Wildlife Awareness" to promote. As a result of this one of the decisions that I made was to set up an extensive Talks Programme geared towards enthusiasts from all walks of life regardless of their scientific backgrounds.

The second of the decisions that I made was to conduct Tours of my own where the numbers would be limited to 4 or 5 and photographers and non-photographers would not be mixed. These took place by Landrover to various Mediterranean countries but, over a period, the whole process became so regulation and Health and Safety Insurance bound that they were abandoned in favour of a less stressful, and certainly less expensive, way of life. Since I am a creature of weak will and am easily led I can still be persuaded to guide such groups, and can, indeed, show them subjects and places that they would never come across on regular Wildlife Tours, but now only on a personal, as opposed to a commercial, basis. Additionally my Landrover is now ageing at a faster rate than, thankfully, am I and the volume of potential business is not sufficient to warrant its replacement at modern day prices.

Whilst all this, my own personal Industrial Revolution, was taking place I inadvertently and unintentionally became, once again, the owner of my former Livestock Accessory manufacturing business. This, of course, somewhat curtailed the picture taking side of life but fortunately provided the wherewithal to expand my Photographic interests without them needing to be financially viable in their own right. This viability is a cross that all Wildlife Photographers have to bear as, contrary to popular belief, and despite what many photographers will assert simply to appear successful, this is, in itself and for all but a fortunate few, an extremely precarious business. It is neither easy as a fulltime profession nor is it a suitable source of "the quick buck". For me, however, those early years were like a preview of heaven on earth. With Wildlife Photography as a hobby financed by other means you can experience all of the pleasure without having to feel any of the pain. However, to anyone thinking of it as a fulltime occupation, I would say "look before you leap". Make sure that during your "apprenticeship years" you have managed to establish sufficient outlets for whatever you decide your photographic product will be, to ensure that you will be in with at least a chance of running a positive balance sheet. For myself I must confess that it has not always been so but I do, nevertheless, feel that the stresses and strains have been instrumental in preventing my brain cells from atrophying as they are always far too busy dreaming up new ventures and ways to make it pay!

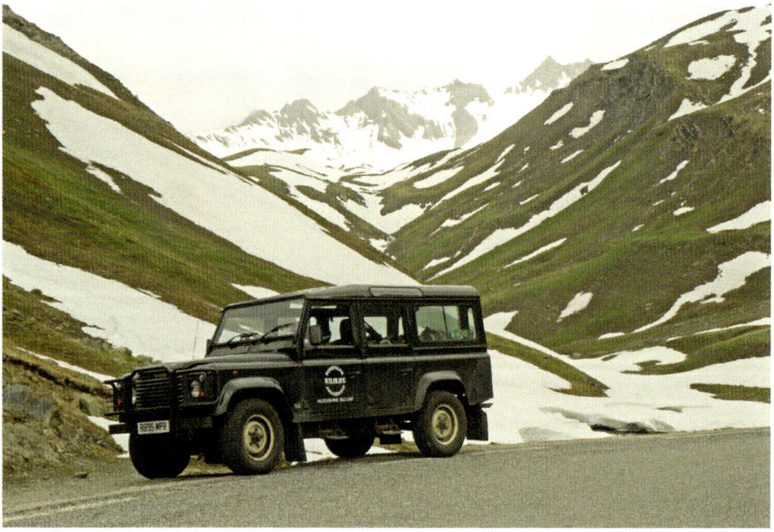

"Landy" in the High Alps

A number of near idyllic years ensued. The Talks side of life thrived, the picture taking also, though a little more free time would have gone down well. Ultimately, however, a certain mental turbulence was brewing on the horizon and a bad case of "Walkabout Fever" felt nigh. I was saved from the effects of these, and other of life's little trials and tribulations, by an offer from an almost lifelong friend to go to Africa to help manage a large Game Reserve of which he had recently become the owner.

There are times in life when you must let your head rule your heart, and there are many more times when you think "may the devil take the hindmost". The country concerned was undergoing a period of unrest (Ha! Some kind of understatement!) and so, since I have always suffered from a hearty head and a headstrong heart and soul, the sensible side of me came out of retirement and whispered "Don't touch it with a bargepole". However it was promptly outvoiced, outvoted and kicked into touch by the "Tally Ho! - let's do or die" part that reminded me that my dotage was rapidly approaching and, being neither an actress nor a Bishop, I wasn't likely to get another chance of such excitement at my age if I turned it down.

Like all good things there always seems to be a price to pay and mine was that I had to virtually sacrifice all the progress that I had made on the photographic front, cancel all outstanding talks and part company with my business for the second time. Caution, however, was cast aside and I set off for the "Dark Continent" full of aspiration and adrenalin. The period which followed was something akin to living a life straight out of a Boy's Own Annual. However, in the fullness of time, this page in my Book of Life eventually got turned and, relatively intact, I returned briefly to the UK and thence back to Spain with a "slidepile" somewhat higher than of yore.

It would seem that financial security and I were never destined to be loving bedfellows and so I cast around for some means of financing my increasingly addictive photographic habit that now seemed to be demanding a certain amount of foreign travel as part of the price for keeping a glint in my eye and hope in my heart. Via another long-term friend an offer in Property Consultancy came my way and thus my career took a temporary diversion from what I had perceived to be its ordained path. As a result I managed to spend some years being able to banish (tho' never very far!) the wolf from the door. However, due to the phenomenal number of hours involved in the job my photography went into a state of near suspended animation.

Nothing seems to last for ever, does it? Once again "Walkabout Fever" forced my life away from a potentially promising future and back onto its preordained and "macro" dominated course. One very hot and windless night I inadvertently opened my bedroom window for some fresh air and lo!, on the slight breeze that developed, I could distinctly hear the Falkland Islands calling out to me. Ever since owning a pair of Flightless Steamer Ducks back in my early Zoo days, the '82 War, and the accompanying graphic TV coverage, I had nurtured a desire to see that desolate land and its wildlife and here it was practically demanding that I make the journey! Property Consultancy requires your ongoing presence on a daily basis as there are always a number of deals only partway to fruition and so, with house construction sometimes taking up to 2 years to complete, part time was not an option. Once again caution was cast into the prevailing winds and I embarked on a lengthy and concentrated study of the world's wild places with three months in the Falklands as a starting point. The Galapagos, South America, the Himalayas, Africa again, the Near, Far and Middle East particularly Kurdistan, all followed over the years with a satisfying increase in the height of the "slidepile" as a consequence.

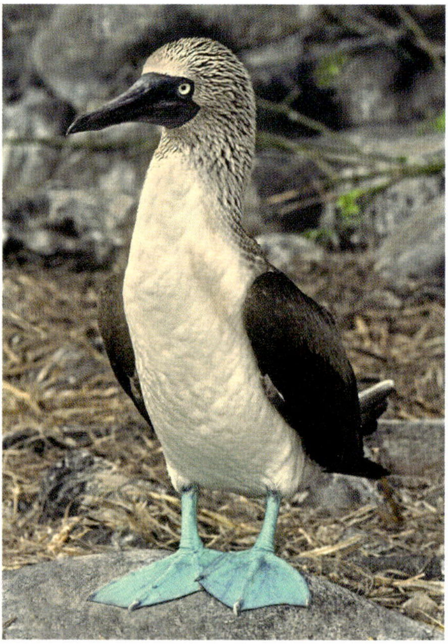

Blue Footed Booby - Galapagos

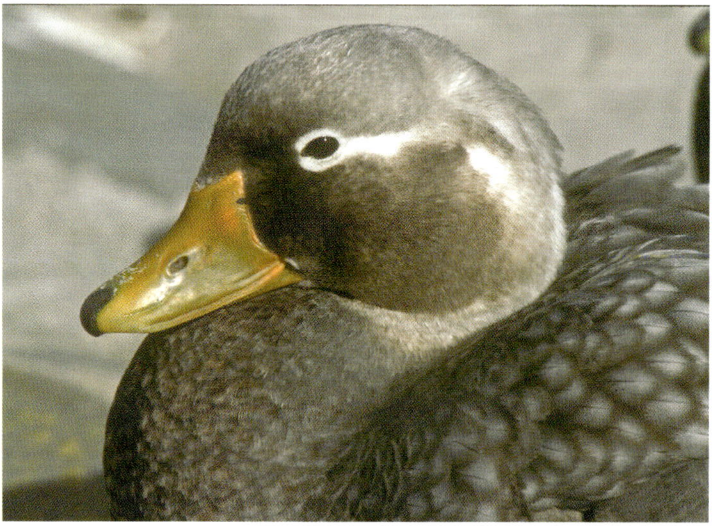

Steamer Duck male - Falklands

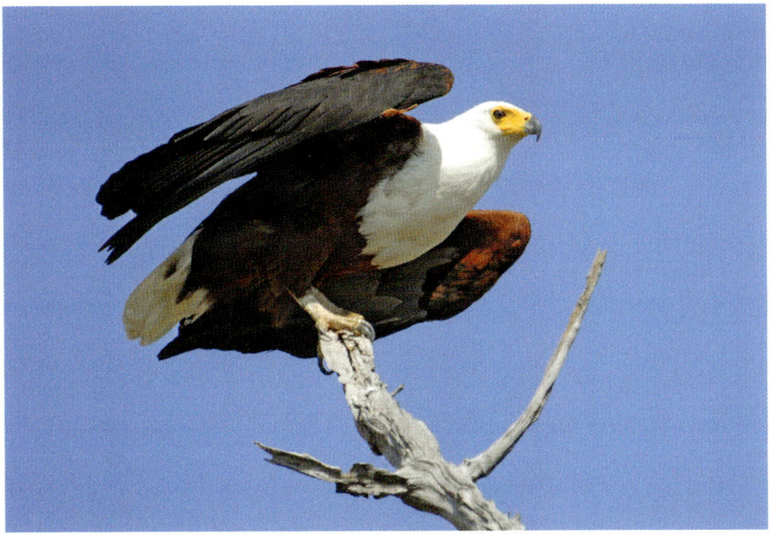

African Fish Eagle - Zimbabwe

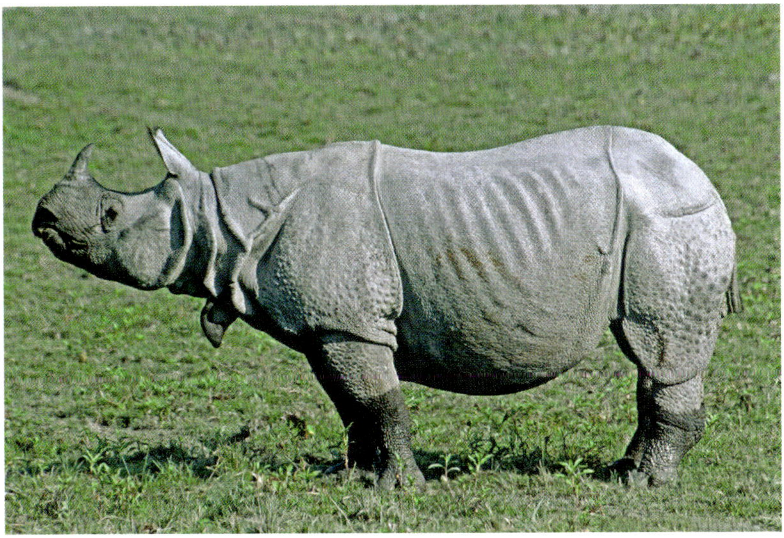

One Horned Rhino - Kaziranga

During the Property Consultancy period I had steeled myself to go where I had formerly feared to tread and invested in a computer. My proficiency with it would have driven a five year old to tears! In fact it still would! (More of this era in the Life of this Brian can be found in the chapter on "Film versus Digital").

Suffice to say that during this period I eventually, and with some reluctance, switched from film to digital cameras and so began the latest stage in the metamorphosis of my life. Because of my travelling, and being based in Spain, the Talks side of life had become comatose. Desperately in need of convincing myself that there was some worthwhile purpose to justify my gallivanting, and with my fortuitously timed switch to digital photography, I changed course in mid stride and put all my efforts into the production and marketing of Wildlife Prints, either mounted or framed, and this still plays a big part in my overall strategy. So followed a further few pleasurable years until I realised that, due to the insistent demands for continuous investment that "going digital" involves, I was in danger of having to subsidise my ongoing financial requirements out of what little "fat" I had gained in previous years. The problem with living on your fat is that you only ever lose weight, and if you lose too much it can prove quite hard to put it on again. As in many walks of life it is often quite difficult to differentiate between the "essential" and the "desirable" when it comes to expenditure and in the world of photographic gadgetry the list of "desirables" seems to know no bounds!

Once again Dame Fortune stuck her finger in my pie and I was asked to go back to Africa to plug a temporary management gap until a replacement could be found. Surely a trip of short duration. "Walkabout Fever" is very much akin to Malaria in so far as, once you have had it, there is always the chance that it will recur again and again throughout the rest of your life. In order to forestall a recurrence I agreed to go for a maximum period of three months. The former mild civil unrest had escalated into something far more serious but, nevertheless, with cameras clutched firmly to my bosom and a fierce expression on my face to deter any potential "ne'er do wells", I set forth again on my short break. Almost two years later what was left of me returned, though this time it was not with a higher "slidepile" but an overflowing hard drive.

By this time my mind was being assailed with visions of not only mounted prints but also websites, DVD's, illustrated Talks again but this time with sound and motion side effects, and a whole raft of other time consuming notions – one of which was to commit the tales of my misspent life to print.

As I said at the beginning of the "Introduction", this book has been a long time in the coming.

Chapter 3

Modus Operandi

This is just a general advice chapter before getting bogged down in the nitty gritty of the book.

Firstly those of you who watch any amount of TV will probably have realised that Wildlife Photography does not rank highly in the list of top spectator sports. If your own interest tends towards the serious then it seldom pays to set out with non-photographing companions. Many of them, with the best of intentions, will think that they are doing you a favour by offering to "keep you company". Believe me what will represent a good day for you will be a bad one for them. Wildlife Photography can be so psychologically intense that you will still be up there in seventh heaven, and oblivious to all but the subject in front of your lens, while their patience and boredom levels will have long gone into the red. It can become so absorbing that you can find that you don't actually need the comfort of having anyone with you so make sure that, if you do take a companion, it is someone whose company you really enjoy and whose presence will really enhance your day.

Much wildlife tends to slow down towards early afternoon and, indeed, some of it, like me, can grind to a complete halt without seemingly trying. Early mornings and late afternoons are, therefore, probably going to be your most productive times of the day. Personally I am a night-owl, given to staying up on the computer till some 3.00am. The passage of time seems to have taken away my ability to burn the candle at both ends. I used to be able to do it as a way of life but the ability, along with other of my faculties, seems to be atrophying at an alarming rate. Accordingly this is a case of "do as I once did" and not "do as I do now". On a serious note you must remember that "the early bird catches the worm" and you should be there, set up, ready and waiting, to take his picture when he does.

Try to wear clothing sympathetic to the area that you are going to be working in. Avoid wearing loudly coloured, loose and flappy garments. Apart from the fact that your red anorak will spoil the view for other country lovers it will make you stick out like a sore thumb and frighten off every living thing for miles. You don't need to doll up like Rambo but most clothing in browns and greens will normally blend in quite well.

Even in ostensibly fine weather it pays to carry a waterproof especially since, these days, you can buy lightweight raincoats that seem to fold up into the size of a pocket handkerchief. Avoid most oilskin type waterproofs as they are normally heavy, loudly coloured, make you hot and sweaty and create a crackly, creaky, rustly noise when you move. Don't bother trying to find something that will cover both you and your gear at the same time. Only a Poncho is likely to be able to do that, and they restrict your movements too much. Whilst that may be alright for a walk in the park it's a helluva hindrance if you're shinning up a mountainside. I always carry two or three bin liners or garden refuse sacks, which often come supplied with drawstrings, which I can then put round my gear in inclement weather and carry on walking normally.

When deciding what gear to carry and how to carry it make sure that you can stow it in such a way that it wont jingle, clank, clonk or rattle just at the wrong moment. Photographic or Fisherman type jackets can be very helpful since they are normally sensibly coloured, and come supplied with an enormous number of practical sized pockets that can be zipped or velcroed shut to cut down on noise and to prevent loss of items when you are crawling through the undergrowth or swinging from the trees.

Here again is a case of "do as I say and not as I do". If at all possible, when going out for a day's photography on your own, try to tell someone at least roughly where you are going to be. My personal circumstances are such that there is often no-one to tell, which complicates matters. (Of course I am always open to offers, so nubile maidens who see their vocation in life as a Wildlife Photographer's assistant should feel free to tender their bids!) This may seem alarmist but, particularly with macro photography, you can become so concentrated on the subject at hand, and working so closely to it, that you lose track of your more general surroundings. With your eye often firmly fixed on your quarry your leg, left to guide and amuse itself, will unerringly find the only rabbit or badger hole in the entire field! In my time I have walked into low branches, fallen off steep slopes (once with my video camera continuing to capture the whole sequence of both the roller coaster journey and, due to its built-in mike, the expletives – many of which I didn't even realise that I knew - that accompanied it), got stuck on cliff faces, forgotten where I left the car and tripped over and fallen badly for no apparent reason. Should any of these kinds of mishap render you unconscious or incapacitated, then the fact of someone knowing your whereabouts may be a critical factor in your recovery when you finally fail to show. For the same reason it pays to always carry a mobile phone with a fully charged battery. Unfortunately many of the sites that you visit will be in areas of either poor, or even no, reception. However, a fully charged battery will certainly improve your odds of getting through, and you may end up needing to be on the phone for some time if you have to guide rescuers to your whereabouts.

Always carry, as an absolute minimum 1/2Ltr water and a full litre if possible. Again if you come adrift it may be some time before you are either located or manage to get out on your own. You can go days without food but sometimes, and particularly in hot weather, only a few hours without water. My own golden rule is that I never touch the last 1/2ltr until I am back in sight of the vehicle, even on those occasions when you feel you are at death's door for want of a drink.

I know that some of this sounds melodramatic but I can assure you that any cautions I issue in the course of this book are based on the fact that the issue concerned has either happened to me or to someone that I, personally, have met. The list of safety measures could be endless, such as always carry a torch and a mini first aid kit, but many of these factors have been covered elsewhere in this book especially in the chapters entitled "To Trip or not to Trip" and "Foreseeing the Foreseeable", and most of the rest are down to just common sense.

Before leaving the area of cautions completely, one final addition to it concerns leaving your vehicle. Many of the more prolific Wildlife sites are, of necessity, in relatively isolated areas. This often forces you to leave your vehicle in a vulnerable position. Although this is commonsense, and not only relevant to photographers, if you can't park in a communal area where potential thieves would, perhaps, stand out then try to park it where it will not be too obvious to cruiseby ne'er do wells. The advice to "empty your car" and "do not leave personal possessions inside" is well documented but is particularly relevant to photographers who may well leave surplus tripod and camera bags on view on the assumption that, since they're empty, then they are no incentive to theft. In fact they are not always obviously empty, especially if their lids are shut, and, in any event, their presence highlights the fact that it is a photographer's car and there is every chance of valuable gear having been hidden under the seat or in the boot. In the UK some years ago, when my vehicle was a small Spanish Renault Extra, I was broken into so many times that, in the end, I stopped having the locks and side windows repaired and left the vehicle totally unlocked all the time. This proved to be the most efficacious cure since, from that time on, I suffered no further damage.

Enough of the darker side of life!

Get into the habit of checking out known and potential sites on a regular basis. With short flowering times, and frequently short emergence periods for many insects, a site can change dramatically from week to week. In my earlier photographic days, when I tended to run about like a headless chicken, I was often guilty of writing off a site which, on a first visit, seemed to have nothing to offer, not realising that 2 or 3 weeks earlier or later would have made all the difference.

Another advantage of regular visits is that you are on the spot, over a sufficient period, to record various stages in the lifecycles of a wide range of species living there and you can also indulge in a fairly basic form of Time-lapse photography. Most of the stunning T/L sequences, particularly in the area of growing plants, that you see on TV, have been achieved under strictly controlled and contrived conditions the likes of which we common mortals cannot hope to compete with. You can try setting up something in your greenhouse at home should you have one but it is likely to be a humble effort compared with what you are probably trying to achieve. In the field, however, there is much that you can do with quite good results.

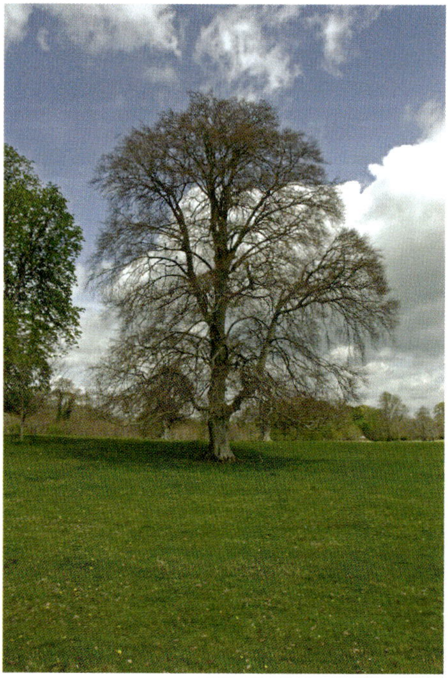

"Time Lapse" 1

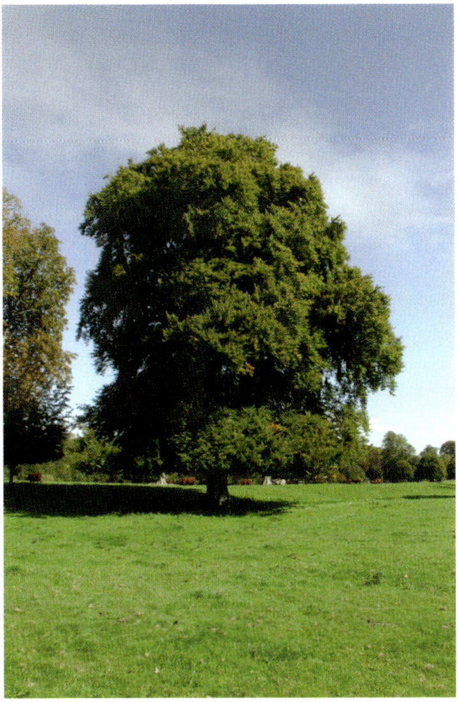

"Time Lapse" 2

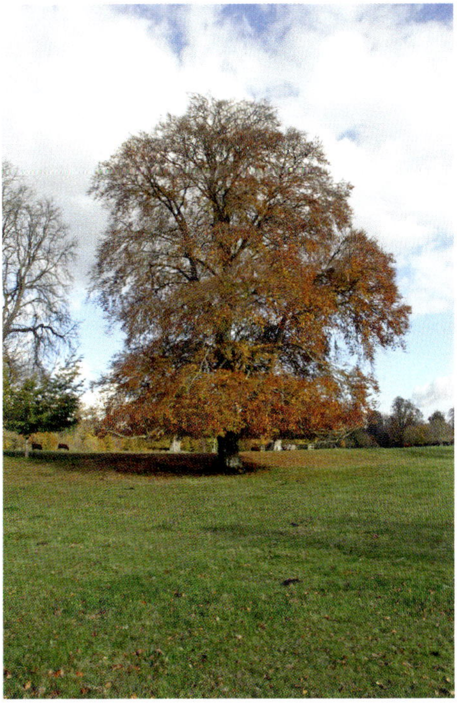

"Time Lapse" 3

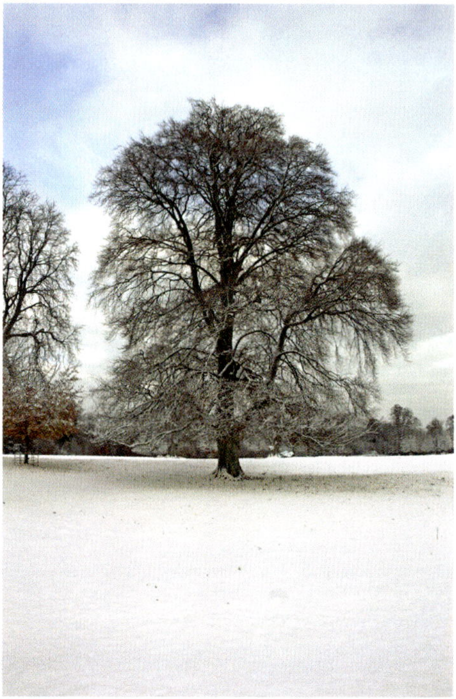

"Time Lapse" 4

Primarily you need to select your subject/s and/or locations. These may be a particularly flowery bank or hedgerow, a specific variety of plant such as an Orchid, a stunning landscape (hillside, wood, valley or coastline), or even just various habitats (pond, stream, river, field, heath or downland) and so on. The safest way to select suitable subjects is to do so at a time of the year when they are at their best. This way you know exactly what the end product is going to look like and you will thus avoid a year's wasted effort working with a subject that doesn't, finally, come up to expectations. Having selected your subject and photographed it at its best you then proceed to photograph it at regular intervals, of your choosing, throughout the following year. This then gives you sufficient images to be able to set up a slide show fading and dissolving them into one another over a full 12 month season, or whatever part of it that you deem desirable. If you balance your transition and duration times correctly you will be able to simulate a continuous Time-lapse sequence.

Take care, however, as things do go wrong! First and foremost you need to record the exact position and height of your tripod and the focal length of the lens you are using. Your camera settings will have to vary as they will be determined by the light conditions prevailing at the time of taking your shots. Differences created by the variations in these settings can usually be overcome in your enhancement programme to create an overall similar lighting effect throughout your series. Position, however, is all important. Don't kid yourself that you'll remember exactly from where you took the previous shot because you most definitely won't. Certainly not with the degree of accuracy needed. Sometimes you can mark the position of your tripod legs but, in many locations, there is a danger that whatever you use as markers will get moved or even disappear. The easiest answer is to accurately record the focal length and focussing distances displayed on your lens when you take the first shot of the series (most lenses will be calibrated in such a way as to allow this), and, additionally, print off a 6 x 4 or a 7 x 5 of your first shot and take it with you each time you go. You can then use all these guides to accurately replicate your original position.

When taking your second, and subsequent shots, allow yourself a cropping margin on your image. Effectively this just means taking a slightly wider angled view than your first one. This will give you working space to tweak, twitch and crop all your subsequent images to exactly match the first one. Never mind how careful you are, you never seem to get it spot on at point of shoot.

A number of situations can arise that seem calculated to doom your venture to failure. My first attempt at this was with an Early Purple Orchid. I found a plant in a hazel coppice with the most incredible black spotting on the leaves and decided to photograph it every few days until flowering was over. The plant was large and robust and in a clearing where it caught the sunlight perfectly. There was another pathetic looking plant, obviously doomed to die in its infancy, just in front of it and several more off to the sides. After each photographic session I left it, and its neighbours, covered very loosely with some small branches to prevent my pride and joy getting inadvertently stomped by size 10 feet. Some 3 to 4 weeks and many pictures later, Spring was turning into "Sprung" and I began to realise that at that time of the year hazel trees begin to produce leaves. The first setback was that my carefully chosen sunny clearing became a deeply dappled and shadowed woodland glade where the sun could scarcely penetrate through the newly opened foliage. The second setback was that the wimpy plant, that was certainly due to die, developed a second lease of life. Whereas I had figured that, by then, it would have been well past its sell by date, in fact it grew at an alarming rate and overshadowed my target plant. Its location was exactly so that I couldn't bypass it without changing my shooting angle and that would have ruined the effectiveness of the series of shots. This was in the days of slides so I couldn't hide behind Mr Adobe and hope that he could put it right. There may be some who would be inclined to say "hook it out" and, naturally, that course was obviously a possibility. You do, however, have to work to a certain code of ethics though, since there is normally no one looking over your shoulder, there is nothing to stop you from breaking it. Only you will know. However, you will know, and you will always know, and if you are able to happily conduct, and live with, yourself in that fashion then you are not one that I would wish to call "compadre". In any event, even had I chosen to go that route, then my series of shots would have suddenly acquired a glaring gap. In my case the "wimp" became such an impressive plant that I considered making it the subject rather that the one with the magnificent leaves. Nature, however, saved me developing a headache over the matter by sending some anti-photographic nocturnal creature to graze off all the flower heads partway up their stems. End of problem!

Some time lapse sequences of individual habitats can be extremely effective especially if you are able to get shots clearly portraying all the seasons of the year, including at least one under snow. Individual trees can produce some stunning sequences as you can portray them through Spring, Summer, Autumn and Winter as they come into leaf, flower, fruit, Autumnal tints and leaf shedding and culminating in the Winter dormancy period.

Have a go. You will know best what sequences will fit in with your own aims and objectives and this kind of photography helps to provide an all year round excuse to be taking photos and gives you a great sense of purpose as you follow through with your carefully drawn up plans.

Never stint on your research and become familiar with all stages in the life cycles of your chosen subjects. Not only is this mind broadening, but it will often enable you to be still actively photographing, through seasons of the year when many other photographers will feel that there is nothing out there for them, in order to capture the entire year round life cycle. As you study more and more life forms you will begin to see an overall pattern and interdependency between often widely differing species. With a little thought some of these interdependencies can become the basis for pleasingly involved and protracted photographic projects spanning many seasons or even years.

Put yourself about. Get to know the wardens and rangers at the various sites that you visit. Be approachable, don't be a recluse and don't be afraid to engage people in conversation. This next is a potentially more hazardous pastime – be prepared to point out the error of their ways to those uninitiated who periodically abuse the countryside – but try to do so in such a way as not to receive a thick ear for your trouble. Read, mark, learn and inwardly digest all that you can on your chosen subjects and, over a period, you will find yourself becoming acknowledged as a serious source of information. There is a great inner sense of achievement to be gained as you progress up the tree of Wildlife knowledge and it will add a huge amount of extra satisfaction to your photographic efforts. Coincidentally being known to all and sundry will stand you in very good stead if you ever decide to commercialise your interest by the sale of prints, writing of articles, giving of talks or whatever. Don't be afraid to voice your opinions and don't hide your light under a self-imposed bushel. We need you to swell the ranks. There are not too many of us out here and we need all the help that we can get to spread the word!

Chapter 4

Film v Digital

Preamble

It is not normally the purpose of this book to attempt to sway its readers in any particular direction when it comes to the choice of either equipment or subjects, merely to offer up the list of options and allow you to proceed on your own path, freely chosen and freely pursued. On the subject of film vs digital I may, however, in keeping with modern times, be accused of showing some bias. This assertion would be true but I would also hope that my following reasoning will both explain and substantiate that bias.

The subject of film vs digital was, until fairly recently, a subject very relevant to Wildlife Photography of the day, and the choice between one or the other warranted careful thought and consideration. However, quite quickly even for these hectic times, I would say that the subject and consequent choices have passed out of the realms of relevance and, in realistic terms, are no longer an option that anyone anticipating a longterm future in Wildlife Photography should need to consider.

Until really very recently the question of whether I photographed in film or digital was posed regularly to me at virtually every talk that I gave. That has now ceased to happen and, although Talk Organisers still occasionally ask whether my presentation will be slide or digitally based, I'm sure that their query relates only to what kind of projector I will be using. I truly believe that virtually no-one, these days, would think to question what photographic format I am using since it would not cross their minds, even for a moment, that I could be using anything other than digital.

Many speakers are still giving slide illustrated talks even though they may, some time ago, have switched to digital photography. The reasons for sticking with the old style illustrations are often based on the fact that digital projectors are certainly very expensive plus the fact that many Wildlife Photographers, who are now firm digital enthusiasts, have not been so for long enough to have accumulated a digital image library to equal their old slide one.

Some clubs have invested in a digital projector but for many others you have to bring your own gear, which needs to be PAT tested into the bargain. Some speakers, especially those drawn from the ranks of their own club members, may only be called on to give one or two talks a year, so what are they to do? Fees for this kind of talk often hover around the level of "a pittance" so they can hardly be expected to carry the costs of producing a digital presentation for such infrequent use. Apart from the equipment problem is the fact that, quite often, a large part of a talk's content will be of such an age that it will have to be slide based anyway, and so then there is the added headache of scanning and enhancing them. With an average talk consuming up to 200 images this can represent a considerable workload and it is simply not worth it for only an occasional outing.

There are still some film diehards, and all credit to them. Long may they be able to buy film! They are a mixture of dedicated souls, some of whom will still be singing "I did it my way" even as they are carried off to that great photographic studio in the sky, and many of the rest are simply resisting change because they are afraid of the unknown. Few of us, and even less as you get older, welcome dramatic change in our lives, particularly in those of our pursuits that may, in fact, form a very large part of those lives. This I know well because "I was that soldier!" What younger generations today often overlook is that there are those among us who didn't grow up sucking on the control stick of a "Game Boy". Some of us are so old, and despite all the odds still alive, that we can still add up two plus two in our heads without having to resort to a calculator, and even spell more than a dozen words without the need for "spellcheck"! In fact many of us, until recently myself included, have lived perfectly fulfilling lives without the seeming need to even own a computer. This does not mean that such people should be considered as figures of fun since, after all, they could still be members of Mensa.

Unfortunately the mere thought of having to come to terms with computer technology, often from a standing start, at a late stage in life can be a daunting prospect, and there are many who are simply not prepared to make the move. In practical terms you cannot become a digital photographer without embracing the inevitable use of a computer that it demands. Yes, the odd argumentative soul might claim that you can just take your memory card to a photographic outlet and let them do the work and print your pictures. Come on! – in the real world how many serious photographers are going to settle for that? Yes, you've guessed it -----! You need to be computer literate to even understand how your digital camera works let alone how to use it. Just checking and retrieving your images requires computer type literacy never mind the subsequent enhancing of them.

Before my incoming email box becomes clogged up with contentious and argumentative nonsense I would ask all my potential detractors to read the following chapter chronicling my own switch before they sit in judgment. It is self-explanatory and was certainly a lot easier to write about than it was to experience. All I can say is that I, personally, am the furthest thing from "technology minded" that you are ever likely to come across, and that if I could make and survive the switch-over then so, certainly, can you. I realise that a number of you will promptly claim that you simply have no wish to change and, after all, why should you? Of course you are entitled to your assertions. I feel, however, that of this number not too many will be telling, or even admitting to themselves, the truth, which is that subconscious fear of the unknown. Far be it from me to mention the Ostrich who, when accused of sticking his head in the sand to avoid reality, promptly attempted to justify his actions by firmly avowing that he was doing no such thing but was, in fact, talking to a mole!

I include this chapter, therefore, not as one of modern day relevance but rather one of historical interest though, to me, the history period in question seems to be but yesterday.

The concluding section of this chapter takes the form of my answer to the, then, frequently asked question "Have you switched to digital, and do you regret it?"

Film v Digital.

"Yes, I switched to digital some years ago" and "No, I would not, by choice, go back." Was it a financially painful switch? Yes I suppose it was. Not only was there the cost of new camera bodies and their associated paraphernalia but there was also the "writing off" of several film camera bodies. Years ago I was a "Mr Pentax" but became a "Mr Nikon" when I decided to buy a 200 mm Macro lens and found that, in Nikon, I could get the equivalent lens plus a body plus another lens for the same price as just the Pentax lens on its own. Something to do with the economics of whether the volume of sales could be divided by or into the cost of production!

However, enough said on that earlier score. At the time of my switch to digital I had to mothball Nikon F5's, F100's, and a trusty FM2 because, by that time, there was no resale market for film camera bodies. The only mitigating factor in my switch was that, by staying with Nikon, I could retain my lenses, all of which were Nikon's own.

In fairness I must confess that I held out as long as I could and I was one of those pains in the backside who was never going to change unless dragged there screaming. However, a friend of mine visited me in Spain with his two newly acquired Nikon D70s's. We had a "good old play" for a couple of weeks and the seeds were sown. I was not without apprehension since the term "not computer literate" was formulated specifically with me in mind. The vagaries and directions of my life may have stood me in good stead from the point of view of acquiring an understanding of Wildlife but they never gave me even a nodding acquaintance with the electronic world. The only "mouse" I ever had to deal with was either a problem in my Zoo feed store or something that I fed frozen to various small mammals, birds and reptiles!

There can be no doubting, however, that digital is the medium of the future, (if only until they come up with an even more expensive alternative), and so you eventually have to decide whether to go with the flow or fight against the tide. I believe a "Mr Canute" tried that once and failed abysmally. Anyway I convinced myself that children, scarcely of an age to even talk, seemed capable of using computer like products – so how hard could it be?

Nikon was about to launch its D200 so, to dip my toe in the water, I settled on a D70s and a D200. Unfortunately, I have found in practice, and especially on a trip, that I need at least two, and preferably three, camera bodies. Apart from potential breakage, loss or whatever, it is often not feasible, particularly with highly active Wildlife species, to have to change lenses halfway through the charge or chase. It is also helpful, in the heat of the moment, if the bodies you are using are identical so you don't have to realign your memory banks, every time you switch cameras, to cope with a different range of knobs, dials, buttons and twiddly bits.

With my two new acquisitions still hot from the press I embarked on a trip to Zimbabwe for some weeks where most of the picture taking would be on the hoof and in the bush. Photography on this trip would be playing almost second fiddle since actual Wildlife itself is also my business and I was to be involved in the translocation of a large number of animals, including a group of Elephants, from one reserve to another. I have worked in Africa on a number of occasions, before and since, but this was my first visit with a digital camera.

The disadvantage of not being familiar with my new equipment was, to a large extent, offset by being able to check the results each evening along the way by camera playback, or via the storage unit I was using to download my images. Whilst I didn't exactly grow to distrust the D70s I quickly found myself loathe to use it if I could use the D200, which felt far more comfortable, instead. To cut a long story short, on my return to the U.K., I traded in the D70s, bit the financial bullet, and now have a full complement of D200's. I have been tempted by the D2 and, more recently the D3, ranges but, thinking back to my film days, can well remember that, whilst my body arsenal once consisted of F4's with F90x backups and later F5's with F100 backups, it was only the lighter backup bodies that I took on overseas trips. This was not only for the weight consideration but also ease of use in fast moving situations. In fact I can truthfully say that the F100 was the most efficient and comfortable to use body it has ever been my pleasure to own – and the D200 equates to this in its physical characteristics.

However, past equipment apart, how does film v digital compare? Personally I feel that it is not a fair comparison to make because you are not comparing like with like. The two technologies are so completely different. Unfortunately the more recent one looks to be a bottomless pit of financial input if you are not careful. Its potential is vast, but so is its propensity for expensive backup. Like many of our Wildlife subjects it is an evolving species early on in its development. There is a game of leapfrog between camera development and backup component development and innovation, and to stay abreast of the game can prove to be expensive.

For the aspiring Wildlife Photographer does it need to be ongoingly expensive? Assuming you are going to be using an SLR camera then I would say "Yes, to a certain extent, but not necessarily to an unlimited degree". If you are determined to keep up with developments then, indeed, you need to keep digging deep. However, ongoing costs are, to a large extent, determined by what you require as an end product. If your photographic "raison d'être" is to produce prints to enter into competitions, or images with a view to publication, then you are going to come up against others to whom outlay may be of no consequence. If this is the case, and you wish to compete with them, then I guess that you have to bite the bullet and continue shelling out. If, however, your aspirations are somewhat more humble and you just want pics for yourself or friends, or even images for projection as a slideshow, then ongoing costs need not be significant once you have acquired your basics. There will always be a new camera just coming out, using more pixels, but you have to ask yourself "how many do you actually need to achieve your desired effect?" Some of my most successful African images were captured on the original D70s, with which I parted company so early on, and I often doubt whether I could really better them today.

Rather take time out to become truly proficient with the gear you have got before moving on in a constant spiral. Reach for the stars by all means but do so when the time and finance suits you rather than feeling obliged to keep up with the Joneses. Try to avoid convincing yourself that acquiring "this phenomenal brand new product" will transform your life and raise your photographic excellence through several levels – because it probably won't. It will more likely force you to replace the rest of your gear to keep up and remain compatible!

When deciding which way to go don't let the ridiculous carrot of "look what you will save in film and development costs" be the only determining factor. By comparison to the cost of the software and gadgetry you need to invest in, the old cost of film and developing was a drop in the ocean for many photographers. Admittedly, particularly in these days of airline baggage restrictions, the physical transporting of film had become difficult. I usually allowed 5 rolls of film a day on a trip to a new area and was always afraid to send it through the hold baggage scanners, they being, or so I understood, much stronger that those used on hand baggage. A three or four week trip could, therefore, involve carrying some 150 rolls or so as hand baggage together with all the equipment and, towards the end, this was becoming a major logistical problem.

In summation I can only say that, despite all the minor headaches involved, you should "Gird up your loins and Go West young man for that way lies the future!" -----, and if you don't you'll most certainly be left behind!

Chapter 5

Image Storage

Whichever route you choose to follow, be it digital or film, one of the problems that will rear its head is that of how and where to store your images. If you have opted for film then this problem does not come under the heading of "major". There are a superabundance of tried and tested methods of storing film negatives and, if you are using film positives, (slides), then there is also a wide range of options to deal with them as well. Personally I always took slides and I stored them in the small plastic boxes in which they were returned from the developers. Some time ago (we are now going back into pre-history), I arranged to buy several hundred spare boxes from Kodak, who did all my developing (I used Kodachrome slide film), and this gave me enough spares to be able to store slides of each subject in their own individual boxes. They were then held in a series of shelves and racking, tailormade for the purpose, and which made retrieval straightforward. Towards the end of my slide taking days I had in excess of 150,000 slides and, shelf system or not, it was stretching the logistics more than a little. However, then came digital and all my problems were over, as I could simply store my images in my computer, which was surely big enough to hold as much as I would ever take for years! My first laptop, which it seems I acquired as if but yesterday, had a hard drive of some 20 or 30 GB which was more than adequate for the task – for about as long as it took to blink! The latest one, and there have been one or two in transit in between, has 500GB capacity and I am already having to be careful just what I keep in it. Camera resolutions increase, image sizes go through the roof and the number of shots that you take on digital would have bankrupted you had you tried to take that many on film.

As an on-going problem I think that film image storage, for other than just a few, can be consigned to the past and does not represent much of a problem for the future. Where digital images are concerned, however, I have read much learned piffle about image storage by a succession of pontificating persons who obviously are not very prolific photographers. It can be a problem. Fortunately it is a problem to which the solutions are evolving on a day to day basis. Hard-drives, both in the computer and as separate items of hardware, are increasing in size at an exponential rate but so, too, are image sizes. I fear you will always have to play leapfrog to a certain extent.

The problem is exacerbated for the Wildlife Photographer because, for many of us, there tends to be a fairly short season within which we capture the bulk of our year's images. For those of us who are UK or Europe based this will normally be Spring/early Summer. During this period it is all happening and you will be hard pressed to keep up. The inevitable result of this is that you create a backlog. In effect this means that you will have a build-up of unenhanced images taking up space on your computer. The pundits will advise you that this is no problem since you just "bung 'em on a hard-drive" until you have time to deal with them. In essence this is correct but, in practice, it is not always the same thing. If you can imagine having such a number of photographs that the only way you can store them is to stick them in a box up in the attic, just imagine what a pain it will be when you want to go through them. It's not that it's difficult – it's just a pain, and will seem like a tremendous waste of time. Not only that, but because they've been out of sight and out of mind for some time, you will have forgotten exactly what you have there and which folder/binder/envelope you put them in, so you will have to check around to find them. In the same way, once you place an image on a separate hard-drive its retrieval is quite simple and straightforward but if, like me, you are impatient and in a hurry then the pfaffing about involved in finding and moving your image back into your computer will drive you potty, especially if you have a number to deal with. As a result of this you will probably find that you would prefer to hold them in your computer, where you have instant access to them, until you are ready to work on them.

There are many who will give you a never ending list of advantages of digital over film. In many instances they may well be correct and they will invariably offer up a number of different carrots, all aimed at making you think how lucky you are to be part of this digital revolution. Many of the carrots will relate to the various amounts of time saving that can be effected with the new technology. One of the carrots that is frequently offered, and which always make me smile whenever I hear it, is to the effect that, with digital photography, "at least you can check and delete your mistakes as you go". This is often said in such a way as to imply that it simplifies the whole process and takes any effort and skill that you may lay claim to out of the equation. This is blatantly misleading, to be polite, and a "crock of something else" to be realistic. If you, in fact, try this "as you go", the first reality that you come up against is that, unless you are totally different to everyone else in your approach, you will end up taking vastly more shots in digital than you ever would have done with film. Because of this, and the sometimes frantic nature of photographing highly active Wildlife subjects, there is often little or no time during actual shooting to do more than cast a quick glance at a histogram to monitor your exposure values. This means that any checking and deleting in the field will have to be done after the action is over and, by that time, you are like to have a sizeable number of shots to look at. If you are going to check them in any great detail then, apart from the potential waste of valuable shooting time, you will need a bag of spare batteries. Additionally, with field editing, you will come up against a second harsh reality and that is that the image portrayal on your camera back or storage unit is not good enough to justify making irreversible decisions to delete anything other than the most outrageous and obvious of "cock ups". If there is a shortage of shade, or an abundance of sun, you are likely to scarce be able to see your image display anyway.

Best to get a few extra memory cards and leave your deleting till you can get home and check things out on your computer, where at least you can see what you are doing!

This, of course, leads on to the Boogeyman I have mentioned elsewhere – the computer time involved. This is exacerbated by two principal factors. The first is that you now have a superabundance of images to edit because of the increased number of shots you have taken. The second is in actually deciding exactly what to get rid of. With slides, in the days before "in house" scanning and enhancing became a practical proposition, it was relatively straightforward. If the slide wasn't right then it was wrong, and that was often the end of it. Now, however, you will find it much more difficult to decide. Firstly there will be the obvious discards – like your shot of the perch where a stunning dragonfly was sitting when you started to press the shutter release but wasn't by the time it triggered, and glaring and obvious exposure and movement problems. These are easily dealt with and, in practice, you will probably surprise yourself by how few of these there are. Once you have achieved a reasonable degree of proficiency the numbers of out and out horrors that you take are often quite small. Equally easy to deal with are those shots destined to become Front Page or Centre Spread of the "National Geographic" where that innate expertise, that you have long kept hidden from the world under a proverbial bushel, has finally blossomed forth – surely as a sign of things to come! Unfortunately the reality is that there won't be many of these either but those that there are can be immediately filed away for later attention – if you can bear to wait that long!

In between these two extremes, however, is a huge grey area. Gone are the days of the clear cut decision making that pertained in the era of film, when you could either use it or not as the case may have been. Software programmes now are so comprehensive that many slightly lacklustre shots can be salvaged and turned into something quite worthwhile. This is especially so if you are only after 6 x 4 or 7 x 5 prints, at which size many minor faults are apparent to only the most discerning eye. Even these shots are not too time consuming at this stage, as you quickly become proficient at recognizing them and can file them accordingly. No, the headache is all the rest. With the virtually unlimited potential of what you can do to an image in any half decent enhancement programme you will find that an incredible number of your shots will contain at least one, if not more, redeeming features that "just might" be useful at some future date. The ostensibly easy answer to this might seem to be to hang on to them all just in case you one day want to use "that top left-hand corner!" However there's no such thing as a free lunch because now you have to decide where and how to store all these "maybe's" so they don't clutter up your workbench. You can hardly store them in your main computer otherwise, if you are a prolific picture taker, it will soon become full – no matter how much room there seemed to be when you bought it! Spare hard drives are now a viable option and probably offer the easiest retrieval or, of course, you can burn the images to disc.

Image storage on overseas trips, in particular, can be a headache. I download images onto an Epson 40 gig storage unit at the end of every day's shooting and make sure that I have enough memory cards to get me through even the most successful of days without having to delete along the way. That's fine as far as it goes but I shoot RAW and JPEG simultaneously and, on my camera settings, this gives me roughly 40 images per GB or, in effect, about the same as one roll of film would have done. This puts my storage unit capacity at the equivalent of about 40 rolls of film. Not a lot on a decent trip, especially in view of the increased number of shots I now, in keeping with most other digital photographers, seem to be taking. Whilst I am not always in reach of mains electricity nevertheless, in practice, on most trips, then at least every few days some form of civilization rears its head so I can make a beeline for the nearest socket. I am loathe to have to carry a laptop with me just for downloading or disc cutting as, apart from its size and weight, it, and of course my storage unit and cameras, are very "nickable gear" in some locations. This is a risk that is sometimes unavoidable if you want to be where the action is and, to minimize its threat, I try to stick to gear that I can carry on my person. I usually wear two lightweight camera jackets giving me an inordinate number of pockets to play with. If you have a laptop with you then, in reality, it usually gets left at whatever your base is during the day due to the impracticality of having to shin up trees and clamber down gullies with it and the rest of your equipment. This unattended period is when it is most likely to "get took" with "walkabout fever". I have partially overcome this problem by buying a disc cutting gadget that fits in my pocket and cuts a disc from a memory card. It is both mains and battery operated and enables me to cut discs regularly. I normally make two copies, one to be mailed back to the U.K. at the earliest opportunity and the other to stay with me. It is really just a "belt and braces" option in an attempt to minimize the potential loss of my work. My theory is, without being too dramatic, that even in countries where you can be relieved of your equipment at gunpoint, and there seem to be an increasing number of these, then there is always a chance of at least saving or getting your images out one way or the other.

Assuming that one way or another you have got yourself, your computer and your images all together at the same time then where to from here?

If, like me, you are a bit of a Magpie then the important thing is to develop a system that suits you and the way in which you work and try to stick with it. Try to get it right because, however you decide to tackle the problem, you will still be retrieving images from within your system for years to come so that it would be an enormous benefit if you could think it through and come up with a system that will stand the test of time. There are new developments constantly cropping up and, since I started putting this book together, the position has changed more than once. As I write this now, at some unmentionable hour of the morning, the current best option seems to be a separate hard-drive. It wasn't always so, but, at least for the time being, it is at the moment. The way in which I handle it is covered in a little more detail in the following chapter but, in essence, I download from my camera, or field storage device, into my computer. I have a natural and in-built distrust of modern technology and feel much happier if I can hold an image in my hand in some form or other, rather that just accepting that it is there somewhere floating about in the ether or in my computer, which could wipe itself clean at any time just because it's having an off-day, so once the images are downloaded I burn them to DVD (I use 4GB memory cards and one of these just fits nicely onto a DVD which takes, theoretically but never in practice, 4.7 GB as opposed to a CD which only takes some 700MB). I then have a separate hard-drive onto which I put all my downloads. In fact I have several separate hard-drives for various purposes and one of these is used to backup all the others. I then copy this one onto another master at regular intervals and this second one is then held in a different location for extra security. That way, if the housc burns down and I lose it all, then at least I can retrieve anything and everything. I shudder to think of the work that would be involved, mind, and would probably have to do a deal with that great Wildlife Photography Producer in the sky to grant me an extension to my allotted span so that I have time to follow it through.

Chapter 6

Image Editing And How Far To Go

It is impossible, in this day and age, to ignore this aspect of modern photography, whether dealing with scanned, or straight, digital images. In the early days the main use of an editing facility was merely to improve or "enhance" your image to produce a more pleasing hard copy "photograph".

The disadvantage of slide photography was always that the slide was the slide was the slide and if you got it wrong you were, to all intents and purposes, stuck with it. Now, of course, it is a straightforward process to have slides scanned to become digital images and, furthermore, you can then even have those digital images reconverted to slide so that there is now an opportunity, in between times, to "enhance" some of those slides that, at the time, were lacking in some respect. This is especially useful for anyone who is a user of slides or giver of old style Slideshows as you can now upgrade your presentations without having to switch to digital projection with all that entails. The above mentioned disadvantage of slide photography was, however, not all one sided. Knowing that you could do little to alter your final slide image was tremendous incentive to make sure that you got it right in the first place. Yes, shutter speed and aperture variations could be covered by bracketing, but composition and cropping, or the removal of unwanted objects were all but impossible to remedy. The danger of today's photography is that it can all too easily include an element of "never mind I can put that right in Photoshop" and that can lead to sloppy work. Yes, you should certainly use and consider all the tools at your disposal, including these subsequent image editing possibilities, when taking a shot, but try to avoid letting future enhancing potential lead to rushed and careless photography. Remember it is far easier to edit a good image than an "iffy" one.

The scanning of slides can be a minefield in itself. If you take your slides to one of the multiples that offers this service you are likely to get them scanned on average settings which may not be good enough for your particular images. I have a very good quality Nikon slide scanner and we scan all our own. Because of the vast number of slides involved, however, it is not possible to scan them all on an individual setting basis, and so we, too, have to settle for an average, but at least it is an average set by us, for us. What seems to be the biggest stumbling block is that when I was taking slides, mainly to be used in illustrated talks, then the camera settings chosen at point of shoot were those that would produce a slide viewable via a slide projector on a white screen. If the subject contained potential highlight areas, such as Penguins and many Waterfowl, then the exposure settings chosen were done so to produce a viewable slide and not necessarily to favour the highlights. In effect this must have caused what we would now describe as a degree of burnout, or near burnout, with the highlights, but because of the nature of viewing them on the screen it was not as apparent as would be the case today with a digital image. Had the slide been taken on such settings as to retain detail in the highlight areas then it would have been far too dark to be viewable on the screen as a slide. The net effect of all this is that if you are scanning your old slides you are likely to find a number of them in which the highlights are distinctly burnt out and there seems to be little that can be done to cure it during the scanning process. Sometimes a little skillful enhancing can rescue some of them but some of the others may have to be abandoned.

Which leads on to what, for me, has become the Boogeyman of modern photography, and that is the amount of computer time involved. It is no longer just about taking pictures. Today cameras and computers seem to go hand in glove. It was bad enough at one time when you seemed to have only enough time to spend one day a week taking your shots and then six days a week in the office working out what to do with them. Now you have to add several days of editing time into the equation and the percentage of your life that you can spend in the field is reduced even further.

Before dealing with the subject of image editing in any detail you have, first, to decide whether you aim to be a Wildlife Photographer, out there where it is all happening, or a slave to a computer, in there where it is not happening. Part of your answer to this question will be decided by your answers, if only to yourself, to the questions regarding the "purpose" of your photographic venture, that I posed earlier. It is all too easy to become so bogged down in the enhancement side of things that you may end up losing sight of all the reasons that brought you to the world of Wildlife Photography in the first place. I have known some competition photographers who happily spend days, and even weeks, working on a single image. The end product, after all that tweaking and twitching, must be so far removed from its original that it almost ceases to be relevant. Either that or it must have been a pretty "bloody awful" image in the first place, and then you have to wonder why they chose that one to work on?

I'm probably not that much better since, just as I can never remember taking what I considered to be a perfect shot (except in my very early days when, as I recall, they all were!), neither have I yet managed a perfect edit. There seems always to be something that you think could be improved. It is really a question of degree and what lengths you are prepared to go to. To a certain extent this will be decided by the enhancement programme that you have decided to work with.

Before discussing individual programmes one of the questions that needs to be addressed is that of how much enhancement is ethically acceptable? Here you enter really contentious country. I hear many alleged purists maintaining that photographs should not be enhanced at all. To them, I am sorry, but I can only say "Get real". Whether we like it or not those days are behind us and I cannot see them returning. Ever since man designed flashguns and filters then photographs have been enhanced – never mind earlier dark room techniques. There is now a whole new technology out there. Maybe embracing it in all its totality is what gives rise to the oft leveled assertion that it changes us from digital photographers to digital artists. This kind of allegation is always proffered with a slight curl to the lip as if the whole scenario is, in some way, distasteful and likely to stick to the sole of your shoe. In the real world this is an "about to be outmoded" opinion and is only voiced because of the newness of the technology involved. As time goes on people's perceptions of what constitutes photography will change, just as they always have done. There seems now to be an unquestioning acceptance of the rapid pace of technological change and innovation in all walks of life and photography is no different. Unfortunately change seems to come in packages and you generally have to accept the whole package or not at all.

Often the intended purpose for which the image is being prepared will dictate the level of enhancement that is merited. The important factor is to be able to be up front about it without feeling like a second class citizen or the need to lie. Competition entries are usually covered by a set of guidelines, clearly stating what is acceptable. Submissions for potential publication will also normally be covered by the publisher's own set of rules and regulations. Record shots should need little or no enhancement or they cease to be record shots, but it should be borne in mind that many cameras record basic images, devoid of any in built enhancement, under the right and proper assumption that the images will subsequently be subjected to some kind of editing programme.

It is with pictures to be hung on the wall that the greatest potential discord arises. I would submit that, in this new era, if you can do something to make the original image more pleasing to the eye for display purposes then you should be entitled to do so. After all, should the enhancement of a picture be of concern to a prospective purchaser, then he or she can always ask for a certificate, or confirmation as to whether it has been enhanced and, if so, to what extent.

There are those who would long debate the difference between enhancement and manipulation but I would suggest that they are merely playing with words. Once you change a sky, clone out a telephone pole or pylon, or delve into the realms of "layers" then you unquestionably change that image out of all context with its original. Whether this be enhancing or manipulating and whether it changes you from a photographer to an artist then I say "Good luck to you and go for it". It is plain nonsense to suggest that some editing aids are more ethical than others and I would suggest that those who hold back and maintain that view will be overtaken, and may not even finish the race.

For myself I am fortunate that by far the bulk of my images are of individual Wildlife subjects, and their backgrounds and surroundings are often not really relevant. Indeed a great many, and particularly my Macro shots, are taken on exposure settings deliberately chosen to blur the backgrounds and make the subject stand out. I say that in this I am fortunate since this type of image often demands only a minimum amount of tweaking and this can frequently be achieved using pretty basic and non time consuming programmes. Many of my enhancements take no more that a couple of minutes and involve using only one or two "tools". Of course I kid myself that this is because I take a good picture in the first place! There may even be an element of truth in this as my earlier days of slide photography rammed the message home to me that a little extra effort at point of shoot usually pays off in the end product.

I am further fortunate in that my main commercial outlet is the sale of prints, either direct or through wholesale outlets, to the public. I am not a competition photographer, and so avoid most of the preparation time demanded by that vocation, and I am not too bothered about publication, and so avoid the inordinate amount of office time that aspiration inevitably involves. Time is of the essence to me and I have found, at risk of contradiction, that 90% of enhancement effect is achieved in 10% of the time that could be spent on an image. The final 10% of the effect takes the remaining 90% of the time. Your own personal set of standards, and search for perfection, may demand that you spend this extra 90% of effort but I would suggest that the bulk of the non photographic public is not discerning enough to appreciate your dedication. Their buying impulses are, in the main, triggered by factors far more mundane and as basic as simply whether the picture appeals to them or not, for whatever reason. Your degree of technical perfection and ability seldom enters into it.

I am, myself, my own worst judge of my work's saleability because, being so involved with it, I use a biased and blinkered set of criteria by which to judge it. I have to use Mother or Sister to give me some idea of whether I'm on the right track or not. Neither of them has the faintest idea of any of the technicalities involved in producing a final image, nor are they remotely interested. They only know whether they "like" a picture or not. It's a bit similar to liking strawberries or not. How long it took, or difficult it was, to grow them plays no part in the decision of whether to have them for tea. You either like 'em or you don't. It's not explainable – it's just how it is!

Their opinions often cause me to entertain thoughts that bring their mental ability into question, but I have learnt to keep these thoughts hidden in a dark recess as they often prove to be right when the images finally go on sale.

So ------- you've now reached make your mind up time. For a whole host of reasons you now have to decide which images to work on, and to what extent, as well as what programme to use to do it with.

Now I'm going to be really contentious. I'll bet that if you have read any amount of literature on the subject you will have come away with two distinct feelings. The first of these is that you should shoot in Raw and the second is that Photoshop's CS range is the answer to all your enhancing prayers. They may well be right on both counts but as to whether they are really necessary in your initial apprenticeship period I leave for you to judge because, with both, there are potential headaches and pitfalls. Incidentally when I refer to items such as "your apprenticeship period" or "in the initial stages", these are, in a way, figures of speech and not meant in any way to denigrate your status. However, the whole photographic scene is so involved that you do need an "inauguration" period and it is no reflection on your abilities to admit to being within it. It's rather like driving a car. You may like to think that you were born with the innate ability to drive already in you, and the need to stick up those L plates is an affront to your finer feelings and machismo. If you have ever travelled to any of those countries where going through a "learner" stage is not a legal requirement towards getting a license to drive, and looked at the complete nightmare and lack of driving skills exhibited by so many of the drivers, then you will appreciate the need to grin, bear it and take the test!

The benefits of working with both RAW and CS are well documented and propounded by all and sundry. However, I have always believed that you should learn to walk properly before you break into a sprint otherwise there is a distinct danger of tripping over your own feet. There is a potential element here of too much too soon, and much of it may be surplus to requirements. My following suggestions may seem to deal with the subject at too amateur a level but they have the advantage of allowing you to produce final images quickly and with relatively little pain. If you find that my methods leave you with unsatisfactory results then upgrade, or move on, from that aspect of the process that has given rise to the dissatisfaction. By the time that you are able to make that sort of decision, however, you will have a far better idea of what you are doing and can base your ideals on your own experience and not have to depend on that of others.

Some of you may be using cameras that take only JPEGs, and to those I would say that you have nothing to worry about, save only that you should set your cameras to take the absolutely best quality of JPEG that it can handle. Generally speaking the higher the setting that you select then the fewer images you will get on a memory card, but I can assure you that the pain of the cost of extra memory cards is far less than the pain of working with poor quality images just to gain a few extra shots per card. Others of you will have the option of shooting either JPEG or RAW or both. Being a belt and braces man I would suggest that you opt for the latter but, again, make sure that you set the camera to take the best quality of JPEG that it can though this will, of necessity, limit the number of shots per card dramatically. Don't even give this aspect of it a second thought. Memory cards have become very reasonably priced and are reusable countless numbers of times. Once your images have been downloaded they no longer need to remain on the card and if you get into the habit of downloading every night, even if it doesn't seem worth it when you may have taken only a few shots that day, then your cards can be cleared on a daily basis.

Generally speaking I use two programmes for the bulk of my downloading and subsequent enhancing. Many digital cameras come supplied with basic downloading software and I use the Nikon programme that came with mine, which is called Picture Project. This is a very basic programme and I use it simply for downloading into and as an initial viewing platform to decide which images I am going to work with. Although it does contain some enhancing tools, I do not use them as such other than occasionally, and temporarily, during the viewing process. If you do not have the benefit of one of these "free" programmes with your camera don't worry as there are a great many out there, and any of the major retailers can advise you accordingly. Remember, you don't need this programme to do anything other than downloading and viewing, so don't spend money on additional features that you will not need to use.

Most of these programmes will locate your various downloads in separate files and offer you the opportunity to place selected images in a "collection" or a holding file. My Nikon programme offers the "collection" facility and I set up one for each downloading session. The only time I ever delete from a memory card before downloading is if I know that I have made an almighty boo boo with a particular shot since I do not accept that the camera display is detailed enough to base a deleting decision on. Accordingly I then download the entire card, in my case I shoot both RAW and JPEG, into the computer. The next step is to then burn the entire download to disc and, in addition, copy it to a hard drive on which I store all my downloads. At this stage I can draw comfort from the fact that all the images are backed up somewhere other than the computer, and I can start to play with them knowing that if that computer goblin that eats images for a living gets any of mine then I can easily replace them.

Now, just when you would think that it was "safe to go into the water" you have to start making life determining decisions. The first of these is whether you are going to work with RAW or JPEG if you have the choice of both. My advice, at this stage, is to forget all about RAW. You have got all your RAW information well backed up and if, at some stage in the future, you decide that you want to work with it then it is not a problem to retrieve it. This advice may go against much that you will hear from other quarters but I am a firm believer in that the more you can do to an image then the more you will want to do, and you will certainly convince yourself that you simply must do. RAW can undoubtedly offer advantages on a few occasions such as very contrasty subjects like Penguins, Magpies or some Waterfowls, or on those occasions when you have only been able to get one or two shots of a subject and have managed to muck up your exposure settings. However, if you have bracketed sufficiently, as advised in other chapters, then you should have a sufficient choice of images to be able to select one that doesn't require you to plough through the huge range of options that your RAW converter will offer you. Believe me if there is anything of the real "out there amongst it" Wildlife Photographer about you, you will come to value any time saving that you can effect. For those of you who have decided to stay with me a little longer we will move on to the next step.

Having decided to work with JPEGS I would then go through the JPEG content of the downloaded card and select those images that I feel I want to work with. These I then would place, as I selected them, into the "collection" prepared earlier. Having worked through the whole card you are then left with your selected images in their "collection" and you can export these to your final enhancement programme. At this stage I would convert them from a JPEG to a TIFF since a JPEG image can degrade with constant opening and closing whereas a TIFF remains the same. In my case this converts the size of my image from +/- 5/6Mb to 29Mb which is a substantial uplift. This is where the use of the two separate programmes comes into play since it allows you to keep your basic downloads separate from your "workons" and avoids cluttering up your "workbench". Once you have transferred your selected images you can, if you wish and are not likely to need them for future comparisons, delete your download file from the original programme as the conversion to TIFF will, in effect, have produced a separate image that will not be linked to, and deleted with, the originals.

You are now clear to start enhancing your images but, of course, at some stage of the game you need to have decided what programme you are going to use. Here, again, I am likely to be contentious as I would advise against CS at this stage. It is a wonderfully all embracing programme, but also wonderfully complex to the uninitiated. There are a number of mid-level enhancement programmes available by such as Adobe and Paintshop, as well as a host of others, that may well be better suited to you at this stage. I feel that, on this subject, I am only qualified to speak of what I know from personal experience and so, whilst I normally tend to shy away from advocating specific products, in this case I would be inclined to recommend Adobe's Elements. This is a programme with which I am very familiar and I would go so far as to say that I would find it very difficult to imagine what you could want to do to an image that you cannot do with Elements. It is not expensive and is very user friendly. Like any of these programmes, of course, it takes a bit of getting used to but there are so many instruction guides available on it that if, unlike me, you can understand the jargon used then you should have no trouble in coming to terms with it. CS is so comprehensive that there is a great danger that once you pass through its doors we won't see you again for decades. There is almost no limit to the changes you can carry out with CS but many of them are so minor that only the most discerning and, may I say it, pedantic eye, can spot the difference – and they all take time to effect, and often quite a lot of it.

Before closing on this subject I would just say the following. Unfortunately, as in many walks of life, you will find some in this vocation who obviously seem to feel the need to adopt superior airs, often to cover their own inadequacies. They are few in number and, indeed, the vast majority of people that you meet in conjunction with your photographic pursuits will be the most kind, pleasant and helpful you could ever wish to encounter. If you have the misfortune to meet any of the former do not let them sway or influence you. You will know them instantly as, apart from viewing you over the top of their glasses, they will immediately pooh pooh whatever you are doing and promptly start to tell you how to do it better. Be polite and listen, with seemingly avid interest, as some of what they say may inadvertently be beneficial or enlightening, even if it is only a lesson in how not to behave. Never let yourself feel inadequate if you don't have monster lenses, high resolution cameras, use fancy computer programmes or even know the Latin names of your subjects. All these are things to which you can aspire but at a time when your circumstances permit and not when you have felt railroaded into it.

Further to this, and in conclusion of this chapter, I would offer you a challenge. To those of you to whom time is of no object then it may not represent a challenge, but to the rest of you who, like me, just want to get out there and take pictures, then it is really relevant. I would ask that you bear with me, follow my advice, and become proficient with the enhancement of JPEGs. When you have become sufficiently competent select one of your final images with which you are well pleased, and then go back and retrieve the RAW version of it. Either do it yourself, or give it to a colleague who is conversant with RAW, and work on that format of your image. Keep a record of the amount of time involved in achieving both versions of the final image, as well as taking into account the cost of whatever programmes are used, and compare them. If you feel that the RAW wins the day, taking all your own personal budgets into account, then there you have your answer and can head in that direction. If, as I suspect, the difference is so slight that you are indecisive as to which is the better then take the line of least resistance and stick with what you already know best and to hell with what anyone else thinks. Conduct the same experiment with just the difference between working the same image in Elements and CS and, taking the above criteria into account, see what you think. At least, that way, you will be able to make up your own mind based on your own circumstances, and not have to worry about what anyone else may seek to talk you into.

If you are one of those people who has never attempted anything like this before and are apprehensive to the extent that it is putting you off from "having a go" then worry no more. You are perfectly normal and not cerebrally challenged. We all experience a degree of "collywobbles" from time to time so you are not alone. Bear with me, have faith and we'll get you under way in the time it takes to flip a computer's on/off switch. Here I have to assume that you have a modicum of computer ability and also that you have followed my advice and installed a copy of Adobe Elements. Download your images as I instructed above and select the ones you want to work with and copy them to Elements as TIFFs. Open Elements and select "Edit" from the welcome window. Wait while Adobe does its commercial credits bit and a blank Editor screen will open surrounded by tool bars. Go to the top rt-hand corner and click on the word "organiser". Your browser will open up. A window called "Watched Folders" will come up and offer you the chance to add a number of images to your "browser". Say yes. This Watched Folders window will eventually drive you potty as it seizes on anything and everything that you put into your computer and tries to kidnap it into Elements whether you want it there or not. What it will do is open a window into which will flow all your recently downloaded images in their entirety and, at the very end, will also come those that you selected. One of the options you will be offered at this stage is to "deselect all". Do so. Now go through the images on offer and put a tick in the small box alongside those that you have selected (they will be the ones showing as TIFFs so you should be able to identify them without too much trouble). Hit OK (at the bottom of the window). Things will flash and zoom about and then Element's import window will come up. Hit OK again. All the images you selected will now be displayed in their own Browser window without being mixed in with any other images already there. They will remain in this isolation, from where you can work on them, until you switch off or reboot, at which point they will be added to your main Browser which comes under the heading of "Organiser".

Choose the image you want to work on and click on it. When the image shows as having been selected (a blue box appears around it) click on the word "Editor" (top right hand corner of screen) and select the "Full edit" option from the drop down. If your luck holds then, joy of joys, a large version of your chosen image will suddenly appear and you are now in the "Editor" which is the place where you do your work. Click on "Enhance" (Towards the top Left-hand side of Toolbar). Ignore all "Auto" settings and click on "Adjust Lighting" in the drop-down. Click "Shadows and Highlights" in secondary drop-down. This opens up a window containing three sliders and initially I would suggest trying about 13% each for the top two and 10% for the bottom one. The effect of each of these sliders on your image will be immediately apparent and if any of my suggested settings are obviously wrong for your particular image then adjust them to suit. You can check whether you have effected an improvement by using the "preview" button which will show you your image just before your latest editing action. By switching the preview on and off you can compare the "before" and "after". When you are happy with this stage click OK. Go back to Enhance and Adjust Lighting and this time choose Levels from the final drop-down. Click on "Auto" (halfway down on rt hand side of Levels window) Normally, in most cases at this stage, you should now have a wonderfully improved image. Click on OK. If you still need it brighter or more contrast then return yet again to Enhance, Adjust Lighting and this time choose the option for Brightness/Contrast and adjust the slider to suit. Click OK. If you are happy with the image hit the Editor Close "X" (top rt-hand side of Editor window. Don't hit the very top right corner X or you will shut down the whole caboodle. You want the second X down). This will then give you the option to save. Say yes. This opens a "Save As" window. Save the image "as a copy" (tick small box in the middle towards the bottom of the Save As window.) Click the "Save" box. Click OK in the TIFF options window that comes up. Your image will then be saved as a copy in your browser alongside the original unenhanced image from your download.

If all that sounds daunting and a foreign language don't worry. Just keep this page open and follow it slowly and see what happens. OK, I know it won't be perfect because I obviously can't see your image and so I don't know what needs doing to it but it will at least improve your image and give you the courage, I hope, to start poking about to see what else you can do. Don't be too proud to go buy an "Idiots Guide to Elements". If you're self conscious then make a spare cover for the book out of a thick brown paper bag and then you can read it in public without passers-by knowing what intelligence category you obviously feel you come under!

Chapter 7

To Trip Or Not To Trip

(Photography on Organised Trips)

Whilst prices, taxes, volcanic dust clouds, striking Cabin Crews and the World Economy may all fluctuate in both their intensity and the effect that they have on our daily lives in general, we live, nonetheless, in an age when International travel has never been more affordable in terms of cost in relation to income. I am all too painfully aware of the fact that, for many, any form of travel, even the local bus into town, is almost a cost too far and takes some considerable thought as to whether it can be justified in the face of a strict budget. However, like it or not, it seems to me that, no matter how hard the times, a vast number of folk seem, somehow, to come up with the wherewithal to embark on at least one annual holiday.

At the risk of strident contradiction I would suggest that, in a great majority of cases, an overseas trip may be no more expensive than a UK based break. It will certainly be more productive in the supply of subject matter that you may not encounter again for the rest of the year. After all, you can cover what the UK has to offer on odd days out and short breaks as and when you can fit them in, but once across the channel a whole new world opens up. Yes, I know the £ is weak against many currencies but you will still find it eagerly sought after by all and sundry from the Tour Operators to the market traders of whatever country you decide to visit. One of the advantages of holding a sought after commodity is that your possession of it, and no doubt reluctance to part with it unnecessarily, normally has the effect of forcing down prices amongst those seeking to become its new owners.

For those of us with a Wildlife Photography bent I find it hard to convince myself to settle for the newly invented "staycation" (what sad soul dreams up these words?) when the old tried and tested "vacation" is still on offer. This is especially so since, in the long term, the latter can often turn out to be considerably cheaper.

However – all that apart – for those of us who wish to combine our interest in Wildlife Photography with our normal breaks, of whatever frequency, times, in my memory anyway, have never been better. A number of Tour Operators have sprung into being to satisfy our needs with the result that you can now access almost any part of the known world, in the company of like minded souls and under the guidance of leaders whose very livelihood depends on them making sure that you enjoy your trip. "Quids in" or what?

Admittedly this does not constitute a guarantee of enjoyment since the "best laid plans of mice and men etc" but it does go a long way towards dotting most of the i's and crossing most of the t's. Added to this is the fact that many of the operators have run trips to the same area for many years and so have had time to "suss things out". The benefit of this manifests itself, not only with carefully chosen accommodation and eating facilities, but also in an acquired knowledge of local customs, highspots and the best locations to find whatever you are seeking. I ,myself, know several localities and sites in my own home area in Spain (see article on Castell de Castells in the "sites" section of this book) that host an infinite number of beautiful things, whereas similar looking sites only a few hundred meters away are virtual deserts. The chances of a casual visitor coming across these hidden oases are practically zilch. Whether you initially find these places by accident or not you do, nevertheless, need to be in the area regularly to stand a chance of being in the right place when the "accident" happens – and this is where the Tour Operators score as a result of their regular visits. They will also have worked out the best time of year to visit certain areas since a difference of only a few weeks can be all that stands between success and failure.

There is also the old saying of there being "safety in numbers" and here again the organised trip scores over independent travel in certain areas. Apart from spreading the often considerable cost of transport over a greater number of bodies, the chances of being mugged, robbed or ripped off are considerably reduced. Additionally you get the chance to visit places that many would-be independent, solitary, travellers may be better advised to avoid.

First glance at a brochure may make you feel that some trips are expensive compared to what you feel you could visit the same place for independently. You have, however, to remember that in many cases, other than the cost of getting to and fro your UK airport, you may not need to spend any more money at all since many of the trips on offer are on an all inclusive basis. Of course you may wish to buy souvenirs and drinks etc, but apart from these most other expenses are included. Added to this is the fact that from a responsibility point of view you will be virtually "stress free". Part of what you are paying entitles you to sit back and enjoy it while someone else sorts out the myriad niggles and problems that an overseas trip inevitably engenders. No more worrying about where to stay, what to eat, how much to tip, have you got enough fuel and if not where is there some more, no more language problems and if the vehicle breaks down in the back of beyond then Jim – if that is in fact your leaders name – will fix it (or find a man who can)!!

There are a great number of Tour Companies operating and I can only speak as I find. I have always used the same company and so I cannot speak for any of the others, though I have no doubt that their continued existence is testament to the fact that they are offering value for money. The Company that I always used when embarking on trips of this nature (no pun intended) was Green Tours of Leigh Cottage, Gauledge Lane, Longnor, Buxton, Derbyshire, SK17 OPA. – Phone 01298 83563, and I would recommend anyone to contact them if only to ask for a brochure. I have a collection of these going back over many years and just reading details of some of the trips on offer warms the cockles of your heart on a winter's day.

All the above said there are several factors to be borne in mind if you are considering embarking on one of these getaways and their relevance is probably greater the more ardent a photographer you happen to be.

Over the years I have been on a great number of overseas Natural History / Wildlife Photography Tours both as a client and as a leader. The nature of the photography that one is able to conduct on these trips is frequently a far cry from the way you would normally be able to operate on your own and at home. A degree of preparation is often required without which your chances of success, and retaining your sanity, will be severely diminished.

At risk of sounding like a schoolmaster I offer my own experiences and solutions in the hope that whilst, to many, my advices may sound mundane and obvious, perhaps one or two may benefit and their results be enhanced accordingly.

Most Natural History Tours, perforce, work to a fairly fixed itinerary and the leeway to stray from it will obviously vary from trip to trip. However, having to make advance bookings for accommodation normally dictates the time that can be spent in any one location, particularly on those trips where you are constantly moving from base to base.

Whilst there are a number of specifically themed Photographic Trips on offer most tend to be of a more generalised nature. On these not every photographer will necessarily be interested in just wildlife in general, per se, and many will have their own specific fields of expertise and interest. Birds often seem to demand, and receive, more than their fair share of time and attention and, whilst your interest may be less specific, you may find that you have to go with the flow of the group for the sake of peace and quiet.

Tours normally seem to consist of smallish groups of only 10/20 people but they will, invariably, cover a wide range of ages, interests, abilities and dietary requirements and preferences. Trying to fulfil your own aspirations in the face of the above can sometimes prove a daunting task. Taking into account the fact that you may never have met any of your fellow travellers before and given the diversity of personalities, quirks of behaviour and individual idiosyncrasies that will have come together in the one melting pot for 10/14 days, there often needs to be a greater than normal degree of give and take if the trip is not to degenerate into a fractious disaster.

The potential for dispute is often triggered by the time allocated to a given location. On a trip covering mixed Natural History interests each and every location is likely to appeal to one set of enthusiasts more so than to another. Human nature being what it is there is obviously the chance that at a Botanical site the Birders are going to get a bit twitchy waiting to move on – especially if the next stop has been promised as Birdy Heaven – whilst the flower followers carefully "garden" and prepare their subjects and wait for the never ending wind to drop so they can get their shot.

Another bugbear can be that on a site with a limited number of potential subjects a queue can often form at the best looking specimens leaving the dedicated photographer with a guilty conscience – and no-one to talk to at dinner!- if he takes too long and the dreaded cry of "back to the bus" goes up partway through the queue. Often when that cry goes up and everyone is back in the vehicle - grudgingly or otherwise - a head count will reveal someone missing. If you are one of the righteous ones ensconced in your seat it is more than a little annoying. If, however, you are the guilty party you will find that you can get away with it once by offering some jocular explanation based on the effects of the change in diet. Twice is pushing your luck and three times leaves you ostracised and persona non grata for the rest of the trip. I, myself, have been known to tarry over the odd shot and I well remember, on a trip to the Galapagos, that the guide made the whole group stand and wait each time until I caught up. Try that a few times and you soon discover how not to make friends and influence people!

Mealtimes can often provide a little light hearted relief. You will be surprised at the range of anti-social eating habits that can be displayed. Furthermore you will probably be dealing with cuisine alien to your norm and there will always be at least one to whom it is not suited. The success of your meal in many countries where English is not the language of choice will often depend solely on the abilities of your leaders to converse with the waiters in the local vernacular. Despite their undoubted expertise there is always plenty of room for error. It often pays to be somewhat forgiving should the need arise and it frequently pays to shut your eyes and swallow rather than inquire too closely into the antecedents of the suspicious offering that ends up in front of you and looks nothing like what you thought you were ordering.

Bathrooms can sometimes be a fraught experience. Apart from the general state of the plumbing, which can be mind bending in its complexities, there can be local customs and idiosyncrasies that sit ill with our reserved English natures. I have never yet come to terms with the requirement in many locations, such as Greece, not to put toilet paper down the loo. This is obviously to avoid blocking up the pipes or the septic tank with that which may not be biodegradable. This leaves you having to put the used paper in a bag hung beside the loo for collection by some unknown person later. I do not believe that there are too many Anglo Saxons with whom this practice sits too easily. I well remember once being on a trip to the Amazonian Rainforest where the lodge was built on stilts in a swamp and the same rules applied. To ram the message home, when we were given our "indoctrination lecture", the guide was at pains to point out that, should we disobey the rules in this regard, then the person responsible for clearing the certain and inevitable blockage that would occur also happened to be the Chef. He added, almost as an aside, that if we were prepared to have dinner cooked by a chef who, only moments before, had been up to his armpits in who knows what, then it was up to us.

There are other bathroomy things that sit ill with me. As a wet shaver the habit in some countries, such as Spain, not to supply a plug for the washbasin, drives me to delirium. Supposedly some ethic dictates that you shouldn't wash in dirty water – hence no plug. I also hate those showers where you have to hold the unit in your hand because there is no hook on the wall to hold it for you, or the one that is there has gone floppy. Often there is no accoutrement shelf either. How you are supposed to hold soap, shampoo, your alltogethers and the showerhead all in one hand at one time defeats me.

Even more so than a shower cubicle without wall mounted "hooker onto" is my intense dislike of a bathroom where, instead of a shower cubicle there is a bath with a combi tap/shower head unit, but still no hook on the wall. I can never make my mind up whether to stand up, sit down, kneel down or lie down. If you stand up there is normally no shower curtain and you soak the floor. If you kneel down you can't get at your feet and your knees hurt and if you sit down or lie down you can't reach the shampoo and soap that you left perched on the end of the bath – and you still can't reach your feet!

Over the years I have also got used to "mine hostelry" supplying shampoo and soap. Even if the soap is in such small bars that you can't hold it once it's wet I still make sure that I use it, particularly so on a trip where you are moving around. If you are forced to use your own bar, probably of a decent substantial size, you have to return it to your plastic soapbox when you pack to move on. Once ensconced in this plastic mausoleum it cannot dry out properly and so the next time that you use it you have to fight your way through a thick layer of viscous sludge!

Enough! I'm writing this whilst on a Botanical trip to some of Europe's major mountain ranges and I need no further reminding since much of the above is contributing to my current daily discomfort. Let us lay my pet dislikes to one side and return to the photography.

One of the biggest problems of dealing with a possibly tight schedule is that you find yourself having to cope with the conditions prevailing at the time. You cannot, normally, come back next week when conditions may be more clement and so you have to make the most of what is thrown at you. This really is often a case of take the shot despite the conditions or risk not getting a shot at all. Do not rely on assurances that you will see many more of this particular "thing" later in the trip because you may well not and, even if you do, conditions at the time may be worse.

I have one or two failsafe strategies to fall back on, particularly when photographing plants. If it is raining I have waterproofs for both myself and my gear and I try to avoid using flash for fear of the inevitable searchlights of reflection from water droplets. If it is windy I have a fold up length of plastic plus some light tent peg type supports to make a windbreak. Additionally I carry some spare bootlaces to either tie the subject down or tie back overhanging vegetation. I also have some large green clothes pegs to pin foliage back or pin the subject to a supporting strut if necessary. I use green ones since, often, your image edge can come close to a peg and a green reflection tends normally to be much more in keeping than a red or blue one.

I don't much bother with mammals or other distant subjects in the rain since the power of modern digital technology is such that it can capture every raindrop and leave you with a nightmare of an enhancement job on your hands. A further problem with most mammals, and some birds, in the rain is that you end up with images of what resembles a drowned rat or a wet feather duster.

I also carry two of those "fold up into nothing" umbrellas. One for me and the camera, and one for the subject. This latter one has a spike on the handle so that, with luck, it can be fixed over the subject without having to convince some poor soul to stand there and hold it. You have to be careful shading a subject from rain since it is often impossible to exclude raindrops without excluding what little light there may be as well. You also need to be careful if shading a subject from bright sun. There is a great danger that some of the bright surroundings that fall outside of your shaded area may end up in your image. If this happens you may find that the resulting lighting contrast is too much to overcome, even if you are an Adobe Adept.

Perhaps the biggest problem is accepting just how little time you may have to play with. Just because the brochure says that there is plenty of time for photography that doesn't necessarily mean that there will be time for you, personally, to carry on as if you were at home. You have to get in and get out ASAP. In times gone by, when slide was the order of the day, much precious time was wasted at each stop in looking for the best specimen or view. Whilst I would never advocate settling for second best there is a case, in these digital days, of settling for an "acceptable" shot provided that any shortcomings are such that they can be put right in your enhancing. The days when you were loathe to accept a flower with a minor blemish on a petal or an insect with slight damage to a wing are, fortunately, long gone. With birds and mammals there are many variables but whatever enhancement software you are using it is a nonsense to ignore its capabilities in situations such as these.

In ideal, or near ideal, circumstances I would always advocate going for as perfect a shot as possible including selecting the best image available to work with. However, on a trip, you do not always have the benefit of those kinds of conditions and you are often flying by the seat of your pants. My advice is to get the best shots you can as quickly as possible so that, at least, your subject is "in the bag" and then search for perfection if the timeframe permits.

If you are taking prescription medicine make sure that you take more than enough to last the trip. As we have seen recently it only takes an untimely volcanic eruption, or other unforeseen circumstance, and your trip could suddenly be extended by several days. You cannot depend on obtaining prescription drugs in foreign countries even if they are major players in the EU. Things can go wrong and it is "sod's law" that they will. Weather, unexpected and lengthy Bank Holidays, strikes, social unrest and the ever present terrorism threat, to name but a few, can all play their part in forcing shops and surgeries to be closed unexpectedly. Also take plenty of the more obvious remedies like plasters, pain killers, anti-inflammatories and germicidal cream. Your leaders will no doubt have a good supply but, apart from your own requirements, you can easily find yourself having to share what you have with someone who has come unprepared. Make sure you have a decent sunblock and "après sol" cream. Windswept hillsides may not seem all that hot but with a normally unexposed skin, especially if you are involved in a heavy and protracted photographic session, you are constantly at risk of burning and may not notice it happening.

Last but by no means least, even if you do not normally need them, take some of those remedies geared up to ensure the smooth running of your own internal combustion engine. A change in water, local bugs and beasties, and a plethora of other organisms that bear you ill will can cause a certain looseness, of which we are all only too well aware. What is often overlooked is that a succession of unexpectedly late nights and early mornings can play havoc with routines of metabolism that have taken you a lifetime to perfect. This, coupled with the all too easy mistake of not drinking enough to suit your changed conditions, means that it is as important to have "un-bungers" as it is to have "bungers-up". Personally I have found that the best cure for the "looseness" that accompanies much foreign travel is to forgo the pleasure of all foodstuffs and beverages, other than plain water, for a full 24 hours. This normally works a treat and clears things up completely without ruining the balance of your digestive system. Many of the undoubtedly effective "bungers up" only alleviate the symptoms temporarily without addressing the cause so that, at best, they only delay the suffering.

Apart from ensuring the smooth running of your own internal processes it is obviously of paramount importance to keep your photographic systems flowing sweetly. In this digital era this can put you in the position of needing to have reliable battery operated, as well as mains, downloading and backup facilities. On some trips you cannot always rely on a mains supply. Personally I have dual purpose mains/battery operated downloader and disc cutter. In addition, of course, where possible, I have my laptop. I also carry several memory cards and sticks and, one way or another, I get by. Remember that you are probably going to be taking far more photos than you would, perhaps, normally do at home especially since you could well be on a once in a lifetime experience. The downloading capabilities that would have been more than enough to cope with a stroll up your local hillside in the UK will prove woefully inadequate in foreign sites where you are likely to find yourself surrounded by all manner of wonderful things and no chance to come back next week and have another go!

In closing I would only advise that you avoid the politics and in-fighting that, all too often, seem to arise on trips of some duration. Best to do your own thing, remember why you are there, and get on with it. Leave those who wish to squabble to do so amongst themselves and maintain a firm stance on the touchline. Close confinement for periods of up to 2 or 3 weeks can bring out the worst in folks and it really is best if you can stand back and leave them to get on with it. People are often not themselves under the stress of foreign travel and 2 to 3 weeks is too long to maintain a false front so it is not surprising that, occasionally, the niggles come out and get an airing.

Finally I would reiterate – do your homework, cover your options, don't forget essential items and I'm sure you will have - and my best wishes go with you - the trip of a lifetime!

Chapter 8

Foreseeing The Foreseeable

There is nothing worse than planning the photographic trip of a lifetime, often at considerable expense, and having it ruined, partially or totally, by some foreseeable circumstance. It is bad enough if it goes wrong for some unforeseeable circumstance but at least, in that case, you can console yourself with the thought that you probably couldn't have done anything to prevent it. The foreseeable circumstances, however, are usually, to some extent or other, under your own control and you will have only yourself to blame if they occur. No doubt one or two of your acquaintances, when your long planned trip goes belly up, will offer that ridiculous platitude of "Well I believe everything happens for a reason" as if that makes your holiday ruin whole again. Of course it happened for a reason – you forgot or overlooked something!!

I do not pretend to have a magic answer but for those with a less than perfect memory, or no sense of planning, I set out below the steps I take to circumvent, as far as possible, any one of a number of potential disasters.

First and foremost I am one of the worst in the world for making lists. However, in the case of foreign, or even extended UK based travel, I have been known to capitulate. It is courting disaster to leave packing to a last minute dash. In the excitement of finally setting off on your trip of a lifetime there is no way that the average humble brain can remember the contents of an extensive mental list of essential requirements - let alone details of where you last put them all.

Better to start a list some time in advance and select a place, or a container, to gradually accumulate those items that are not in everyday use. Then, when the time comes, you have just to grab the receptacle concerned and your only worries will then be how to fit a quart into the pint pot of your luggage. If you are travelling solo then yours are the only items to be accommodated and you have only yourself with whom to argue. If you are travelling with partner and sharing luggage allowances then be well prepared with valid arguments to convince him/her that your extra camera body - weighing at least four woollies, three sets of underwear and a bag of cosmetics - is actually completely essential to the continued well being of your body, soul and quality of life and that, without it, the whole trip would be meaningless!

Since the earlier days of film I have always been loathe to risk any of my essential gear in the hold. Apart from the vagaries of the performance of scanners, especially in obscure locations, I will always remember coming back from an exotic location and seeing the first two dozen or so cases onto the carousel spewing forth their contents from where, presumably at point of embarkation, they had been neatly slit along their zipper lines with a carton cutter or Stanley knife in order to get at their more valuable contents.

In days of old I also carried my tripod with me since, in many locations, there is absolutely no chance of replacing such an item should your hold baggage fail to arrive in the same place as you. However, a change in regulations some time ago decided that a folded carbon fibre tripod and a deadly weapon were one and the same thing. Thereafter it either had to go in your hold luggage or into a special bag in the care of the captain. Whether he sat on it or not I have no idea but wondering exactly where it was caused me endless worry, particularly on trips to such as the Falklands where the aircraft on which you arrive at destination can be two or three times removed from the aircraft on which you originally embarked. The only saving grace if you fell foul of this regulation was that the bag in which your Weapon of Mass Destruction was incarcerated for the journey was a wonderfully large thick yellow thing with a stout drawstring, which could be inestimably useful thereafter for wet landings, or in rainforest settings, to prevent the elements wreaking havoc with your gear.

Many flights now have relaxed the weight limits on cabin baggage, though normally size limits remain due to the need for hand luggage to physically fit in the overhead lockers, and this has made life a little easier. However for those flights where you are restricted not only by size but also to only 5 or 6 kilos of weight then my modus operandi is as follows:-

Firstly I make sure that my main camera carrying bag falls within the allowed size limits. I then pack it with everything that I want with me other than what I normally carry in my pockets. This ensures that it all fits, regardless of weight, in the carrying bag you will be using abroad if you can only get it there. At this stage it will probably weigh far more than the weight allowance. I then don two lightweight photographic jackets, with at least some of the pockets large enough to take a camera body or a decent lens. From the bag I then set aside one camera body and my largest lens, which is only of an 80/400 zoom size, since it normally seems permissible to carry a camera round your neck on a strap without it being weighed, and I then unload the other contents of the bag into my various pockets until it comes down to the proscribed weight limits and, Voila!, we're ready to roll! Once through check in and security you can reload your bag and shed your Michelin Man image, as you're not likely to be checked and weighed again. Due to its weight the tripod head now accompanies me in a pocket as well, whereas the tripod body is consigned within my hold luggage wrapped up in socks and underwear. Apart from the contents of your pockets make sure that there is enough room in your carrying bag to pack away the camera you are wearing, after security, otherwise you will have to babysit an unprotected camera for the whole trip. Just imagine someone's steel toecaps resting on it when you are told, in no uncertain terms, to put it under the seat for landing!

I hardly ever keep a diary of a trip, and then spend years thereafter wishing that I had done. My advice is that if you can, then do so. If you never have to refer to it again then so be it, it cost you nothing. However, if you ever want to make a return trip, or advise someone else of where to go and what to do, it could be invaluable. However brilliant you think your memory is I can assure you that, once back in your normal surroundings, many details of the wheres and whens of it will fade into the sunset with little chance of recall.

I realise that everyone will, no doubt, have their own tried and tested routines but I take the liberty of detailing below those items which appear on my list, which is far from perfect, on the off chance that it may prompt one or two to add or remember items that may otherwise have been overlooked. I will not be so presumptuous as to list items that no doubt form part of your everyday photographic kit as you will be well aware of what they are and they will, no doubt, be ready to hand due to their frequent use. The items are listed in no particular order other than the haphazard one in which they come to mind:-

1. Lens cleaning gear, especially a good "puffer" to cope with frequently hot and dusty conditions.

2. A decent, robust and manageable sized torch. Don't skimp on this and make sure you get one that takes conventional sized batteries. You stand a much better chance of obtaining replacements of multiple small ones than those often single large heavy batteries on which some torches depend.

3. Enough battery power for all gadgetry. Try to acquire as many of your items as you can with a common battery size such as AA's. If you use

rechargeables then carry 2 or 3 spare sets of Lithiums in case you cannot connect to the mains for a period.

4. Sufficient memory cards and other backup facilities to fulfil way beyond your wildest image taking dreams – just in case they do become fulfilled. Certainly have enough memory card capacity to carry you right through the day to avoid having to take time out to make hasty, and sometimes later regretted, deletions in the field.

5. Waterproofing for self, camera and equipment bags (see more under article on Trip Photography).

6. Put clearly printed Home Address labels inside all containers so that there is at least an outside chance that any lost bags or containers may get returned to you.

7. Spare bootlaces for tying back and 101 other jobs.

8. Try to carry a spare camera body, or even just a point and shoot, over and above whatever you feel is the minimum requirement for recording your photographic brilliance.

9. A travel type mozzy net for relevant areas. Even if you are not going to a malaria area biting insects can become a nightmare in many places. In addition have plenty of insect repellent wherever you are going. Most destinations have some form of biters or stingers and, especially near water or out in the country, you could well meet most of them.

10. Your inoculation card with an attached note, clearly printed in block capitals, detailing any allergies or medical conditions that you may suffer from in case you are rendered unconscious or cannot communicate in dire circumstance.

11. Passport and tickets of course and then give serious thought as to what form of monetary exchange you want to take. Consider carefully, in the light of your particular destination, whether you really want to risk using a Credit Card, especially if you are on an all expenses paid trip. If taking travellers cheques make sure you record the numbers and keep the list somewhere other than your wallet. If you are relying on good, old fashioned, cash then make sure that whatever currency you take it in is readily acceptable in whichever country you are visiting. Invest in a comfortable body belt to carry the bulk of it and only have in your wallet what you feel you may need to use that day. This way if you are mugged or pickpocketed there is a good chance they will miss your main stash as long as your wallet contains a sum reasonable enough to satisfy them.

12. Decent soap. Especially in hot climes a change in soap can be enough to trigger a number of skin conditions. I try to take dettol soap as it discourages a plethora of skin complaints, insect bite infections and parasitic

invasions by such as ticks. In addition to this some form of medical kit is a good idea.(More of this under the previous chapter on trip Photography)

13. A travel dictionary if you feel that you will need it. I never bother since I can get by in English, French, Spanish and one or two African dialects but what is more to the point is that, these days, I can never remember newly learnt phrases anyway. I can learn several words and phrases each evening but can also guarantee to have forgotten all of them, plus a couple more besides, by morning! The more that you travel then the more that you will be happy to rely on a lingua franca of arm waving, pointing, miming and grunting and you will be amazed how many other people speak the same language! As Brits we are often embarrassed to "have a go" and this is our downfall. My advice is to get stuck in and see how you get on.

14. I always take a few plastic carrier bags and bin liners. You will be surprised at just how useful they can prove to be and you cannot rely on being to obtain them locally in many foreign climes.

15. Footwear is normally too heavy to consider carrying spares just for the sake of it, especially walking boots. However make sure that the boots you are taking are worn-in but relatively new and not on their last legs. Cobblers are often few and far between and a separated sole early on in your trip can play hell up with your ability to scale the highest peaks.

16. Some kind of travel wash can help maintain appearances. Not all locations offer a laundry service and you may find that you have to rinse your smalls by hand every so often. If you are going to risk your general clothing to whatever laundry facility is on offer then take the trouble to identity mark your items. This often means that you stand a chance of getting a higher than average percentage of your own stuff back.

17. If you are on an organised trip make sure that the leaders have details of who you would like to be contacted in the event of a mishap. If you are travelling solo make sure that you stick a piece of paper with the same info on it in your passport and write clearly in capital letters. Again for solo travellers make sure that someone at home has as much detail as you can provide in advance of your proposed itinerary just in case you fail to show and someone has to instigate a search. I am, myself, very lax in this regard and so it is a case of do as I say and not as I do. Again, to conclude the section for solo travellers it may be a good idea, albeit a pain in the backside, to arrange to check in with someone, somewhere, at some kind of pre-determined intervals.

18. On organised trips especially, a travel alarm clock or some means of being woken up is not a bad idea. Early morning sorties are often on offer and it would be a shame to miss an opportunity just because the local vintage the night before packed a heavier punch than you are used to.

19. If you are lucky enough to be going somewhere exotic like the Galapagos, where beach landings from inflatables are the order of the day, then I would advise two things. The first is a waterproof bag large enough to stuff all your gear in other than your tripod. There are two kinds of landings – dry and wet. The dry ones are where you will be able to tie up alongside some kind of landing facility and you should be able to disembark with dry feet.

Sometimes, though, there are no such facilities or the swell is too much and you have to resort to a wet landing. This is where the boat just pulls onto a beach and you leap over the side into whatever level of surf is prevailing at the time. This can be a messy business with arms, legs, bodies and equipment flying in all directions. No one else will be much worried about your gear and so its wellbeing is down to you. Have a waterproof bag (just a heavy duty plastic bag such as the tripod bags mentioned above will do) with a drawstring or roll over top and stuff all your gear into this before you disembark from your main boat and then you need have no worries from spray or surf and are free to join the melee of the landing with all the rest.

The second thing is a pair of sandals that you don't mind getting wet. You may be promised a landing on sand but sod's law is that the only stony outcrop on the beach will be right where you need to put your foot. You also have to remember that whilst you may land on sand your round the island walk may take place on volcanic or coral outcrop and bare feet are not too bright an idea.

20. Reference books. I seldom bother with these as they can account for so large a part of a precious baggage allowance. If you are on an organised trip your leaders will have suitable reference books to look at and if you're going it alone you might be better advised to wait till you get home to identify those species that you are not sure of. Just make sure that your photos include all the salient points that will be needed to make an identification! Of course there is no real problem with one or two small field guides but, unless you suffer from tunnel vision, there is such a diversity of subject matter on a foreign trip that to try to cover all your options with reference works is somewhat over ambitious. Take the picture and worry about what it is later!!

21. Specific Travel Insurance for your gear need not cost the earth. Look into it well before you go. In any event take identity numbers of all your major items just in case of loss or theft.

I cannot promise that the above constitutes a foolproof list and should you feel there are items that I have failed to include then let me know and I will add them on. Neither do I wish to appear alarmist with some of the suggestions but I have seen most scenarios unfold in this respect and it is always traumatic for those on the receiving end especially when just a little fore thought could have made life so much easier. Far and away the majority of trippers have a wonderful time without mishap (but we seldom hear about them). With this article I would just hope that I might have helped one or two of you avoid becoming one of the few unfortunates that we all read about.

Have a good trip!

Chapter 9

Subject Provenance

I never cease to be amazed at the importance that some potential print purchasers attach to the question "where did you take it?". The question is often posed in an almost accusatory and belligerent manner as if, merely by offering the picture for sale, you are some kind of potential conman. I suppose, in reality, that people want to think that you hung over a cliff on the end of a rope for three days, surrounded by killer bees, in order to get the shot. You just know that if your answer is that you simply walked up to it in a field and pointed your lens at it's ear, or that it was a pet one in the back of Joe's Diner and you bribed it with a cheeseburger to pose for you, then you are not going to make a sale. I can appreciate that some people acquire a second hand feeling of derring-do by association with a photographer, or his work, but have never been able to understand why the original location and circumstances of a subject should determine whether the picture should be bought or not.

If the image contains some scenic content above and beyond the inside of a bramble bush then, of course, the "location" of a "location" can have some bearing, but with many wildlife photos, and certainly many of mine as I specialise in close-up photography be it a grasshopper or a lion, the subject occupies the bulk of the overall image area and, quite often, the background has been deliberately blurred by camera setting to further highlight the subject. In cases such as this there can be no sense of location derived from within the image and so why does the "where" of it apparently seem so important as to mean the difference between making a sale or not?

No doubt stating this will bring a flurry of correspondence pointing out the error of my thought processes in far from dulcet tones. However I would reiterate that I, personally, cannot see what difference it makes where a photograph was taken as, surely, it should stand on its own photographic merits, and for what it is a picture of, and not for where the "of" came from.

Like it or not the whole world has become a zoo and the only qualifying difference between establishments is the distance between, and the nature of, the boundaries. Much of the world's wildlife is, these days, contained within some kind of barrier be it physical, as in the form of bars or fences, or merely delineated by boundaries of human tolerance. Outside both of these restraining influences an animal will inevitably be shot if it is dangerous, eaten if it is palatable or turned into cash if some part of it constitutes a trophy.

"Living in the wild" is, to a large extent, often something of a myth. Procreation and the "survival of the species" is frequently a carefully monitored, rather than random, process and consequent population levels are strictly controlled and maintained by the myriad of owners, rangers, administrators and officials involved, and are normally subject to specific, long-term, development plans and not the haphazard vagaries of nature. Practically all constrained, and many ostensibly free ranging, wildlife populations are subject to strict culling regimes either by so called "sport" shooting interests or by some form of "cropping".

Wildlife populations occupying less constrained habitats can normally only lead an unfettered existence while ever they toe the local party line. Once they step over this then outside control quickly takes over as evidenced by the rapid retaliation exacted by man in the case of stock eaters, crop raiders, knockers down of fences or even just what are deemed to be perpetual or even occasional nuisances. Even wildlife that becomes a so called nuisance, menace or threat through no fault of its own is often rigorously dealt with.

I well remember the case of a "wild" Bull Elephant in an African country with which I have recently enjoyed a lengthy relationship. This Bull took to "loitering", initially seemingly "without intent", around a campsite provided as a facility to accommodate those who came to view the wildlife. What prompted his original interest I have no idea. Perhaps to him it was the equivalent of going to the Zoo for the day as the view of such establishments is often more entertaining for those on the outside looking in than it is for those on the inside looking out. I do not doubt that his original intentions were fairly honourable as he caused no trouble other than a sharply increased metabolic rate in those who nearly bumped into him on their way to the loo after dark. However, in the fullness of time, and because he didn't seem to be much of a threat, certain of the visitors, in their wisdom and understanding, took to throwing him fruit and veg in much the same way as people both insist and persist in feeding New Forest Ponies and the like. Despite the alien nature of these offerings he developed a marked predilection for oranges and any other product flavoured by them. Juice, yoghurts, trifles, jellies, the fruit itself, anything with even the slightest whiff of orange ranked very highly on his "wish list". Rapidly, and with great and original thought, he was nicknamed "Oranges" and he became something of a celebrity and a firm favourite with the visitors. Such was the strength of his craving, and such was his ingenuity, that he ultimately worked out a way to use his tusks as "car openers". I expect he'd always wondered what they were for! His preferred method of entry was via the roof which he quickly learnt could be neatly ripped open and peeled back, much like the top of a sardine can, thus granting free and easy access to whatever delights lay therein. Both oranges, and the feeding of "Oranges", were quickly banned and, though the latter continued surreptitiously by ill advised but no doubt well intentioned visitors, the orange ban was generally accepted, if only from the point of view of personal safety. However, in a country where oranges are almost a staple, there are not many vehicles which will not have had oranges or one of their by-products in them, if not at the time of visiting, then certainly at some time in the preceding few days. The super sensitivity of an elephant's olfactory system does not seem to be able to differentiate between "they're in there now" and "they were in there up until recently" where lingering smells are concerned and so his depredations continued. He was shot dead by a ranger!

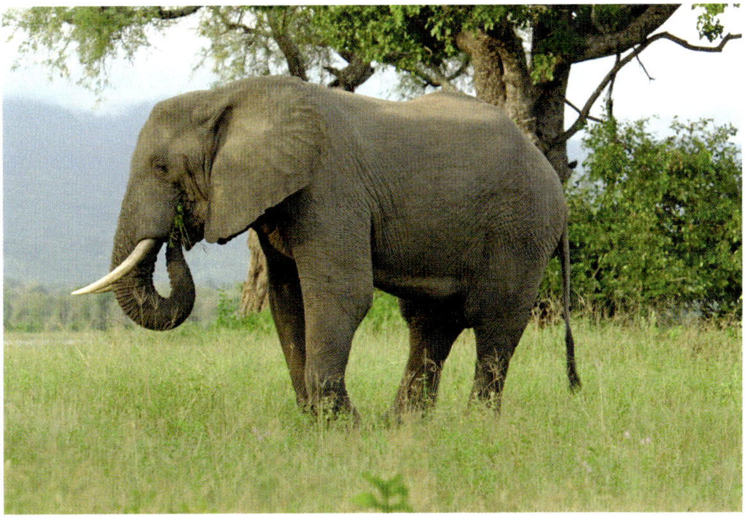

Not "Oranges" - but one like him!

Before I am taken to task for apparent cynicism I would say that I fully realise that there are some truly wonderful "wild Places" (well – almost wild anyway!) because I spend a great deal of my time visiting them but they are few and far between, dwindling in both size and number and often lacking the amount of financial support needed to secure their future size and number. It is almost impossible to find areas capable of sustaining decent wildlife populations that do not also have to sustain, or help support in some way, shape or form, a human population as well. This invariably leads to conflict, with farm stock and crops being the most common catalyst.

Many of the world's leading wildlife viewing destinations are, in fact, reserves, and are controlled and administered accordingly. Human activity in and around these "Parks" is normally constrained to some extent or other, at least on the surface, but intrusion and encroachment are all too frequent. Increasing human population levels, local wars, poaching and eco-tourism are all adding to the pressure. Even the time honoured pastime of game viewing is taking its toll. In many of the better known locations species such as Big Cats are finding it increasingly difficult to find the opportunity to hunt, eat, mate and successfully rear young surrounded as they constantly are by a circle of zebra striped mini buses. Don't think that your unexpected safari encounters with rare and exotic animals are the result of skill on the part of your driver. Normally spotters will have been out, often all night, keeping track of the better known "must see" list and locations are radioed in long before your dawn game drive sets out. Truly random sightings are quickly passed on from one driver to another and this is what leads to a convergence of vehicles where you will be lucky to take a photograph that doesn't include at least one, and often several, other Game Drive Vehicles. Add to this the fact that, even as far back as the 50's and 60's, it was not uncommon for various species to be lured to certain areas either by regular feeding (especially Big Cats) or by provision of salt licks, water holes and other attractants in pre-determined and selected areas suited to maximizing game viewing encounters. Don't get me wrong. None of this is necessarily a bad thing as eco-tourism is probably one of the least damaging guarantees for the future of wildlife but we need to see the picture for what it really is and not kid ourselves with over emotional delusions. Wildlife is exploited at almost every level and the areas most likely to thrive are those where the benefits to mankind, either pecuniary or otherwise, are the greatest.

One of the effects of human encroachment has been to convert many reserves into virtual "islands" or "oases" in a hostile environment simply by surrounding them with cultivation. By our European concepts of open spaces some of these "islands" can seem vast, or even constitute "the wild", but when you consider that to an Elephant anything smaller than a continent represents confinement you will realise that it is a question of degree. If you live on an island then whatever constitutes the shoreline is as much a barrier as a fence or set of bars.

In evolutionary terms the creation and isolation of many reserves has occurred so quickly that wildlife levels within them have become cut off from the invigorating effects of new bloodlines moving in to expand what can quickly become a very limited gene pool. Most wildlife, (even many species of birds that can fly), will not move from one area to another, even if not that far apart, unless it can do so along a corridor providing both food and cover. A busy road or track across these corridors can often become, in effect, the most efficient of barriers.

This is why, at risk of committing a faux pas along the lines of a leading Wildlife Presenter's recent comments on the future of Pandas, I have to admit that I view many "return to the wild" schemes with a great degree of scepticism. This is especially so with animals that are the product of several generations of close captive breeding. As with the island reserves mentioned above many captive populations also often have a limited gene pool to draw on with the result of an increase in the rate of mutational factors creeping into the species. Most mutational factors have a deleterious effect on the species and in a truly wild situation they would normally be quickly weeded out in the battle for life and the survival of the fittest. The immediate effects of some mutations are obvious such as Albinism, melanism, five legs or two heads. Many, however, are of a far more insidious and less apparent nature. These, combined with a complacency borne from the absence of threat and the consequent atrophying of senses no longer required for survival in a captive environment, can have a serious effect on the chances of a species regaining its original abilities even if released into the most ideal of locations.

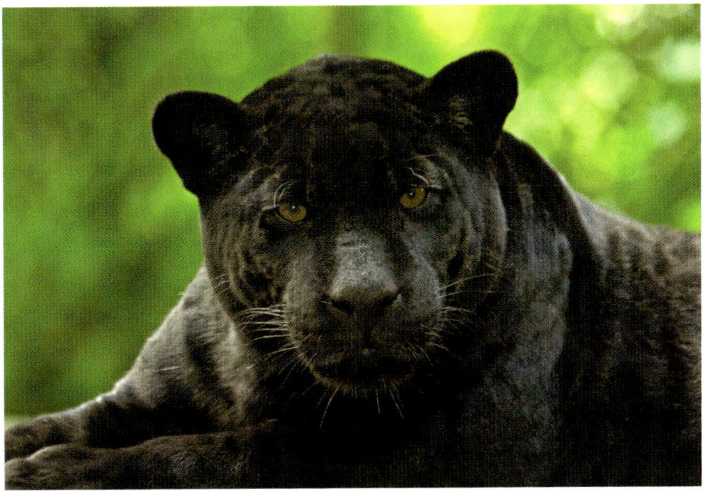

Black Jaguar - Mutation

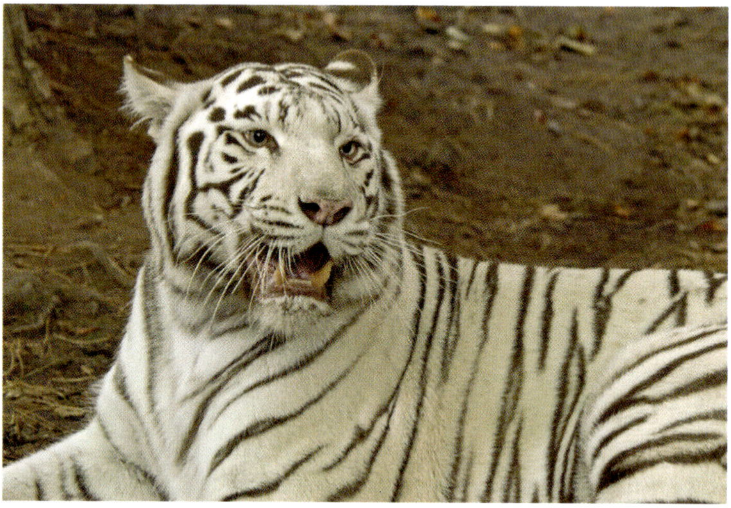

White Tiger - Mutation

Factors such as the albinism mentioned above can often have secondary effects far less obvious than the primary one which, in this case, is colour. One of the more critical secondary effects with albinism is how badly eyesight, particularly in bright light, is affected. In the wild this would seriously hamper the ability of a predatory species to see and catch its prey and would severely restrict the ability of prey species to escape their predators.

Unfortunately some of the more visually startling mutations attract a greatly enhanced financial or trade value due to their uniqueness and exclusivity and this can often be the road to ruin for the species. Controlled breeding programmes often select partners based on an unnatural selection of features deemed desirable from no other than a financial point of view. Add to this the fact that to establish or "fix" certain factors it is initially often necessary to breed from very close relatives, with all the inherent risks that this implies, and you will see that within a very few generations an animal can be irrevocably changed from its original "wild" forbear.

For these reasons I view many avowed declarations of intent to return certain captive species to "the wild" as, at best, well intentioned nonsense such as would, in the past, have expressed itself in the building of those "rich man's follies" that can still be found littering the landscape, or, at worst, a cheap publicity or fund raising stunt geared more to the benefit of the scheme's promoters than the creature concerned.

I do not deny that there are many well funded and scientifically serious release and reintroduction schemes taking place and these I applaud soundly and loudly - PROVIDED - that they are geared towards, and can be practically expected to, safeguarding a species in perpetuity. There needs to be a relatively low "post release" requirement for financial and manpower input. Future generations, particularly in developing countries, may not be so altruistically inclined to maintain such schemes. I accept that these laudable conservation efforts should not be curtailed merely as a result of negativity in forecasting their longterm future but neither, I would submit, can they be justified as "saving the species in the wild" if all they can reasonably be expected to achieve is to merely "delay the evil day of extinction" just a little longer.

Better to devote the efforts and resources to providing a secure captive environment under optimum conditions where an ongoing chance of serious and scientific control is a real possibility. Worldwide there are now several well funded and academically controlled breeding registers and programmes being set up in the Zoo world in an attempt to obviate the effects of too close breeding within limited gene pools. Undoubtedly these captive populations will undergo changes in the coming generations that will be different from those that they would have undergone had they been able to survive in a truly wild environment, but who is to say which set of changes would be for the best? Wild populations change too due to the ongoing process of evolution which basically means that to survive a species needs to adapt to the constantly changing conditions and circumstances under which they live. However we argue it, if the world's biodiversity is to survive, it must adapt to coexist with mankind (for the time being, at least, until we manage to wipe ourselves out!), and I would submit that those species and habitats that fail to do so will, one day soon, cease to be whether we like it or not.

I wonder what would have been the situation today had, say, a wealthy foundation, philanthropist or conservation project been around to attempt to secure the future of the dinosaurs all those millennia ago? How many of them would still be here and what degree of change would circumstance have forced on them? I suspect that their numbers and gene pool would have been so small that they would have been unable to maintain the vim and vigour necessary to survive in even an ideal environment. In addition how many countries in today's world would have had either the will or the financial resources to continue to secure their future for posterity? Will the future be any different for our own endangered species?

I seem to digress slightly from the original question of subject provenance but I would reiterate that I see no problem with, and attach no stigma to, photos of "wildlife" subjects taken in some kind of constrained area as outlined above. In fact it is often more difficult to come up with a good shot of a subject in captivity than it would be in what we still refer to euphemistically as the "wild". First you have to locate your subject and make sure that it conforms to common acceptance of normal and is not displaying adverse acquired behavioural or morphological characteristics – unless your photographic purpose is to illustrate these. Secondly, to be aesthetically pleasing, you need a composition devoid of bars, fences or railings, which rules out many conventional zoos and safari parks, or at least severely limits your chances within them. Thirdly you need more than a little luck with the light since there is not likely to be too big a choice of photographing position and, furthermore, you need no red anoraks in the background and no kids behind you bombarding your subject with handfuls of peanuts. If, however, you can satisfy these criteria then there is a chance of tremendous photos of a fantastic divergence of exotic species such as you could probably not achieve in practical terms within normal "budgets" of time and expense associated with foreign travel to the world's "wild places". Frame filling, close-up, full body or head shots, of many species are simply, for most people, not realistically achievable in the wild, other than by great good luck, massive computer cropping or a protracted and often expensive stay in the location concerned to allow time for careful planning and study.

Before you inundate me with counter arguments and criticisms please remember I am speaking here of closeups. For habitat, intra-species or inter-species action of course you have to go where, hopefully, not too many feet have trod before to get shots unaffected by the hand of man.

Sometimes, of course, there are very sound and valid reasons for not disclosing the location of a picture. I have often photographed in private collections or on privately owned reserves holding vulnerable and valuable species, the whereabouts of which it would not be prudent to disclose. Additionally there are ecologically sensitive sites where a gang of careless, or even just unaware, size 10 boots could completely destroy a population of such as the diminutive Bog Orchid in a matter of seconds. There is also, of course, the question of commercial competition to consider since many other photographers and conservation bodies offer courses, workshops, field trips and the like and I, not unnaturally, would prefer that clients should have to come on the trips that I offer in order to find out these little secrets!

Perhaps I am naïve in hoping to change the world on the subject of "where did you take it?" and rather I should give in graciously and learn to counter what I fear will continue to be the inevitable question with prevarication and as many polite versions of "mind your own business" as I can muster!

Chapter 10

Introduction To The 'Photographing' Sections

The following chapters are designed to provide an insight into the do's and don'ts of photographing various groups of species in the Plant and Animal Kingdoms. This is obviously such a diverse subject that I can but hope to scratch the surface of it.

For myself I am, indeed, fortunate in that my Wildlife interests have always embraced the Natural World in its full range and diversity. This has meant, in practice, that I have never felt the urge to specialise, with all the limitations that that can place upon you. One of the most practical and day to day benefits of a wide spread of interest is that on a fieldtrip you are never short of subject matter. If the target of the day has proved to be elusive, then you can always switch your attention to something that is, maybe, a little more obliging, without suffering a withdrawal of interest levels. The downside is that the level of knowledge required to cope with such a spread of interest is immense though, admittedly, its depth is dictated by the levels at which you wish to express that interest.

Being cognizant of the fact that many will wish to follow a specialised route I have, therefore, broken the World of Wildlife down into groups that I feel fall within the scope of this book, and have accorded them separate chapters to avoid confusion with other species.

In my own case I started out photographing flowering plants and very quickly expanded my interest to incorporate their associated invertebrates. The grid system of interlocking interdependencies between all lifeforms in the wildworld then took over, leading on to the very general and overall interest that has occupied me ever since. Those of you starting out on a specialist route may well find the same factors influencing and expanding your interest, often at an alarming rate.

However, to avoid a potentially aimless meander through the subject of Wildlife Photography itself I have broken it up into sections that I hope will suit the purpose of both general interest and specialists alike. I have not dealt with the likes of invertebrates in general because it is such a vast field that I could not hope to do more than skim across the surface. Instead I have dealt in some depth with the photographing of a few of the groups that come under the invertebrate heading, such as Grasshoppers, Dragonflies and Butterflies and would hope that the information contained therein can be applied across the board should your interest lead you to other groups. Several come to mind such as the Beetles, Bees and Wasps, Moths, Bugs and Spiders – to name but a few. Generally speaking the photographic tips and techniques covered in my specific chapters should also apply to the other groups mentioned and, of course, the equipment required will be the same.

There are chapters devoted to various groups of plants and, once again, rather than attempting to cover the whole subject in one go I have dealt in greater depth with a limited number of groups and the photographing of them. If any aspect of plant photography falls within your sphere of interest then I would hope that within the coverage of the groups that I have chosen there will be something relevant to your own particular subject. The chapter on Wildflower Photography is a generalised one dwelling more on seasonal subject availability than on actual photography itself. Once again the relevant tips and techniques are covered in greater depth throughout the more specific chapters that follow and it is to these that I would refer you if that is what you seek.

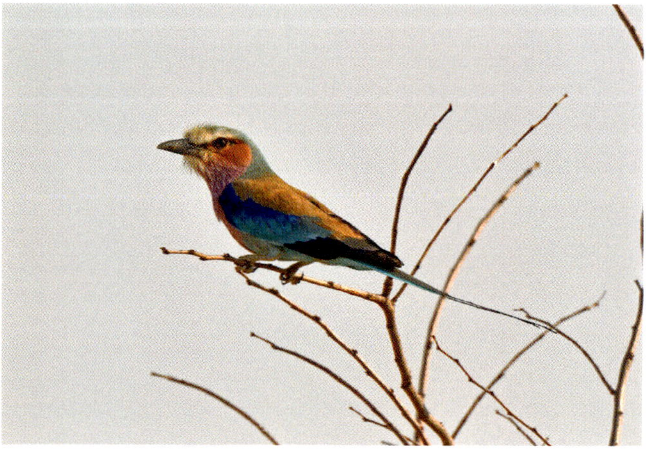

Lilac Breasted Roller - Botswana

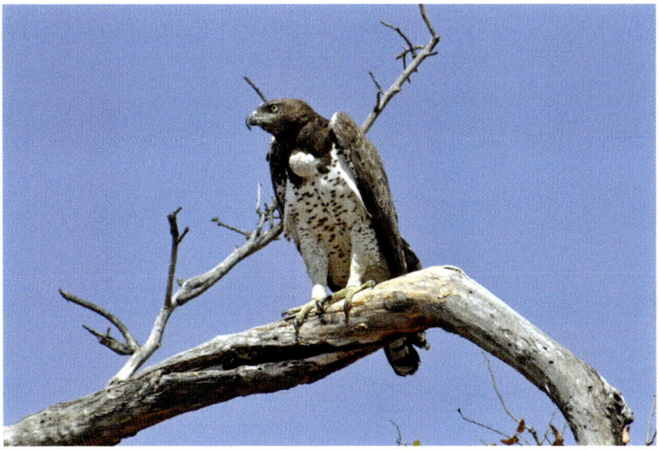

Martial Eagle - Selous

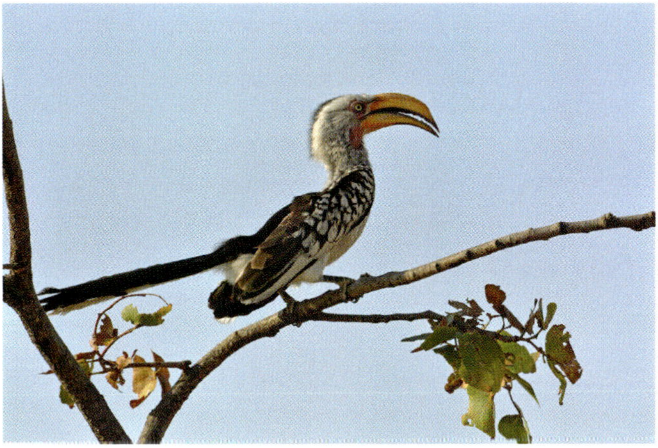

Yellow Billed Hornbill - Hwange

There are further chapters covering the photography of Birds, Mammals and Reptiles in the "wild" and also photographic techniques in Zoos and Safari Parks. You may feel that some, or all, of these scarce qualify under the banner of Macro or Close-up Photography. If you feel that way then I would beg to differ. Close-up photography is what it says it is – taking photographs from close-up. It has little or nothing to do with equipment since, as outlined elsewhere in this book, virtually every camera in the land either has a close-up facility built in or one can be obtained for very little outlay. No the thing that has to be close-up is you, the photographer, unless you are operating some kind of remote controlled equipment the use of which, if this is the case, scarce qualifies you as what would be called a Wildlife Photographer in the commonly accepted meaning of the term. Since you are the prime mover in this scenario then Close-up Photography, where you are concerned, will relate to anything to which you are able to get close. Obviously as your fieldcraft improves so will the range of subjects that you are able to get close to increase. For this reason I have covered subjects that anticipate your prowess in the field and incorporated them under the Macro banner.

Chapter 11

Photographing Wildflowers and Fungi

It would probably be virtually impossible for any devotee, of any aspect of colour photography, not to experience at least a passing dalliance with Wildflowers at some time in their career. The vibrancy of their colours almost begs to be recorded, if not for posterity, then simply in recognition of their inherent beauty and ephemeral fragility.

For myself my circumstances have never allowed for an intense relationship with, or indulgence in, Wildflower Photography per se. Over the years I have, however, favoured certain groups within the Plant Kingdom, especially bulbous plants, as specialist areas, often with unbridled enthusiasm.

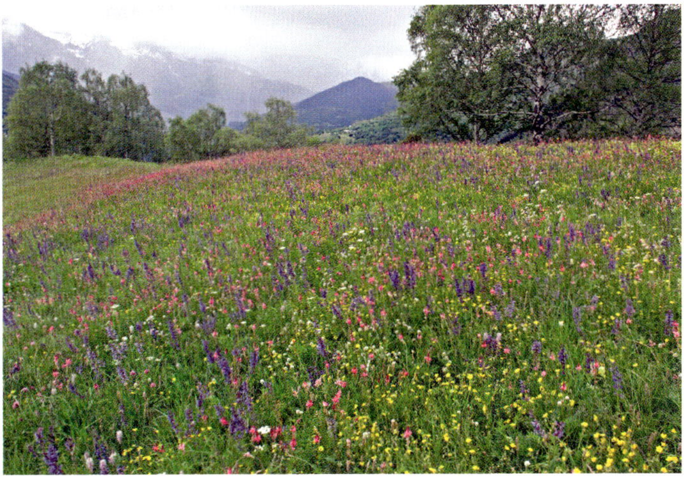

Flower meadow in the French Alps

The ubiquitous nature of Wildflowers, however, often defies you to pass by without taking time out to record their beauty, and so it has been for me over the years. My passion for bulbous plants, several of which are dealt with separately in their specific groups, has taken me to many of the world's wild botanical places. Over the years I have built up a sizeable portfolio of other wild flowering plants that owes nothing to planning and everything to happenstance. Generally speaking most of my Wildflower Photography has taken place as an aside, when I was in search of something else, and there has been no cohesive pattern to my picture taking. In reality my workload is such that I cannot see me making a concerted effort in this direction, at least in the foreseeable future, though I do expect to continue to be as busy on an opportunistic basis as I have always been in the past.

Most of the photographic tips that I would wish to pass on for the photographing of Wildflowers are actually covered in one or another of the specialist plant group chapters elsewhere in this book. On that front I have little to add and would, accordingly, refer readers so interested, to them. In this chapter I will treat Wildflowers across the board without any group splitting, and leave readers to make up their own minds should they choose to take a more specialised route.

We are, indeed, fortunate that even in temperate climes it is possible to find Wildflowers and their associates all year round. If you are interested in flowering plants you cannot, realistically, ignore the vast array of fruits, seeds, nuts, berries and insects that invariably accompany them and this, of course, extends your potential photographing season significantly. I am writing this in late Sept/early Oct and it is definitely berry season. Just a casual walk along almost any country hedgerow can be expected to reveal a wider range of berries than you are likely to be able to fit into one season's photography. There are so many around at the moment that you can get three or four species in one shot. There are also a few field and hedgerow flowers still in bloom as well and if you are lucky with the weather then a day out in the country lanes could well prove to be productive. Many berries persist well into the winter and, in times of inclement weather or snow, they act as a magnet for many over wintering bird species.

As winter wears on into the New Year one or two of our native bulb species begin to show. Catkins of various kinds begin to appear on the trees and bushes and birds begin to adopt their nuptial plumage and behaviour patterns. Snowdrops and Daffodils are quickly followed by a whole rash of field, hedge and woodland flowers. Some of the earlier Orchid species begin to appear accompanied by various Violets, Wood Anemones, Primroses, Bluebells, Archangels and a profusion of Labiates and Composites.

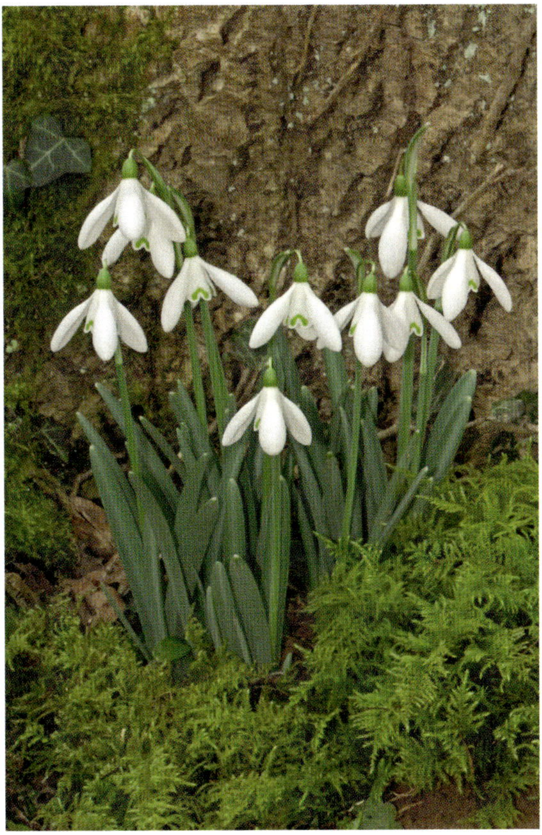

Common Snowdrop - Galanthus nivalis

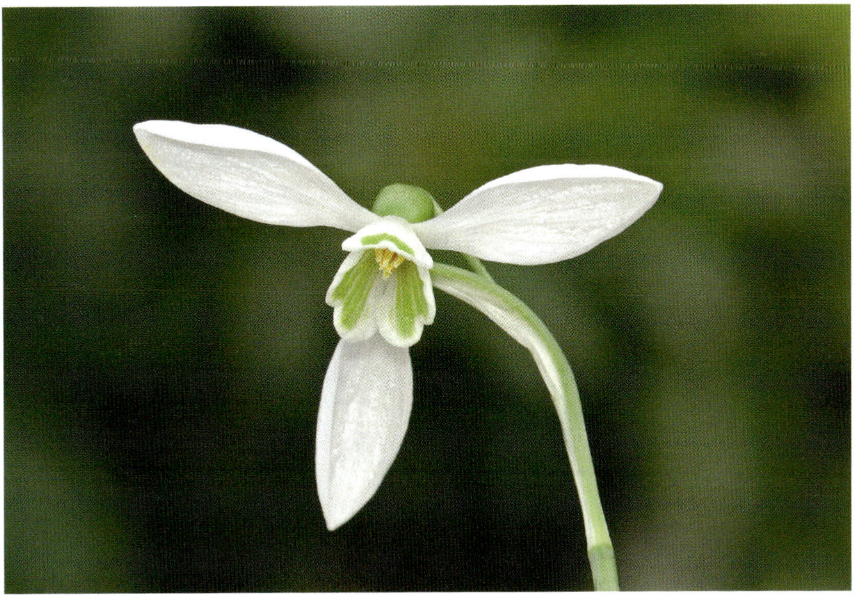

Single form of Snowdrop.

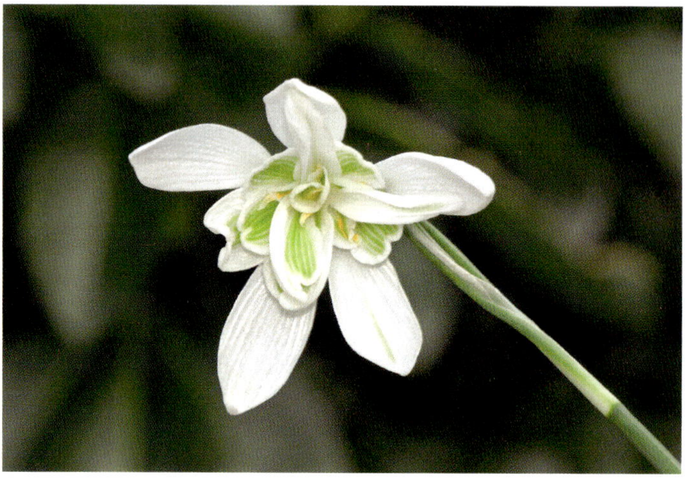

One of several "double" forms of Snowdrops.

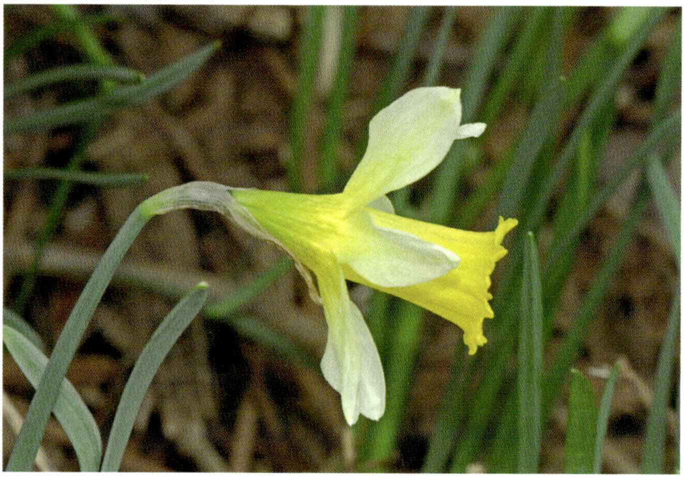

Wild Daffodil - Narcissus pseudonarcissus - near Wimborne

Once the season starts it is hard to keep up with the rush. For Wildlife Photographers it is, indeed, a season of plenty and one in which no time can afford to be wasted. Many species have relatively short flowering times and if you miss them it will be twelve months before they come again.

Because of the apparent plentitude of subject matter it is easy to end up wandering aimlessly because you will seem to be surrounded on all sides. If you break it down into species, however, you may well find that an area, seemingly brimming with Wildflowers, actually contains only four or five species, but in such numbers that they create a false impression of abundance. Surprisingly enough it really does pay, in the face of this avalanche, to draw up a "hitlist" to work to. This will not only give you a sense of direction but of purpose as well. Rest assured that you are not going to get them all in one season, or even several. After exhausting the ubiquitous species that can be encountered for no more trouble than a casual walk down a country lane you will find that research will be required to establish the whereabouts of the rarer and more sought after species. Often some degree of travelling will be required and the learning curve is, thankfully, never-ending.

Over the seasons certain species on your list will, no doubt, remain elusive. This, although it may not seem so at the time, is a boon, albeit well disguised. If it was all too easy then the "been there, done that" factor would take over and dispel some of the zest that this season deserves. The satisfaction of finally discovering a species that you have searched for over several years can be immense and make the wait seem almost worth it.

I well remember (When I employ this phrase of mine, "I well remember", its use often coincides with those who know me losing the better part of their will to live. "Oh no here he goes again" is a phrase often used in conjunction with my own!) ----however, I am hoping that there are enough readers that do not, as yet, know me and will experience no sense of foreboding at my use of the phrase and may, in fact, remain with me long enough to learn the lessons emanating from what was, at the time, a major drama in my life. To recap. I well remember, in the early days of my sojourn in Spain and when I was still on the cusp between video and still photography, that I found a book on the plants of the Costa Blanca that contained a photo of an Insect Orchid called the Early Spider Orchid. For some reason this plant caught my eye, as so many of them do, and since it was supposed to be a local speciality I decided to make a point of finding and photographing it. I spent a number of seasons in its pursuit to no avail. I well remember – duck or abandon hope all ye who enter here – deciding to make a video entitled "In search of the Early Spider Orchid." Of course these were the days of my almost juvenile naïveté in certain matters – Terrestrial Orchids being one of them – when I felt sure that this was bound to be a plant as rare as I thought it was beautiful. How was I to know that I had left behind in Dorset a huge population of the same plant on the Purbeck coast, albeit a slightly different sub-species? How was I to know that in other parts of Spain, and Europe generally, there were places where its numbers were as if 'twere grass? Suffice to say I searched diligently and never found hide nor hair of it. Not even the crushing blow of discovering one that had "gone over" just days beforehand.

One day, with this plant specifically in mind, I set out at dawn – which I have to tell you is, for me, a major achievement – to climb one of the Serella Mountains overlooking the village in which I lived. The day was partially productive in that my shutter release finger was dutifully and repeatedly exercised on various subjects, but of my target Orchid there was not a sign. They do say that "absence makes the heart grow fonder" and I must admit that, by this time, I was "gagging for it". Of course with my ever active imagination this plant by now, in my minds eye, had achieved a stature of 8 feet instead of 8 inches. However, to cut a long story short, which is something that I have never before knowingly done, my dedication went unrewarded. Having risked life and limb all day long and with darkness not too far off I clambered back down to the Landrover with thoughts of Paella and Red Wine gradually forming in my mind, though not necessarily in that order. Less than 3 feet from the door of the Landrover was the loveliest looking bunch of Early Spider Orchids that you could have wished for. Man oh man, could you believe it? They were every bit as beautiful as I had imagined them to be.(Of course having seen, since then, many 1000's of plants of the various sub-species even I, rose coloured specs and all, would have to agree that they are, in fact, rather drab and almost insignificant). But not that evening they weren't!

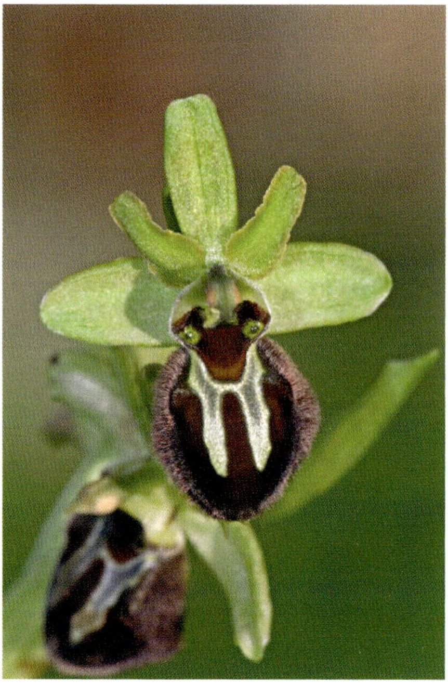

Early Spider Orchid - Ophrys sphegodes

It certainly gives credence to the saying that "beauty is in the eye of the beholder". I was so enraptured that I spent so long on bended knee admiring them that it became too late – these were the days of slide film remember – to photograph them in natural light. Never mind my village was just up the road and I would be back at dawn (two days running!) with all cameras blazing. You are no doubt familiar with the saying "raining cats and dogs"? Well I have to tell you that that night it rained "cows and horses". Dawn was out of the question as it was still bucketing down but by lunchtime the sun was shining and I was back in the saddle. The mountainside was still too wet to drive up so with loins girded up in one hand and cameras clutched firmly in the other I clambered over rocks and precipices to return to what had, by then, become something of a "grail". You know that feeling when you've ticked off the full set of lottery numbers only to realise that it was on last week's ticket? I was on the sharp end of a double whammy. Not only had the rain beaten everything to the ground but Pepe, the local shepherd, had run his flock through and my cherished dream was not only flattened but broken off as well! "Gutted" is too polite a word. I gathered them up with some degree of reverence and returned home to see if I could salvage anything from the wreckage. They were certainly not photographable in that state. Early Spiders, in keeping with many of the Insect Orchids, are extremely "hairy" and we all know what that looks like when it's been caught out in the rain. I needed to dry them off and tried to do so by proximity to the wood-burner. Most of the "hair" is carried on the labellum or "base plate" of the flower. It dried out nicely, and relatively quickly, and when I gathered them up for a tentative photoshoot in the backyard all the labella fell off. To cut another even longer story short all my very early shots of Early Spider Orchids were of plants where all the labella had been neatly repositioned on small blobs of blue-tack – and I even managed to use them in one or two talks without being rumbled! 20 years further down the line and I have still not seen this plant in that area again.

Any lessons learnt? Yes! Ever since that time I have always photographed any subject, for which I have searched long and hard, as soon as is humanly possible once it has been discovered, regardless of conditions prevailing at the time. Any kind of bird in the hand is worth more than a bunch of loose feathers in the bush. Do not leave it till tomorrow because so many things can go wrong. I have lost subjects overnight from so many different reasons that they would be too numerous to list. I have suffered from cross-country runners, mountain bikers, rain, hail, sleet and snow, flocks of sheep and goats, grazing cows, deer with a sweet tooth for flower nectar, nocturnal "varmints" of several different shapes and sizes, not to mention the size 10 boots of "nature loving" walkers.

Often conditions may not be conducive to good photography at the moment that you actually discover this manifestation of all your dreams come true. But take my tip. Photograph it there and then regardless, as if it were your last chance - because it may well be. At least that way you will have something to show for your hard work and if you are able to return and better your efforts on another occasion then you can always "bin" the originals. Better safe than sorry is the order of the day.

As Spring moves forward into Summer many species, and particularly most of the bulbs, disappear but their place is taken by a rush of annuals of every size, shape and colour. Grassland areas and hedgerows become filled with many common-place species but always, amongst them, there is a smattering of rarities to whet the appetite. Many of the Wild Geraniums and Cranesbills are worthy of note and amongst the swathes of Bluebells in late Spring/early Summer there can be found beauties such as Wood Sorrel, Yellow Archangel and early Purple Orchids. Some areas support species such as Solomon's Seal or Polygonatum of which an ancient herbalist once said of its various medicinal properties that "it takes many bruises of women's wilfulness in falling on their hasty husbands' fisties". In this politically correct age in which we find ourselves I do not feel at liberty to discuss the meaning further but that is how "it was wrote". Willowherb, Ragged Robin and Red Campion take over in the hedgerows and a number of the Scabious family begin to make an appearance.

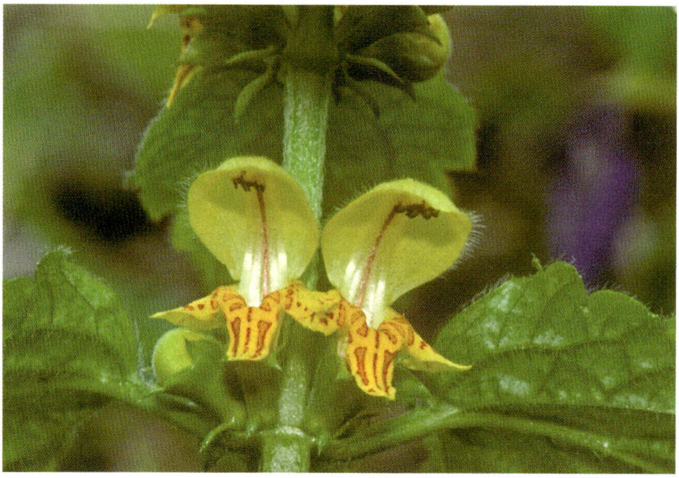

Yellow Archangel - Lamiastrum galeobdolon

Late Spring/Early Summer is the time for many Orchid species to flower and some of these, particularly some of the Helleborines, can be found right through until late July/August. High Summer can be a time of greater scarcity, especially in the open areas, but many waterside plants will be showing well and some of the seeds, fruits, nuts and berries will be appearing. Insects are around in plenty. Butterflies, Grasshoppers, Dragonflies, Hoverflies and the like will be at their most plentiful and, of course, the weather will be as good as it is probably going to get.

Fungi

I cannot discuss flowering plants throughout the year without incorporating some comments on Fungi. It would seem that recent research has established that these organisms, which are classified within a Kingdom of their own are, in fact, more closely related to the Animal Kingdom than the Plant Kingdom. Nonetheless I feel certain that, in the minds of most people, they will invariably be thought of in the same context as plants and so I take the liberty of including them in this chapter.

At any given time of the year there will be one or two species of fungi to be found but it is the Autumn which is the time of plenty. Depending on how the seasons are running then from late August on till late December a great many species can be found with really very little effort. As with any section of the Wildlife World there will be rarities that will take some finding but my initial advice would be to give these a miss until you know specifically what you are doing and what you are looking for. I would start off with species that are startling in appearance and not difficult to come across such as Fly Agarics, Boletus species and some of the more attractive and frequently diminutive species that tend to grow on aged or fallen trees such as the delightful little Porcelain Fungus.

Whilst some species grow out in the open nevertheless a great many of the ground-growing varieties can be found amongst the leaf litter of woodland floors. Deciduous or mixed woodland will probably produce the greatest variety though there are many others that favour, or are specific to, coniferous woodlands. You need to develop a good eye for spotting some of them as they keep their heads well down amongst the litter. This tendency can be a double edged sword for fungi since, whereas it tends to protect some of the more delicate species from weather damage, it nevertheless harbours an abundance of gastropods and other life forms that love nothing more than dining out on fruiting fungi.

Once located your biggest problem is to decide on the best angle from which to photograph. With many species the most seemingly picturesque view will be from above so that you can capture the full beauty of the "cap" which will frequently be the most striking feature of the fungus. Beware though as this can be a classic case where the obviously "best" view, as experienced through the view-finder, may not manifest itself as the most aesthetically pleasing form in your final image. There may be a case for recording shots from directly above as part of your bracketing process but don't overdo them if putting together any form of display or exhibition. Most people hold a subconscious mental image of a Toadstool or Mushroom type fungus as having a flat cap on a relatively long stem and they are likely to need to see at least part of both these features to "please their eye". Additionally the defining characteristic between certain species is, in fact, the patterning and/or formation of the stem and so it is imperative that you capture this feature in at least some of your shots.

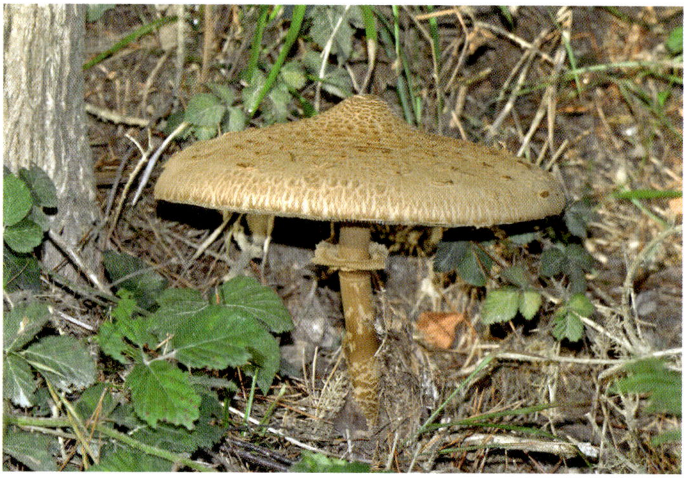

"Nice legs – shame about the head!"
– Parasol Mushroom taken from a 90 degree angle.

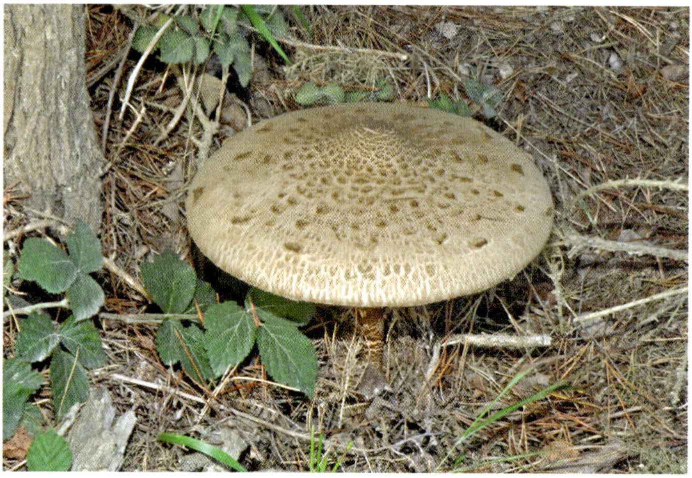

Same Parasol taken from 45degrees above to show better details of cap.

Depth of field will be one of your larger headaches. If you position yourself at ground level you will be in with a chance of a reasonably sharp stem and a reasonably sharp edge to the cap, depending on the size of the specimen and width of the cap, but you will see only the horizontal view of the cap and this might not display it to best advantage, especially if it is an attractively coloured one. The higher you elevate your shooting position then the better will become your view of the cap, but correspondingly the harder it will be to maintain a sharp image of the stem. With the majority of lenses and equipment you will have to compromise and, I would suggest, bracket like crazy for both viewing angle and depth of field or aperture. My normally favourite position, though obviously each case stands to be slightly different, is from about 45degrees to the subject from above and using up to the minimum aperture (highest F stop number) that the light will allow. In many woodland settings you will need to be using either flash, or fill-flash, anyway so you should be able to operate at small apertures without too much trouble. My own trick to achieve the best compromise when I want to emphasize more than one feature at different focussing distances, or am uncertain as to what should be the main focal point in a particular image, is to firstly set the camera into manual focus mode and then view the subject through the viewfinder without letting my eye focus on any one spot. Zoom your focus ring backwards and forwards and let your eye view the subject in an almost unfocussed way, just as if you were viewing one of those computer generated images that are just a mix of dots until suddenly an image materialises as if by magic. You should find that your subconscious eye will know when the subject is at best compromise focus distance and will prompt you accordingly. It may sound crazy but just try it and see what happens. It is a useful technique for many other "macro" situations where you are uncertain as to what point of focus will give you the overall sharpest image.

After a few "practice sessions" with Fungi, experience will quickly tell you the optimum shooting positions and settings for any given situation and you should be able to reduce your bracketing needs accordingly.

In most areas of the country there are now a proliferation of what are termed "fungus forays" at this time of the year, organized and conducted by worthy souls from local Wildlife Trusts and so on. It would certainly pay to go on one or two of these if only to establish what constitutes favourable habitat in your area. It is the practice with many of these forays to collect some of your discoveries and cook and sample them back at base. This is no doubt all part of the fun and I would be the last one to question the efficacy of this process in bringing to a satisfying conclusion what will be, to many, a novel day out.

A word of warning however! If this is a new interest for you then do not become so cocksure of your powers of recall, where identifying various species that you have seen and been introduced to on one of these forays is concerned, that you feel confident enough to go out on your own and emulate the day's success! Before setting forth in search of Fungi with either photographic or culinary intent then make sure that you have invested in at least one Fieldguide to Fungi with the species depicted by photographs and not illustrations. Get more than one if you can so that you can compare images. Don't make the mistake of buying cheap either. Get the best and most comprehensive that you can afford. Once you start photographing Fungi, and then trying to identify your images later at home, you will begin to realise that many species can look remarkably similar and the differences between them, to the untrained and naked eye, may be too slight to differentiate. This is not catastrophic if the result is merely a misidentification when you submit your pristine images as exhibition entries. The embarrassment may make you blush when your errors are pointed out to you by one of the innumerable "experts", who seem to make a habit of attending any kind of photographic exhibition, but your face can go red for a different reason if your misidentification is discovered via the dinner plate. Your newly acquired guide can make alarming reading and the occasional item that gets reported in the National Press from time to time will ram the point home. Some of these seemingly innocuous "good to eat" lookalikes are actually acutely toxic. Apparently some species, which you may have recently relished with gusto secure in the knowledge that you know what you are doing where Fungi are concerned as you went on your first foray just recently and now know all there is to know about the subject, can make you somewhat ill, if not immediately, then certainly not long after eating them. Over the next couple of days, especially if you are of a robust constitution, you may well recover to all intents and purposes. Two to three weeks later when walking down the High Street or driving down a country lane you may equally well drop dead. Alarmist nonsense? Read the book you should have studied more conscientiously before that late night supper of "wild mushroom" omelette you so enjoyed and see what it says on the subject. You can draw some comfort from the fact that there is often a section in the book discussing potential cures should you find that you have inadvertently eaten the wrong thing. The line in this section that boldly states that the only way to extend your active life, if you have inadvertently eaten and digested certain harmless looking species, is a full liver transplant, is enough to encourage me to search diligently and enthusiastically for as many rare and deadly species as I can find, but to limit my interest in them, and their many no doubt "good to eat" cousins, to their photogenic potential and restrict my dietary intake to only those species that have been bought in a supermarket under the label of "Closed Cap Mushrooms"!

On a serious note Fungi make fascinating photographic subjects and can really test your ingenuity in discovering new angles and techniques with which to record them. Many species are very attractive on their undersides, having a wonderfully delicate array of gills that practically demand to be photographed. How you achieve this without turning into a gnome is what photographic genius is all about!

What more can I say than to wish you "Good foraging!"

****

It can also be very rewarding to follow some trees, plants, flowers and bushes through the various stages of their annual life cycles and doing this provides the incentive to draw up a longterm plan. Quite often, especially in your early days of plant photography, you can gain enough satisfaction from random and haphazard excursions because there is so much out there that you will never be short of subject matter. After a while, however, and particularly after you have "bagged" the bulk of the more commonplace plants, you will no doubt feel the need for a more structured approach. A carefully researched list of outstanding species and objectives will often solve this problem and add a sense of purpose to your activities. It will also greatly enhance your feelings of satisfaction as you work your way through it.

Fortunately there is so much out there that you will never cover it all, and there will always be something still to look forward to.

Chapter 12

Photographing Bulbous Plants

With all the photographic opportunities that the Plant Kingdom has to offer this is the one that jingles my jangles. Most of the flowers occurring within this group are so bold and colourful, and show such a phenomenal diversity of form, that I never cease to be amazed by them. I found myself photographing many of the species concerned, as and when our paths crossed, on a haphazard basis during otherwise motivated photographic forays.

To be truthful, when I started photographing plants, it was only ever as a casual occupation and I had neither inkling nor inclination for it to become anything more. My preferences and intentions certainly fell within the Animal Kingdom, on which my entire adult life had been based thus far. It was only after I moved to Spain and photography became a full-time occupation that, surrounded by flowering plants of every shape and size, I began to consider them as something other than just backgrounds and cannon fodder for my talks. As I devoted more time to the subject an inexorable appeal began to manifest itself. At the outset I was no different from anyone else embarking on a new venture and, on reflection, I suppose I spent quite some time photographing anything and everything in the Wild World without any real sense of direction. Over a period, of course, personal preferences began to kick in and dictate the paths that I would ultimately follow.

Again, like anyone else, I found that I began to develop a fondness for certain shots of certain subjects and these were the ones I looked at first when browsing through the results of my labours. Bearing in mind that these were the days of slide photography, and at that time I was involved with video as well, I found myself selecting various images and video clips to incorporate into the Talks I started to put together to present at various social gatherings of local ex-pats. These Talks became my entry ticket to a whole variety of boisterous and well lubricated events. My book reference library in those days was very limited, and the chance of extending it with local acquisitions in early 80's Spain was zilch, so many of the subjects that I had photographed went unidentified. I still had favourites, though, despite having no idea what they were.

I think the breakthrough came when a friend, visiting from the UK, brought with him a copy of David Lang's "Wild Orchids of Great Britain and Ireland". Although it did not cover mainland Europe I found, when leafing through it, that several of my new found plant "favourites" were, in fact, Orchids. The visual appeal of many of the other species depicted was such that I determined, there and then, to find and photograph as many species as I could. My local Town hall had recently persuaded me to give English lessons to all comers and so, without more ado, I paid a quick return visit to the UK to stock up on Wildlife Field Guides and as many aids as possible to do with the learning and teaching of English as a foreign language.

Time and again, over the ensuing period, I found myself concentrating on a wide variety of plants based solely on their visual appeal. I never considered their rootstock. If I was honest I would have to say that the question as to whether they had roots or not probably never crossed my mind. Repeatedly, however, when looking them up in my newly acquired library I would find them in a book I had bought entitled Bulbs – The bulbous plants of Europe and their allies – by Christopher Grey-Wilson and Brian Matthew, and illustrated by Marjorie Blamey. Another Book in which they featured regularly was "Bulbs" by Roger Phillips and Martyn Rix. Many of these names have gone on to become famous in Botanical circles and, no doubt, the books to which I am referring have probably been superseded and surpassed by other publications, often involving the same authors. However, back in the early 80's, Field Guides and Reference Works were far fewer and further between than they are today and I was pretty pleased to have the ones I did. They certainly managed to enable me to identify the majority of the plants that I photographed and, of course, I have added to the library since, as and when new books have been published, so that today I can identify virtually any of the species of plants and animals that I am likely to come across in Europe. The outcome of all this was that, over a period of time, I developed a preference for bulbous plants that turned, ultimately, into something of a passion. It has certainly proved to be the sole instigating force in directing many of my sojourns to some of the world's far- flung places.

One of the advantages of many bulbs is that they flower very early in the year, or season, and so tend not to be swamped by the profusion of indiscriminate under-story growth and grasses that follows shortly behind them. Apart from making them easier to locate and subsequently photograph, they occur at a time when there is not too much else about and the normally photographic "lean times" of winter are just behind us, so they are a fitting introduction to the times of plenty to come through the spring and summer.

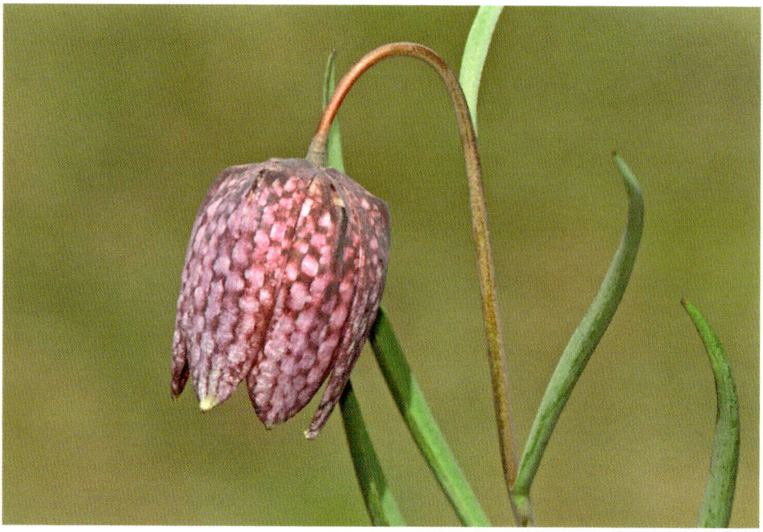

Fritillaria tubiformis - Mt Lozere - Cevennes

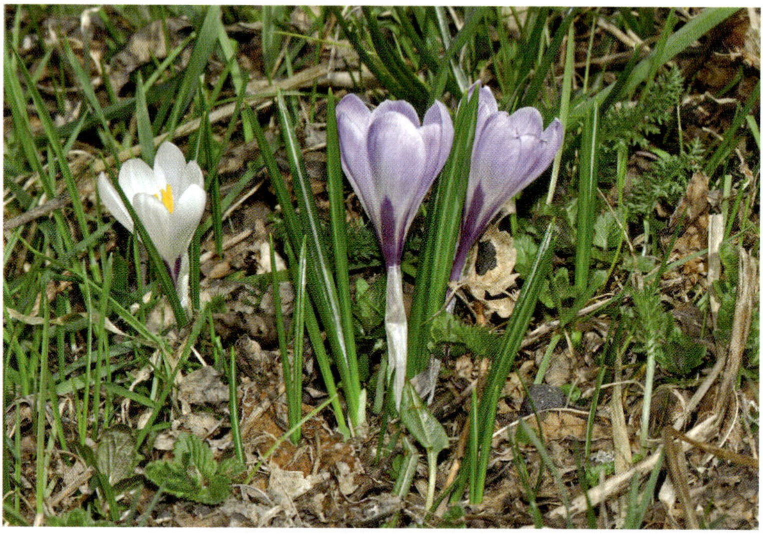

Spring Crocus - Crocus vernus - Mt Lozere - Cevennes

Some of the plants that come under the "bulbous" heading, and which are most likely to be encountered in Britain, are Snowdrops and Snowflakes, Bluebells, Daffodils, Fritillaries, Iris and Gladioli, Lilies, Arums and, of course, Orchids. Mainland Europe offers many more species within the groups already mentioned together with Crocus, Muscari or Grape Hyacinths, Tulips, Gageas, Alliums and Ornithogallums. There are a host of other odd plants but the above mentioned groups provide by far the bulk of what you are likely to become involved with. If you decide to go this route do invest in a decent Field Guide on the subject as your enjoyment of the hunt will be so much greater knowing that you can identify what you have found. Even the identifying itself can add to the pleasure of the whole experience and will undoubtedly add to your knowledge of the subject tremendously since, in seeking to identify what you have already found, you will flick through pages, the contents of some of which will remain in your memory, of plants that you have not yet come across.

Some of my most productive trips in "bulbous" pursuit have been to Iranian and Turkish Kurdistan. To stand in an Iranian desert and have a panoramic display of Tulips, Irises and many other assorted bulbs in flower for as far as the eye can see is an unforgettable experience. In Britain such sights are, indeed, rare these days though a field full of Snakeshead Fritillaries, all nodding in the breeze, can be a joy to behold. There are a number of tour operators offering trips to areas where there is an abundance of bulbous species. Many of these trips are organized in conjunction with the Alpine Garden Society and anyone so interested would be well advised to check with them as to what is on offer.

The only way in which I could cover the whole range of bulbous plants in this book would be "loosely" to say the least. It is such a vast subject. I have, therefore, dedicated the next few chapters to two sub-groups in particular – the Narcissi and the Orchids. The former of these two is presented in a fairly lax fashion with an emphasis on the kind of botanizing trips the pursuit of these unbelievable plants can involve. The latter is covered in more specific depth and relates as much to background and photographic tips and techniques as it does to the plants themselves. Readers will, I am sure, be able to apply the content of the Orchid chapter to the various genera within the other families involved.

Once again I would urge readers to obtain whatever guide books are currently on offer, since this group of plants enjoys such a devoted following that, as a consequence, the quality of the reference works backing it up knows no bounds.

Chapter 13

In Search Of Wild Narcissi

Before delving too deeply into the subject matter of this chapter it may help to briefly discuss the vocabulary commonly used in association with it. Many people seem to accord the name "Daffodil" to those members of the group bearing the large "trumpet" centred flowers, which form the bulk of the larger and more obvious cultivated species, and use the name "Narcissus" to refer to any of the more diminutive, or multiple flowered, species. At the risk of boring the already botanically minded of you I would point out that the plant world is broken up into a number of "families" of which the Amaryllidaceae is the one within which the "sub family" or "Genus" Narcissus falls. All members are either "Narcissi" if being scientific or "Daffodils" if using the nomenclature of common parlance. For a better understanding of the technical jargon relating to this Genus and its origins and background I can best refer you to the book "Narcissus – a Guide to Wild Daffodils" by John Blanchard (ISBN 0 900048 53 0) which is currently the most comprehensive guide that I know of.

My original love of flowering plants has always played a large part in my photographic pursuits, and living, as I do at the moment, in Spain, it is, therefore, a natural progression that Wild Narcissi should, so to speak, raise their collective heads and clamour for attention. The bulk of Narcissus species originate in the region stretching from the French Pyrenees South through the Iberian Peninsula with a number in North Africa and one or two in Northern Europe.

Whilst the characteristics of most of the better known species are well documented many of the descriptions of plants in the wild are based on dried specimens and date back many tens of years and, in some cases, more than a century. On the current status and distribution of naturally occurring species there are very few reference books dealing in any depth with the genus Narcissus.

I decided many years ago to cover as many species as came my way and, accordingly, though never in a position to make a concerted effort, photographed them as and when I came across them. Living in Spain provides a gateway to a veritable Utopia of flowering plants but there is a great dearth of like minded individuals to myself – certainly to the almost obsessional degree that my interest has shaped my life over recent years. As a result of this I often feel like the "Lonely Petunia in an Onion patch" without that gratifying opportunity to exchange information with fellow enthusiasts on a "where have you been and what have you seen?" basis. In the absence of the opportunity to "swap" sites etc there is a good chance of having to wander like a headless chicken in search of your interest of the moment.

Unfortunately for me I recently developed an undeniable urge to cover the genus in greater depth. Living a somewhat solitary and single minded life (nubile and Wildlife Photography orientated maidens please note – but must be able to carry my tripod and spare lenses!), I often find the course of that life dictated by undeniable urges. One of the regular and more insistent of these is my form of "walkabout fever" which can rear its head unexpectedly at any moment and its demands can only be assuaged by reaching for the backpack and travel bag and setting forth into the great unknown.

However this latest Narcissistic urge dictated a greater degree of research than just an aimless meander. No doubt there are enthusiasts in Spain who could have pointed me in the right direction but, as is often the case, I don't happen to know any. I therefore turned my attention to the U.K. I have a great plant growing friend in Cornwall and I remembered seeing some Daffodil Society Handbooks with him some years earlier at a time when the "urge" was not upon me and I consequently paid them little heed. However a trip to the U.K. was imminent, for reasons that I cannot recall, and during it I made Safari down to deepest Cornwall to visit him.

Not only did he have Daffodil Soc and Alpine Garden Soc handbooks going back many years but he also introduced me, for the first time, to John Blanchard's book on Narcissi. This book was like manna from heaven to me and served not only as a most helpful reference work but also as a confirming stimulus to my own plans to locate and photograph each and every one of the species that occurred in Spain. This book has now been delineated, within the terms of my own personal vocabulary, as "The Book" and despite the fact that I have read, marked, learnt and inwardly digested its contents from cover to cover on a number of occasions, it still travels with me whenever I make any trip whatsoever within the regions where Narcissi may occur regardless of the time of year. I read assiduously in the two days of my visit and made copious notes based on all reports of Narc hunting trips or sightings and, in conjunction with maps of Spain, Portugal and the French Pyrenees, came up with a number of potentially viable sites.

Many wild populations of Narcissi have a flowering period of only some 2-3 weeks and so locations are of little use without some information regarding flowering times. Fortunately the various articles, in conjunction with "The Book", had provided a rough guide to some of these and the others I was able to hazard a guess at. I certainly had enough information to feel justified in setting up a planned trip. One potential hazard was that, not only are flowering times very limited in the wild, but also seasons, particularly in high montane regions, can vary significantly from one year to the next and so any information regarding flowering times can only, at best, be treated as a rough guide. There is no greater frustration than to finally arrive at a long sought site only to find the object of your desires wilting and desiccated. No doubt this is quite rewarding for the devoted botanist who may well be after seeds but for the flowering plant photographer the only consolation is in knowing where to come next season without having to search again.

One of the advantages of choosing Narcissi as a project is that the flowering times of the various species span almost a full twelve months period. In the extremely dry and arid Southeast of Spain, Narc. tortifolius can be found from late Dec through to late March and its flowering emergence is closely followed by a succession of different species, right through to several Autumn flowerers such as Narc. viridiflorus, which can be found from late Sept through to Dec. Many of the individual species occur at a number of different altitudes and this, of course, has the effect of extending the period during which you may locate and photograph them. Anyone planning a trip to concentrate on this Genus should look to the months of May and June to maximise the number of species they can expect to find. Whilst several of the early flowerers will be over by then nevertheless many species will still be in flower at lower altitudes, especially in Northern Iberia, but it will be the High Sierras that will provide the richest pickings – no pun intended!

The following three chapters are of a travelogue nature and cover a number of trips I made in search of Wild Narcissi. It was always my intent to come up with a Travel Guide dedicated solely to this subject. Time, as ever, seems to be against me as I have become so busy on the Illustrated Talk front and so I have decided to incorporate what would have been three of the chapters from the new book into this one. Several more chapters are ready written but there are many that are not and it could well be some time before they are.

Chapter 14

Province Of Teruel - Spain - March 2006

Narcissus eugeniae

On checking through John Blanchard's book on wild Narcissi one day in Feb, I came across the section covering Narcissus eugeniae. The opening sentence struck me – "On a remote, windswept hillside overlooking Valdelinares in the province of Teruel ---" ,and he went on to describe how he was lucky, in March 1987, to see 1000's of plants in flower.

Living only four hours drive from Teruel it stuck in my mind. Though, in some respects, 2006 was a difficult season ,late for some species and early for others, when I found myself able, in mid April, to make the trip I figured I would still be in with some sort of a chance.

At the time I was conducting Botanical Tours round the Iberian Peninsula and due to take some U.K. photographers on a Narcissus run. Though we had planned on starting "down South", it was a "distance no object" trip and so N. eugeniae could be included on the menu.

We duly set forth – albeit it later, rather than sooner, in the day – (occasioned to a certain extent by the need, the previous evening, to check the vintage of various village brews firsthand before feeling competent to recommend them to fellow travellers!). This late departure consequently created a need to hurry in order to be on site early enough to photograph in decent light. N. eugeniae has a substantial sized flower-head supported by a stem only 5 to 10 cms long and so photography late in the day, at this time of the year, leads to very long shadows. Furthermore, due to its habit of forming clumps, with a consequent increase in shadowed areas, this can give rise to some very disappointing shots.

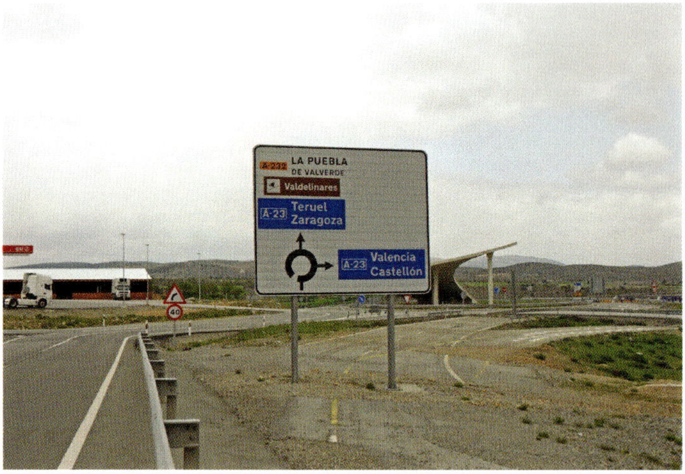

Motorway turnoff for Valdelinares

Accordingly we sallied forth on the motorway past Valencia and took the Teruel turnoff. The road from Valencia to Teruel has been much improved over the last few years and so we made good time. Just short of Teruel we turned off at the signpost to Valdelinares which proudly announced that it was an "Estacion d' Esqui". This translates to it's being a ski slope.

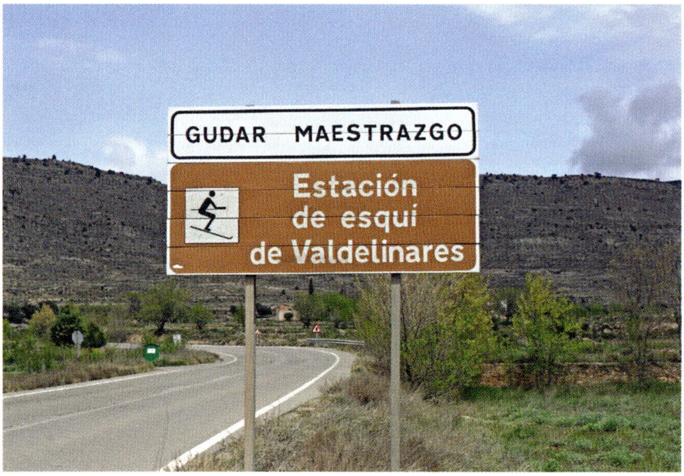

Ski slope sign

From driving on newly constructed dual – carriageway, so fresh the tarmac was barely dry, we suffered something of a culture shock as we hit our first "unimproved habitat" in the form of an unrestored Spanish mountain road. The signs, however, pointed ever onward and upwards and so we progressed with several botanising stops on the way.

We passed through some foothills, which eventually turned into mountains, forming a long arable valley up which, if the signs were to be believed, we would find Valdelinares.True enough, as we progressed upwards and the air grew chillier, we began to see signs for Valdelinares quoting distances in single figures of kilometres. As we came closer to the village the country on the right-hand side of the road consisted of unfenced fields of short turf with unrestricted, open access and which seemed like ideal habitat for eugeniae and photographers alike. On the left-hand side of the road were well fenced fields of a photographer deterring kind with a mixture of both long and overgrazed turf liberally dotted with the picturesque hummocks of recently deposited cowpats. Definitely neither Narcissus nor photographer habitat!

True to form it was in one of these inhospitable places that the first Narcs appeared.

Feeling like Crusaders who had happened on the Holy Grail we piled out to have our first look at the object of our day's labours. Between 20 and 30 plants were in flower and, through binoculars, they looked eminently photographable.

Despite a consensus of opinion that the fencing should be treated as no more than a minor obstacle on an assault course, put there to be overcome, common sense prevailed and, since we had made good time, we pressed on up the valley knowing that we could always come back if we had no luck further up. Several equally well defended fields on the left held scattered populations but the vast expanse of welcoming habitat on the right hosted not a one and, of the serried ranks of hoped for thousands, there was not a sign.

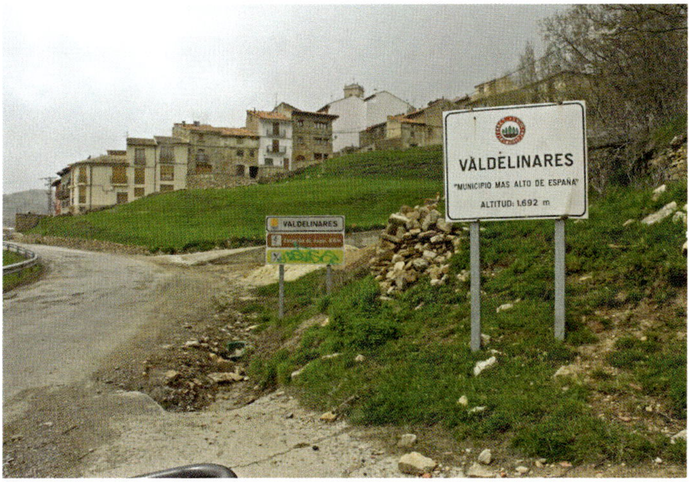

Valdelinares village outskirts

We passed through Valdelinares, which was a typical agricultural mountain village, and carried on up the hill towards the Ski slopes. We were left in no doubt as to the reason for the description "remote, windswept hillside ---" since, had it been a tail wind, we could have used the Landrover as a hang glider.

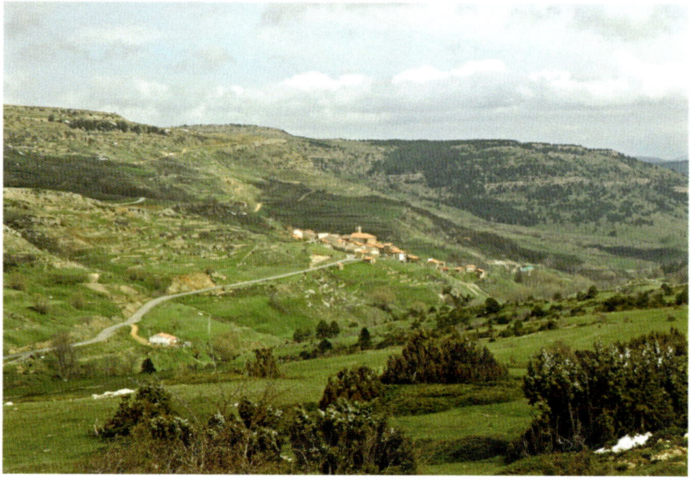

Valdelinares from the Ski slopes

It would seem that when that great plant maker in the sky designed wild Narcissi he used the same pot of paint to colour one or two other species as well. These he then planted in the fields around Valdelinares far enough from the road to look like distant Narcissi from the windows of a labouring Landrover. Several abortive exploratory scrambles turned up only a never ending selection of Narcissus look-alikes including bright yellow ground hugging gorses, mixed compositae, various ranunculus species and some very lovely plants of Helleborus foetidus. Of the hoped for serried ranks of Narcissus eugeniae there was neither a whisper nor a promise.

Be that as it may, as we progressed up the valley between the Gorse and Hellebore laden slopes, it eventually became apparent that the Gorse in question had shrunk somewhat and was only a very few inches high. It was, in fact, sheets of Narcissus eugeniae. They were growing in prodigious numbers though, to be fair, when we came up to them the sheets were not continuous, as had so seemed from a distance, but, instead, comprised densely packed populations in all the dips and gullies on the very undulating hillsides. If you had felt the wind you would have understood their strategy!

The hollows in which they grew were far from wind free (as any of the photographers would agree) but, nevertheless, with patience, we managed to get some very credible shots. Whilst there were very many individual plants

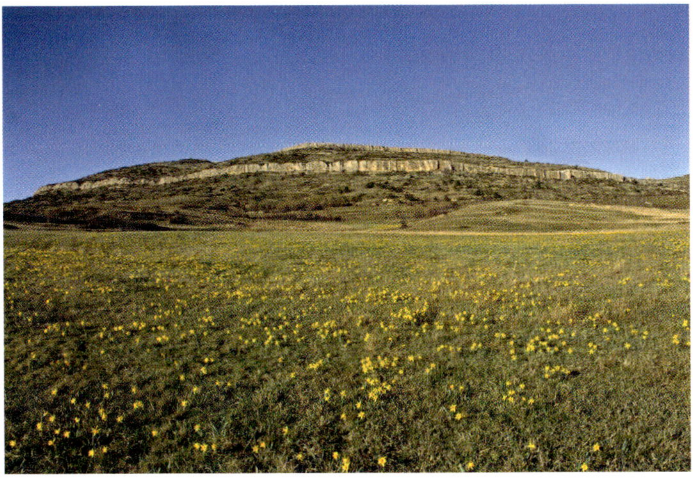

Narcissus eugeniae as far as the eye can see

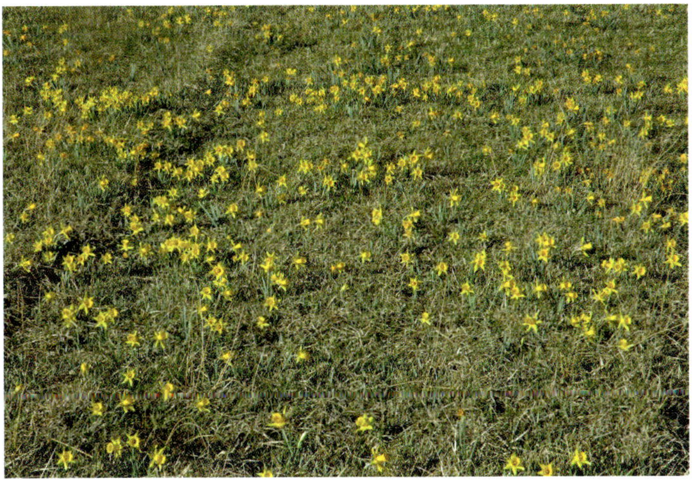

Massed ranks of Narcissus eugeniae

there were, also, a significant number of clumps. With good luck clumps can be very attractive subjects, bringing a great sense of colour and "busyness" to a shot. With my normal luck, however, there is usually, within a clump, at least one flower "gone over", 2 or 3 facing the wrong way, and at least one with a strong sense of imagination so that it persists in nodding in the breeze, even when there isn't one!

The snow had only fairly recently melted and what must have been the very short turf left behind had already, judging by the substantial number of cowpats around, been significantly grazed. Whether this was before the plants' emergence or whether, for some reason such as taste or colour, they did not fall within the preferred bovine menu I do not know, but there was certainly no sign of grazing damage amongst what seemed to be a very healthy population.

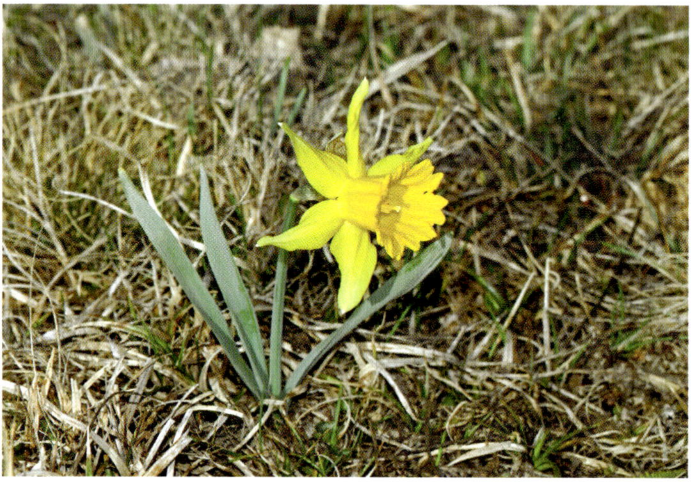

Narcissus eugeniae

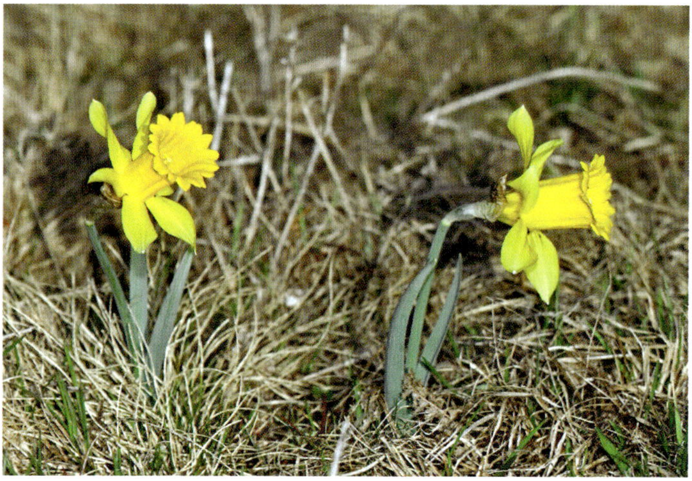

N. eugeniae showing almost top heavy stature

The flowers of N. eugeniae are much akin in size, and casual appearance, to those of N. pseudonarcissus, the common "Wild" daffodil in the U.K. and are, indeed, deemed to be a species or sub – species of that group, but to see these supported on stems only some 2 to 4 inches long and blowing lustily in the wind gives them something of a top-heavy appearance. The wind resistance of such a large flower head, relative to stem length, must be significant and so it is no wonder that they seek what little shelter is afforded from it by the hollows that they favour.

On the whole a joy to behold and, by it's very abundance, gives the lie to the supposition that a combination of skiing interests and cattle grazing are necessarily counterproductive where wild flora and fauna are concerned.

Chapter 15

Narcissus moschatus/alpestris

Two striking White Daffodils featured by photographic plates in John Blanchard's book had instantly taken my eye when first leafing through it. I must admit that, from the photos, I couldn't see much difference between the two but, nevertheless, in the enthusiasm of the moment, they were two species that I determined to see. On taking the time to read the write ups, however, my hopes were dashed on the subject of N.moschatus by J.B's assertion that, whilst its origins were "probably the Pyrenees or Galicia", it "probably no longer exists as a wild plant". N.alpestris still seemed to be on the cards and I filed its details in that nebulous region of my brain reserved for "things to do one day". There the memory remained, as do so many unfortunately, until I was conducting my Cornish "in depth" research on the Genus Narcissus and I came across an article giving details of a site supposedly for N. moschatus in the Pyrenees, which would seem to have abrogated its extinction.. Accordingly this information, together with my original interest, was moved up a notch and placed in the mental file of "things to do soon".

Eventually on the 8th May 2006 I set off with, amongst other things, four target Narcissus species in mind:- N. moschatus, N.alpestris, N.pallidiflorus and N.abscissus together with its hybrid with N.poeticus known as N.montserrati. The latter species are dealt with separately but the subjects of this chapter are the first two.

Using all the reference books at my disposal I tried, in advance of my trip, to define the difference between the two species we are dealing with here because I kept going back to the photographs in which, to my untrained eye, they looked the same. Some books grouped the two together, some included one with the other and some called one by the other's name!

As almost, but not quite, an aside, I am currently trying to pen "A Wildlife Photographer's Guide to the Bulbous Plants of Europe". This is not quite as pretentious as it seems, since the Bulbous Plants do seem to generate a great deal of interest amongst those involved in plant photography at a serious level. This is probably because, containing plants such as the Orchids, Irises, Narcissi, Fritillarias, Arums, Lilies etc, they are so photogenic. Additionally in these days of very economical Continental travel it seems pointless to limit writings to the U.K. when the whole of Europe is but a stone's throw and a few pounds away. What creates a constant stumbling block to my efforts, however, are the often stridently opposing views of many of the "experts" in the various subjects. No doubt similarly diverging opinions pertain in other areas of evolving species but some of these botanical guys take the biscuit. There seem to be two distinct groups, the "lumpers" and the "splitters". The "lumpers", strangely enough, tend to "lump" similar species, sub species and varieties under one heading whereas the "splitters" tend to "split" them up under a number of different headings, on what often seems, to me, the slenderest of justifications. Were I forced to declare myself for one camp or the other I guess I would side with the "lumpers" but I must admit, at risk of severe castigation, to adopting a far more simplistic approach. If, through my camera lens, I am unable to differentiate between two supposedly "different" species then, in my book, "if it looks like a dog, bites like a dog and barks like a dog" then "it's a dog". Many populations of the same species, but living in completely separate areas, are bound to develop certain of their own features and characteristics, for no other reason than the effects of different environment, terrain and local family relationships. That these often minor differences should entitle them to separate specific or sub-specific status does not sit too well with me despite the efforts of the "splitters" to convince me otherwise. I would refer you to my articles on Fritillarias for a fuller explanation of my feelings on this subject. In the meantime suffice to say that I am quite happy for reasonable and established differences to be accorded "varietal" status but for more than that I need to be convinced. (Having read through this last paragraph it makes me sound as pedantic as some of the rest of them!) It does, however, cause much confusion if you are undertaking an amount of research using more than one reference book, as different authors' views and assertions can often be so divergent that, at the end of the day, you simply have to make up your own mind.

Back to the hunt!

The site details for Moschatus, such as they were, were to the effect that, above the village of Benasque, in the Spanish Pyrenees, is the ski resort of Cerler, above which there are two ski lifts and a large car park. The supposed Moschatus was apparently to be found to the West of the car park in surrounding meadows. The general area is one that I am reasonably familiar with from previous Orchid and Lily hunting trips, but I had never been there so early in the season, and never as far up as Cerler. Accordingly I set forth with hope, as ever, springing eternal and dubious weather all round.

The first days of the trip were to be occupied by other species, and also the "dubious weather" as it unfortunately turned out. My route took me through the tunnel of Vielha and I couldn't resist turning off shortly after, in the Val d'Aran, to one of my favourite Orchid spots. This site is as close as you get to Orchid heaven on earth. Early in the season it is host to Vanilla Orchid, Elder Flowered in both its Yellow and Purple forms, Marsh Orchids in prodigious numbers, a very dense flowered and deep purple form of Early Purple Orchid and a very fine assortment of Alpines. An impressive early display of various Blue Gentians gives way a little later in the year to Large Yellow Gentian and one of the best displays of Iris xiphioides I have seen, all growing in an idyllic valley with a picturesque stream running through the middle of it, and overlooked by the towering and majestic beauty of Pico d'Aneto. This time the turf was almost bare but, on the slopes above, through my binoculars I could make out some yellow Narcissi and the massed ranks of Elder Flowered Orchids which occur here in a particularly robust form. Gentians, Early and Trumpet, were everywhere as were Primulas Elatior and Farinosa. The Narcissi, which turned out to be past their best, proved to be N.Bicolour.

It was already late in the day and I have a favourite Hostal just above Vielha that I wanted to get back to for the night. There mine hostess can do things to quail involving blue cheese and other colourful ingredients that makes a meal to die for! Without the stop at the Orchid site I could probably have made it to Cerler and back in good time but I now found myself faced with what, to my sedentary inclinations, seemed an unprecedented need for haste. I therefore flew (as far as third gear in a Landrover can be called flying,) from there to Cerler. It involved a journey of some 80 K's but in the Pyrenees, where straight roads are not only a rarity, they are virtually non-existent, 80 K's can be quite a distance.

I arrived at about 6.30 and found there was only one road up and out of Cerler and there, true to my directions, was a ski lift just a matter of metres from the village. Only one, it's true, but maybe the other had been discontinued or moved. In any event, that this was the place was clinched by the extremely large car park at the bottom of the lift. Home and dry in one! I hurried over to the Western end, as per instructions, only to find a precipice over which had been deposited rocks, household waste and somebody's kitchen sink. This

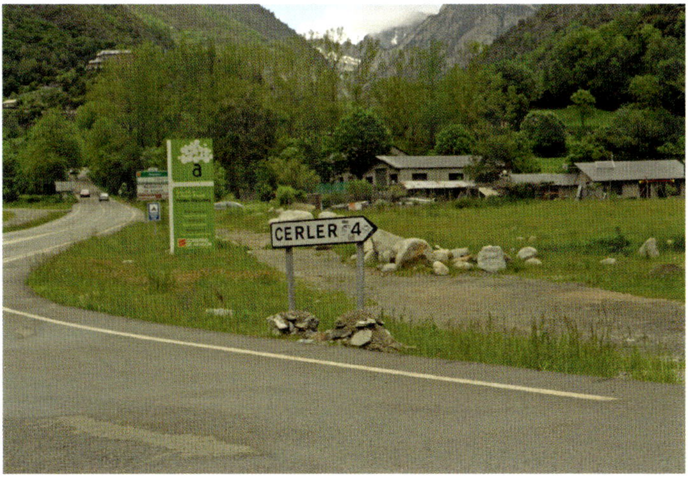

Road to Cerler - almost perpendicular from here on up.

abortive foray was followed by an all points search to the East, North and South to equally no avail. At this stage uncharitable thoughts crossed my mind such as "Could they have confused N.moschatus, which was nowhere, with N.poeticus, which was everywhere?" or, heaven forbid and wash my mouth with soap, could the fault be mine? There was only one lift, and the article had clearly stated two, and there was a very narrow road seemingly continuing on above the village, and so up it I duly progressed. To say that this road kept on keeping on would have been an understatement. Nevertheless perseverance (there are those who, out of my hearing, would suggest that it could be pig-headedness), is an integral part of my makeup and so I duly persevered. The light was fading fast and it looked as though I was well on my way to the back of the moon. Imagine my delight as I finally came round a corner and there, before me, lay not one, but two, structures each of which was the bottom of a ski lift. To compound my joy there was also a largish car park.

Nothing like as substantial as the one down below, mind, but sizeable nonetheless. By now the problem of determining which was the Western end was easy. The sun was sinking fast below the mountain tops and, trusting that that day was no exception to the rule, I assumed, in true Boy Scout fashion, that where it sank lay West. Certainly in that direction were surrounding meadows but already in deep shadow and with not a Narcissus to be seen. Trusty binoculars to the rescue and scan all points fore and aft. Lo and joy behold, there on a higher slope still catching some setting sun was a Narcissus. White in colour, drooping in stature and looking for all the world like I imagined a Moschatus should look. At this point I abandoned all hope of stuffed quail and leapt to the task at hand.

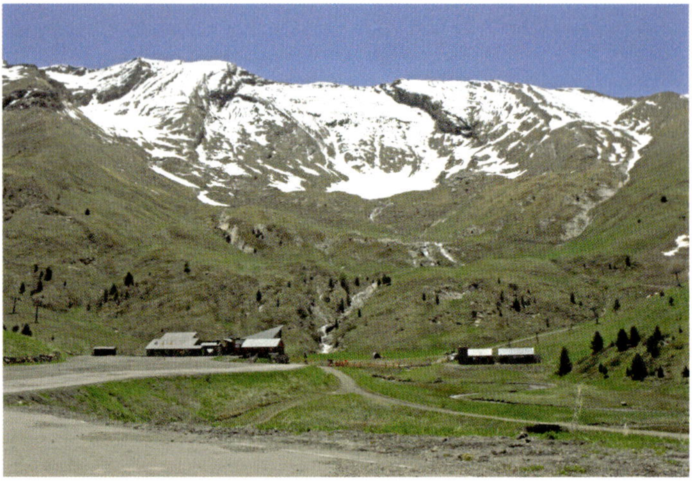

The two Cerler Ski lifts at last

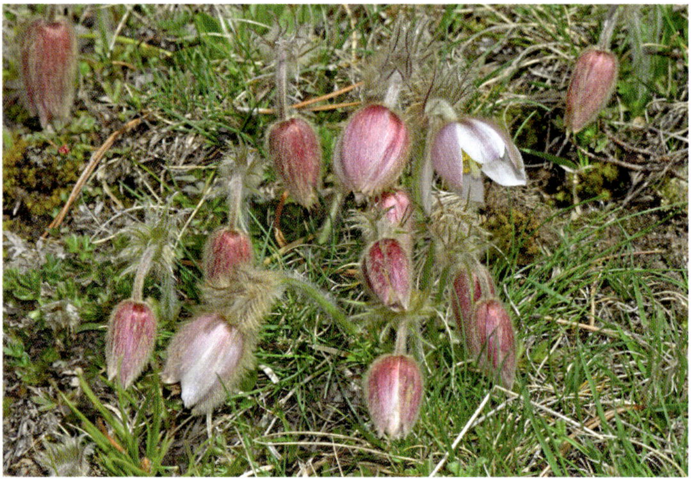

Spring Pasque Flowers - Pulsatilla vernalis.

There were but two plants. Scarcely the profusion I had been hoping for but still two more that I had ever seen before. Spring Pasque Flower - Pulsatilla vernalis - was emerging in vast quantities and through binoculars, at a distance, their nodding heads had a distinctly Narcissistic appearance. However on that far slope could it be? Yes it was! Several more Narcissi. The remaining light could now be counted in minutes. Scarce controlled panic produced one and a half rolls of film in about the time it takes to think "I wish I'd got here an hour earlier." Then, as if someone had turned off the switch, the sun dipped below the mountain rim and it was as if, maybe not midnight itself, but certainly 11.00 pm had arrived, and that seemed to be that. However, on raising my head, I saw one or two higher hummocks still benefiting from a smidgeon of late May sun so I scurried, crablike due to the slope, to a new vantage point. Wonder of wonders – a veritable cornucopia of Moschatus (or Alpestris!?) hove into view. A great many already "gone over" it is true but also a great many others crying out for attention. Stuffed Quails were now right out of the window and a further one and a half rolls were quickly garnered.

Once again the light beat me and I used what little "twilight" time there was to overlook the population. Some wonderfully photogenic offerings convinced me that a return on the morrow was called for, and so I accordingly sallied forth to find lodgings for the night. These I duly found in a village just a few K's down the road. Fed and liquored, to a lesser extent than originally hoped for but to a greater extent than was really necessary, I retired replete and in anticipation of a return to the Narcs in the morning.

Arisen, refreshed, and up the road again on what, fortunately, turned out to be a glorious day. Arriving on site in full light, now from the East, the whole scene was transformed. The dark mountain and meadows of the night before to the West of the car park now turned out to be covered with extensive patches of Narcissi. (The altitude here was considerably greater than that of Cerler itself, and the plentiful N. poeticus of below had petered out on the way up, leaving me up on top with only the one, other, or both species that I had come for). Cameras to the fore I surveyed a likely looking hummock that hosted a goodly population. Confusion and consternation entered the scene! Two days earlier I had photographed what, at the time, I had assumed was N. pallidiflorus. (I was subsequently told that this was, in fact, N. moleroi, a plant I had never heard of and could find no reference to in my books, so whether this is an old plant with a fancy new name or a newly discovered plant with a new name to go with it I do not know.) However, before me, amongst the population of Moschatus /Alpestris / Whatevers were plants that, to my untrained eye it is true, were ostensibly identical in every respect to the plants of two days ago. Certainly there were very many individual plants and clumps of pristine white Narcs which I took to be the Mosch/Alps. However, amongst them in some profusion – certainly far too many to be described as "an odd plant or two"- were these pale yellow ones identical in every respect other than colour, as far as I could see, with the white ones. I would not dream of raising hackles with opinions based on my rudimentary knowledge (that's not true because really I wouldn't mind at all) – but!! Whatever the truth of the matter may be, and I suspect that truth would vary depending on whose opinion you took, both my cameras and I agreed amongst ourselves that it was either one species with two distinct colour forms (there was no gradation of colour displayed between plants), or it was two completely separate, though remarkably similar, species growing side by side. It seemed to me to highlight the problems I outlined earlier on in this chapter and a repeat of the N.graellsii /citrinus syndrome (see separate article on Bulbocodiums) all over again. Anyway – whatever they end up being called they were very beautiful and I was delighted to be there photographing them on such a lovely day.

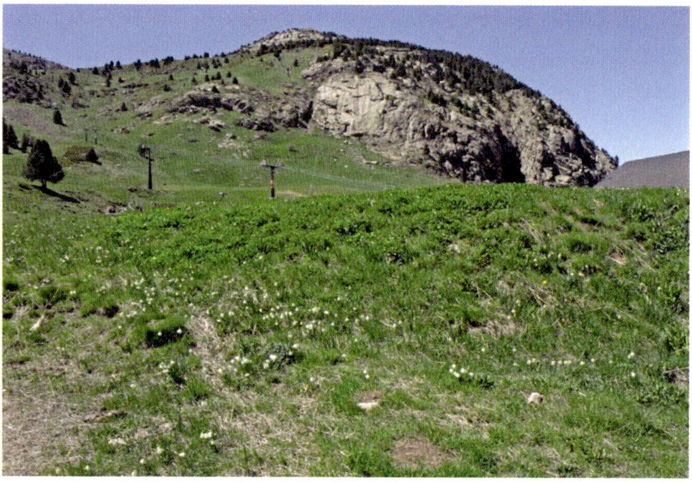

Bank of Narcissus moschatus

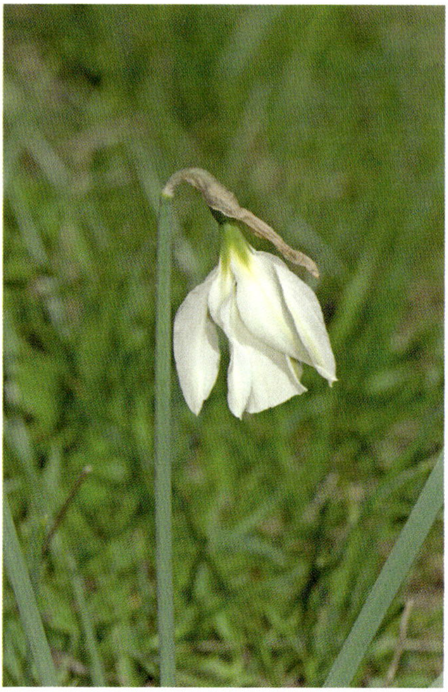

Normal colour form of Narcissus moschatus.

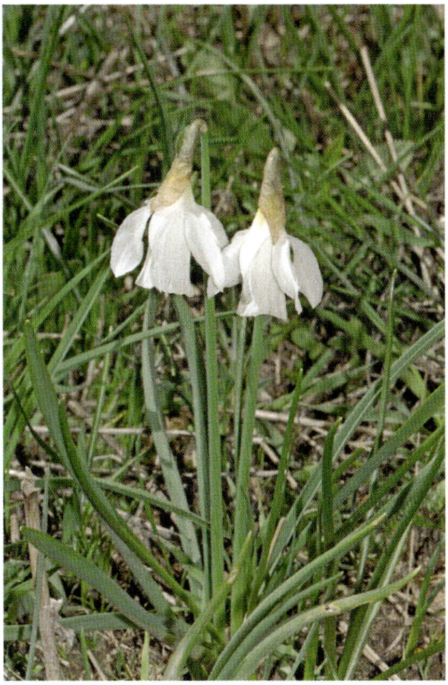

Exceptionally white form of Narcissus moschatus

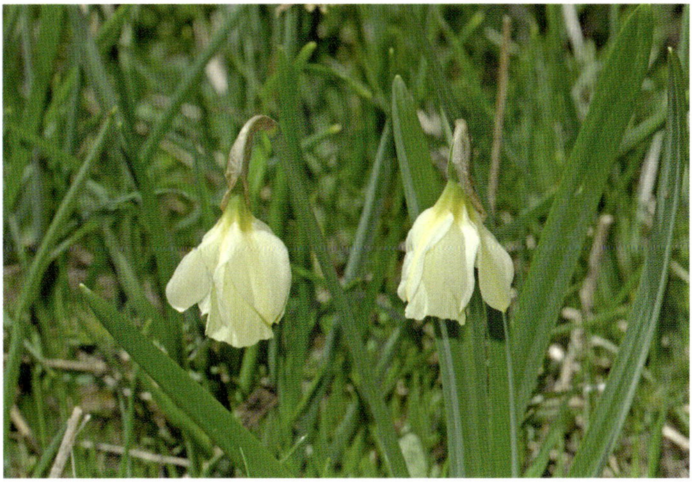

The pale yellow colour form of moschatus or whatever

You would have thought that my confusion regarding species identification would have already been tested to the limit, but no, more was to come. I drive a fairly distinctive Landrover which often attracts an undue amount of attention from conservation Jobsworths who, here in Spain, have only recently sprung into being with a newly acquired awareness of Spain's "Natural Heritage". I am delighted to acknowledge their newfound existence but must confess, that secret part of me that cannot be openly portrayed, wants to yell "what do you think I'm doing?" accompanied by suitable expletives when, cameras trained on a subject from all of 12ins away, the inevitable "What are you doing" inquisition begins. Fortunately my Spanish is good enough to explain that "No, I do not want to cut it down, dig it up, eat it or stick it in my ear – I just want to photograph it". The genuine and helpful ones are a joy to speak with, and from them you can often learn a lot, but those bustly ones, brimming with self importance, often make me wish them elsewhere – like the bottom of a deep muddy ditch! However, during my Mosch/ Alps sojourn just as I was trying to sort t'other from which, a white van slowly crept up the slope towards me. At least it wasn't the Guardia so hopefully only a minimum amount of paperwork would be needed to establish my bona fides. Out stepped two guys, one of whom approached me and said, in an accent from somewhat North of Dorset, "Hello, you must be from the Alpine Garden Society." Taken aback is the polite phrase that springs to mind. It turned out that, for probably the first time in my life in Spain, I was in the company of fellow plant enthusiasts and photographers. These seemed, in fact, far more knowledgeable than was I and they further compounded my amazement by saying they had John Blanchard, he of "The Book" fame, in the van with them. Having long looked to him as the veritable "guru" of Narcissi and exchanged some letters with him only weeks before, you can imagine my astonishment and pleasure at such a chance meeting, virtually on top of a Spanish Pyrenee.

Having met him and finding him to be an exceptionally pleasant and human "guru", my obvious question was – "Are they Moschatus or Alpestris?" The answer of "I suppose they're probably Moschatus" turned many of my preconceived notions of precision identification techniques on their head. I am now left with the situation that I have "probably" now seen and photographed N.moschatus but - if so - then not yet N.alpestris!!

Roll on next season!

Chapter 16

Narcissus pallidiflorus

I thought that I had this species cracked and in the bag until I met John Blanchard, author of what, for me, is the definitive guide on Wild Narcissi, out of the blue one day on a Spanish mountaintop. He promptly disabused me and informed me that what I had taken to be Pallidiflorus was, in fact, a species newly named as Narc moleroi. I have, since, covered this species more fully in an article on Narc moschatus. After a Narc hunting season spent happily adding to the "been there, done that" list I was somewhat saddened to have to reduce the target list by one after our chance meeting.

Shortly after this I was returning to my home in Spain from a trip to the Cevennes, in the Massif Central of France, and wanted to photograph a fairly late flowering Orchid – Orchis cazorlensis – on the way. Normally, from the Cevennes, I return via the coast road but this time I cut further across France to drop down through Larzac where I hoped to photograph two of Europe's rarest Insect Orchids – Ophrys aymonini and Ophrys aveyronensis (in which aspiration I was successful) – before cutting further across to take in the Corbieres Mountains just north of the Pyrenees. From there it is a straight run down to the site I had in mind for Orchis cazorlensis at Tragacete in the Provincia de Cuenca just east of Madrid in central Spain.

Having passed through the Corbieres with several excellent Orchid species encountered, including Serapias cordigera in significant quantities, I then drifted over towards Andorra. It was many years since I had passed that way and it was on a more or less straight line to my destination. I approached it via Pas de la Casa and, after a seemingly never ending series of hairpin bends, I arrived at the lower outskirts of the town.

Most towns and villages in this region derive their living from the side benefits of skiing and at this time of the year, May, with the snow all but gone they have a bedraggled appearance. Almost bereft of residential life, there is a flurry of construction in an effort to generate even higher returns next year, and loads of decorative glitz now out of season, and so out of context, and looking somewhat tarnished. The consoling factor was that, as I came up the road, I could see Narcissi flowering on both sides. However, due to its switchback nature, and the fact that no provision at all has been made to allow parking or pulling off, then the large volume of traffic travelling at manic speeds ensures that you have to keep going rather than park on the carriageway. I was, therefore, grateful at the outskirts of the town to find a lay-by to pull into. The upward hill to the left, and the downward hill to the right, both hosted a population of Narcissi thus obviating the need to backtrack on foot and, particularly off to the right, some very handsome Pulsatilla alpina were in full and open flower.

The Narcissi turned out to be the true Pallidiflorus and were, for me, not only a first but also a very satisfactory ending to a lengthy season's Narcissi hunting.

As to photographing them – that was a different story. The force 9 winds prevailing at the time were a mere bagatelle in the melting pot of a Wildlife Photographer's life and I foolishly thought that was all I had to contend with. The downward slope seemed more sheltered than the upward one and so I opted for that with fingers crossed. Although, due to its rocky nature, there were several virtually wind free pockets on the slope not one Narcissus had opted for these seas of tranquillity but were, instead, firmly ensconced in the teeth of the gale. Nothing for it but patience and so I chose my plants with care and waited, and waited, and waited. Seriously there were, as almost ever (except in the Falklands, but thereby hang several other tales), gaps in the wind and I did, indeed, finally achieve my objective.

Having, at long length, photographed the Narcs to what I felt was a sufficiently comprehensive degree I turned my attention to a few side shots of a particularly delightful pair of Pulsatilla alpina that had been nodding pointedly in my direction and, in all but words, demanding "Take me, take me!" Mission accomplished I then readied myself to climb up what now, from below, looked like a precipice, which I had much more easily climbed down, when a gust of wind and a virtual blanket of fog blew up behind me. Almost dislodged, much to the merriment of a group of workers from a nearby industrial unit, I looked up towards the Landrover only to see it disappearing into the mist. Never mind I figured that if I kept going up I would bump into it eventually. Unfortunately that great Narcissus designer in the sky intervened by placing, almost beneath my very feet, the most photogenic N. pallidiflorus ever seen by man. I don't know how most would have reacted in the circumstances, but as an obsessional Wildlife Photographer I'm afraid that once the radar locks onto a target then no amount of man made, or even divine, intervention is going to get in the way. Accordingly, as clouds of cloud or mists of mist rolled by, I proceeded to photograph a plant that I could only see in fits and starts.

I remembered, once before, photographing European Bison from a horse drawn sledge in the snow and finding, when I got the slides back, that they were all blanketed in a fine white mist and totally unusable. It took months and a return visit to work out that it was a mixture of my breath, horse's breath, steam off the horse's rump and airborne water vapour that were to blame and here I was like to repeat the performance.

I must admit that John Blanchard's written description of Pallidiflorus did, I thought, exactly fit the "Moleroi" plants I had found earlier. Face to face with the living proof, however, even I, in my Narcissistic naïveté, could see that this was an entirely different kettle of fish. Actually very attractive. Of medium height (on this site anyway), with foliage of a height with the flowers, it looked like a pale version of Narc pseudonarcissus though to my eye more appealing. Very subtle shades of creamy yellow in the petals contrast only slightly with a deeper coloured corona. For me its winning feature was its fantastically flared, and at times recurved, flange at the end of the corona, up inside which was a pleasant mix of shades of cream. I found it an altogether pleasing plant to see. It looked nothing like the Moleroi and Moschatus I had seen only a few days before and was, for me, a fitting finale to my year's Narcissus hunting and photography.

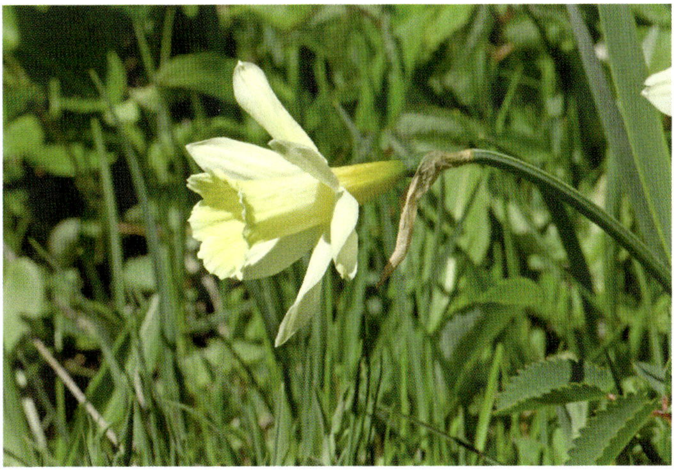

Narcissus pallidiflorus

From Pas de la Casa I continued down towards Spain via Andorra la Vielha. The first major town I encountered was Soldeu, and as I dropped down (in Andorra you are always either dropping down or climbing up) towards it the road, on entering civilisation, turned sharply to the left. Directly to the left and "up a bit" in the curve of the hairpin was what looked like a reasonably new Ski Village. Between this village and the road that I was on was a fairly extensive grassy area already provided with a service road, no doubt indicative of its designated future as an extension to the "des res" development alongside. That apart, at the time of my visit, this area was completely carpeted with Narcissi. One side of the green held a large population of Narc poeticus and the other side one of Narc pallidiflorus with a small stream separating them. My mind immediately switched into "Hybrid mode" and I turned off to investigate. True enough there they were. Although the Pallids were just "going over" and the Poets just coming, nevertheless, on the line of demarcation between the two species, were a number of hybrids. They were not unlike the hybrid between Narc abscissus and Poeticus though, in this particular case, the petals were much whiter creating an especially attractive flower. As I dropped further down the valley the Pallids became fewer and fewer and eventually ceased to be.

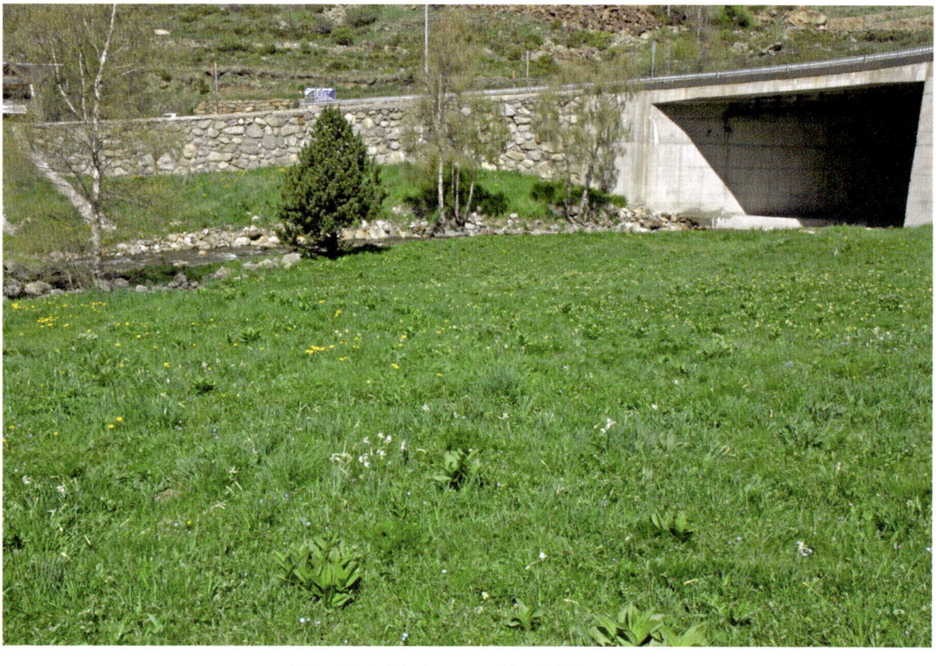

The Hybrid site outside Soldeu

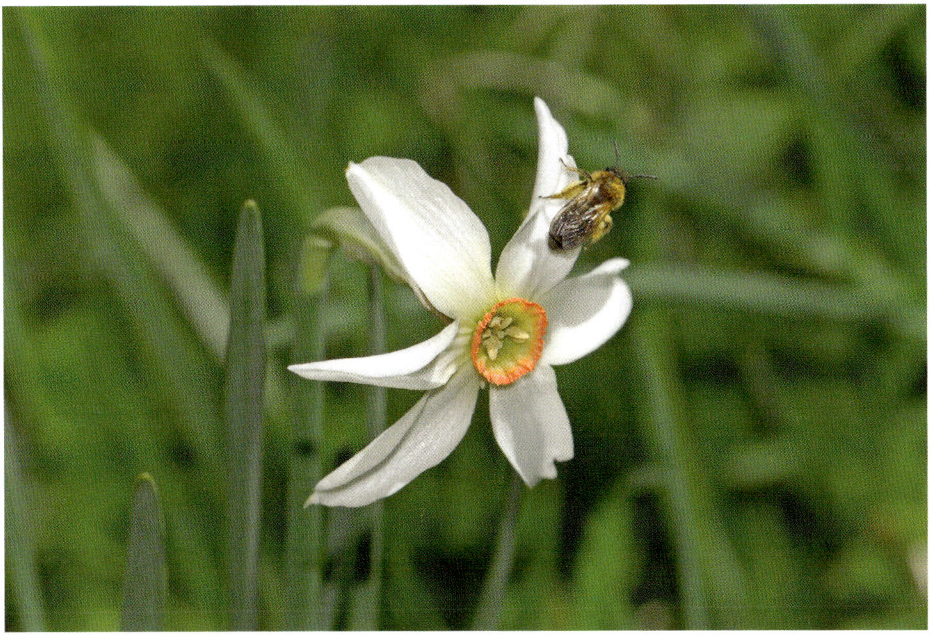

Narcissus poeticus - The Poet's or Pheasants Eye Narcissus

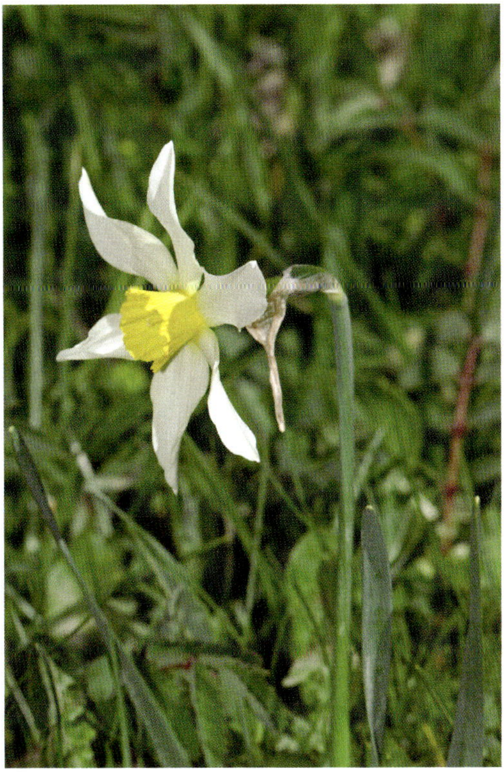

Narcissus aranensis - hybrid between poeticus and pallidiflorus

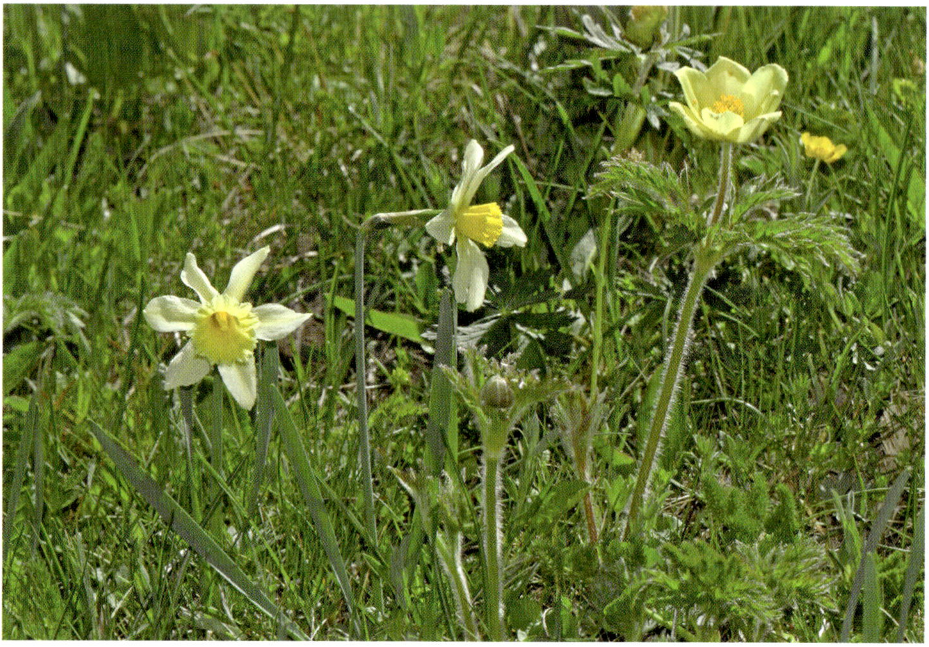

N. aranensis, pallidiflorus and Pulsatilla alpina or Alpine Pasque Flower.

Their place was taken by a colourful array of cranes, building sites, traffic lights and jams, duty free shops and filling stations – all in full bloom! Never have I seen so many filling stations per capita of residents. It must have equated to at least one each! After the serenity of the mountains for so long I must confess that this was something of a culture shock that I nevertheless had to endure for the greater pleasure of passing back through into Spain. (Diesel, by the way, was almost exactly half the price it is in the U.K.)

Through Customs, which seems to be much of a formality these days, and "onwards and upwards" as they say, to Orchis cazorlensis.

Chapter 17

Photographing Terrestrial Orchids

My own love of bulbous plants came about as a result of my fascination with Terrestrial Orchids. In its infancy this bug caught hold of me when I was first living in Spain and my photography was mainly video. I wasn't really even sure which were orchids and which were not but researching to find out what I had managed to photograph made me realise that it was the undeniable appeal and appearance of Orchids that had caught my eye.

How thankful I am that they did for since those early days my pursuit of this oft elusive quarry has taken me to many parts of the globe that I would probably not otherwise have visited and led on to an all consuming interest in bulbous plants in general. The Orchids remain King, however, though the incredible diversity of the rest does take some beating.

Initially I will deal with those species to be found in the UK. There are in excess of 50 species and, in keeping with many other groups of Wildlife, the exact number is debatable and depends on where you fall between the "lumpers" and the "splitters". At risk of repeating myself the "lumpers" are those who "lump" together similar individuals and possibly sometimes sub-species, as one species. The "Splitters" accord what are frequently only marginal differences, specific, subspecific or varietal status. They frequently insist on granting full specific status to populations of what, ostensibly, are merely populations of the same species but living in different localities, based on what can often seem to be the slenderest of justifications. I have covered this subject more fully in my articles on Narcissi and would refer those who may be interested to check under my article headed "Narcissus moschatus/ alpestris".

Essentially, to my Botanically naïve mind, many, if not all, lifeforms are actively evolving. Some to a more noticeable degree than others. If you locate populations of the same species in a number of different habitats it seems, to me, inevitable that over the course of time family relationships and factors beneficial and possibly peculiar to the particular location will begin to have some bearing on the appearance of the subject concerned. At what stage these differences warrant specific status is, of course, the moot point. I have just completed a long promised trip through the major mountain ranges of Spain and France and have encountered, several times, the "same species" in nearly all locations. There is no way these populations can come into contact or be influenced by one another as the sites are often hundreds of miles apart. They are, then, evolving at their own individual paces and developing features that suit their own exact locations and so of course there are going to be differences. Often, it seems, it is decreed that the difference warrants specific status solely for the aggrandisement of he who supposedly "found" this new thing. I would have thought that in this day and age of DNA and other technology that there should be a more definitive method of determining when a species is sufficiently removed from others of its like to warrant a name of its own. That way we may be spared the ongoing onslaught of names of the various wives, daughters, mothers and grandmothers of the so called "discoverers" as happens at present.

In keeping with other groups within the Wildlife network the British Orchids have a finite number of species (give or take a few!) and are well documented both generally and scientifically. The number of species and the wealth of information relating to them is such that, for the diligent, it is possible to bag a "full set". This always seems to be a tremendous incentive in many walks of life and Orchid photography is no different. Whatever brings you into the interest you will quickly find that Orchid photography is a highly addictive pastime.

Of the fifty odd species available to you between 20 and 30 can be located and photographed relatively easily. The rest will demand varying degrees of effort and expertise in their identification and location before you can add them to your "been there, done that" list. The hardest part for the newcomer is to recognize when he/she is actually looking at an Orchid. Their shape, size, colour and locations are so diverse that it takes time to realise what you are looking for.

Many sites can be identified via the internet under either Wild Orchids in general or by punching in the names of individual species. There are also some very good books available on the subject. I suppose the most definitive of these at the moment are those by Delforge though their content is too Continental for them to be really relevant to the UK per se. Neither do they give specific sites but rather just general areas. When you become more proficient a general area is often good enough because, within it, you will probably become able to pick out likely sites by eye. In your early days, however, it would always help if you knew to turn left at the fourth rock on the right, take five steps forward and then look under the tree straight in front of you. Unfortunately there are not too many books that go into this much detail but there are some that help.

I haven't, personally, bought Orchid books for some years and so am not truly aware of what is currently out there on the market. However for Hants and Dorset there are two very good ones by Martin Jenkinson and much of the information in them would apply to the various species wherever they be found. These are "Wild Orchids of Hampshire and the Isle of Wight" ISBN 1 873035 04 7 and "Wild Orchids of Dorset" ISBN 1 873 03502 0. There are also a number of general "finding wild flowers" books and the one relevant to my home area in Dorset that comes to mind is "The Wild Flowers of the Isle of Purbeck" by The Rev Ted Pratt ISBN-13: 978 0 9553928 4 9. Of these latter I have no doubt that there are others throughout the UK that are probably more applicable to your home areas. I expect that David Lang's "Wild Orchids of Britain and Ireland" ISBN 0-19-282599-2 is still one of the best if it is still in print, failing which a check with Amazon will no doubt prove fruitful.

By far and away the best site guide, however, is word of mouth. If you can take the time and trouble to meet other like minded souls you will find that every one of them knows at least one site that you don't, and many of them will know several. So get talking! Once you start out on the trail you will inadvertently bump into others on a similar quest. Don't be a "shrinking violet" and don't go all broody and possessive over sites that you may have discovered and are convinced that no one else knows about. Be prepared to swap information and you'll be surprised at just how helpful other people can be.

If you are not already a member of your local Wildlife Trust then perhaps you should consider joining. Most of the Area Trusts have several sub groups within them and they publish an Events Diary listing forthcoming events and talks. If you keep your eye on this list you will no doubt find one or two talks that will appeal to you but, in any event, if you make the effort to attend one or two of them you will have the opportunity to meet other enthusiasts and share information. If you are lucky enough to be able to attend a talk on Orchids or Wild Flowers it will not only give you an opportunity to learn something about the subject but also to judge the quality of photography that is currently "doing the circuit". If, after seeing one or two, you feel that you are still "an aspirant" then get aspiring! If, however, you feel that you are already "up there with them" then get giving talks and sharing your knowledge and expertise. In reality this is not easily achieved and you should not be downhearted if you find that you are still "on the ladder" provided that you are moving in an upward direction. This is not just about Photography but fieldcraft and a feel for the subject as well. Some of the best photographers in the world would not be at home on their knees in a muddy field surrounded by cowpats and with the Orchid, of which they need a closeup, nodding in the breeze that has been blowing continuously for the last two weeks and doesn't seem to be about to give up.

So - - you are now genned up on what you are looking for and have a reasonable idea of where to find it. Now the problems begin. The primary one is that it is not only a case of "what" and "where" but also of "when". Most wild flowers, compared to their garden counterparts, have a fairly short flowering period of only two to three weeks. This season varies from year to year by up to as much as 3 or 4 weeks one way or the other. Take it from me there is nothing more frustrating to a plant photographer than to arrive on a long searched for site and find that all the subjects are, in fact, there but you are two or three days too late and they are all in the "seedhead" stage. At least you'll know where to go next year! Always check the state of the current year's season as to whether it is early or late and be guided accordingly.

However, assuming that all prevailing factors have conspired to smile in your direction for once and there, in front of you, is the object of your desires, how do you set about photographing it? I think closeups are the stuff of every plant photographers dreams but a succession of only these quickly becomes boring. I usually work to a three point principle. Firstly you need an "in habitat" shot showing the whole plant and enough of its surroundings to conjure up a mental image of the "where" of it. Secondly I try to take an "in between" shot showing the Orchid head, a bit of stem and, hopefully, the rest of it out of focus and not intruding in any way. This takes care of those that just want to see the plant for what it is. Thirdly, and finally, there is the closeup. In days of slide this often took at least two different shots. One of the complete flowerhead, as large as you could get it in the frame, and the second of just one or two parts of the flower or florets depending on the species concerned. In these days of digital, if you are careful, one shot will fulfil both these latter requirements. If your full frame headshot has been carefully composed and taken you should be able to crop it with your software programme to show any parts of the flower that you choose whilst still maintaining subject sharpness.

When it comes to the actual taking of your shots you will find that your subjects are split into two main groups. One group will consist of those species that grow in amongst other vegetation in a field or hedgerow or similar setting and will need a degree of "gardening" to show off the whole plant. This "gardening" can be something of a controversial issue with the opposing camps taking varying views as to whether you should take the shot "as is" regardless, or whether, to make the shot more aesthetically pleasing, and certainly to show the subject off to full advantage, you should engage in a little of what is euphemistically called "gardening".

I subscribe to the latter though you do have to be careful. First and foremost take care not to destroy any vegetation that may have been sheltering or supporting your subject and may actually be partly responsible for the pristine condition that presumably prompted you to select it in the first place. Most offending vegetation can be temporarily pinned down with small stones or sticks and some of the heavier and stronger stuff can be tied back with spare bootlaces. Do not uproot anything since roots can travel with a mind of their own and often a plant some distance away can actually have its roots entwined with those of your subject. I carry a pair of surgical scissors to carefully snip off grass stems and the like that may be in between lens and subject and some of those long seeding grasses that, though not directly in the way, nevertheless deliberately lean over and ruin your view every time the slightest breeze blows. Make sure you do not get cut ends in your final image otherwise you will have further enhancement to do. Finally return things to as near normal as possible when you have finished so that not only your subject, but the surroundings also, can continue to thrive to whatever extent the weather and local herd of cows permit.

The most persistent problem with the above group will be coping with the wind. In reality, and provided that you have the patience, most winds do have occasional lulls. You just have to wait! Sometimes this can take some time and you have to remain focussed with your finger on the shutter release ready to seize the moment. Digital cameras give you a greater range of shutter speeds at the twitch of your ISO settings than did the film cameras of old. However, I always prefer to wait until the subject is quite still, even if I have a square eye by the end of it. The effect of wind causing subject movement is more easily overcome with your "in habitat" shots due to various factors such as your choice of lens and the increased shutter speeds you can obtain from the increased amount of light if using a "short" lens. Additionally there is the unarguable fact that a quarter inch wobble at fifty feet is going to be far less noticeable than the same wobble at eighteen inches.

When you come to your flower headshots there are a couple of support systems that you can use to reduce the movement somewhat. Many Orchids consist of a flower/s on the end of a fairly long stem. I look for three lightweight forked twigs of a suitable length and lay them up against the stem, just below the part you are photographing, in the form of a tripod. You do not normally need to fix them either to themselves or the plant as the forks usually bind them together. This has the effect of stilling the stem movement whilst leaving the head free to be photographed without any supports showing up in your shot. The wind will still affect those parts of the plant above your "tripod" but the movements will be greatly reduced and the periods of complete stillness will be increased. You can also try sticking a twig of suitable length in the ground (some way from your plant so that you don't damage its underground parts) in such a way that your subject is, in effect, just "leaning" against it. This is not as effective as the "tripod" but it is very quick and often serves the purpose.

I also carry a folded up length of plastic sheeting about 18ins high, and some lightweight tentpegs for support, to provide a bit of a windbreak. In practice it's not very efficient as most winds seem to enjoy going round corners or even over the top. There is also a danger that you may convert the gentle, elegant, swaying in the breeze motion of your subject into a movement more reminiscent of a bad case of the DTs. It is far harder for the eye to judge when this latter movement has ceased than it is the former and so you stand a very good chance of taking your shots in mid-shiver and ending up with a blurred image.

The other group will be growing in either a woodland or open setting where other vegetation is not a major problem. Often, however, they will be in the shade or, even worse, dappled light filtering through branches overhead. This group poses slightly different problems. Wind is not quite so critical though it does still find its way in. Gardening is probably not a problem either as many woodland understories can be relatively bare. By far the biggest problem in the woods will be the light especially if conditions are such that it is dappled. You will be surprised at how fast the sun and its associated shadows can move. Often an Orchid, perfectly outlined in a ray of sunshine, can have faded into insignificance by the time you have unslung your gear and set up your tripod. Sometimes you can tie back branches to create more light but all too often the offenders are many feet off the ground and out of effective reach. Better to wait until your subject is either fully lit or fully in the shade before taking your shots. Unless you are very lucky most shots in dappled light pose an exposure and enhancement nightmare at the end of which you may well wish that you hadn't bothered or that you had waited a little longer. Before someone points out to me that dappled and filtered light can produce some dramatic and stunning effects I would agree, but repeat that, far more often than not, it is just an exposure nightmare and a mess – But hey!- you're the photographer and it's your decision how and what you take and not up to anyone else to make the choice for you – so go for it!

With the photographing of both the above groups a flash unit can be an invaluable aid. There is, in my mind anyway, no question but that flash brings out a degree of detail, in many situations, that would not be portrayed in a non-flashed shot. How important this lack of detail is to you is, of course, a very individual consideration and will probably be determined by what you have as an end requirement for your image. If all you want is a 6 x 4 print or a screen image then you can probably get away without flash and brighten your image with your software programme. If, however, you want to substantially crop your image, or go for a larger print, then the extra detail provided by flash may assume a greater significance. You may feel there is no need for flash in an open field with sun shining fit to burst but this is not necessarily so. I normally set my flash unit on a "fill-flash" setting as this just lifts heavy shadows caused by bright light and "reaches parts of the flower that other photographers may have missed!" I seldom, if ever, use full flash as, though it can admittedly freeze movement, it creates black backgrounds and provides a fairly harsh image which my eye does not find pleasing.

There is, however, no such thing as a free lunch and so the extra detail from flash comes at a price. I have been "doing this thing" for many years now and I still find it impossible to accurately predict the varying degrees of reflectivity of all the background vegetation some of which, rather than being nicely blurred, can become quite intrusive. Additionally, with many plants, and some Orchids in particular, there can be a fairly mega problem caused by reflections from dust and pollen particles. When illuminated by any kind of flash these have the propensity to become mini searchlights since they can be highly reflective and can, sometimes, spoil your shot completely. Many Orchids, especially those of the Ophrys or Insect Orchid group, seem to act as a magnet for dust and pollen due to their frequently sticky and "hairy" flower parts. The problem is that not every particle or water droplet will reflect to the same extent, nor do so in a direction that will show up in your image. It is all but impossible to predict the extent to which your image will be affected and you will not truly know the position until you get home and display the image through your computer as your naked eye, and most camera playback systems, are not detailed enough, especially in bright light, to show the true scale of the problem. The upside is that these mini-highlights are normally easily removable with your healing tools but it can be yet another tedious process, particularly with heavily affected images. It is not necessarily an answer to the problem, as each set of circumstances will be different, but if you take some shots with, and some without, your flash then you will give yourself the widest possible choice of images to work with.

Because of the varying conditions under which you will be working it is often impossible to accurately predict exactly which camera settings will provide the most pleasing images. It pays, therefore, to take numbers of shots using different settings. This is known as "bracketing" and allows you to cover all your options. I bracket as much as circumstances and prevailing conditions permit. Bear in mind that the most pleasing shots do not always come from the smallest apertures. Do not fall in love with high F Stops just to be able to claim that you normally work at F22 and above since, although this type of setting gives you the greatest depth of field, this is not necessarily a plus if you want your subject to stand out from its background. BRACKET !! I suspect that, were I to check back, the bulk of my full plant shots will turn out to have been taken on F8 or F11 and not until taking extreme close-ups will I have switched to the smaller apertures of F16, F22 or smaller depending on the lens of the moment. Quite frequently when taking fairly distant shots of some of the Ophrys Orchids I may use apertures as large as F5.6 since the often "spindly" design of the plants will make them disappear into their backgrounds at a higher setting. At the end of the day it is all about what you want and so you are the best one to make the necessary decisions but, in the meantime, if you are not very experienced, then do yourself a favour and bracket like hell! Not only for your speed, aperture and flash settings but also for shot angles. Remember that many of these plants flower for a very short period and it is far better to have to discard the majority of your shots than it is to spend a whole year champing at the bit whilst waiting for another crack at it because you goofed. A wise man once said that when he came to be lying, dying, he wanted to be able to regret things that he had done rather than things that he hadn't done, and your Orchid Photography might well follow these lines.

Most of the Orchis and Dactylorhiza species which, between them, comprise by far the largest part of the British range of species, have a fairly cylindrical shape when in full flower. As a result lighting and focussing are fairly straightforward – just make sure that you get the best angle. Some species have basal leaves on opposing sides of the stem and it gives a nice balanced image if you can get at right angles to these when taking your fullbody shots even if that is not necessarily the best angle for the flowerhead. Super closeups, however, of head and/or individual florets will have to be taken so as to show them off to best advantage, and this may involve a completely different angle of approach.

My own personal favourites, the Ophrys or Insect Orchids, pose a slightly different problem. They tend to be far more diminutive in size and so, whilst the full plant shots are fairly straightforward and normally lend themselves to portrait format, the closeups are more difficult. It is not easy to make a full length Ophrys shot look exciting since the plant comprises little more than a relatively long, spindly stem with up to a dozen or so very small flowers sprouting from it. The whole thing from a distance is relatively uninspiring but it is in the intricate design of the individual flowers that the beauty of these plants lies and your objective will be to portray these to their best advantage. You may be forgiven for thinking that a full frontal approach is best for this purpose but, in practice, this is often not the case. Fly, and some Early Spider Orchids, can show well from this angle but others such as Bee and Late Spider are arranged in such a way that, with lifesize images, the flower is too deep from front to back to get it all in focus at one time. With Bee, for example, it is not possible to focus on the front of the labellum and the sepals, which normally curve backwards, in the same shot. With these I find that a half sideways shot probably does the best possible job and if you look at one or two of my Bee Orchid shots under the Orchids of Europe heading on my website you will see what I mean.

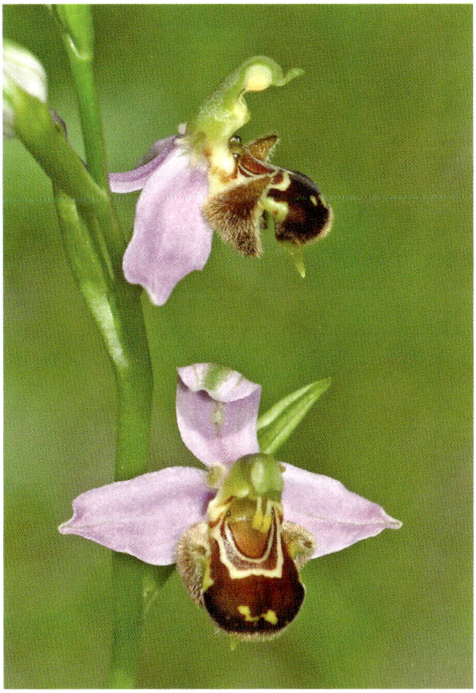

Ophrys apifera or Common Bee Orchid
showing two shooting angles

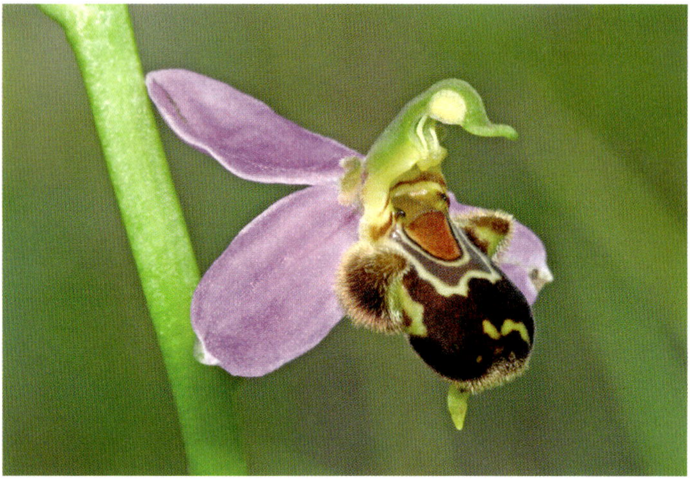

Bee Orchid from my preferred shooting angle.

Mainland Europe is home to all the species that we have here, though often in far greater density of numbers, plus a range of species that we do not have despite our being only a short distance away. Many of the European islands host the more common species plus an often significant number that are specific or "endemic" to that particular island only. This is brought about by the fact that in island, and some mountain, settings many species of plants and animals have evolved over the millennia cut off from, and unaffected by, other populations. The longer the island has been isolated then, normally, the greater will be the diversity and significance of the evolutionary changes effected.

In the case of our own "island" it is only a very few thousand years since the thawing of the most recent ice age and the consequent rise in sea levels cut us off from Europe. At that point in time we were stuck with the limited number of species that were already present here and able to survive in the conditions prevailing at the time. The difference between Europe and the UK, however, is that as this part of the planet warmed up species which had formerly existed only in the Southern parts of Europe were able to spread Northwards, often fairly quickly and in significant numbers. In our own case, though only separated by a short distance across the Channel, many of the more sedentary species unable to cross water have been unable to establish here. We are, therefore, limited to those species that were already here before the landbridge disappeared and the odd few that have resulted from either accidental or, sometimes, deliberate introduction since.

The net effect of this is that, for the Orchid Photographer, a short trip across the Channel can seem like coming out of the desert into an oasis where all manner of good things abound. Often species which in the UK can be counted by individual plants such as Man, Monkey, Military, Lady, Ladies Slipper, Red Helleborine and others can be found just across the water in huge numbers and throughout vast ranges of distribution. There are, of course, for the reasons outlined above, a much greater number of species and subspecies and, if there is a downside to this, it is that it is far more difficult to locate and photograph a "full set". This is particularly so in view of the current spate of reclassification that is taking place at present.

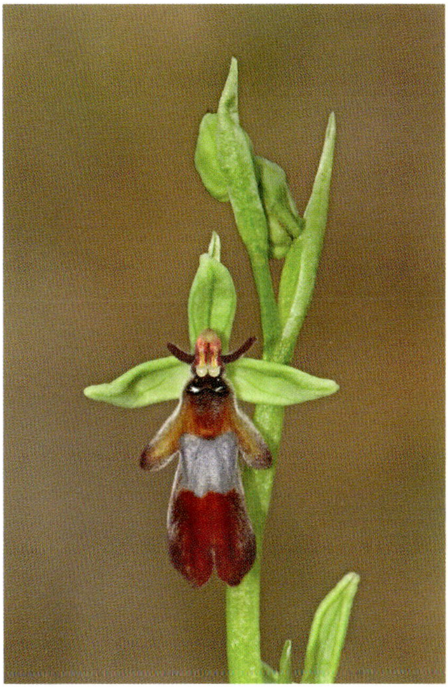

Fly Orchid – a full-frontal shot made possible by the "flat" nature of the image.

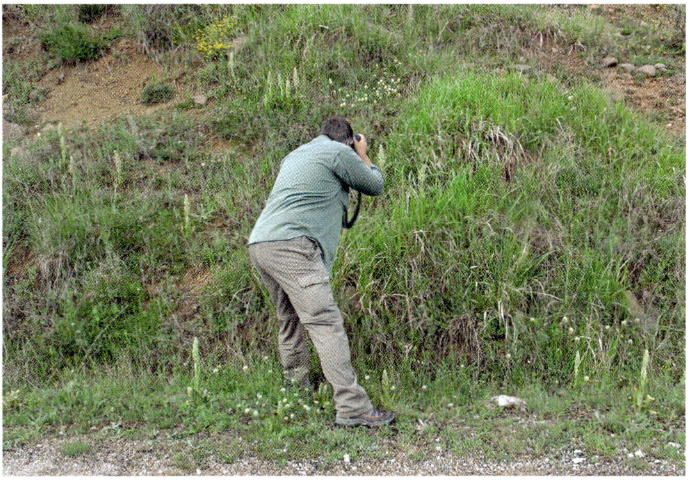

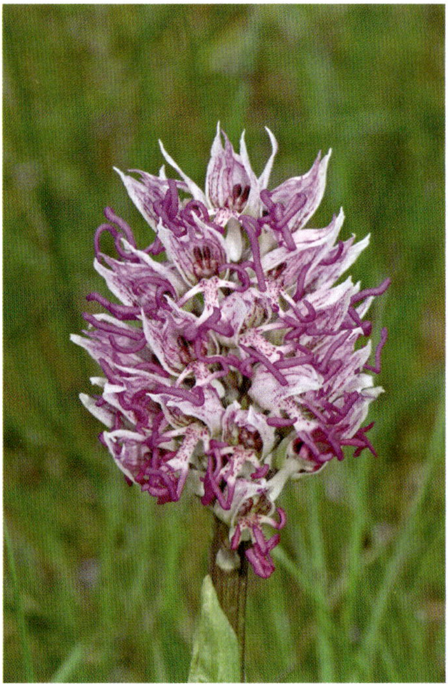

Monkey Orchid - Orchis simia

I also wonder if, perhaps, it is as much fun as the search can often be over here. There is much truth in the old saying that "the thrill of the hunt is in the chase". Certainly for me, and no doubt others who, like me, are dedicated to the subject to an often all consuming degree, the excitement is definitely still there in Europe – but we have served our apprenticeships over here and moved on. I suspect that for many newcomers Europe could be too much too soon. My advice would be to cover the UK fully before looking abroad so that by the time that you do, eventually, get there you know what you are doing, what you are looking for and what you expect to get from it.

But - - Hey Ho! Hey Ho! – all life is a compromise so I suppose there is no reason why Wildlife Photography should be any different. Bracket like crazy, cover all your options and above all -- Enjoy!

Any help I can offer that you may require is freely available via the "contact us" button on my website. I ask only that you be somewhat patient in the Spring/Summer months as I am often out of civilised and email contact for varying periods at this time so my reply may not come by "return post"!

Have Fun!

Chapter 18

Photographing Waterfowl

Sometimes seemingly simple, often more than somewhat difficult, and frequently all but impossible!

One of the major problems with photographing waterfowl has been brought about as a result of their physiques. They are almost invariably of chunky build, well muscled, with dark and succulent flesh and taste wonderful cooked in any number of different ways. The result of this is, of course, that they have been hunted by man for millennia and have inherited all the nervous dispositions that this kind of lifestyle engenders.

Behaviour patterns exhibited by waterfowl given to gathering gregariously and often frequenting public parks, ponds, lakes and suchlike can, and do, undergo a complete transformation when the same individuals are paired off or feeding in a more natural and rural habitat, for it is there that if they are going to be predated upon it is more likely to occur. The same pair of Mallards that come waddling up to you for a piece of bread in the park will allow you no closer than the first carelessly broken twig if you attempt to approach them on a pond in the countryside.

What does this mean for the potential Waterfowl Photographer? It means, chum, that you've got a job of work on your hands particularly if you are "purist" enough to insist on only taking photographs "in the wild" – wherever that may be in this day and age.

How you set about your waterfowl photography really is dependent on what you want from it. There are only 150'ish species in the world. The exact count depends on where you fall among the "lumpers" and the "splitters" (more of this under Photographing Narcissi). The species are then divided into various categories and sub-categories such as Ducks into Diving Ducks, Dabbling Ducks, Sea Ducks and Aberrant Ducks; Swans; Geese; Shelducks and Sheldgeese; and Aberrant Species. This categorical list can vary from publication to publication and from time to time as species are reclassified.

Only a percentage of the species can be described as British Resident whilst others are regular migrants, some are occasional migrants and others are vagrants that have normally been blown off course during migration when strong winds have managed "to get up their tail pipes".

If your objective is to capture shots only of British species in wild habitats then your modus operandi is fairly straightforward. After you have exhausted parks and public places where some species are regularly present and approachable then you will need to work essentially from hides, often with significantly long lenses to guarantee you any degree of success. I would warn you now that you need to be of a particular temperament to be able to undertake and withstand this as a sole course of action. Many public "hides"provided by various management and conservation bodies, whilst no doubt normally sited in ideal locations, are often like Piccadilly Circus where through traffic is concerned.

There is nothing more frustrating than to find yourself bursting at all extremities, having been installed since dawn, and frightened to leave your gear unguarded whilst you make an ablution break, least it go walkabout during your absence and/or, if you take it with you, you risk losing your hardwon place at the prime viewing window. Often, just as the main object of your desires paddles into view a coach party, or even just some careless soul who allows the door to open and close with a bang, comes stomping in and distracts you or terrifies your subject and all the previous nerve-taut hours of patient vigil are destroyed in a moment. The alternative, of course, is to look for smaller and more private hides, set up your own, hide in the reeds or float flat out in a punt. Unfortunately you cannot, realistically, expect to notch up significant numbers of species using these methods and the time demanded in pursuit of them can be significant. Neither can you realistically expect to achieve a succession of shots of rare and exotic creatures, set against aesthetically pleasing backgrounds, since many of your Waterfowl shots will comprise no more than your subject, surrounded by water, as it floats or paddles serenely by. Unfortunately water is water is water and the surface of your neighbours garden pond will not look significantly different to the surface of the most photogenic of lakes, set in stunning surroundings and which it has cost you an arm and a leg to get to, when viewing only the microcosm, captured by your lens, on which your subject is floating.

One alternative is simply to take Waterfowl on an opportunistic basis as you go about your normal Wildlife Photographing activities. This I did for many years, making the most of opportunities as and when they arose. Undoubtedly this approach can result in some nice images as, normally, you only feel moved to take a shot when all the right conditions and surroundings come together. The downside of this tactic is that you need to be a far younger person than am I, at the outset, if you wish to acquire a respectable portfolio of species in the duration of your active lifespan, since your haphazard opportunities may be few and far between.

Fortunately there is a viable option that can result in an impressive hitlist of species in surroundings that, with care in taking your shots, can often provide natural looking backgrounds. This option owes its existence to other aspects of the Waterfowls' psyche and appearance. As an overall group they can become quite trusting and confiding in captivity and this aspect of their character, coupled with their often stunning plumage variations, has made them popular for many years as "collectors items". As far back as the Romans, and no doubt even further, Waterfowl have been kept in captivity and, in addition, certain breeds, almost invariably derived from the Mallard, have been domesticated and/or selectively bred for specific characteristics and purposes. Some species, such as the Eider, supplied down for duvets and pillows and the like, some like Muscovies have been used for their egg laying capacity, whilst several others have been redesigned in various ways for either egg laying, eating or both. Additionally, for centuries, there have been collections of so called "ornamental" Waterfowl maintained simply for their sheer beauty and it is to the modern day equivalent of these that you may be advised to direct your attention if you are after quicker results.

In the UK, apart from those larger private collections that open to the public to help defray maintenance costs, we have the added benefit of the WWT and the RSPB who, between them, own and/or control a significant number of reserves situated across the length and breadth of the country. Many of these, particularly those of the WWT, boast a resident population of both native and exotic species as well as playing host to huge numbers of migrating and over wintering birds.

I thoroughly recommend these as venues capable of bringing a wide range of species within reach of your lens. Huge numbers of overwintering Swans, Ducks and Geese can be found here grazing on the marshy ground where these reserves are normally situated. If your equipment is not up to the task of tackling the sometimes distant grazers then, certainly in the case of the WWT, most of them will be represented "in captivity" in the "home" part of the reserve together with other rare and exotic species from across the world.

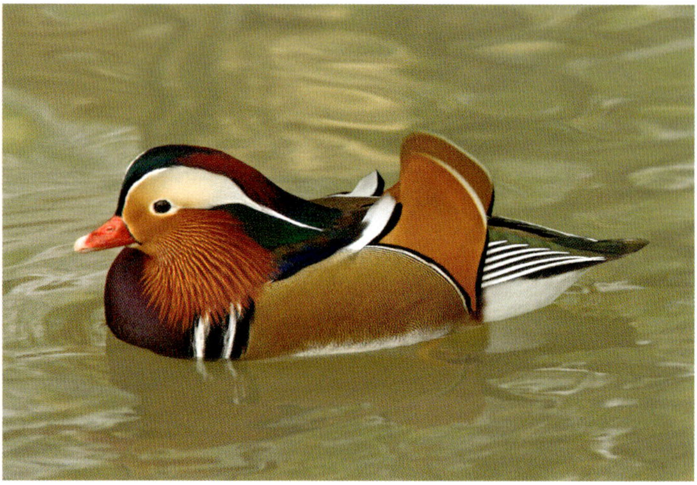

Mandarin Duck - a Chinese Ornamental

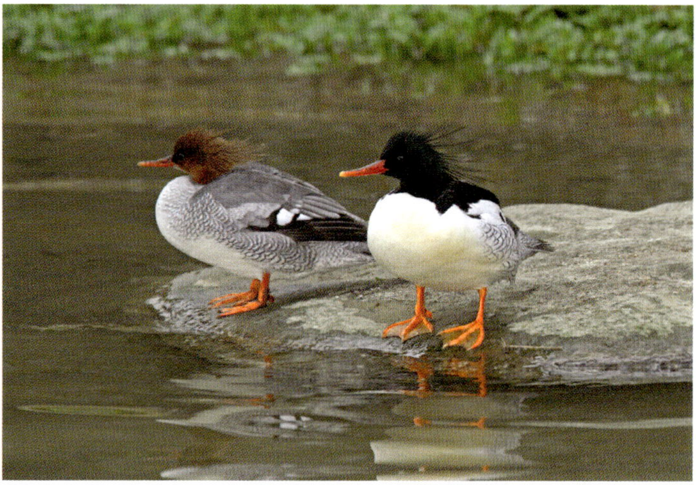

Pair of Chinese Mergansers at Arundel WWT

Do not turn your nose up at photographing those species to which photographic access involves merely leaning over a fence or setting up your tripod on a tarmac path. In reality, where some species are concerned, this is the only way you can practically expect to photograph them without embarking on long and expensive trips abroad, often with no guarantee of success and, furthermore, even with your subjects well within range, it is not as easy as you might think!

I will first deal with some of the problems associated with photographing Waterfowl per se and then move on to those peculiar to a captive environment.

First and foremost of the problems is posed by the basic patterning of many species' plumage. The majority of them do tend to be highly colourful, even gaudy, especially during the breeding season, and many of the colours displayed are often a direct contrast to one another. If you have chosen a sunny day for your sojourn then just try balancing your aperture settings for both the black and the white of a male Goosander or Eider and see how you get on! Apart from the dangers of highlights created by the contrasting colours you have to remember that strong sun equals harsh shadows. Much of the time your subjects are going to be sat on, or swimming in, a large expanse of water which, in itself, is a well known exposure hazard in much the same way as snow. You are likely to be somewhat limited in your choice of shooting position and, frequently, will not be able to get the light on your side, in which case you will have to expose for what is, in effect, a backlit subject. If you manage to expose the subject correctly for its own colour patterning then just sit back and be amazed at the kaleidoscope of colours and patterns provided by some of the water reflections in your shots.

Most water that carries Waterfowl has some degree of colour to it either on its own account or attributable to the Waterfowl themselves. No two ponds, even though adjacent, seem to be the same and can vary from clear to green to brown and all shades in between. In addition they will often have an inordinate number of foreign bodies floating on the surface. Bits of foodstuffs, water vegetation, dust, down, feathers, other unmentionables and lumps of that unsightly mess that seems to continually break away from the bottom of natural ponds and float to the surface. All will conspire to spoil your shot. In reality, at point of shoot, you have to ignore all these, for their number is legion, and rely on your enhancement programme's healing tools to clean up for you.

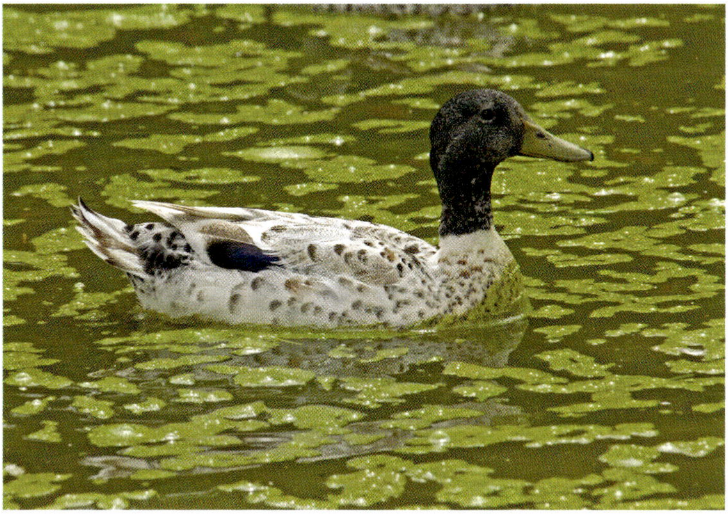

An attractive Mallard variety swimming in scummy algae.

In captivity there is another hazard to contend with and that is the "pinioned wing". To prevent often expensive species from flying away into the sunset captive birds are routinely pinioned. This involves either clipping the primary flight feathers of one wing to put the bird chronically off balance so that, if it does take off, it flies in ever decreasing circles until it disappears to somewhere other than the sunset, or else surgically removing that part of one wing that will carry all, or part, of the primaries. The former is, at best, a temporary measure and will need to be repeated more than once a year causing considerable stress to all concerned. The latter can seem somewhat callous at first glance but I feel that in the long run it provides the best option since, in practice, the Waterfowl quickly learns to gear its life to the loss of some of its flying abilities. In a captive environment it is shielded from the problems of having to find its own food and having to escape from a constant supply of predators. Unless it is a migratory species the above two activities would probably have accounted for the bulk of its flying time and the birds normally seem to settle into a contented lifestyle, since they breed, and otherwise behave, in a natural fashion. Whichever course of action has been applied to our subject in question the net effect is to leave it without all, or some, primaries on at least one wing. This may not offend your eye, of course, in which case it is immaterial, but if it does then the only practical answer is to wait until the subject turns its "good side" to you. After all, unlike in a "wild" setting, you can afford to wait since, in the circumstances, it is hardly likely to fly away!

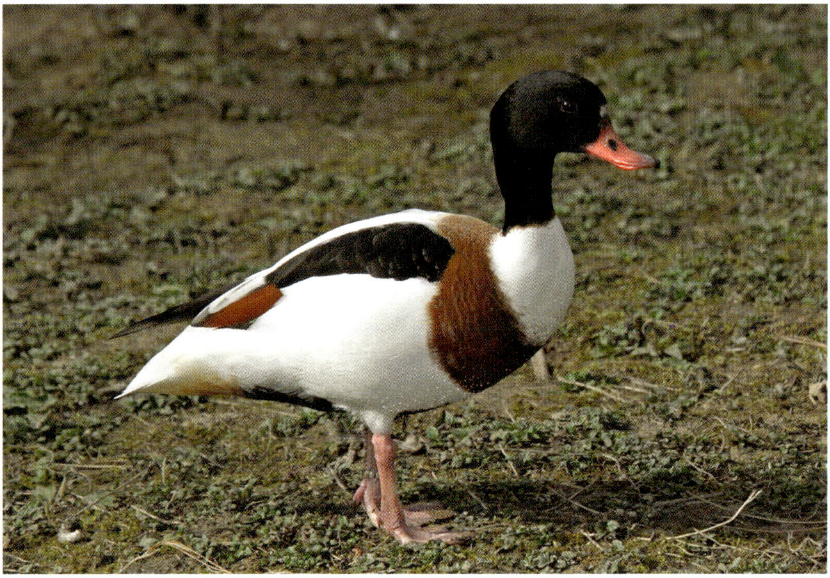

Female Common Shelduck showing effect of pinioned right wing.

Another hazard of bright light is reflections from ripples in the water which manifest themselves in highlit lines along the sides of your subject. I'm afraid that you are stuck with these but, with diligence, should they prove offensive to your eye you can probably minimise their effect, if not eradicate them altogether, with your enhancement software. They are exacerbated by using a flash, even on only a fill-flash setting. You will have to weigh up the pros and cons of using flash and, bearing in mind that the problem is worse the brighter the weather, it may well be that you do not need the added boost of flash in those conditions.

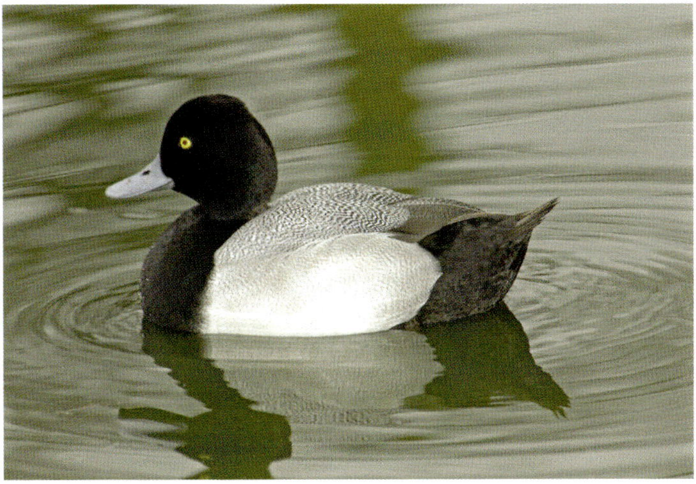

Greater Scaup male showing water ripple reflections.

All Waterfowl, whether divers or dabblers, that derive any part of their diet from underwater will, almost inevitably, be covered with water droplets. In certain light conditions, particularly if using flash, these droplets will show up in your image like searchlight beams. Again there is not too much that you can do to circumvent this but draw comfort from the fact that they are normally perfectly round and, as such, lend themselves ideally to the touch of your healing brush tool. I would advise you here that, if you are determined to erase them completely, do not zoom your screen image up to work on any larger than the size you intend to view or print. If you close in too much you will end up having to take out hundreds, if not thousands, of mini droplets that wouldn't have shown up anyway at normal image display sizes.

Remember also to set a decent shutter speed. Waterfowl are almost constantly on the move either swimming or looking around. Their motion tends to be very jerky and so the fastest shutter speed that conditions allow is the order of the day. Having said that I have just realised that with today's technology the fastest shutter speeds can be enormous and not worth the compromises that you have to make to get them. I would, therefore, probably change my advice to read that a shutter speed of at least three times your lens length should suffice.

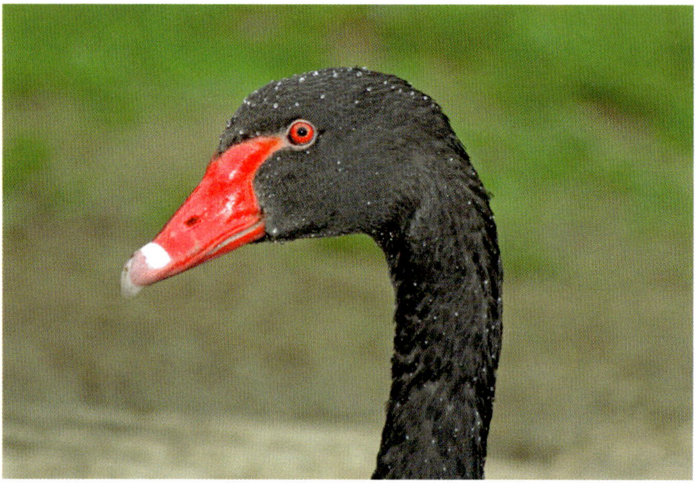

Black Swan showing effects of sun or flash on water droplets

Having read what I have written thus far I realise that I probably sound like a prophet of doom. There is, however, light at the end of the tunnel which I will come to shortly but, before I do, there is one more scenario to bear in mind.

Many of the problems outlined above pertain to fine sunny weather and they can be reduced by operating under less clement conditions. However, in winter and on duller spring/summer days, there is a further problem that manifests itself – that of "noisy" backgrounds. Unless you are prepared to accept a highlight burnout you must expose, or underexpose, your shot accordingly. Unfortunately on dull days, and in the case of most Waterfowl, your potential highlight danger is posed by a very small percentage of your overall image. Just a white wingbar, forehead or chest patch may be the only white in a sea of dark colours. To avoid the burnout you will have to underexpose the shot to such an extent that when you attempt to brighten the overall image in your enhancement programme you are likely to generate very noisy water and/or other background features.Unless, as I have said above, you are prepared to accept burnouts there is not much you can do about this at point of shoot and you will have to rely on your enhancement programme to put things right. One thing that you can do to alleviate the problem is to make sure that the subject is as large as possible in the frame. That will mean that the water and background will have less effect in your finished product and is one less contrasting feature to worry about. Don't rely on cropping during enhancement to achieve your ideal sized subject – try to get that size outlined through your lens.

Having listed many of the potential pitfalls involved I feel obliged to offer some, or partial, answers to them. I am always loathe to offer specific and definitive enhancement tips, if only for the fact that I cannot cope with the deluge of email traffic pointing out the supposed error of my ways every time that I attempt it. There is no single quick fix but there are many, many partial remedies that can be undertaken to suit both your own capabilities and those of your various software programmes.

So ---- whilst I would not wish to be seen as trying to teach my dear old grandmother to suck eggs, nor would I attempt to advise those many readers who are undoubtedly far more proficient than I at handling the vagaries of Photoshop and the like. I will, nevertheless, take the liberty of outlining what I do in various circumstances. For those of you to whom it is a help I would say that I am grateful for your existence, and for the many of you who feel that you can do it better, differently, quicker or more correctly I beg your indulgence and ask you not to read further. (Of course a secret inner part of me, which I would never dream of disclosing, wonders whether many of the more proficient enhancers have become so since the quality of their recorded images is such that they demand an infinite degree of enhancement expertise to make them acceptable? Or is it simply the arrogance of an innate conviction that you can improve upon nature, or whatever your chosen subject is, and a refusal to accept that the billions of pounds spent in development costs has still not resulted in cameras that are capable of accurately recording what is "shoved in front of them"?)

I have known people who will spend days and days, or even weeks, working on an image. (If the Bible is to be believed even God only took 6 days to get it right!)

I can accept that many digital "creations" can take an inordinate amount of time but in this chapter we are dealing only with producing presentable images of Waterfowl and so I would hope to put across what my own experience has taught me and how I obtain and process my images without seeking to inflict my ways upon you by suggesting that this is the one and only way to go about it.

Basically my gear for Waterfowl consists of a digital SLR and an 80/400 zoom lens with a flash unit that offers a "fill flash" option. This length of lens allows me to take the odd "wild" shot, distant "captive" shots and certainly helps me achieve frame filling images of closer subjects. If you do not have this length of lens then shorter zooms are OK – you just have to learn their capabilities and limitations and work within them. Even "point and shoot" and, sometimes, phone cameras can capture perfectly acceptable images, especially if taking them at somewhere like the WWT at Slimbridge, Arundel or Martin Mere where subject distance is not always a problem. However, to obtain prolific and consistently high quality images my personal recommendation is an SLR and appropriate lenses. Whilst accepting that not everyone can afford, or even cope with such gear, I would not wish to seem to belittle the results of the enormous variety of picture taking gadgets on the market. Photography is a very personal thing and if you are happy with the images that you are producing then there need be no further argument. It is only when you, yourself, cease to be content and decide to improve either your technique or your equipment that the problems begin.

Armed with what, compared to some, may seem to be my fairly cumbersome gear which, by its very nature, also needs a tripod for support, I try to set out on a day that is preferably not too sunny. Many of us cannot choose our days with such abandon and so will have to make the most of our allotted time despite the prevailing conditions. I set my camera to give me a flashing highlight/lowlight display and work entirely to that. I start off with camera settings that are a mixture of what I think that they should be and what the camera thinks, set on full matrix metering. I then work entirely from the display and adjust the settings until there is not even the slightest highlight flicker shown unless, on occasion, it is in the sky and which you will sometimes have to live with. Lowlight is nothing like the same problem and can almost be disregarded. If you work this way at least all parts of your image will contain some detail. As explained above I take care of potential movement of both myself and my subject with a tripod and a high shutter speed.

Water ripple reflections I leave till later. There is not much that you can really do about it at point of shoot and you're often left with the choice of either taking the shot under adverse conditions or going home without one. Careful work with whatever "healing tool" your system offers can usually reduce this to an acceptable level and, indeed, some of it doesn't look out of place anyway.

Water surface kaleidoscopes can be minimised to a degree with various of your enhancement tools and if you keep your subject image as large as possible in the frame you will be able to live with all but the most futuristic of the effects.

Noise anyway, but engendered by lowlight in particular, is a pain. All I do if I feel that it affects the image display, or would show up in a print, is as follows:-

I section off the subject in its entirety and there are, of course, normally several ways in which you can do this depending on the limitations of your software. Having sectioned it I then apply the "inverse" command which puts my "line of ants" around the outside of the frame and limits any work done to the area between the selected image and the overall image boundaries. To this area I then apply up to the full "noise reduction" facility that my software permits. I then deselect and keep my finger well away from the "image sharpen" controls. Whilst this process does tend to soften the background this is normally incidental in most Waterfowl shots and the subject image itself is sharpened by default as all around it softens.

The normal lighting and colouring effects can then be applied before, during or after the above as you see fit.

Whilst all the above will not necessarily lead to National Geographic front pages, or maybe not even win at your local club competitions, it will, nevertheless, provide you with a portfolio of Waterfowl pictures most of which, apart from one or two of the more pedantic viewers, will satisfy many of the people much of the time.

Good shooting!!

Chapter 19

Photographing Birds

The various requirements that have to be met in order to photograph birds successfully on a regular basis break too many of our "budgets" for me to devote a fullblown chapter to them under that banner.

All is not lost, however, as there are several opportunities that can be exploited if your leaning is towards that subject. Birds tend to be a specialist area mainly because to consistently succeed with them as a sole interest demands undivided dedication, much planning, many frequently wasted hours and some fairly expensive equipment.

I could be leaving myself open to criticisms here because, although I have firsthand experience of photographing all the other subjects covered in this book and have, in fact, done so in such depth that I feel that I can hold my own with anyone, I have to admit that my bird photography has only ever been conducted on a happenstance basis, as and when opportunity has arisen. By this I refer to general birds and not such as Waterfowl and Penguins which I have treated separately as subjects in their own right and not under a group heading. I have, however, had enough of the happenstance occasions arise over the years to be reasonably conversant with the requisites and the potential pitfalls and so feel qualified to include this chapter, though not in as great a depth as some of the others.

You will see a great many extremely beautiful bird pictures in a wide variety of places on virtually a daily basis, and to their photographers I give all credit. They feature in newspapers, books, magazines and periodicals, greetings cards, food packaging, advertising of a wide range of products and a whole host of other locations.

Part of their success as photographic subjects is due to their generally endearing characteristics, frequently very striking colours and the fact that practically everyone, from whatever walk of life, comes into direct contact, or proximity, with at least some of them on a daily basis. As a sector of Wildlife they attract a huge number of followers and adherents, and organisations such as the RSPB and some of the Wildlife Groups have sprung up to continuously campaign on their behalf, do what they can towards their conservation and generally promote their case to ensure their wellbeing in any way possible. Feeding the local Swans, and birds in the garden, brings children into contact with birds from an early age and on a benign basis.

It is generally only some farmers and other livestock producers, whose incomes can be badly affected by bird predation of their crops and livestock, who have a bad word for them, and then those bad words are usually limited to those species that directly affect them, and are not applied to the birdworld in general. OK, in addition, some inner cities, parks and seaside towns sometimes suffer a localised problem from noise and faeces of birds such as starlings, geese and seagulls, but this is a very limited problem, particularly in the UK, and is really only relevant to those directly on the receiving end and so does not colour the outlook of the general public.

By and large then they are held relatively dear in most peoples' hearts and this, in large part, contributes to the size of their following.

All this apart, however, we are dealing here with the actualities of photographing them and not the motivations for doing so. Suffice to say that for the reasons outlined above, and many more besides, they are able to command a devoted and, sometimes, fanatical following and this is reflected in the number of photographers who choose them as their principal, and often only, subject.

This chapter, therefore, is not aimed at the truly dedicated, who see Bird Photography as a lifelong vocation with no expense spared, but rather at those who wish to include it in an overall wildlife portfolio to whatever extent is possible bearing always in mind the "budgets" which this book is all about.

If you do choose to go this route with any serious intent then you have to accept that you will almost certainly need a lens longer that the short zooms that we have discussed earlier. These, and many of the compacts now in use, will still give you the odd flukey Garden Bird shot particularly if you have access to a tame Robin or Blackbird or the like. By and large, however, you will not, generally speaking, be able to get close enough on a regular basis to provide you with the kind of shot that I would imagine that you would want. Maybe initially, in the excitement of a new venture, you may be prepared to settle for a small image in the centre of the frame, especially if you crop it up, but I suspect that, in reality, this will soon begin to pall and your aspirations will become more demanding.

Many of the bird pictures that you will see will be seemingly taken from close quarters. Whilst this may well be the case, and if it is then a hide of some sort will no doubt figure in the equation, more often than not they will have been taken at some distance using long, and frequently very expensive, lenses. When your photography has been limited by using only short zooms up to 100mm then you often form the impression, leading to an almost firm conviction, that a jump to a 200mm would be the answer to all your prayers and completely transform your photographic output. Do not be misled by this supposition and the frequently optimistic sales propaganda of the lens suppliers. For birds I am afraid that 200mm is still not very big. My main lens in the bush, where you never know what is going to pop its head up next, is an 80/400 zoom. At full size on my digital camera this equates to a 600 mm lens on an old fashioned film camera. (For those who want it, full explanations of this phenomenon are best researched in specific photographic publications and will probably be found under either "sensors" or "lens sizes".) Even at this size you have to be very close to a sparrow sized bird to get a decent sized image of it. For the purposes of most of us, and bearing our various budgets in mind, I would make the following suggestions. There are a great number of medium range zooms on the market of, say, 70/80 to 200/300mm. at fairly reasonable prices. You can also buy, again at not unreasonable prices if you do not insist on camera manufacturers' own, converters of, say, 1.5 or 2X capacity. A 2X converter has the obvious effect of doubling your lens size and will upgrade your 2 or 300mm to a 4 or 600mm which is probably more than enough for what you will initially need. The potential downside of this equipment is that it will limit your maximum aperture and probably demand better light than you may be experiencing under certain conditions. However, it is probably the best "budget" option and compromise to allow you to serve an "apprenticeship" in bird photography. My contention has always been that if you need the full size of your lens to get a reasonably acceptable shot then you are too far away. Certainly, initially, you would be better advised to devote your efforts to improving your techniques and fieldcraft to enable you to get closer, than to devote your hopes and life savings to monster lenses. Many of the large prime lenses are a logistical nightmare to carry, particularly if travelling abroad, and their sheer physical size will often demand that they be consigned to the "hold baggage" with all its inherent risks.

Moving from one type of photography to another, such as from closeup to mid distance, often demands a settling in and familiarisation period. Once you have become proficient with the type of equipment that I am suggesting then you can make your own mind up as to what size and value of gear that you wish to aspire to and you will then pass out of the range of this book – but thank you for being with us thus far! As a final word on this subject, and going back to my earlier listings of "budgets" in Chapter 1, the one on which I placed great emphasis was that of "purpose". Because, for Bird photography, you can be involving yourself with some really serious expenditure, it is all the more important to determine your "purpose", and the strength of it, before joining the financial spiral. Most people will not truly know the answer to their "purpose" question until they have tried it for a while – and I don't mean just for the weekend. You really do need to "have a go" for a full 12 month period to experience all weathers and to maximise the number of species that you can expect to see since many are seasonal visitors only and not present all year round. The equipment that I have mentioned will be good enough to get you through this trial period and I really would recommend trying it before you commit to "big end" long distance lenses and the appropriate camera bodies to go with them.

If you are expecting to obtain meaningful pictures of birds whilst taking a pleasant stroll in the woods or out in the countryside then, from a practical point of view, you may as well forget it as your chances of success are more than a little remote. The likelihood of getting close enough to other than the odd pheasant, pigeon or partridge is limited. The one chance that you do have on this kind of outing is if you opt for the fairly recent innovation of "digiscoping". In effect this involves fixing a camera to a telescope by means of an adaptor. You do not need to buy them as a matched pair as many cameras can be made to fit many telescopes by a variety of different adaptors. This gives you the opportunity to shop around for "best buys" but do make sure, especially if you are buying the components of your intended setup in different places, that they will, in fact, be compatible when they do, finally, come together.

With this equipment you can, obviously, photograph whatever you can see though the scope. I hesitate to pass comment on the drawbacks, pitfalls and image quality of this method of photography since it is fairly early on in its evolutionary development and comments that would apply today are likely to be outdated by tomorrow. Of course I am hoping that this book will be around for some time and I do not want future readers to think that I've spouted a load of twaddle because, by the time that they read the book, the technology may have moved on.

At risk of being shot down in flames I would say that, at present, based on those images that I have seen, their quality does not compare to images gathered by more conventional means. That this will change I have no doubt, and probably quite quickly, especially if it gains any volume of followers. This it could well do since it will no doubt appeal as a means of getting record shots, for which purpose the quality is already quite acceptable, for that vast army of bird watchers to whom the photography would be just a means to an end and not an occupation in its own right.

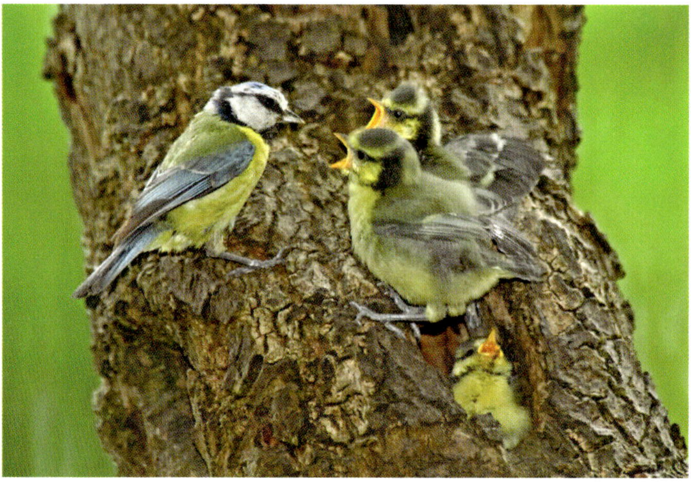

Blue Tits nesting at Arne

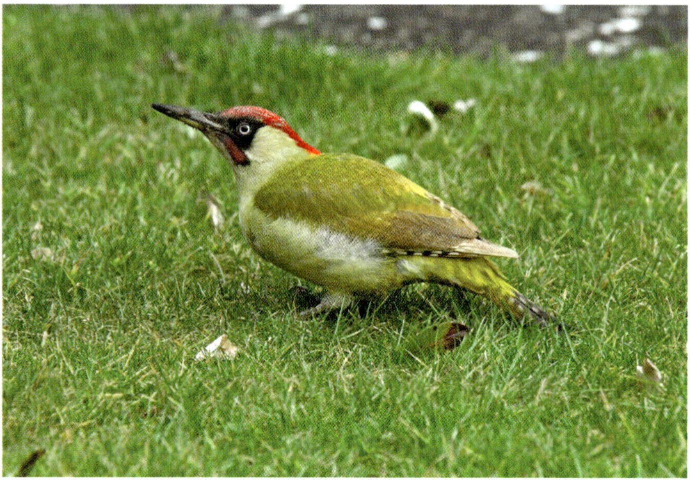

Green Woodpecker after ants.

Moving on, if you are fortunate enough to own, or have access to, a garden in almost any location, be it urban or rural, then there are a great many birds that you can attract to within reach of your lens. The secret is to consistently offer them as wide a range of foodstuffs as you can all the year round. I know that there is a lot of controversy from time to time over the rights and wrongs of bird feeding and the times of the year when it should or shouldn't be done. My own personal opinion is that I cannot see the harm in it. I can certainly accept that if all you offer is dried bread, and no-one in the neighbourhood is offering any better, then in the breeding season some youngsters could end up being brought up just on this which is not, in itself, nutritious enough to sustain them through their development and the coming trials of life as a garden bird. However, over the millennia, bird populations have always adjusted themselves in line with available food supplies of both a permanent and temporary nature and garden bird tables are just one more source for them amongst many.

The best bet is to offer as wide a choice as possible so that your visitors can effect a balanced diet. Of course, like children, they will have favourite foods, probably selected for taste and not for goodness, but if you keep an eye on things you should be able to work out quite quickly whether the reason that a certain food disappears quickly is the result of a few birds over doing it and eating a lot or whether it is the result of a lot of birds managing to get just a little. If it is the former then don't rush to replace it and if it is the latter then increase the amount until you strike a balance bearing always in mind that the choice of various foodstuffs will vary throughout the year. Table scraps, assorted seeds and cereals processed or otherwise, fatballs, nuts, suet and so on can all be offered. A quick visit to your local Petshop or the Pet section in your supermarket will probably provide all the items that you want, and some that you didn't even know existed.

In conjunction with your feeding programme you need to establish somewhere from which to take your shots without scaring off your subjects. You may be able to locate your feeders within reach of a window or a garden shed where you can hover behind a curtain. On the other hand you may have to resort to erecting a tailor made hide of some description. It need not be elaborate. Just enough for you to get inside with sufficient slits or slots to enable you to photograph in more than one direction. The advantage of using your own garden is that you can leave your hide up all the time allowing the birds to accept it as a normal feature of the landscape. Take care in its positioning, or when choosing your vantage point in an established structure, to ensure that the light will be in your favour as much as possible. Some of the most active periods around the feeding station will be in the early morning and the evening when the sun will be low in the sky and the shadows long and sometimes quite hard. You will find that many bird shots where the subject is half in shadow and half in light can be very disappointing and may be beyond the capability of you, or your enhancement programme, to put right afterwards.

One of the disadvantages of a mixed feeding station, of course, is that you will attract birds that you don't want as well as those that you do. I would advise against shooing off the unwelcome guests or your feeding station will gain a reputation amongst the local bird population for having an eccentric waiter who charges wildly in just when you're settling down to dinner. My own mother has taken against a pair of Wood Pigeons and a Grey Squirrel who repeatedly turn up to check out the menu. She avows that, between them, they "scoff the lot" and she is always rushing out to scare them off. The pigeons, in particular, are of a nervous disposition, probably because they're good to eat and we live in a semi-rural location, and so it doesn't take much more than the opening of the patio door to make them beat a hasty retreat. The other birds, of course, take advantage of their nervous nature and use their presence as an indicator that all must be well and it's safe to visit the restaurant. When the Pigeons depart in a panic the others accompany them and it is often some time before they trickle back. It is also a fact that they will, thereafter, be constantly wary in an environment subject to repeated threat as opposed to one where they can come to depend on peace and tranquillity.

My advice would be to keep your feeders and waterbowls down fairly low and then arrange a mixture of photogenic branches above, behind and to the side making sure always that there is a sympathetic background behind them. Most birds coming in to land will do so facing the banquet so try not to place any perches between you and the feeders otherwise the birds landing on those will tend to be facing away from you – unless, of course, you want shots of birds from the rear! You can also drill holes partway through some of these landing perches and stuff them with nuts, acorns or suet to attract species such as Jays and Woodpeckers. Take care to drill the holes in such a way that neither they, nor their contents will show in your shots and that will save you having to clone them out later in order to achieve natural looking settings. Seagulls and Pigeons can be excluded from your feeders, if you wish, by erecting netting barriers of such a mesh size that smaller birds can pass through easily, leaving their larger cousins wondering just what it is they have done to deserve such treatment. It is so easy to develop preferences and pet hates but do try to be dispassionate in your overview and remember that they all have to eat and rear families – even those you would love to "chuck a brick at". Additionally there is always the danger, when using mesh barriers, that the smaller birds inside can, if leaving in a panic for some reason, forget the mesh and injure themselves by trying to fly through it.

If you want to photograph nesting birds or young being fed then be careful. Before setting out on this course check the current state of the law protecting birds, particularly those on the nest, from disturbance. You can look it up quite easily on the internet. I seem to recall that "birds and the law" will bring up the information that you require. Do abide by this law even though it may seem galling at times. You do need to establish a set of personal standards to work to and abiding by existing laws is a pretty good way to start. In any event, if you do contravene the law, you will never be able to show your images anywhere lest someone, somewhere, sometime asks you to explain how and where you got them!

If you are fortunate enough to have a pair of birds actually nest in the garden then, realistically, whatever the law says I guess you are going to want to photograph them. At least in the garden there is a chance that they won't be too disturbed by your presence since you, personally, will have been a pretty regular feature on the landscape. Birds that cannot tolerate you and yours going about your daily business would not nest in your garden anyway. Take care, however, that your activities do not broadcast their whereabouts. The village in which I live in Spain is overlooked by some pretty impressive mountains and on the top of one of them is the remains of a Moorish castle from which the village gets its name. Throughout the surrounding mountains there is a long line of these castles built in a huge circle some 100's of K's long. They were designed and positioned in such a way that each castle could see two of its neighbours – one to the left and one to the right. Apparently their occupants had a kind of semaphore system which they could use to pass messages round the circle, each castle receiving its message from the next on one side and passing it on to the next on the other. In this way news spread pretty quickly – and El Cid never could sneak up on them unannounced! Of course, not knowing where you live I cannot be sure but I'll bet that if you're in an area where birds are given to nesting in gardens, then you will have neighbouring Magpies too. There are 9 regulars in the area where I live when in the UK and they spend most of their time spread out individually around the rooftops and high points, apart from their occasional social get togethers. From these vantage points they don't miss a trick and, just as in the case of my castles in Spain, if one spots something interesting it seems able to pass the message on and before you know where you are they're queuing up to come and have a look. Unlike the Moors in Spain I don't think that they use semaphore but, come to think of it, I do seem to have noticed one or two of them waving their wings in a strange fashion! Seriously, they can be a menace at such times, beautiful and exposure setting nightmares though they are. Fledglings are a very welcome part of a Magpie's diet and you will find it pretty hard to live with if those cute little chicks that you have been photographing for the last few days end up being swallowed whole because you inadvertently betrayed their location. This will be especially so if you happen to be watching at the time and the undoubtedly unique shots that you may have managed to get won't make you feel any better when you watch their anguished parents trying to salvage something from the wreckage.

Sea shores, estuaries and public parks, are all pretty good venues as many of the wild birds there will be used to a regular throughput of people and will probably tolerate you quite well. Zoos, Bird Gardens and Safari Parks are also well worth a visit as, apart from the regular exhibits (covered in the chapter on Zoo Photography), many of the local wild birds will have become people tolerant. The vast majority of the public that visits these places is wildlife minded, otherwise they wouldn't have visited in the first place anyway. As a result the wild birds, especially in restaurant and picnic areas, will have become used to being fed by these sympathetic visitors and so, once again, you can probably approach quite closely. Much of the accommodation that contains the resident animal population will have been built in such a way as to house and confine its occupants, not to keep out feathered intruders many of which can then enjoy almost unfettered access. As a result many of these places boasts a permanent wild bird population of a density exceeding even well fed house gardens since they can benefit from an almost never ending food supply as the exhibits are fed on such a regular basis. Many of these institutions also have one or more open feeding stations and, whilst you may not be able to stage manage things as well as you would at home, a patient wait in the area can sometimes bring rewards.

If the above information and advice doesn't help you fill those odd moments when you would otherwise just be littering up the landscape, or getting in someone else's way, then I would suggest you check out specialist literature, specifically covering bird photography and nothing else, of which there is a great plentitude. I would suggest that you first check on the internet followed by the local library and then, should you wish to buy, try Amazon or one of the leading local bookstores.

Chapter 20

Photographing Mammals

Perhaps not a normal subject to be found under the "close up" banner but there are many species which with patience, commonsense and the fieldcraft that you should be improving on day by day, can be approached very closely, and as you become more proficient you'll get even closer.

You don't need expensive African Safaris to come to terms with mammals since there are plenty to go at in the UK. The safaris, of course, should not be written off, especially if it's mammals that jingle your bells. Safaris do, however, tend to be rather expensive and so I guess that, for most folk, they will come under the heading of "trips of a lifetime" and are probably better covered by the chapter entitled "To Trip or not to Trip".

I will deal with the situation that pertains in the UK and, if you get the chance of mammals abroad, then most of the same principles will apply.

Small Rodents.

If you wish to photograph that group of very small mammals such as rats, mice, shrews, voles and so on, which you would normally expect to be close-up subjects then, personally, I think that the only way to do it satisfactorily is in setup surroundings such as an aquarium. The chances of locating them in the wild in circumstances that make them photographable is, to say the least, remote. Yes, I know, I will now be inundated with claims from people who have photographed Harvest Mice, Dormice etc in the wild and have excellent shots to prove it, but I'll bet that those who have done it did so by accident and I'll further bet that their species hitlist is not very long. Sometimes you may be able to locate and stake out water based mammals since they often tend to live for prolonged periods in a fixed area, especially if they are breeding. Once located then the use of a portable hide or even just a replica of a boyhood den in the bushes can bring good results. Patience and persistence will be the orders of the day.

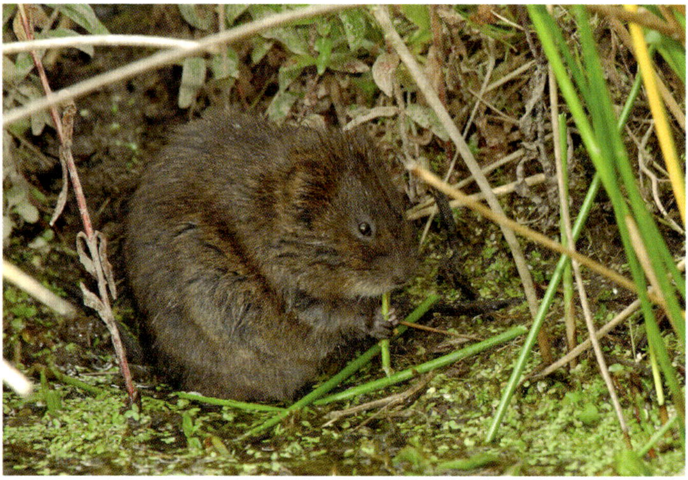

Water Vole having lunch.

Some species can occasionally be found in animal rescue centres, and may even have become used to people. Usually the offer of free photos to the centre will bring a degree of co-operation and you may be able to establish a mutually beneficial relationship.

Failing that you will have to work with trapped animals and this is an area that is very regulation bound. It is not a path I have ever trodden and so I can only advise you to make sure of the legal position before embarking on this course. If you end up taking shots in an aquarium, then I would advise you to check the chapter in this book on "Photographing in Zoos", to see how to photograph through glass without creating reflections.

****

The mammals, currently resident in the UK, that I would put forward as potential subjects are as follows:- Squirrels, Rabbits and Hares, Badgers, Foxes, Hedgehogs, Deer of several species such as Fallow, Sika, Red, Roe and Muntjac (I understand that Chinese Water Deer are now established in the wild, but I guess that you would have to be in the right area to see them as I'm sure that they do not, as yet, enjoy nationwide distribution), and a few Mustelids. Additionally, of course, there is a whole range of domestics that provide very suitable material. I know that we're discussing Wildlife but that doesn't mean that you have to be blinkered to any other subjects that offer themselves up to your lens.

Squirrels.

Taking the above groups in no kind of order we'll start with squirrels.

In the UK we are concerned with two species, the Greys and the Reds. Many people believe that the introduced Greys killed the Reds off, which is not strictly the case. They compete more successfully for food, it is true, but in many areas there is enough food for both especially since they have slightly different preferences. The main killer of the Reds is a viral infection, carried by the Greys and to which they have developed a degree of immunity, but which decimates the Reds in double quick time. I well remember going to Scotland's Isle of Islay some years ago to photograph Red Deer and deciding to stop off at Formby, near Liverpool, on the way, where they boasted the country's most approachable population of Red Squirrels. On arrival at the park gates my enquiry as to where was the best place to see them was greeted by "If you manage to see one, let alone photograph one, I'll give you £50". Apparently they had contracted the pox and been all but wiped out and may well, since, have been completely so. (Addendum:- Since first penning this chapter I believe their numbers have started to recover and, from a handful of fortunate survivors, have managed to reach about 200. This, now, is late 2011.)

Living in the South I am fortunate in that we do have a couple of populations, living in areas where they come into regular enough contact with sufficient numbers of people to be reasonably approachable – well, sort of! Brownsea Island in Poole harbour and a couple of places on the Isle of Wight come to mind. I find the best time of the year to be Autumn when the sweet chestnuts are falling. They're industrious little souls and seem to spend their entire daylight hours finding and burying nuts. The secret is to find a tree where one is working, choose a good spot and sit tight. You probably won't need a hide but it will definitely help if your features are vaguely reminiscent of a lichen covered rock or a gnarled old briar. If not don't worry, just keep reasonably still, be sensibly attired, don't make a racket and you will find that it will keep on working as if you are just another part of the landscape. Most Red Squirrel sites, certainly in the South where they are a rarity, are on reserves or National Trust land where feeders are also provided. Hovering in these areas can also pay dividends, although you run the risk of having a man made feeding table in your shot. A medium range zoom should be enough to get decent sized images.

If you live close to, and can access, a site on a regular basis, then you can try pre-feeding an area. Peanuts are probably the easiest and most acceptable "bait". I would suggest you spend some time reconnoitring the site until you have worked out the areas most frequently used by the squirrels. Try to choose a place where you are not too much in the shade, and certainly avoid anywhere where you are likely to be faced with dappled light if the sun is out. Also make sure that you are not likely to be photographing against the light, as a backlit Red Squirrel can be a nightmare to enhance. Their coats are very shiny and highly reflective, and to get your exposures right you need them completely in either the sun or the shade. Spread nuts on a regular basis over the patch you think they will use and check it regularly. Spread the nuts thinly so that they have to work for them and, when you decide to give your photographic prowess a go, they will be too busy searching for this unexpected manna from heaven to worry about you. Once they have eaten a few you will find that they are completely wrapped up in burying the rest. They stuff an enormous number into their mouths at one go so if you lay your "bait" in piles they will be able to fill up at one stop and this will limit your opportunities when the time comes to photograph them. Make them work for it. They are constantly on the move and so, when deciding on your camera settings, lean towards speed rather than small apertures especially since, with something as exciting as a Red Squirrel, you are not likely to be too worried about getting the background in focus anyway.

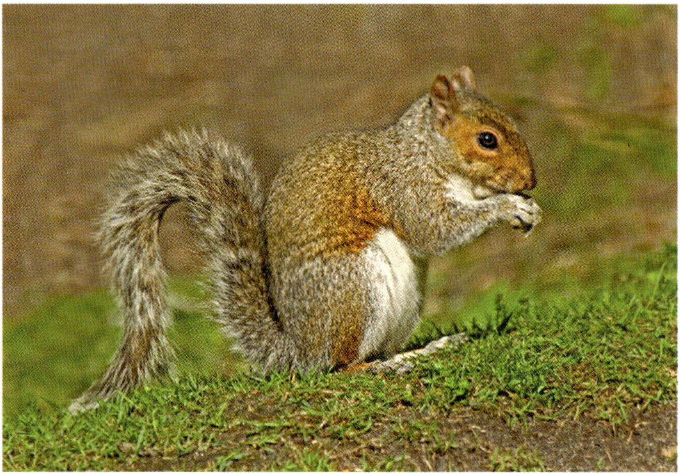

Grey Squirrel - a North American introduction.

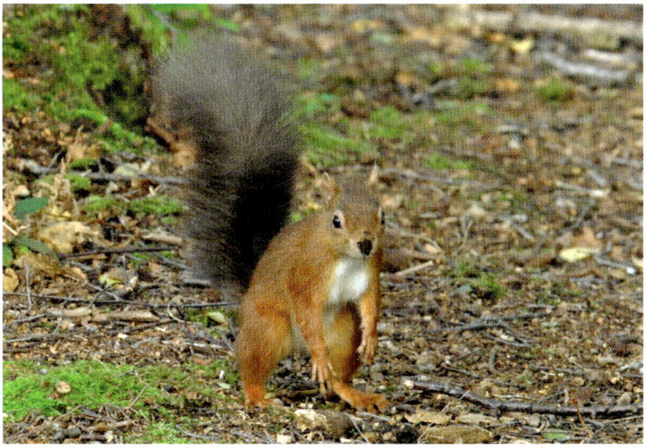

Red Squirrel just after burying a nut

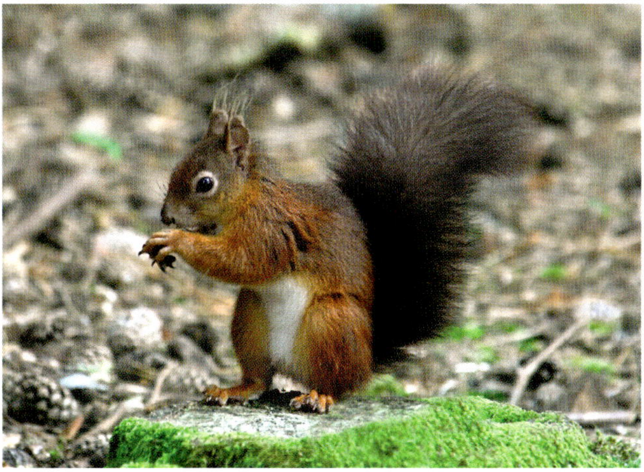

Red Squirrel in classic pose.

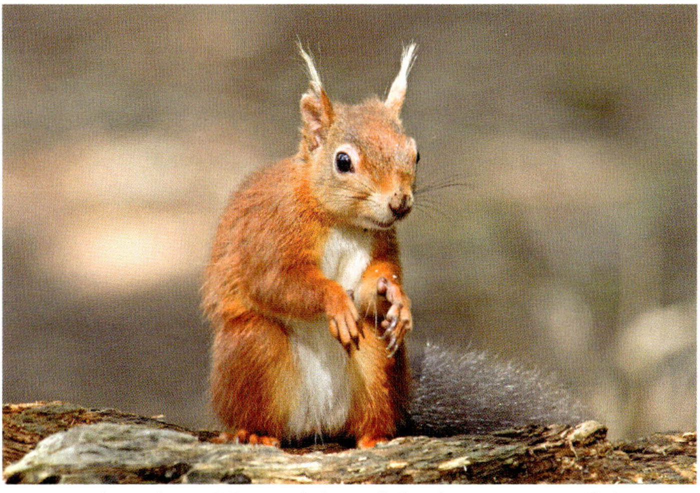

The only Red Squirrel shot of the day in open sunlight.

The Greys are different in that their distribution is much wider, though it is only in urban settings, parks and public open spaces where there is a chance of them being fed, that they can be classed as approachable. Years of persecution have taught them to be wary. Even in my own boyhood (not long ago I know!) I can remember there being a bounty of something like 2 shillings for each Grey Squirrel tail. Such a background does not give rise to tame and compliant subjects. Better to set up for them in the garden - where they will visit your bird feeders whether you like it or not - or in the park. I well remember in the days of my Zoo, which was in a park, that the Greys were the most lovable and approachable creatures ever. They would come up to you all twitchy and wiggly as they do, and take nuts gently from your fingers, until the bag was empty and then the little darlings promptly bit your fingers to the bone instead! They take nestlings and dig up the most carefully planted gardens in winter. However, whatever anti-social traits they may have, they are certainly entertaining and photogenic subjects and well worth spending some time on. Just as a tip, try to get them used to being fed with chestnuts as opposed to peanuts. Apart from making you the favourite Gourmet Restaurant in the park, when all about you are just offering fastfood like peanuts and popcorn, it will also give you a tremendous edge when you finally get that classical Squirrel shot where he sits, holding his nut in both "hands", and chewing it industriously. How much better to have him chewing on a chestnut - which you can leave in - as opposed to a peanut - which you will have to clone out, and then face the problem of what to replace it with - to simulate wild and natural conditions in your photographs? One final word of warning if photographing Greys in your own garden. Don't encourage them, or it (most gardens seem to have territorial singletons), to take food from your hand. Let them visit your bird feeders by all means and get used to seeing you around, but once they come to associate your hand with food they'll never leave you alone. In addition they'll know when you're in your hide and want to come in with you. I can assure you that, even if you're wearing long trousers, being in an enclosed space with a squirrel running round your feet is no joke as you can never be sure where he'll run to next!

Rabbits and Hares.

Photographing these tends to be a far more active pastime. If you are lucky enough to know of, and have access to, an active rabbit warren then your day is made. You can get flukey shots of rabbits in places where they have become somewhat used to people but you have to remember that just about anything that eats meat rates rabbit very highly on the menu. They therefore have the misfortune of having to perceive a huge variety of other life forms as a threat. This, of course, makes them far twitchier than many other prey animals that are predated on by only one or two species. Sometimes you can be lucky. I can remember two rabbits at Arne Nature Reserve in Dorset some years ago that loved peanuts. Their problem was that the nuts were in a squirrel proof tit feeder some 6 or 7 feet above the ground. The result was that they had to hang around and wait for the broken bits to fall from the tits who were feeding continuously. While they were switched into "peanut mode" they were oblivious to all around them and you could have taken their picture with a pinhole camera had you so wished. However, they are the exception and this kind of shot is often a bit sterile being just of a rabbit sat on a patch of grass. Hardly riveting stuff.

No, the Mecca of Rabbit photography is a large and active warren. You can buy, from various places, an assortment of hides and camouflaged netting at fairly reasonable prices. I have something that is called a baghide. This is a shaped and camouflaged contraption rather like a large poncho, with various slits and apertures, which you put over your head and wear and then do your best to look like a cross between a rock and a hard place. It sounds hilarious, and so it will appear to any passersby who happen to see you, but it is often

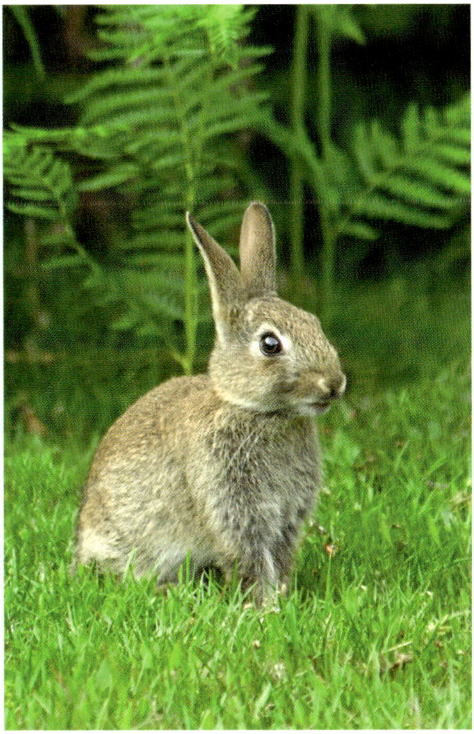

Juvenile Rabbit in relatively photogenic setting.

good enough to fool the rabbits, especially if you have the patience to sit there for some time. The advantage at a warren is the diversity of shots that you can get. There are normally babies of all shapes and sizes popping in and out of holes playing with one another. There are adults feeding, cleaning themselves, cussing one another, making more baby rabbits and so on. One other advantage of this type of operation is that, if you don't have much success with the rabbits, then you can draw satisfaction from the fact that you will have given those passersby, who saw you earlier, something to talk about at dinner for years to come!

Hares are somewhat different. They are not all that gregarious though, admittedly, if you find one then there are normally more nearby. I suspect that this is not necessarily a reflection of their natures but rather that the area happens to suit them. They are notoriously difficult to approach in the open except early in the year during the "boxing season". The frenetic sparring that you can see occurring at this time of year, and which I, in keeping with many others, always assumed was two males squaring up to one another is, I am informed, rather a case of a female gently passing on the message that it's "not tonight with this Josephine" or, in common street parlance, "you must be joking Jimmy!".. If you saw the amount of fur that sometimes flies then you could be forgiven for hoping that it is not your lot to come back as a Hare in a future incarnation. Whilst we're on that subject do try, if you are granted any choice in the matter, not to come back as a male Spider or male Preying Mantis either. The former often gets eaten completely just after claiming his conjugal rights and the latter has his head bitten off just as his breathing starts to become erratic!

In my part of the South of England, Hares are not all that common, though they do seem to have made some sort of a comeback over the last few years. I can well remember those News clips back in the days when they were campaigning to ban Hare coursing with dogs, and the fields that they used for filming seemed to have a Hare every few yards. I have never actually seen this myself and can only assume that the Midlands, or wherever these clips were seemingly filmed, must boast what would amount to huge populations by Southern standards.

As mentioned above, Hares are not easy to approach on foot, as they lie up well out in the open and can see you coming while you're still convinced that they're just a clump of earth. There are only a couple of ways in which I have struck lucky. The first is to find a "Harey" area with hedgerows. If you're careful you can sometimes creep along the hedgerow on the side opposite to your quarry and occasionally get quite good shots of them at work, or at play, without them realising that you are there. If you are fortunate enough to find a field that usually boasts a goodly population then you can stake yourself out in the early hours with your hide on your head, or even a fixed one if that's what you have, and just wait with fingers crossed. The other answer is to make yourself known to a farmer who has Hares on his land and get his permission to drive over his fields, those that are not under cultivation that is, in your vehicle. You will often find that you can drive very close to Hares without alarming them unduly and, of course, once you are in amongst them you can just switch off, sit tight and see what comes your way. For those who can't tell a Hare from a Rabbit I think the most straightforward differentiating factor is size. On average most Hares are up to 50% larger than Rabbits. If you are unfortunate enough to have a large Rabbit and a small Hare running away from you at the same time then the Hare will be the one with black tips to the back of his ears! Hares also have much longer back legs than Rabbits but it's a devil of a job to get them to stand still while you measure them!

Hares produce and keep their young, called leverets, above ground in a rough nest, usually in long grass. If you happen on one of these while walking through a field then you should be able to photograph them as long as you don't get too close. They work on the principle that they are invisible as long as they stay still so don't move in on them. If you do, and you make them bolt, then they'll go every whichaway but loose and there is a good chance that their mother may not be able to recover them all. If it's in an area where your hide won't grow legs and walk if you leave it there, then set it up quite a way off and move it in closer, a little at a time, over the next two or three days. If you are careful, and don't alarm the mother, then you should get some magnificent shots. A word of warning. If you've been in your hide most of the day, and the mother has not returned towards nightfall, then pack up everything and clear out completely because it will probably mean that she's "sussed" you out and is frightened to come back. I know it means that all your work has been for nothing, and that you won't get the shots you were hoping for, but that's just tough luck and part of the course. Don't be tempted to go back later and try again, leave her alone and try to find another one that might not resent your presence quite so much.

Badgers.

Badgers, I believe, are almost the Holy Grail of the British Mammal scene, especially if you can get them in daylight (to view this veritable phenomenon please visit my website!).I warn you now that whatever light you photograph them in they are an exposure nightmare. There is a central patch in the white of their foreheads that almost seems to "glow" white, if such a thing is possible, and another in each of their cheek patches. To prevent these from "burning out" you need to under-expose and since, at best, you are likely to be working in fairly low, late evening light, this makes for very dark shots which can create a lot of "digital noise" in your pictures. I cannot advise a magical cure for this other than to take them earlier in the day when the light is better. Since they're essentially nocturnal by nature then this is a lot easier for me to advise than for you to do.

However - there is a way. First and foremost Badgers have Laws protecting them from all manner of interruption to their quiet lives. Rather than quote you the "Letter of the Law" as it stands today, I would advise you to check its latest status on the internet before going out to photograph Badgers. These laws have a habit of changing from time to time and , since I cannot know at what point in the future you are going to read this, I do not want to be in a position of advising you that it's OK to do something if, by the time that you come to do it, the Law has changed its mind – so check it out. Stick "Badgers and the Law" into your search engine and words of wisdom will come pouring out.

Assuming that, for photographic purposes, you will still be able to work at, or near, a sett, then first find one and then start baiting it. Badgers would leave home for a peanut and a handful would have them jumping through hoops. Some of the modern dry dog and cat foods are also taken readily. If you decide to go this route you must be prepared, and able, to put your bait down every day for weeks, or sometimes months. Wherever you choose to put it make sure that there is a well concealed spot nearby where you can set up for your picture taking. A hide is not a lot of use with these animals, especially if you cannot leave it there as a permanent feature. Their senses of smell and hearing are so acute that they will know that you're there whether you are doing your best impersonation of a bramble bush or not. Their sight, however, appears to be pretty poor so, as long as you don't jump around and are reasonably well hidden, they probably won't see you even from pretty close to. Don't kid yourself that you're fooling them, however, because they will definitely know that you are there so don't do anything that will make them associate potential threat with the smell of you. Highly scented cosmetics and insect sprays are not the best idea that you could have even if the midges are treating you as Sunday lunch. You need to smell the same every visit so do develop some kind of a routine to enable this. Personally I would avoid washing, bathing or showering immediately before going there. They need to come to accept your body smell as benign, which I guess means that you need to have a smelly body!

Put your bait down at roughly the same time every day and don't be too afraid of making a noise , within reason. They will know that you are there anyway and so it's best if they come to accept your smell, your noise and the contents of your goody bag as all part of the same happening. Time your trips for about one to one and a half hours before sunset and, after putting down your bait, wait around quietly for at least an hour. If you get the chance of a shot don't be too hasty in the early days as, at the first click of a shutter release, they'll be off like rockets. Eventually they will get used to it and come to associate that noise with food as well. If you're lucky then after a few weeks just the rustle of a food bag will be enough to bring them running and your biggest problem will not be how to get close enough for a shot but how to get far enough away for the minimum focussing distance of your lens. Once you have been accepted as one of the family, so to speak, you should find that you can encourage them to come out a little earlier than they normally would, when the light will be better and you may be able to photograph without having to use flash.

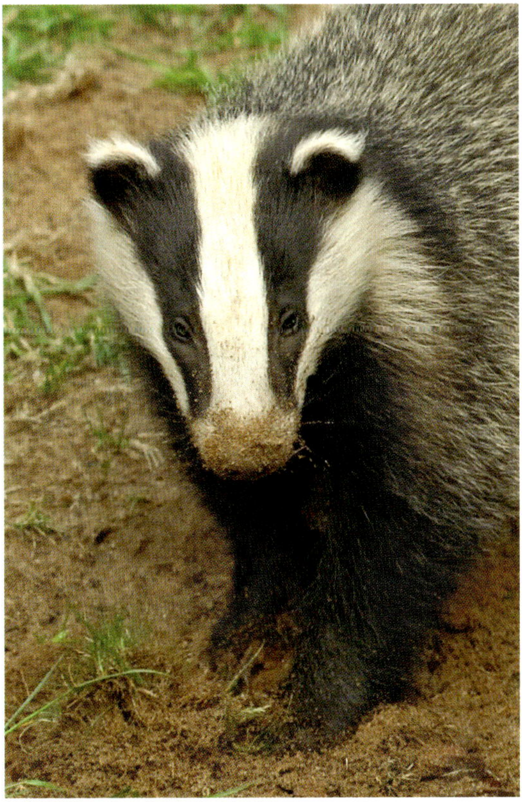

"Who you looking at Jimmy?"

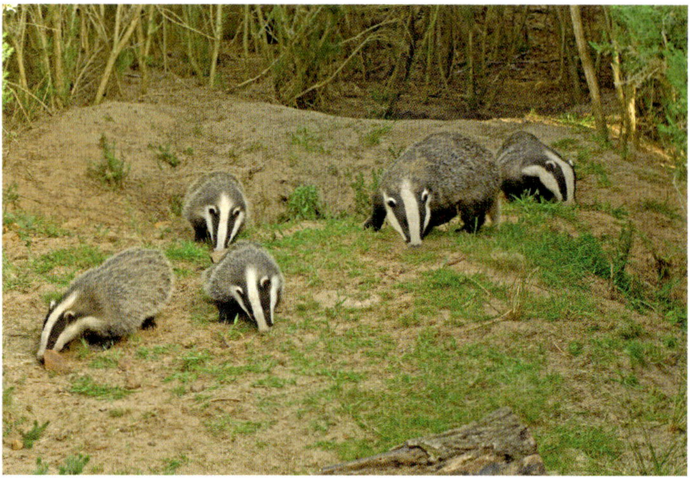

Heathland group of Badgers.

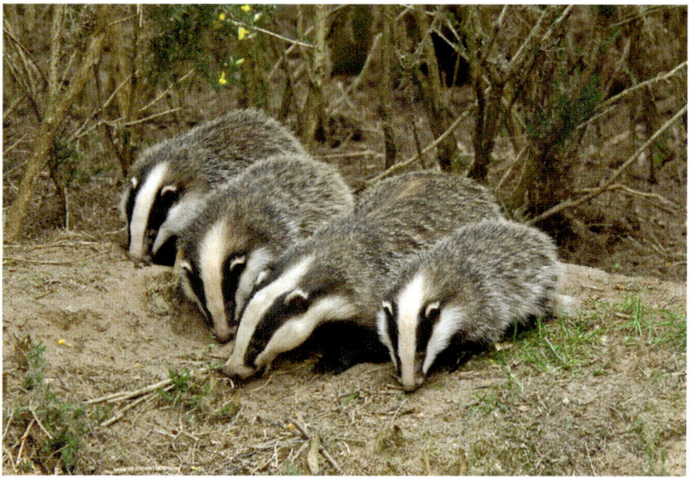

Feeding time for Mum and the Kids.

A word of warning! In some areas Badgers are still dug up for "sport" since they are such fierce protagonists when pitted against dogs. I will refrain from going into the harrowing details of this so called "sport" but, believe me, it's pretty grim. Never, ever betray the location of your "spot" unless it is to someone to whom you would trust your life. Don't forget that even friends have friends that have friends. In the world of entomology there is a saying along the lines of:- "big fleas have little fleas on their backs to bite 'em, little fleas have littler fleas and so ad infinitum", and so it can be with friends and especially with acquaintances. You don't want to spend three months setting it up and then get there one day to find a coachload of photographers has beaten you to it, or that there is just a large hole in the ground where the sett used to be.

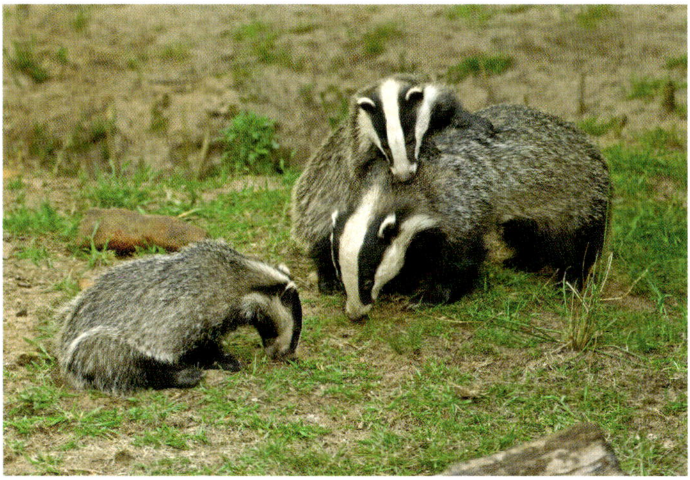

Playtime.

Obviously many people will not be able to devote the time required for the above method and so they have far less chances – but chances there are. Badger tracks through bushes and down the sides of banks are pretty obvious even to an untrained eye. You can try staking one out in the hopes that a Badger will come ambling by but they do tend to use these tracks fairly late on in the day and you will likely need to use flash for lighting. The other chance is to keep your ears open for someone who has Badgers visiting their garden on a regular basis. These will already have been habituated to people to a certain extent so you can probably get quite close. Invariably, however, these encounters will take place after dark and so flash will be the order of the day. Taking black and white subjects with a flash can be somewhat trying to say the least, but if you are working with regular garden visitors then you should be able to keep coming back until you get it right.

I usually find that the offer of free photos is enough to open doors. Once again keep it to yourself, or the hapless householder will be bowled over in the rush of photographers all wanting to emulate your success and you may not find yourself so welcome if you ever wish to go back.

The final opportunity is that some landowners, and/or Wildlife Trusts, have set up Badger watching venues many of which are free or cost very little. Once again you will be working with habituated animals, thus saving weeks of getting to know one another. You may find yourself sharing a hide or a platform with several others but at least you will all be on the same mission so their behaviour shouldn't be a problem.

Foxes

The photographing of foxes follows much the same lines as for Badgers. Once again the chances of a successful wild encounter on a pure chance basis are somewhat remote. If you can find a den – farmers and farm workers often know of them – then you can use much the same techniques as for Badgers. The advantage with Foxes is that they are not as nocturnal as Badgers and, due to their all over colour scheme (except for a small area of white), they do not present quite the same exposure headaches. With the advent of the Urban Fox I would suggest that far more people have Foxes visiting their gardens than have Badgers, so that you stand a much better chance by taking this route. Often they breed in places such as under the shed, or the wooden decking with which the gardens of so many "bijou des res" properties are turfed these days. If you are lucky enough to drop on one of these then you are in for some tremendous photography, especially once the "kids" start to come out to play.

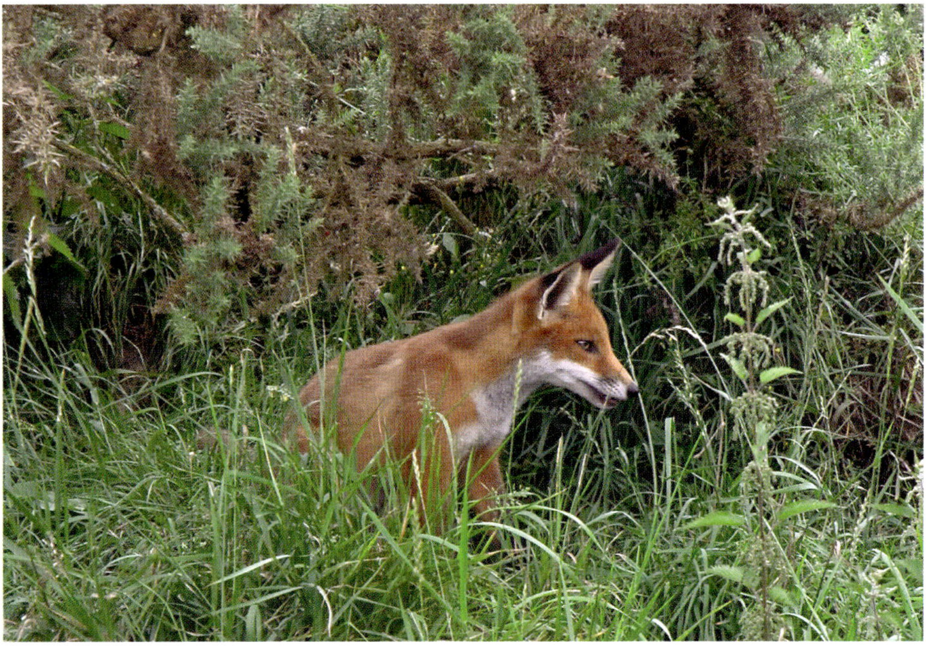

Fox cub about to pounce.

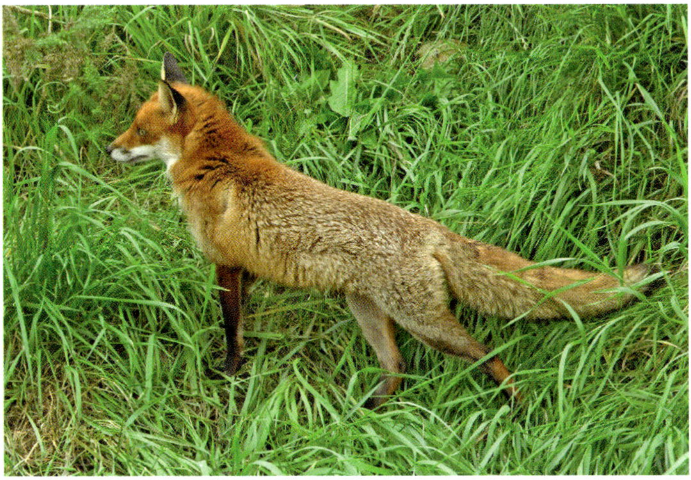

Red Fox.

Personally I have never enjoyed much success with Foxes in the UK as I have never managed to get round to having a serious go at it. However, I can well remember a visit to the Falkland Islands some years ago which was very Foxy in its content. Back in the 1930's the owner of Weddell, Stats and Beaver Islands imported a vast range of exotic birds and animals. One of the aspects of his former aristocratic lifestyle that he missed was Fox Hunting and so, in the new menagerie that he imported, he included some Foxes from Patagonia and released them on his Islands together with many of the other recent arrivals. These Foxes are a striking silvery colour and they took to life in the Falklands like ducks to water or rather like foxes to ducks – and geese – of which the Falklands are full. They must have thought that they'd arrived in heaven with huge flocks of Geese, many of them unable to fly for large parts of the year due to moulting, and the more sedentary rookeries of Penguins often several 1000's strong. Needless to say in no time the foxes became a problem and decimated the local wildlife. Over time they also turned their hands to sheep stealing and took so many newborn lambs that they became declared public enemy no 1. Fortunately they were only ever on the three islands and so their effect on the endemic species was very localised. Shooting, poisoning, fencing and so on have all helped to control their numbers but they have never been successfully eradicated. Now that sheep farming is no longer the sole occupation of the Falklands they will probably make a comeback as there will be no concerted effort to get rid of them. Despite this harsh treatment, however, those that there were, when I was there, were possessed of very trusting natures and one pair took to accompanying me every day as if I was taking them for a walk. The Vixen in particular was very confiding and walked to heel all day long.

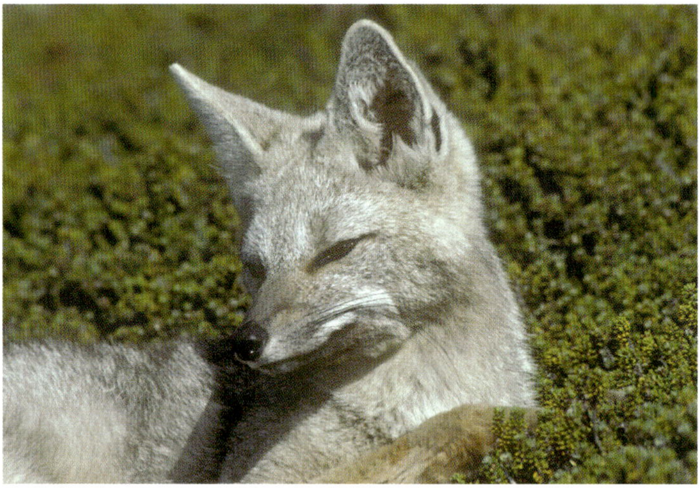

Patagonian Fox introduced to the Falkland Islands.

Many rolls of film later I had to leave praying that they would escape the current owners' poisoning regime.

Deer.

Deer can be a real boon to a Wildlife Photographer as they are around to be photographed twelve months of the year. There are now several species established in the UK and whilst they are not all endemic, most were introduced at various times in the past, nevertheless they have managed to survive and breed in the wild to the extent that they must, by now, be classed as naturalised. Sometimes this has been the result of deliberate intent and introduction and at other times the result of inadvertent escapes. Taking the Sika as an example, they were purportedly introduced onto one or two of the islands in Poole Harbour in the 1890's. Whoever engineered the introduction does not appear to have done the amount of research into his subject that I have urged you all to do throughout this book, so he overlooked the fact that they can swim just about as well as they can walk or run. Surprise, surprise! Once released they promptly hopped it by swimming to the mainland where they proceeded to become established and can now be numbered in the low 1000's. Another population in the New Forest was the result of a slightly later escape, followed by a subsequent deliberate release, from Beulieu.

It would seem that all deer, from whatever country of origin, sizzle nicely on a spit and taste delicious, especially if accompanied by almost any kind of alcoholic beverage! The result, of course, as is the case with so many species of Waterfowl, is that they have been consistently hunted for centuries. Not unnaturally the consequence is that they have become very twitchy by nature, and are almost impossible to approach in the wild to what one could, even optimistically, call "close-up" distance. You can, however, often "ambush" them either by hiding in the bushes or a skilfully placed hide, or even by using one of the many "platforms" erected in likely spots and from which culling often takes place. This method is, however, pretty haphazard since, with you in a fixed position, it is simply in the lap of the Gods as to whether anything comes along. Having said that, with some of the species such as Roe, Muntjac and Water Deer, this is probably the only way you are likely to achieve anything since they are not gregarious, other than in small family groups, and they do not tend to be kept as ornamentals by many establishments mainly due to the difficulty of constraining them.

Red, Fallow and Sika, however, live in substantial groups and have long been attractive to various parks, estates, conservancies, Stately Homes and forestries, not only for their obviously ornamental value but also for sport or even as "farm" animals. Some of the larger estates, especially in Scotland, depend on the income from the various aspects of their deer keeping for their very survival. Since poaching has, generally speaking, become a thing of the past except in a few localised areas, deer, in the UK, have virtually no predators to worry about, certainly once they become adult. Their grazing can be destructive in many kinds of habitat and their numbers are now having to be controlled by culling in many areas. Because of their appeal it is often quite difficult to accept that the extremely lovable deer that you have just been photographing over the last few days may end up being shot as part of a culling regime but I'm afraid you have to adopt a practical outlook. There is no point in becoming emotionally over wrought about it. Over the last few years deer populations have exploded in places and numbers have to be controlled somehow, not only for the sake of the habitats involved, but also for the benefit of the animals themselves. If you have ever been witness, as I have on more than one occasion, to the heart breaking effects of overpopulation on a species within a restricted area then I can assure you that you would be out there at dawn wishing the "cullers" a "good day". Overpopulation is not a pretty sight and the domino effect on other species can sometimes be all but unstoppable. The whole world has become one big Zoo and, unfortunately, someone has to be the Zookeeper. If a conventional Zoo or Safari Park crammed its pens to bursting with animals then we would all be unanimous in our condemnation and so-called "Wild Habitats"(which as far as I am concerned is an extinct species in most of the world) are no different.

Most of the animals held on the farming and sport shooting estates have retained their wary natures and are not the best of subjects for close-up photographic work. I would suggest that anyone setting out to photograph deer under these conditions will need to be in a position to finance some decent gear. To be sensible a lens capacity of some 600mm is probably what you'll need to be in with a chance of some decent sized images. This can still be achieved at a reasonable cost by using 3 or 400mm zooms with a converter. Another alternative is to buy a mirror lens. These are not normally too expensive but their downside is that their maximum aperture (lowest Fstop number) is such that you need pretty good light for them to be effective. With a 600mm capability you should, with careful stalking, be able to obtain some meaningful shots even in ostensibly "wild" settings and I guess, if you are one who gets his thrills from the chase, that this is the route to go. If, however, your prime purpose is to obtain as stunning a collection of images as possible then I would suggest that you go the ornamental route and just top up, if you must, with the odd shot from the "wild".

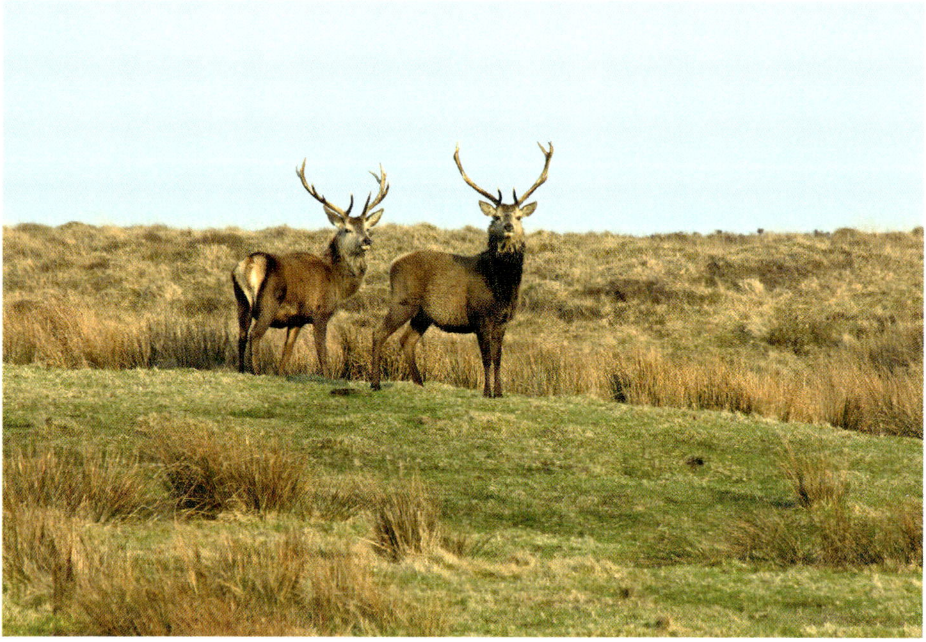

Red Deer on the Isle of Islay.

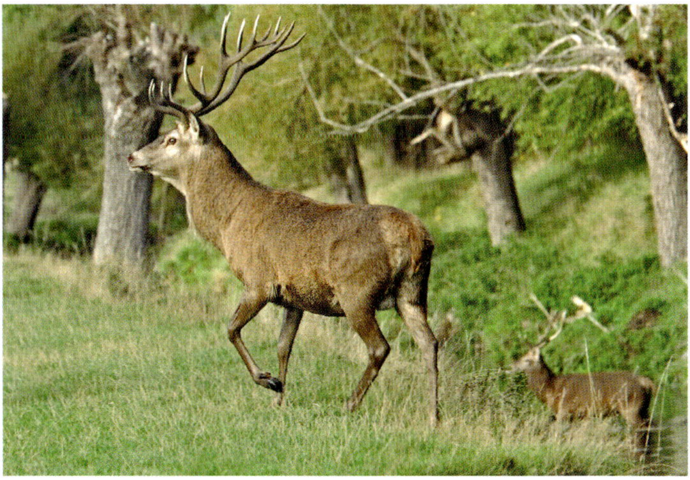

Red Deer stags early on in the rut.

Throughout the country there are a great number of venues hosting populations of various of the three species of Sika, Fallow or Red. Many of these places have a regular throughput of people in sufficient numbers for the deer to have become accustomed to them and they can, therefore, be reasonably approachable, especially in the non-breeding season. All three of the above species enjoy very similar annual cycles during the course of which there are sufficient physical changes taking place to provide for year round photographic activity. An obvious change applicable to all is the transition in their coats from winter to summer and back to winter again with all points in between. In the case of Sika and Fallow they are very prettily white spotted against an autumnal red background when they are in their summer coats. In winter, however, the spots can be scarcely noticeable as their coats become quite dark and shaggy. Spring and early summer reveals the transformation, even in the Stags, and, at a distance, it is often quite difficult to differentiate between Sika and Fallow females and fawns.

Apart from the "cute and cuddly" appearance of the youngsters it is the Stags and Bucks, with their often magnificent antlers, that appeal to both sportsmen and photographers alike. The "horns" of African and Asian Antelopes are permanent structures that grow gradually throughout their lifetime. With deer, however, the "antlers" are shed every year and a new, larger pair grows to replace them. Basically the three species we are discussing shed their antlers sometime in the spring and then regrow them through the summer in time for the "rut" or breeding season in the autumn. Photographically through the winter you have the chance of Stags with their antlers at their finest but their coats somewhat shaggy and often a bit of a

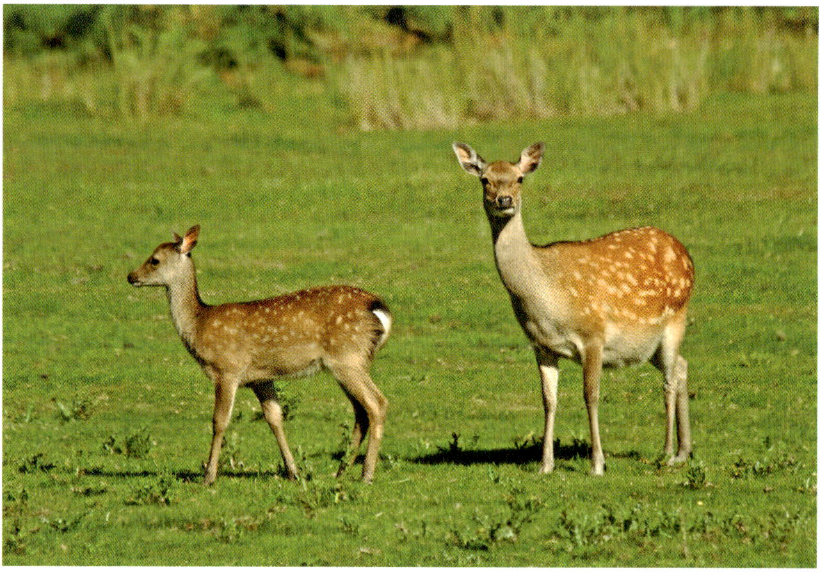

Sika mum and young.

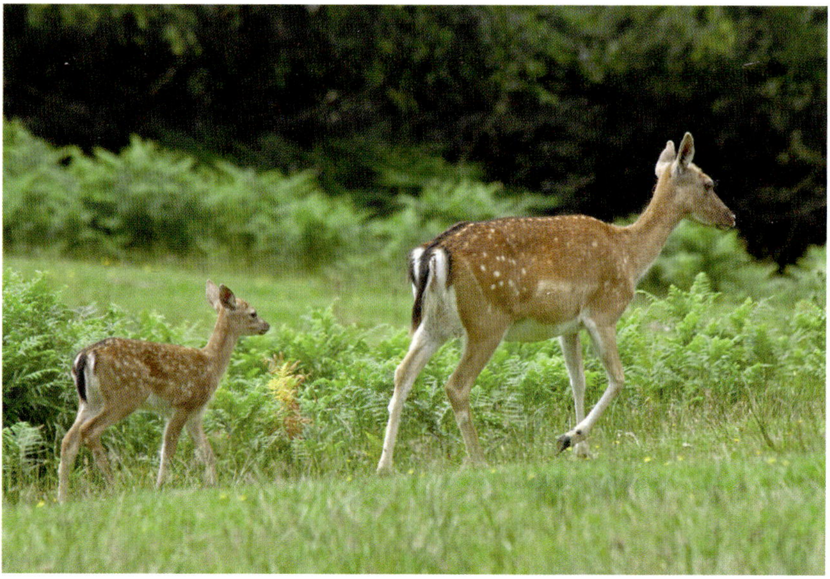

Fallow mum and young.

mess. Spring brings the shedding of the antlers with the associated behaviour of trying to "bash" the old ones off against trees and bushes and the transition to their beautiful summer coats. Late spring and early summer is calving season when the females usually disappear off on their own to give birth and then trickle back to the herd over the next few weeks with their new offspring proudly in tow. Throughout the summer the stags' new antlers are growing and covered with a blood rich layer of tissue referred to as "velvet".

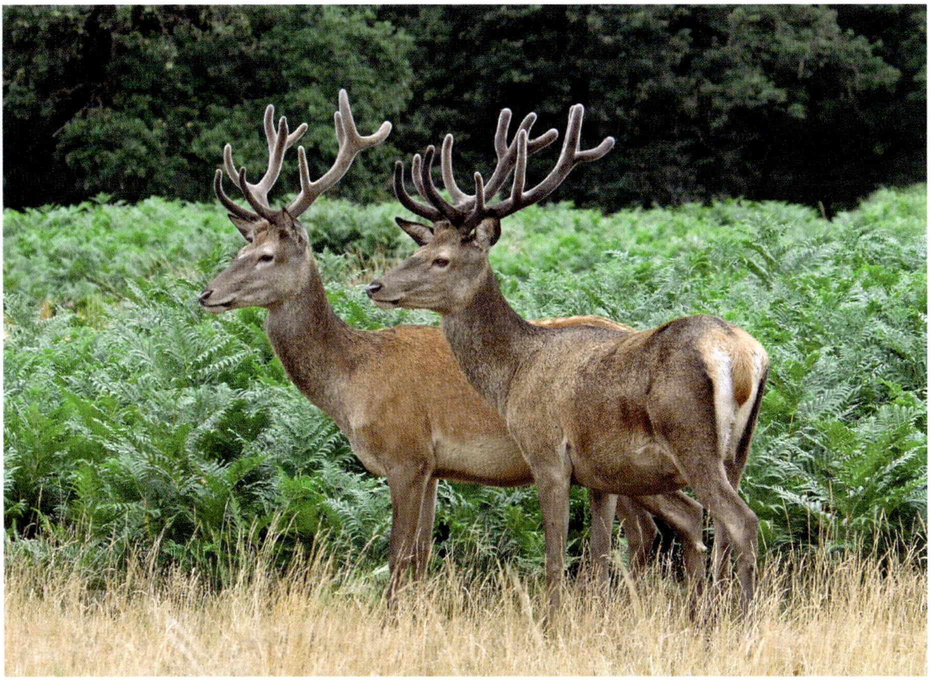

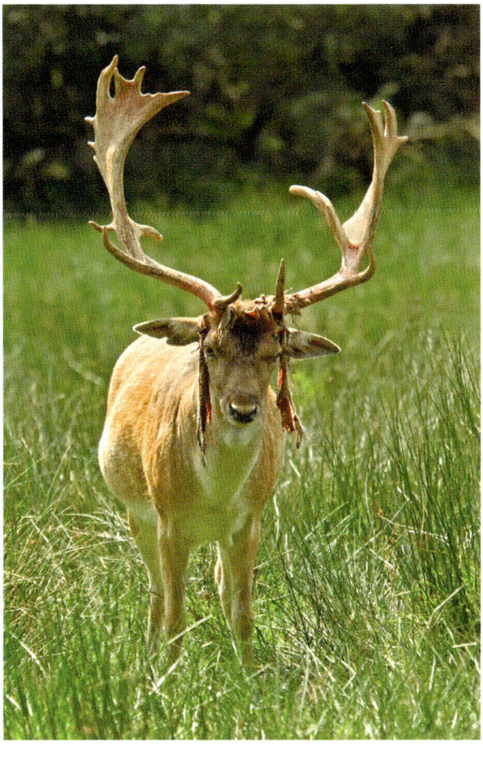

Fallow buck in "Tatters".

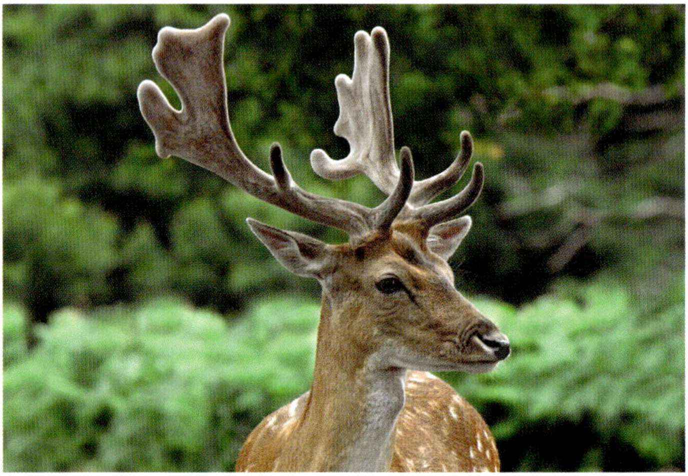

Fallow Buck in velvet.

Late summer sees this layer being reduced to "tatters", again with much "bashing" of bushes, to expose the bone of the antlers underneath. Autumn sees the "rut" or mating period much favoured by photographers, or even those just interested in Wildlife, because of the sometimes spectacular noise and activity that is such an integral part of the mating game.

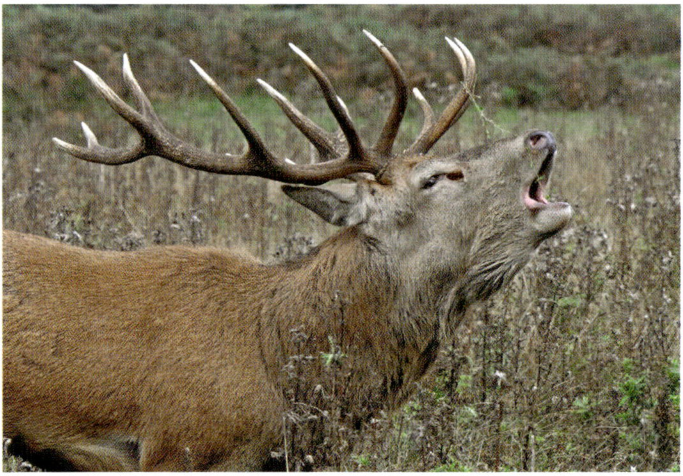

Red Deer stag in the middle of the rut.

Once this is over the summer coats disappear, the females and youngsters herd up, and the males move off in small groups to recover from the rut and, no doubt, to enjoy a little peace and quiet away from the women and kids. Through the winter these stags become the main point of photographic interest since they really do look their "macho" best.

Personally I have only ever seen one colour of Red Deer though you do get some very dark and some fairly pale individuals. In Sika I have seen occasional white ones. These tend to be mostly females but I have seen one white stag, and a very beautiful creature he was too. Fallow, however, come in a variety of colours. At one time different colour forms were much sought after and many mutations were thereafter "fixed" by artificial selection giving rise to the range of colours that you can still see to this day.

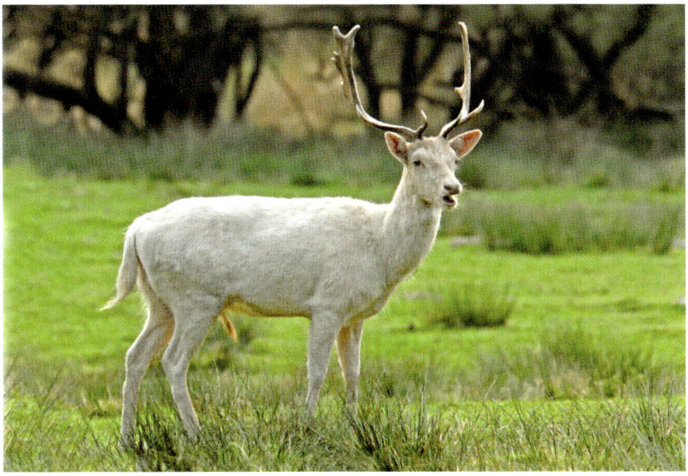

White – not Albino – Fallow buck

You will find that in many of the Deer Parks and similar venues you can actually get quite close to the deer particularly if you go about it calmly and non-aggressively. Remember not to let your body language become too much of the hunter. At some sites you can get so close that you can get shots on a mobile phone so whatever gear you have rest assured that there will be somewhere for you if you can manage to find it. There are also many forests carrying numbers of deer of all species. In my case the New Forest is very close and at one place, Boldrewood, the Fallow Deer are fed through the summer months by forestry staff at a public viewing area. This offers a chance to get quite close to a large number of animals. They are, however, "wild" deer and not fenced in any way and so in between feedings they revert to their "wild" behaviour patterns making them very difficult to locate and approach.

Quite often a stealthy approach is not actually the best method. Generally speaking deer senses are so acute that you stand no chance of getting close, especially on open ground, unless they are prepared to let you. You may kid yourself that there is something of the Great White Hunter in your genes but

I can assure you that the deer have been at it much longer than you and have perfected their techniques accordingly. With animals that, whilst not exactly being tame are, nevertheless, used to seeing humans around you can often get closer with an up front and casual approach. Talking in a soft voice, even if only to yourself, can often have a calming effect. Never approach in a straight line but rather adopt an angled approach with an air of apparent unconcern, across their front, and don't "look 'em in the eye", as this is sometimes taken as a challenge or sign of evil intent. There is another technique that I learnt in Africa and which often works well even with completely wild animals, especially if you are downwind of them. Bend at the waist and lean well forward, letting your arms hang down rather like a Chimp, and shuffle along rather than striding out as you work closer to them. Maybe you walk like that anyway in which case you are definitely in with a chance! This technique doesn't actually make you invisible, nor does it automatically get you accepted as friend rather than foe, but at least it alters your silhouette and may well turn you into a subject of puzzlement rather than fear. In addition, as entertainment, it will give any passing non-photographers who witness your performance something to talk about for decades!

Insectivores.

Of the insectivores I suspect that only the Hedgehog is a likely bet. Almost invariably nocturnal you will be dependent on flash for lighting. You can often find them if you go out on a night walk with a good torch, but your chances of good shots will, to a large extent, depend on luck. They also snore quite loudly when they're asleep and they can also make a heck of a racket when they're mating. I don't think that this din is engendered by the obvious dangers inherent in the mating of two creatures covered in sharp spines but rather the result of sheer exuberance. Whatever the reason, if you're moving about quietly, you will most likely hear it from some distance away. Again photographic opportunity is probably pretty poor since, if you try to get close enough for a flash shot, you will almost certainly scare them off.

As is the case with Badgers and Foxes your best bet is probably to find someone who feeds them regularly in their gardens. This way you will again have the chance to work with habituated animals that are not likely to curl up into a ball as soon as you breathe heavily or shuffle your feet. If you wish to attract them to your own garden then you will have to put food down regularly and cross your fingers. I am going to "cop out" of recommending what to feed them with as thoughts on this subject change regularly. It used always to be bread and milk but I believe this is now frowned on and catfood has taken its place. Check with your local Wildlife Trust or Hedgehog rescue centre and I'm sure they will be pleased to advise you.

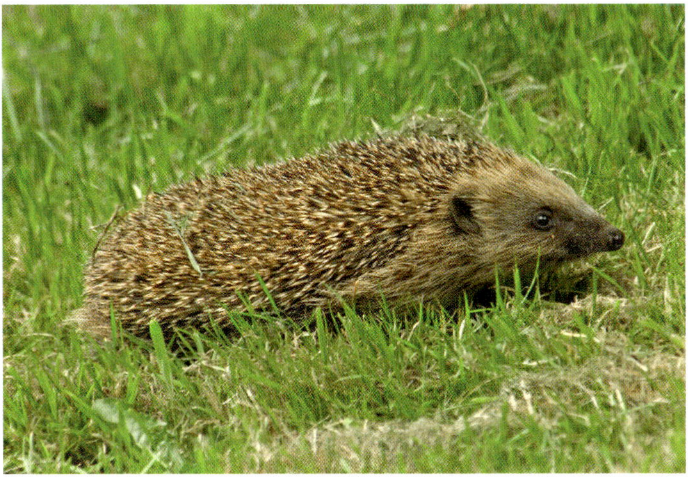

Hedgehog.

A word of warning if you are handling Hedgehogs. They often carry the biggest, hard bitingest fleas that you will ever have seen. I carry a long handled butterfly net in my Landrover at all times so that I can move snakes, toads and hedgehogs from off the road and I no longer pick them up by hand if I can use the net instead. Obviously the snakes might bite you or cover you with a foul smelling anal secretion, the toads will cover you with a slimy liquid which in some cases is toxic and the hedgehogs have no objection to sharing their flea population with you. Do yourself a favour – get a net!

Mustelids.

The final group of mammals is the Mustelids with the exception of the Badgers which we have already covered. Seems strange, doesn't it, that Badgers and Weasels should come from the same family? The three species that you are most likely to come across in the South are Weasels, Stoats and Otters (possibly Mink depending on your area). Further North you may be lucky enough to find Polecats and Pine Martens. By and large all of these will be a fluke encounter in the wild so there is not too much advice that I can offer. The possible exception is with Otters since they are purported to be making a determined comeback. A check with your local Wildlife Trust will ascertain whether there are any likely sites in your area and, failing that, you may be able to turn up something on the internet. Early mornings and late evenings are your best times of day. In actual fact Otters are frequently not all that nervous. You will have noticed in the many Scotland based documentaries on the subject, that the photographer often just pulls up when he sees an Otter working and gets on with the filming of it. It's just that they tend to keep themselves to themselves but quite often, if you can actually manage to locate any, they may well be prepared to let you snap away. Because of the recency of their expansion then many will be new arrivals in an area and extra sensitive because of it. Once they settle in, however, and become established you can find yourself with some good opportunities, especially if you can find a holt and stake yourself out nearby (with your baghide on your head of course!).

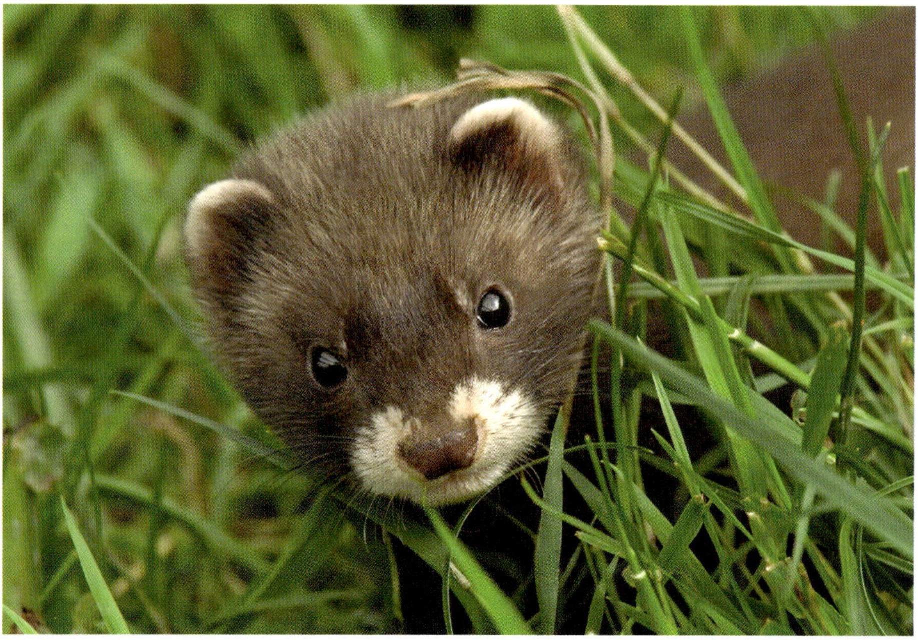

Juvenile Polecat.

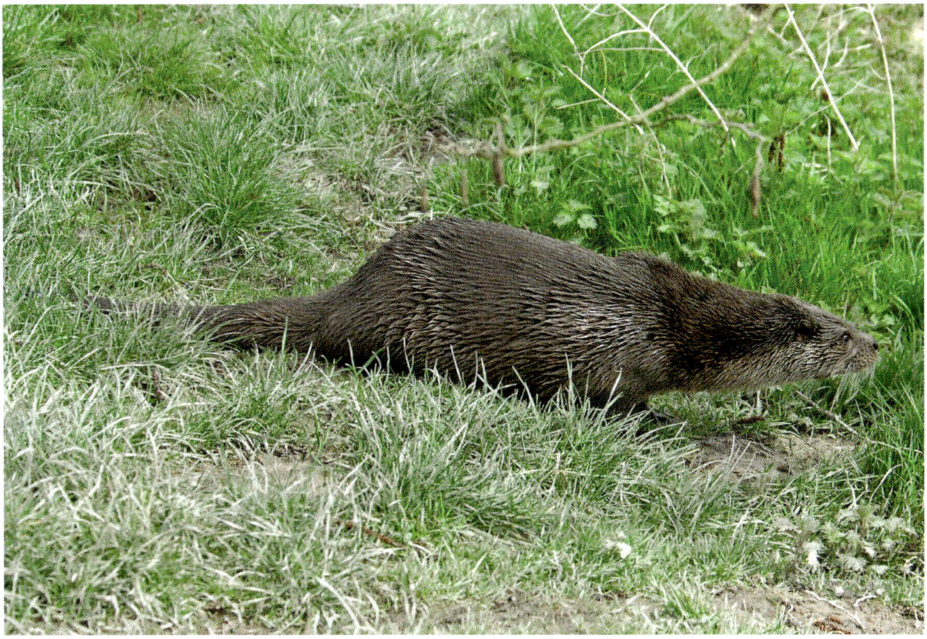

European Otter stalking.

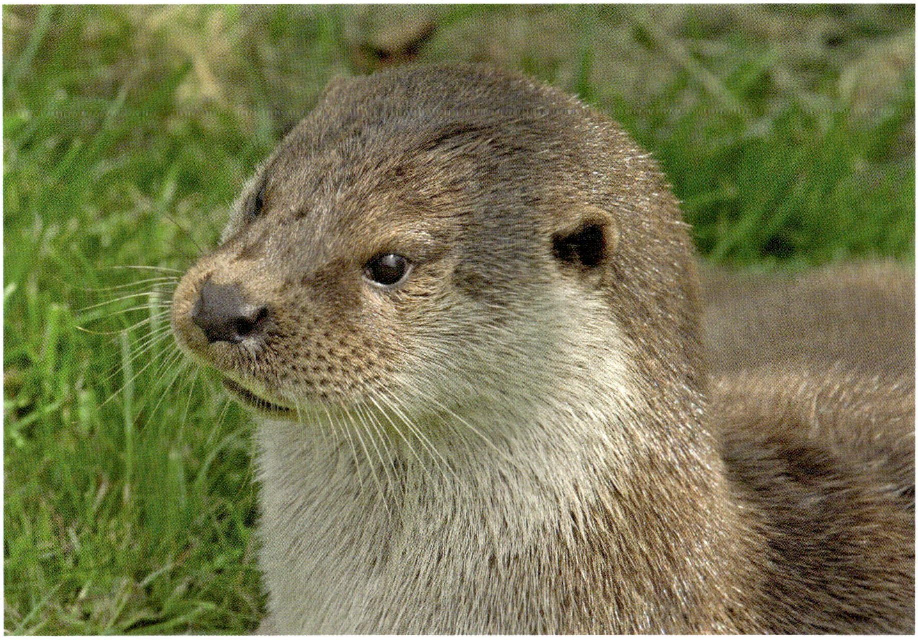

European Otter

Chapter 21

Photographing In Zoos And Safari Parks

My sentiments on this subject have been well documented in the chapter headed "Subject Provenance" but, to recap, – there will be those, and many of them, who will denigrate your efforts and claims to be a Wildlife photographer if you consistently work in Zoos or with captive collections. Ignore them! In the real world, in which we all have to survive, these may be the only places where you stand a chance of photographing some of the species that you have chosen as subjects without embarking on protracted and expensive overseas trips, undertaken with no guarantee of success at the end of them. For most budding Wildlife Photographers, (and some well established ones too,) this is where you are most likely to get stunning close ups of such a wide range of species that you would otherwise have to be lucky, wealthy and live 200 years, to come into contact with.

However, it is not easy and don't let anyone try to infer that it is. The difficulties are, obviously, of a different nature from the ones that you would experience if working in the bush, but they have just as much bearing on your output and need to be acknowledged and overcome if you are to stand a chance of obtaining decent images.

Firstly you need to establish your "budget" of purpose. If you just want to obtain record shots of as many species as possible, or even to cover specific groups such as the Big Cats, and you are not troubled by man made backgrounds or surroundings, then that's fine and you can just bang away as you see fit. The major problems arise when you want shots that are aesthetically pleasing and free of unnatural features. If at all possible try to wait until your subject is in a position where as natural looking as possible a background is behind it. If you cannot achieve this then opt for as uncluttered a background as you can since you may be able to clone it out later and the less cluttered that it is then the greater the chances of retaining and either cutting or cloning around the subject details. Take your images on as large an aperture as you feel that you can get away with and this will blur your background and help you to make a cleaner job with your processing.

In these establishments you probably won't need as much as 600mm of lens but 300 or 400 would be useful as a top end. Remember that the more of the subject that you can get in your frame then the less of the background you have to worry about. If you are lucky then the subject size in your final image can be achieved at point of shoot, but you can also take into account the potential cropping possibilities during your final enhancement process when composing your shot.

Whatever quality or type of image you are after you will probably have to accept that within any given Zoo or Safari Park setting there will be a large number of subjects that, for one reason or another, you will not be able to photograph satisfactorily no matter how much you may wish it. With these you will just have to take it on the chin and hope you get a better chance somewhere else. With modern perceptions of what is acceptable by way of animal pens being so different from those of the Victorian era, we are fortunate that old fashioned cages have given way to a more "open plan" type of accommodation. You will still find, however, that a large part of your photographing will involve coping with bars, mesh or plate glass.

I am somewhat fortunate in that I get to undertake a fair amount of promotional work for captive collections and so can often get "behind the barriers", but it was not always so and, indeed, with many of the animals of the type that can eat you, or even just give you a nasty suck, they cannot be gone in with anyway and so I am frequently no better off than a casual Zoo visitor.

Many Zoos now incorporate plate glass viewing windows into their pen fencing. With a little effort, a bit of planning and a lot of luck you can often make use of these. If you know in advance that you are going to have to deal with glass then there are steps that you can take to overcome its inherent difficulties. My "modus operandi" is as follows. Firstly I always carry some kitchen type "wipes" to clear the glass of candyfloss, sticky bun and greasy fingerprints. Pick an area where the glass on the inside is relatively clean and work from there. On cold mornings there is often the danger of condensation on the glass and, take it from me, it will always be on the other side where you can't get at it. I would suggest either that you have a lie-in, or work a pen without glass, until the sun comes up and warms the condensation off. When you consider the millions of pounds that manufacturers have poured into lens development over the years it seems almost sacrilegious to be contemplating taking pictures through thick plate, or even laminated, sheet glass but, believe me, you can still achieve some stunning results.

Having got your window cleaning out of the way you now come up against the biggest problem of photographing through glass and that is reflections from behind. In my early days I frequently managed a better shot of myself via reflection than I did of the animal that I was trying to photograph. If you could stick your lens flush up against the glass you would be OK but it seldom works out like that. You invariably end up holding the camera at an angle as the animal moves about and that is when the reflections creep in. My solution is fairly simple. You need to make something that will end up looking like a butterfly net, with a hole in the bottom large enough to fit over your lens. You need to use solid black material and not net so that it keeps the light out. In my case I used a black T Shirt and a ring, about 12ins diameter, made of fence straining wire. You will also need to use a tripod or monopod for supporting your camera as you may have to operate it with one hand. Stick your lens through the hole in your "net" from the outside and hold the wire ring up against the glass. Allow the camera, on its support, to rest against the glass and you will be able to support and trigger it with one hand while the other hand holds the wire ring end of your reflection preventer up against the glass. In effect you will be photographing through a blacked out tunnel and you should be able to hold your camera at any angle, or even away from the glass, without fear of any reflections creeping in. Make sure your flash, if you have one, is outside the material otherwise it will, itself, create a reflection.

Bars and mesh both pose a similar problem. Ideally, if you are able to get close enough, you can stick your lens end between the mesh or bars and shoot through them. Bars are the most difficult because if you can't get between them then there is not much else that you can do. Mesh, however, does offer one or two chances. Ideally, if the mesh openings are large enough, such as chain-link, and your lens end small enough, then shoot through it if you can. Frequently, however, your lens end will be too big. If this is the case then hold your lens as close to the mesh as you can and make sure that the centre of your frame is exactly in the middle of the mesh opening. Settle for a subject image small enough to fit inside the clear area where it will not be affected by the vignetting effect caused by the mesh and then crop out the affected areas when you come to enhance your shots later. If the mesh size is fairly small like "chicken wire" then you can sometimes get away with it by standing back so that the mesh comes about 25% of the way between you and the subject and then using a very large aperture (small F stop no). Your field of focus will then be very shallow and there is a chance, particularly with a long lens, that the mesh will not show unless it is very shiny. If it is then either look for a patch of it in the shade or wait for the sun to go in.

If you are working in a drive-through pen in a safari Park then you will undoubtedly have to keep your windows closed. Make sure you clean all your windows, inside and out, with wipes before you go in, and make sure that you don't go through the baboon enclosure if you can help it, otherwise you'll end up with a wrecked car and filthy windows. You can then use the same contraption that I described for the plate glass and you should be free to photograph in any direction without any fear of reflections creeping in. If circumstances permit and you can get the back seat to yourself, assuming that you're not driving of course, then so much the better because you will be free to operate to either side or behind you without someone else's head creeping into your shot.

Bear in mind the nature of wildlife. Much of it is given to lunchtime siestas, especially in hot weather, and this is not normally a very productive time of day. Check the feeding times of the various animals that you wish to photograph (you can often get this information off the Zoo's website before you go) and get to that pen about an hour beforehand. Most animals have a very accurate, built-in time clock and they know when it's almost "grub up". They will normally begin to get restless and start to move around from at least an hour before they are due to be served. If the food is brought on a trolley then they will certainly start to react as soon as they hear the wheels in the distance, so don't leave it too late to get there.

Most sleeping quarters are left open all day and, on those days when it is stifling hot, raining, or just plain miserable, then many animals will spend the greater part of the day inside where your photographic opportunities are often limited. Try to choose the sort of day for your visit that you, yourself, don't mind being out in and you'll probably find that the animals feel the same way too.

Most exhibits are labelled these days with both English and Latin names. Take a note of these because, with many animal species, there are a number of sub-species and the Zoo will obviously know which one they have and, unless you are very familiar with them, you may find it difficult to identify them later. You can never know what you will eventually be doing with your images and there is nothing worse than to find yourself on show somewhere with an incorrectly named subject. Mind you, you won't be left in doubt too long as everyone, and their Aunt Sallies too, will take great delight in pointing out the error of your ways. Don't give them the satisfaction – take notes. If you find that you have forgotten pen and paper then take a shot of the sign and retrieve the image later from your computer, but don't go away without the info!

You may not have much choice of course, in which case you will just have to grin and bear it, but if you can avoid School and Bank holidays for your visit then you may well find that you will enjoy a higher success rate, and certainly have a less stressful day. Get to know the behaviour patterns of your chosen subjects and this will help you to be in the right place at the right time and able to anticipate what is likely to happen next.

To those of you who choose to go this route I wish you well and I know that, with diligence, you will come up with some super shots. Ignore those superior souls who try to "pooh pooh" your efforts because most of them won't know what they're talking about!

Chapter 22

Photographing Butterflies

Butterflies and I have had a recurring number of encounters over the years. I must confess that I was more fond of them in my earlier days of budding photographic genius when both I, and my gear, were not so demanding of accuracy. Most of my butterfly photography was conducted with a 90mm macro lens, mounted on I recall not what body, and supported on a monopod for ease of manoeuvre amongst the brambles which seem much favoured by so many species. Have you ever noticed how far from the main clump brambles actually begin? Many a time, before I have even switched into stealthy approach mode, an invisible hand has reached out and vigorously shaken the bush whereon lay my quarry. Often I have looked round ready to render instant physical retribution to the guilty party only to find that 'twas I, standing on a lengthy bramble side shoot busily seeking to establish an independent existence as far from parental influence as possible!

Where I live in Spain butterfly photography, as an all day pastime, is virtually a "no no", as it is in most hot countries. In the UK and other temperate areas you are in with a chance as the weather is unpredictable to say the least and hot, sunny days can be the exception rather than the rule. The trick to success in the UK is to establish where they roost, and then be there the next morning before they wake up, or the next evening before they retire for the night. Depending on the weather prevailing at the time you have upwards of an hour in the morning, while they are warming up to face the rigours of the day. In the tropics or Southern Europe where I live you seem to have about two minutes!

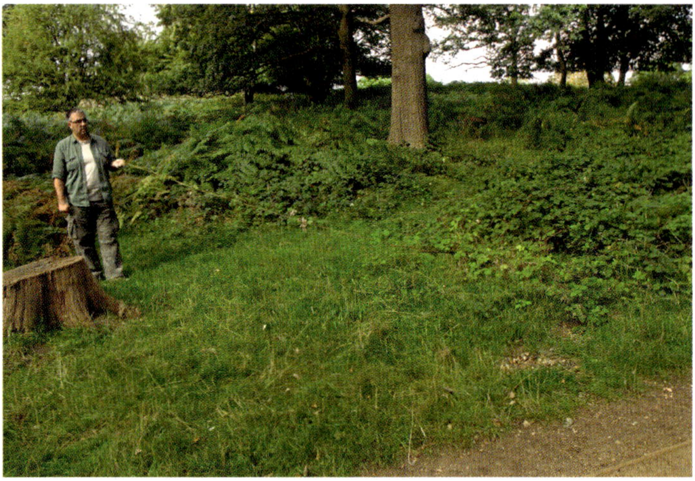

Bramble showing length of sucker.

The advantage of cooler climes is that butterflies spend more time during the day with their wings "akimbo", so to speak, and wide open for photography. Here, in Spain, their wings are continually up and down exercising their own particular system of air conditioning, and it makes close-ups well nigh impossible. Yes, over a period, I have managed to get some nice shots but they were mostly garnered on a "purely by chance" basis where, suddenly, "there it was" and "there was I". I have wasted many a fruitless hour on various trips chasing what, ultimately, proved to be the end of the rainbow and the result is that I have relegated butterflies to the back burner unless specifically called on to do otherwise.

Anyone who is a butterfly specialist needs to plan their trips carefully in order to achieve a modicum of success. In the UK and similar climes it can surely be an all day long occupation but, in warmer regions, it will, at best, be limited to a couple of hours in the morning and a couple more in the evening. The hours in between will be on the basis of "you pays your money and takes your chance". It would help, in these warmer areas, to have a second interest, such as Botany, to plug the gaps in your productivity. The advantage with plants is that they do not move very fast, other than in the wind, and so they can be approached any time of the day or night without too much danger of them running away! If not botanically inclined there are many other subjects that do not display the same anti- photographical traits as do butterflies themselves. There are a host of insect species available in most areas including, of course, Orthoptera which are my own particular favourite and covered elsewhere at some great length. Most of my advices are based on areas where there is a reasonable chance of being able to obtain close-ups of decent quality and I would ask you to bear in mind that, though much of the advice will hold true anywhere, butterfly photography in hot regions should be approached on a "catch as catch can" basis. I would not, personally, dedicate an entire trip to hot climes solely on the strength of butterfly photography unless I wanted an extremely long siesta through the heat of the day!

However, the above said and done, my memory is still sufficiently intact to be able to recall the satisfaction I used to get in the days when butterflies and day flying moths were uppermost in my photographic thinking. The strong colours and the excitement of having to "get up close", and the undoubted beauty of a really good butterfly shot are tremendous draws. I would not want to put off anyone who has determined, if for only a short time, to go the route of butterfly photography.

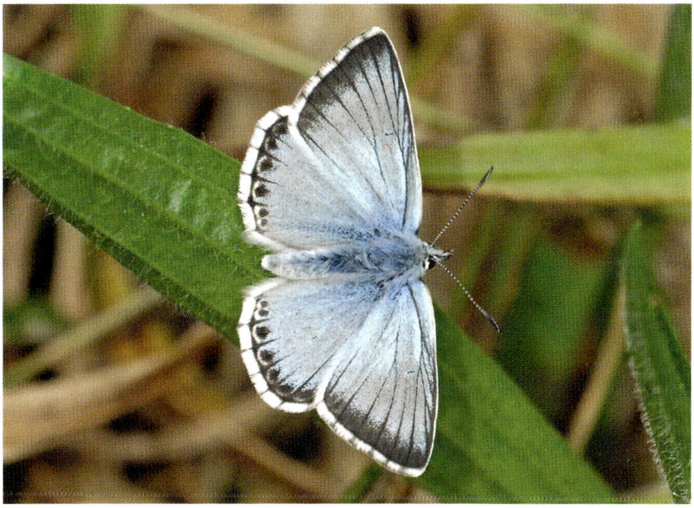

Male Chalkhill Blue catching some "rays".

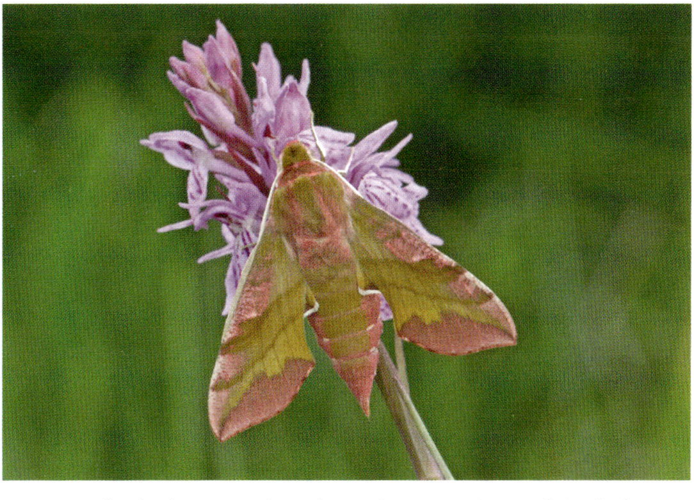

Small Elephant Hawkmoth on Common Spotted Orchid.

Like many aspects of photography it should not be approached in too lackadaisical a manner if you are hopeful of any degree of successful outcome. The days when you could have just sallied forth into the countryside and been surrounded by a myriad of butterflies of many different species at almost every turn are, in this country at least, a thing of the past. Nowadays changes in the countryside and its management have severely reduced areas of habitat suitable for large numbers of mixed species. The vast acreages devoted to single crop cultivation, such as Rape and Linseed, coupled with the associated change from many small mixed farms to far fewer large specialised ones, have led to a grubbing out of hedgerows and borders and fairly stringent chemical controls before, during and after cultivation. Any question that this has had a deleterious effect on butterfly population densities is quickly answered by comparing the numbers to be found on any of the many "unimproved" nature reserves existing only a barbed wire fence away from large arable areas, when the evidence will be clearly apparent.

In practice most butterfly devotees, or even those with just a smidgeon more than superficial interest, ultimately seem to develop a desire to see, and/or photograph, as many species as possible. Whilst it is true to say that the first few of the UK's some fifty odd species are easily achieved the task becomes quickly and considerably more difficult as the list of "outstandings" gets shorter. It becomes increasingly necessary to research and study each species individually if you want to get consistently within closeup distance. Fortunately, in this day and age, there are many aids to this aim readily accessible.

There will invariably be a local branch of Butterfly Conservation that you can join and the number of good quality reference books and field guides available at any decent bookstore is ever increasing. Do spend "a few bob" and get as good a selection as you can afford. I always place emphasis on those which use identifying photographs since, no matter how representative an illustration is, it can often look significantly different to the live creature when it is in front of you. Of course drawings have the added advantage of being able to depict "upper and under" and "fore and aft" wing colours and structures but, nevertheless, with a photograph normally what you see is exactly what you get and identification is often easier. Because of the inherent advantages of both formats then, if your budget allows, I would go for playing safe and get at least one of each.

Many of the best butterfly sites now come within managed Nature Reserves (which tells a story in itself) where, once located, access should present no problem. One or two may require a permit to visit but they are the exception rather than the rule and, in any event, an application to the managing body should be quite straightforward. A diligent search of available literature, and internet websites if you are able, should serve to locate sites for most species and a journeyplan can be made to encompass as many of them as suit your circumstances. Once actively in the field, especially with camera clutched firmly in hand, you should start to come across other like minded souls and word of mouth should identify other locations and recent sightings. Don't adopt the often typical British standoffishness of passing and ignoring strangers as if they were invisible. Often a little sociable effort can be rewarding not only in terms of immediate information but also in the founding of ongoing friendships with kindred spirits. We wildlife enthusiasts are few in number as it is and you are not likely to be able to pick out and identify many others walking along your local High St, so better to make friends where you find them.

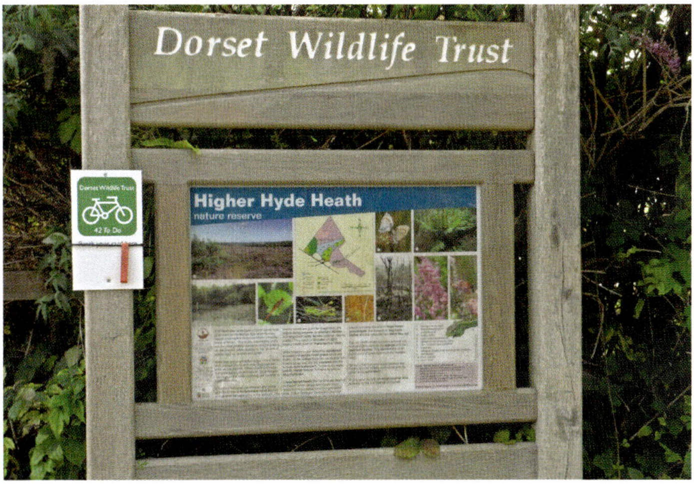

Typical Nature Reserve entry sign.

On the subject of the most suitable equipment to use I am often hesitant to be too specific because of the vast range of affordable gear now available. However you achieve it you will need some sort of closeup facility be it physical, in the form of a lens, or digital, in the form of an in-camera function. You would also be advised to have a flash facility of the "fill-in" kind. Use of this allows you to still depend on ambient as the principal source of light but, nevertheless, lifts and emphasises the colours without creating the black backgrounds that spoil so many full flash shots.

There are many in-camera zoom facilities available these days as an integral part of a camera's functions. However the results from depending on this as a means of obtaining frame filling insect shots is seldom as successful as a closeup shot gained by actually being close to your subject. Some wildlife subjects, as potential closeup material, will stand being "soft" in some areas in order to emphasise others but a good butterfly shot needs to be sharp all over in order to avoid disappointment. Lack of direct exposure setting controls in many "point and shoots", I would suggest, precludes them from being suitable for butterfly photography no matter what their zoom capability is. Taking into account the fact that, at certain settings, the depth of your field of focus may be no greater than the thickness of a piece of card means that your butterfly would need to be dead flat and you to be exactly at right angles to it to get the whole image sharp. These above two sets of circumstance hardly ever coincide in real life though you will be fooled into thinking, at a distance of some feet that may well seem to be in digital zoom range, that they have. Often it is not until much later when you get home and zoom your shots up on your computer that you realise just how far out of square you actually were. This, combined with a questionable viewfinder that you probably can't see the image through if the sun is shining, or even no actual viewfinder at all, limits your chance of a National Geographic centre spread to zilch – however brilliant your subsequent computer skills may be!

I do not wish to denigrate the efforts of those thousands of people who just want images to show at home, or to use as memory jogs on a cheerless winter's evening, for their number is legion whereas the number of seriously dedicated photographers is but few. The ranks of these few will inevitably be swelled by recruits from the legion who will "get the bug" and so they should be helped and encouraged as much as, and whenever, possible. I cannot abide the superior airs sometimes adopted and exhibited by some of the so-called experts in their various fields – wildlife amongst them. Just because someone doesn't know the difference between a Dark Green and a Silver Washed Fritillary, or isn't sure where the shutter release is on his new camera, doesn't make him a lower life form. After all, in his "day job", he may well be a brain surgeon or rocket scientist! Beginners, and especially raw beginners, should be encouraged at every turn as their first impressions on entering a hobby, pursuit or pastime are often lasting and can colour their outlook for years to come. I would be mortified if I felt that I ever appeared condescending or patronising and doubly so if I felt that someone had failed to ask a question for fear of appearing foolish.

However, bearing the above in mind and that apart, my advice, such as it is, is geared to those who want to make the most of the photographic opportunity that butterflies offer. I am not sufficiently up to speed on the proliferation of digital equipment now freely available but even if I were I think that my recommendation would still be to go for an SLR with interchangeable lenses. There is a vast amount of information available on this type of equipment from books, magazines, the internet and even from staff in the photographic equipment outlets, so I do not, here, wish to go the route of specific recommendations. Suffice to say I would suggest an SLR with some sort of closeup facility. The ideal, of course, would be a macro lens but if the cost of one of these is daunting then there are many add-on closeup filters available that produce results that are perfectly satisfactory to all but the most discerning and pedantic eye. Added to this would be my recommendation, as mentioned above, to acquire a separate flash unit with a "fill-in flash" facility. This is far more satisfactory than a built-in camera flash as, with a hotshoe extension lead, you can alter the position of the flash unit in relation to the camera to overcome the problems, not only of prevailing light directions, but also of obstacles, such as vegetation between you and the subject, that may cast unwanted shadows. Remember that, unlike with plant photography, in the case of butterfly photography you are not likely to be able to "garden" intruding vegetation out of the way unless you want a "rear ender" view of a butterfly in flight!

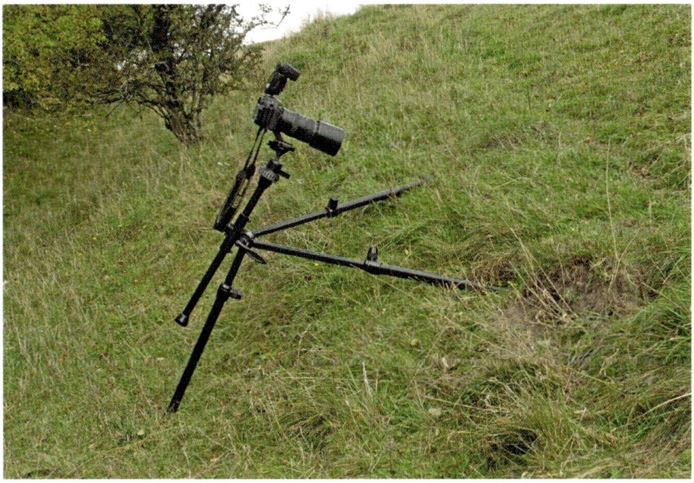

Typical camera and tripod set-up for working rough ground.

Additionally some sort of camera support is of great benefit. Ideal, of course, is a tripod. "Ideal" in theory and "ideal" in practice are sometimes not the best of bedfellows and anyone who has fought a bramble bush with their own two feet, and three more from a tripod to accommodate whilst remaining in "stealthy mode", will appreciate the problem. For species frequenting open grasslands a tripod should be manageable. For other more heavily vegetated habitats, however, a monopod may well be adequate. Whilst it does not prevent camera movement as well as a tripod would do, nevertheless, its potential shortcomings can be put to advantage. Once the monopod foot is in place you can gently sway from front to back to achieve best focus and from left to right to achieve best point of view of what, particularly if it is nectaring, could well be a moving subject, without having to continuously make minor camera adjustments with the consequent potentially alarming hand movements involved.

With the above equipment you should be in a position to go forth and be successful and my only other suggestion would be to take some water and sarnies because once you start following up on a butterfly you can end up miles from base and many hours later without even trying!

Bear in mind, when you finally catch up with your quarry, that a full-spread shot is not the only option to consider. In fact with some species the only upper view that you are likely to get is if you photograph them in flight since they always perch with their wings closed. I well remember in my early days (of photography that is, not of life!) that an acquaintance showed me some stunning close-ups of many species, wings akimbo, almost posing for the camera. Inspired, my own subsequent efforts, by comparison, were undeniably deficient in certain cases and it was not until many years later that I, bolstered by a somewhat enhanced understanding of the subject, got him, loosened up by a certain level of alcoholic input, to admit that, in fact, the Brimstones, Graylings and other species that seldom, if ever, pitch with open wings were dead specimens from a collection which he had carefully placed against a suitable background!

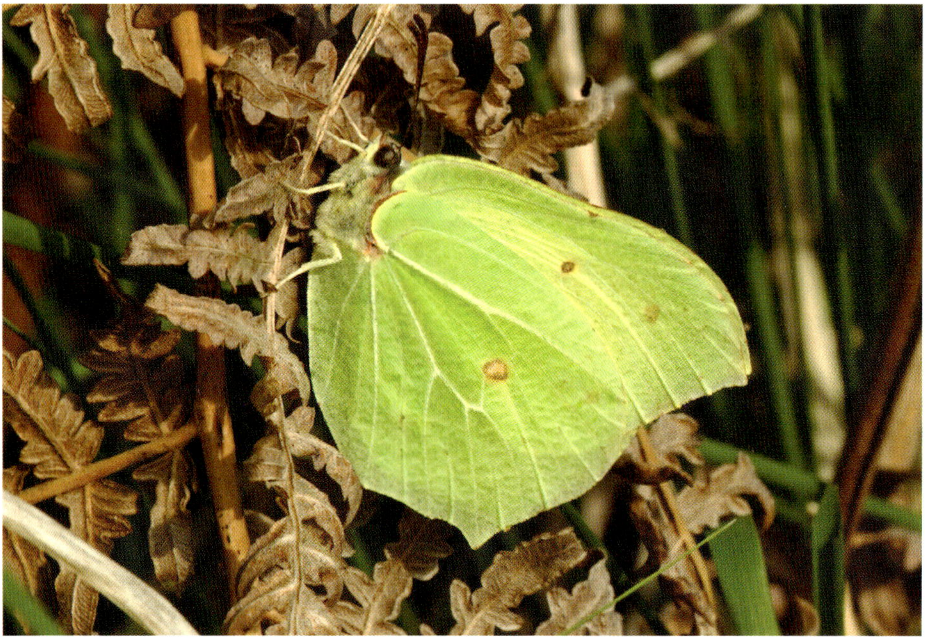

Male Brimstone at rest.

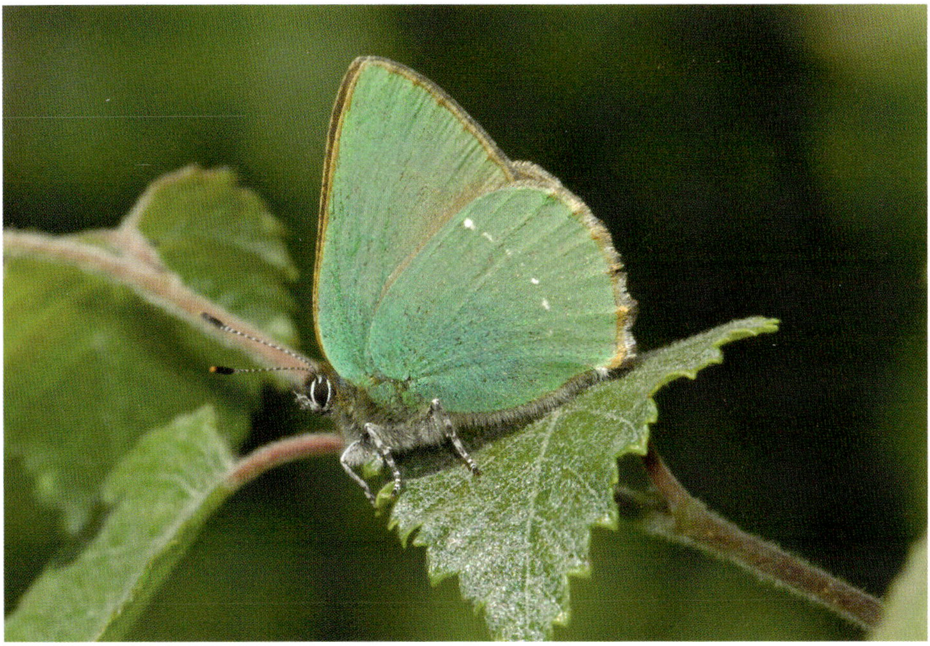

Green Hairstreak.

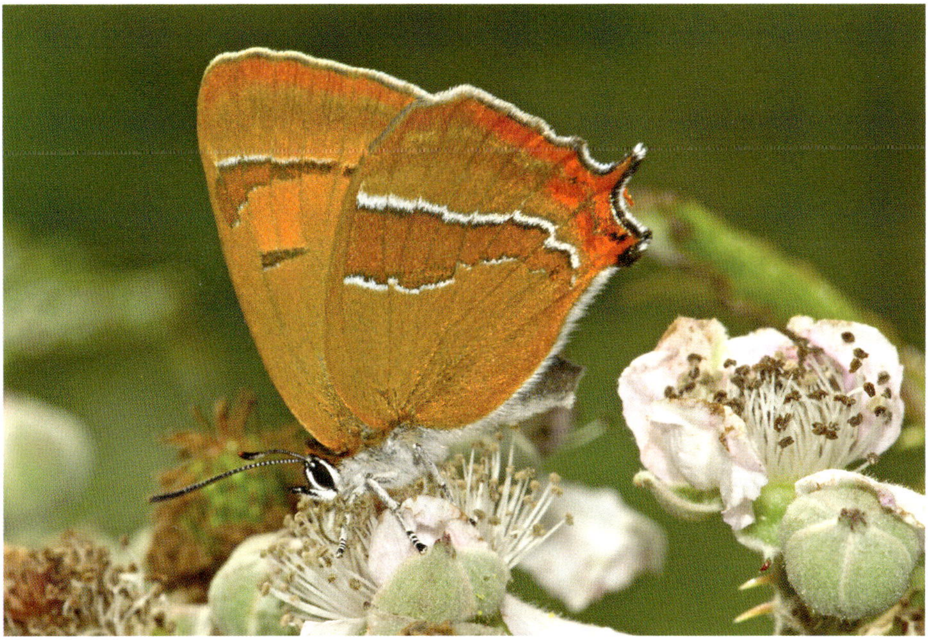

Brown Hairstreak showing "tails".

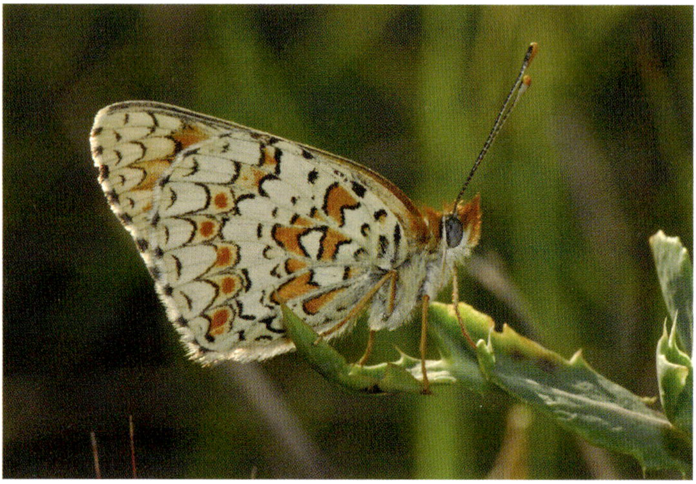

"Ready for bed" - Provencal Fritillary showing it's "better" side.

Many species have an under-wing colouration vastly different but also often as, or even more, attractive than their uppersides. With some species, such as Pearl or Small Pearl Bordered Fritillaries, and often some of the Blues, it is frequently the easiest way to identify them. Photographing the under-side also has the advantage that, with only one wing on view, it is not so difficult to get a dead flat subject. This enables you to use a large aperture setting to divorce your subject from its background. Unfortunately, in practice, you will find that you are able to photograph a dead flat subject far less times than one with raised, or partially raised, wings. In fact some species, such as some of the Skippers, often rest with one or more of their wings raised and angled rather like an aeroplane propeller.

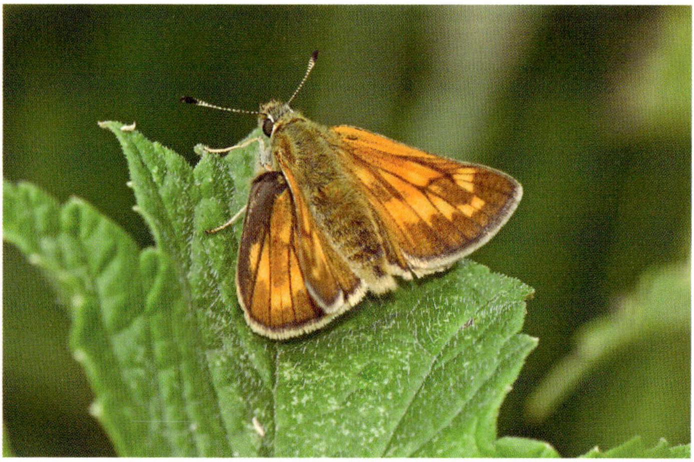

Female Large Skipper.

In the interests of obtaining an all over sharp image, or as near to it as is feasible, you will have to decide on what aperture setting will best suit your circumstances. The situation will seldom, if ever, be perfect but the whole of life seems to be a compromise and photography is no different. This is not the place to delve too deeply into apertures and other settings and I would refer anyone so interested to publications devoted to the subject. Suffice to say that a large aperture (small F stop number) gives a shallow depth of field and lets your subject stand out from its background. In some circumstances this is desirable and a setting of F8 or F11 will probably suffice. A small aperture (high F stop number), however, gives a greater depth of field and so, with butterflies in particular, some of the background vegetation is also likely to be in focus to some extent or other. This can pose problems for some subjects such as, say, a Green Hairstreak in a green bush. Fortunately most butterflies are strongly coloured with clear outlines and should stand out accordingly enabling you to use whatever aperture is necessary to obtain a sharp image. There is no easy rule of thumb that you can apply and my advice is to go out and try it. If opportunity and circumstances permit then bracket your shots. This simply means to take the same shot on a number of different settings. Later, on the computer, you can compare results and learn what setting best suits what circumstance.

As a hitlist of potential shots to aim for per species I would suggest the following possibilities:-

Male, Female, Upperwing, Underwing, Mating, Nectaring, Egglaying, Caterpillars and/or chrysalis.

If that list isn't enough to keep you from having to wander the streets for the sake of something to do for the next few years then I don't know what is!

Have fun.

Chapter 23

Photographing The Dragonflies And Damselflies Of Great Britain

I have made reference in other chapters to the fact that we are fortunate in Britain in having a finite number of species in several sections of our Wildlife diversity. I say fortunate simply because, with a finite and limited number, it is possible for the assiduous to bag a "full house". I think that I have also stated that there seems to be a bit of a collectors instinct in all of us and it often comes into play, albeit uninvited, in wildlife photography. Most of us like to feel some kind of purpose to what we do, even if we exaggerate its importance for no reason other than to justify ourselves to ourselves, and there is no greater incentive than the chance to get "a full set".

To coin a technical phrase Dragonflies and Damselflies come under the order Odonata and are one of those groups of Wildlife that are represented in the UK by between 40 and 60 species. From a photographic point of view this means that, with a little diligence, it should be possible to locate and photograph all of them. The better known groupings that I include here are primarily those that seem to be most appealing to photographers such as Terrestrial Orchids, Dragonflies and Damselflies, Butterflies and Grasshoppers and Bush Crickets. In practice most of us drift into the pursuit and study of any one particular group by accident. Usually you just happen to be in the right place at the right time and manage to get one or two stunning shots of whatever the subject may be. I suspect that most photographers, particularly if they are unsure as to what species they have managed to photograph, then take recourse to some sort of reference literature, if only for identification purposes. Ploughing through details and pictures of associated species frequently sparks an interest and, before you know where you are, life cycles, seasons, prey and predators, foods and foodplants, visible sexual differences and so on begin to rule the day.

Dragonflies as a group pose some photographic problems all their own. You can be one of the most proficient and prolific of photographers and still not get your lens on a particular species. There is a phenomenal amount of luck involved and no degree of knowledge or expertise can guarantee you success. Yes, the research that, as with other branches of wildlife photography you, of necessity, have to undertake can improve your odds. Certainly it will help you to identify and locate potential sites and inform you as to characteristics, habits and behaviour patterns, flight seasons etc. Your research is essential to get you on the right river bank at the right time of year and to know just what to look for when you get there but, unfortunately, it cannot make the creature land in front of you or, indeed, even close to you. Anyone who has patiently watched and waited for a male Emperor to land will tell you that you could be in for a wait of hours. Many dragonflies are tireless in flight and can, and do, feed on the wing and so have no real need to land other than to roost at night – and this is often effected in the treetops just out of reach of your longest lens!

Damselflies are somewhat different since, whilst a particular species may be rare overall, nevertheless, where it does occur it normally does so in some quantity. Most are not as strong on the wing as dragonflies and, in breezy conditions and at roosting time, can be found in tall grasses and low growing shrubs and bushes, thus greatly improving your chances of up to lifesize images. They are also fairly approachable with a reasonable degree of care and often stay in one particular spot long enough to allow a "good old photoshoot" covering all your options at some degree of leisure.

Many of the smaller dragonfly species such as Skimmers, Chasers and Darters are also photographable with a reasonable guarantee of success if approached properly but the larger Hawkers are "something else".

One of the advantages of tackling these groups of insects is that any body of water that supports one species is also likely to be supporting others. This, at least, provides you with another option if your particular target species is proving uncooperative. Not many Odonata trips pass without you getting your lens on something even if it wasn't the object of your desires.

I shall deal with them group by group since different rules and techniques apply. Common to them all is the equipment required which is much the same as that which I have discussed in some detail, in the section covering butterfly photography, elsewhere in this book. Basically you will need a decent closeup capability, a flash unit with a fill flash facility and either a tripod or a monopod for support. In addition, and differently to butterflies, in this case wellies or waders would be a smart move. A change of socks and underwear might also be a good idea. I have often been unexpectedly forced to strip to my underpants and wade in to get "up close" to some elusive subject. I would not recommend this in some tropical climes but, in the UK, apart from the danger of stepping on a broken bottle or a dumped supermarket trolley, at least there is not much that might eat or swim off with you lurking about and so, from that point of view, you can wade out in many waters relatively safely bearing in mind strong currents and glutinous muddy bottoms. Gravel pits and other steep sided bodies of water should be treated with care and I would never advise anyone to enter any water, however shallow seeming it may be, unless you can swim and certainly have someone with you.

I appreciate that this "elf 'n safety" advice may seem unnecessary but you can all too easily find that the photographic equivalent of "Berserkers Rage" can come over you, when all thoughts of personal safety are cast to the four winds. It is normally triggered when the finest specimen known to man of an elusive species, which you have been arduously pursuing for years, suddenly lands on some rushes out in the water. Close enough to see in all its glory as it takes the sun, but just beyond the reach of that lens for which you paid a fortune! I can assure you that in this situation it's "Bob's your uncle, Sally's your aunt, off with the pants and into the water" without so much as a backward glance or a second thought. I speak as one who has been there and has a drawerful of T shirts to show for it. I would quite happily eat grass and say Moo in a field full of bulls if I thought that would get me a shot of some new Orchid species that had chosen to grow there. For many of us it is probably true that the thrill of the hunt is, to a large extent, in the chase and can lead to a determined intent to "take the shot" at risk of any threat to life and limb. It is very easy to become overfocussed on the subject at hand to the point of being oblivious to all around you. This can be an invitation to disaster, especially in places like Africa where I have recently spent so much time. Whilst your attention is directed at the cute cub in front of you its mother and father can be tossing a coin just behind you to see who gets first crack at your juicy bits!

Damselflies, although diminutive in size compared to their larger cousins, are, nevertheless, normally approachable to such an extent that their stature becomes irrelevant in view of how close you can get. The main disadvantage of their size is in being able to distinguish the various species at any kind of distance. Here, and also in the case of grasshoppers and some butterflies, a pair of close-focussing binoculars are a tremendous help. The best I ever had for this was a pair of Pentax 8 x 25 x 6.2. Generally speaking the males are not too difficult to identify being much more colourful than the often drab and very similarly coloured females. The area of greatest confusion probably lies with the group of Coenagrion species. In these the males all have very similarly coloured bright blue and black bodies. Whilst the mix of blue and black markings does differ from one species to another they can be somewhat variable individually, to the extent of causing an overlap of patterning with other species. In any event the difference between species at a distance is probably only discernible to the most highly trained of naked eyes. I like to kid myself that I can identify most of them at a glance but I frequently get caught out. The easiest way to differentiate between them is by study of the small black "mercury mark" that appears on segment 2 of the abdomen and which differs – though not always greatly - from one species to another. I would suggest, however, that in many circumstances , particularly in dense vegetation and in low light , if you are going to go for this mark as your main means of identification then binoculars or a hand lens will be essential as your naked eye will not be good enough. One of the advantages of the closeness at which you can photograph these insects is that, with a decent closeup lens, and especially with the zooming potential of digital images, you can take head and shoulder shots that will display this feature clearly. I have recommended below two books which have proved invaluable to me. For identification of potential sites and details of insects, larvae, habitats etc then I would suggest that if you are serious about photographing Odonata then make an effort to obtain the two books, read, mark, learn and inwardly digest their content, and then get out there amongst it and give your newfound knowledge an airing!

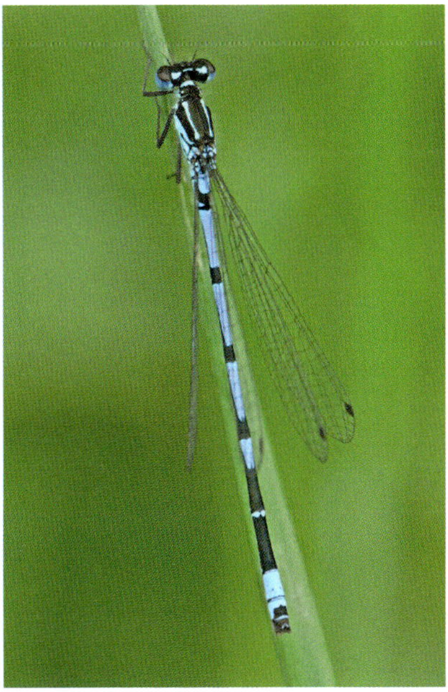

Male Variable Damselfly showing "mercury Mark"

From a practical photographing point of view all the damselfly species can be treated more or less the same. Even in favourable conditions they are nowhere near as active as are most of the dragonflies. Normally their movements are restricted to short flights from one bush to another within fairly confined areas. They are relatively low flying and do not spook too easily. I find it pays to keep down low to avoid your body blocking out the skyline and so you can expect to spend an amount of time on your knees. You will be kneeling in many and varied unmentionables so either wear kneepads or be prepared to get your trousers, that will never look the same again, wet and mucky!

Most damselflies, at rest, fold their wings back along their bodies with the possible exception of the Lestes species which normally, but not always, hold them out at right angles. The two main points of focus that it is absolutely essential to have sharp if you are to be pleased with your close-ups – and here I would say that unless you are prepared to put in the time and trouble to obtain close-ups then, with damselflies, you are wasting your time – are the near eye and the genital region of the abdomen. If you can get both these sharp in the viewfinder then all points in between will normally be sharp as well, including those wings that are lying along the body.

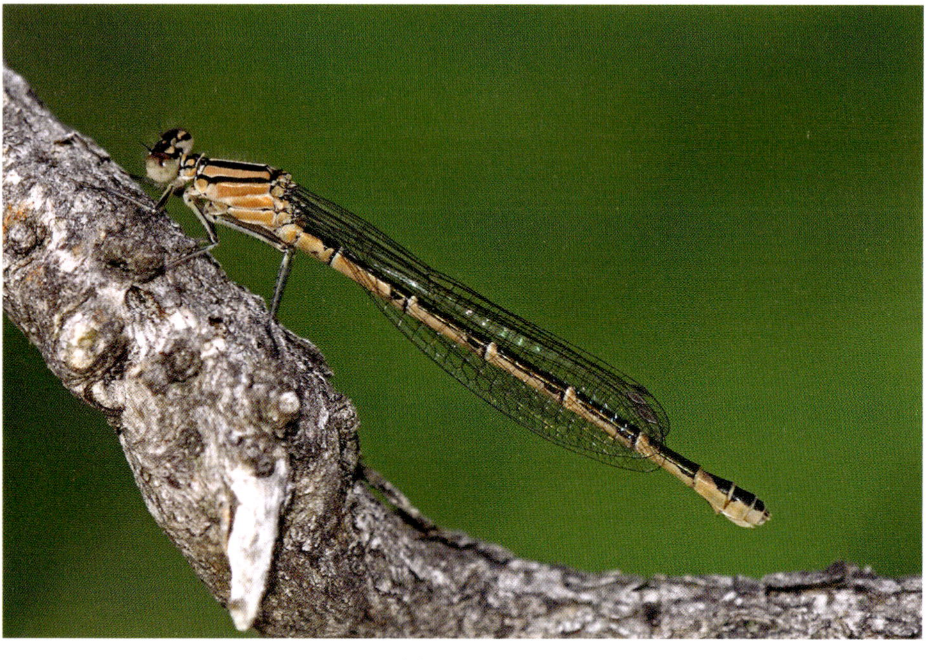

Brown colour form of female Common Blue Damselfly

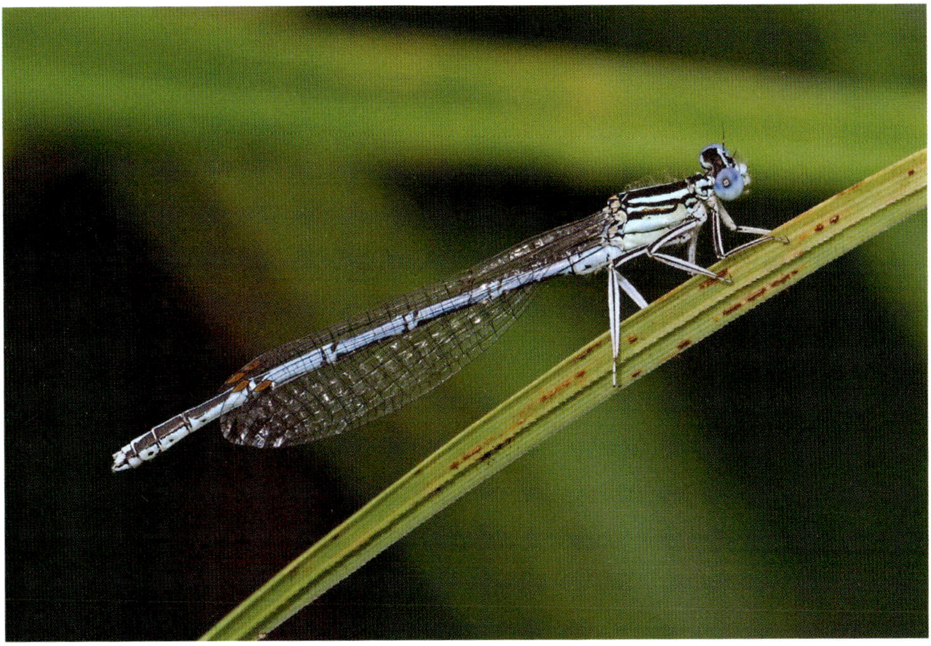

Male White Legged Damselfly.

I normally work on damselflies with a maximum aperture of F8 but go down as far as F22 on occasion especially if there is no foliage in the near background. If I had to choose only one aperture at which to work it would be F11. If you are working at, or near, lifesize you need to be very accurate in your focussing and it will take some wriggling round to get both yourself and your camera in position. Beware the deceptive eye! This is not always as easy to focus on as you would think. Damselfly eyes are a little like translucent goldfish bowls, with no hard and clear surface on which your own eye can easily focus – unlike with most dragonfly eyes. You will have to move your focus backwards and forwards a bit until you find the optimum position.

Once you have developed a technique that gives you satisfactory results you can stick with it and apply it to virtually all the damselfly species

Other than transitional colour changes from juvenile to adult, male damselflies normally occur in only one colour form with occasional, but very minor, variation. Females of some species, however, in addition to the transitional juvenile to adult variations, can occur in a number of adult colour forms which makes for an identification nightmare but certainly adds excitement to the chase, especially if you are determined to photograph them all.

Skimmers, Chasers and Darters I will lump together since, from a photographic point of view they exhibit similar characteristics. They all tend to occupy low level perches, skimmers even preferring to perch on the ground, and seem to have favourite spots to which they repeatedly return. If you stand back on a site and quietly watch you should be able to identify some of these places and slowly move in accordingly. Provided you use a cautious approach you can often get your lens within two to three feet, or even closer, without too much trouble. If the insect zips off during your approach be patient as it will probably return. Looking like a rock or a tree would help but if your best impressions of these leave a little to be desired then you can certainly help by wearing subdued and non-flappy clothing and restraining any natural exuberance between shots!

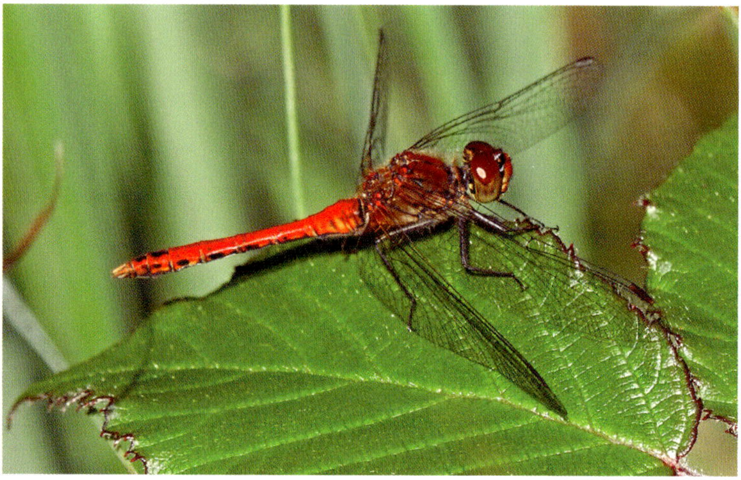

Male Ruddy Darter showing "propellor-like" wing position.

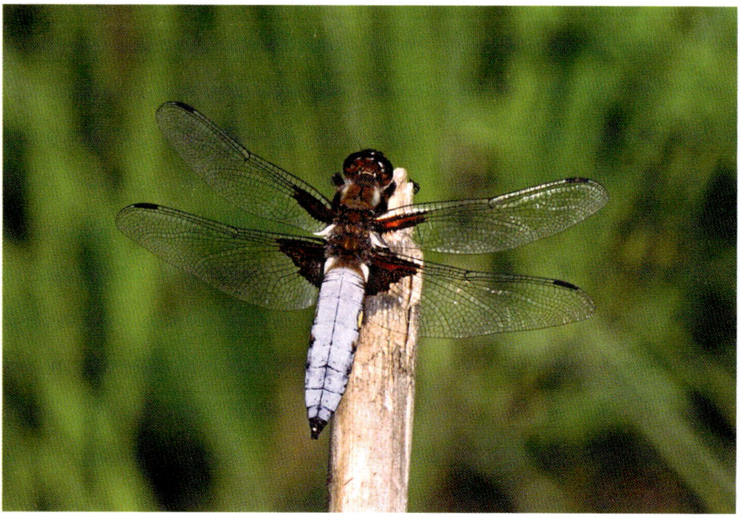

Male Broad Bodied Chaser in New Forest.

Not unlike the damselflies, often, where these species occur, they do so in reasonable numbers and so, with patience, you should be able, assuming that you have done your site homework, to locate and photograph all the species. There is one significant difference between them and damselflies that it is as well to point out. Dragonflies do not fold their wings in along their bodies. This means that, if photographing from the side, no equipment that I know of is physically capable of getting the body and both sets of wings all in focus since the subject depth, from wingtip to wingtip, is far too great. Occasionally they may twist towards you in the wind, or in response to a close approach by another dragonfly, but this is a flukey chance and cannot be anticipated. With these side shots I am afraid that you will have to accept that the wings will not be in focus, and so make doubly sure that you get the body bang to rights to compensate. Whilst chasers normally hold both pairs of wings out flat they sometimes, and darters and skimmers frequently so, twist their wings like an aeroplane propeller. If the wings are flat then a shot from dead above or behind can give you an overall sharp image but if the wings are twisted then you will have to compromise. Actually it is no compromise because you cannot afford to have the body anything other than sharp and so you will have to settle for whatever depth of field your aperture setting allows you on the wings. Again bracket your shots if you have the chance, and choose those that are most pleasing to your eye. If you do get the opportunity for a flatwing shot then try to work on as large an aperture (low F-stop no) as you can get away with as this will emphasise the venation of the wings, which can often be quite beautiful, and divorce them as much as possible from the background. Heathland acid pool species often perch on heather or bracken and in these cases you may have to settle for a shot where the wings may be barely visible against their background. Use of your fill flash facility will help to highlight the wings and emphasise colours without creating the black backgrounds that you can get when using full flash. Beware the wings, however, as at certain angles they can be very reflective. If you are operating on a sunny day and the wings are already reflecting sunlight when looked at through your viewfinder, then I would turn your flash unit off or you will just make matters worse – well no-one said it would be easy!

The larger Hawkers are in a class all of their own. The best that you can hope for with them is to locate potential sites and go there as often as possible with fingers crossed. Other than Goldrings, which perch relatively frequently and seem, with care, to be semi-approachable, most of them are very skittish and if you are lucky enough to "get on one" then make the most of it while you can since it probably won't give you much of its time unless you have been lucky enough to find one roosting or having a siesta. I cannot offer any more constructive advice where the hawkers are concerned and can only wish you the luck I would wish myself in the same circumstances.

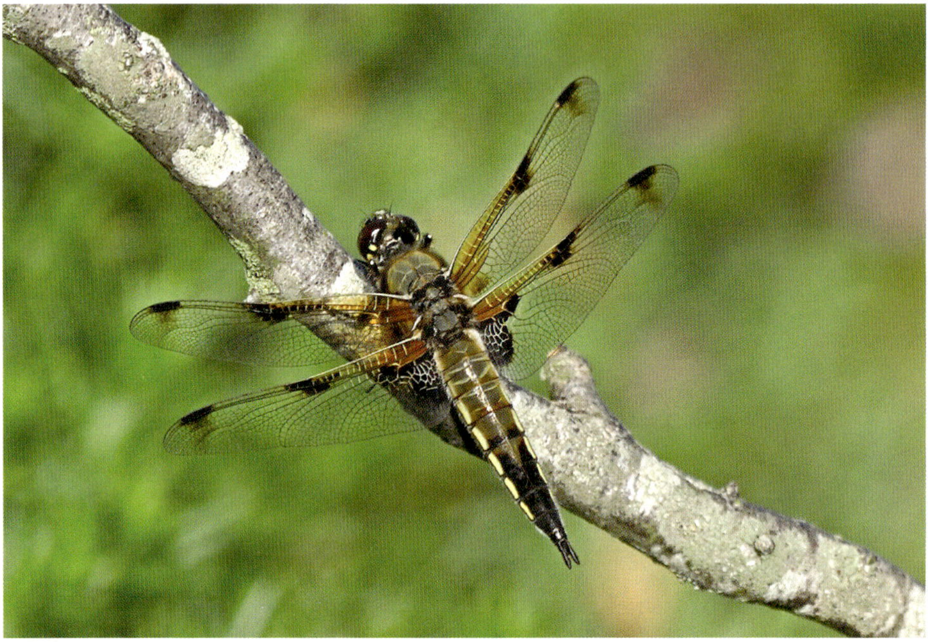

Four Spotted Chaser at Studland.

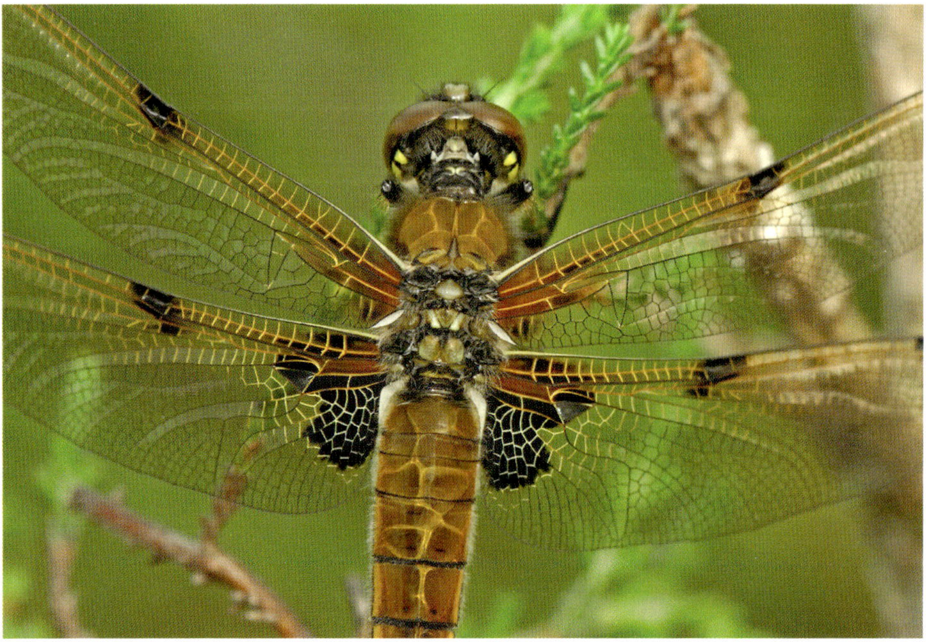

Close-up of Four Spotted Chaser to highlight wing venation.

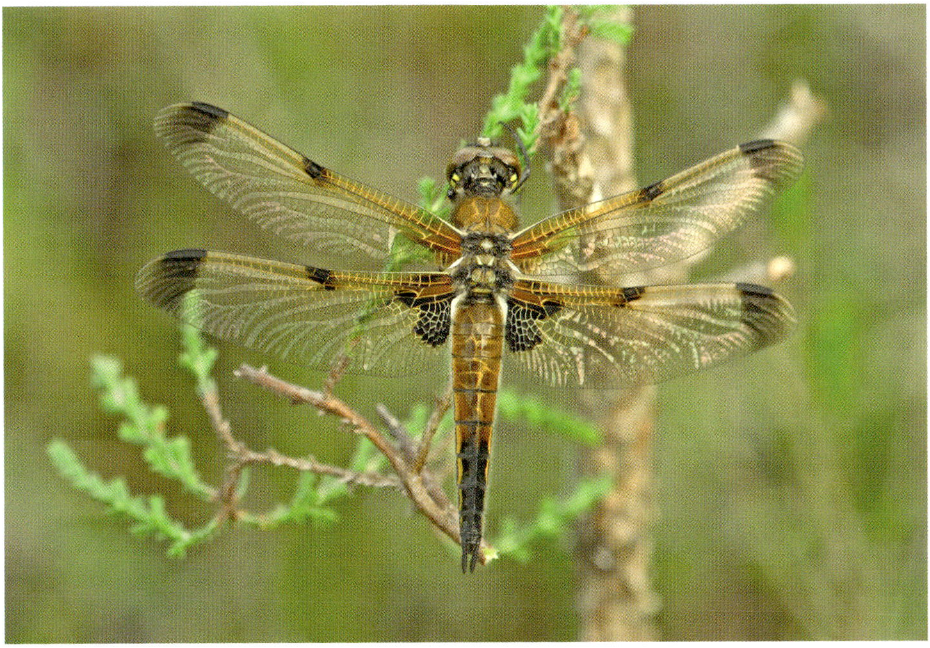

Four Spotted Chaser taken at F8.

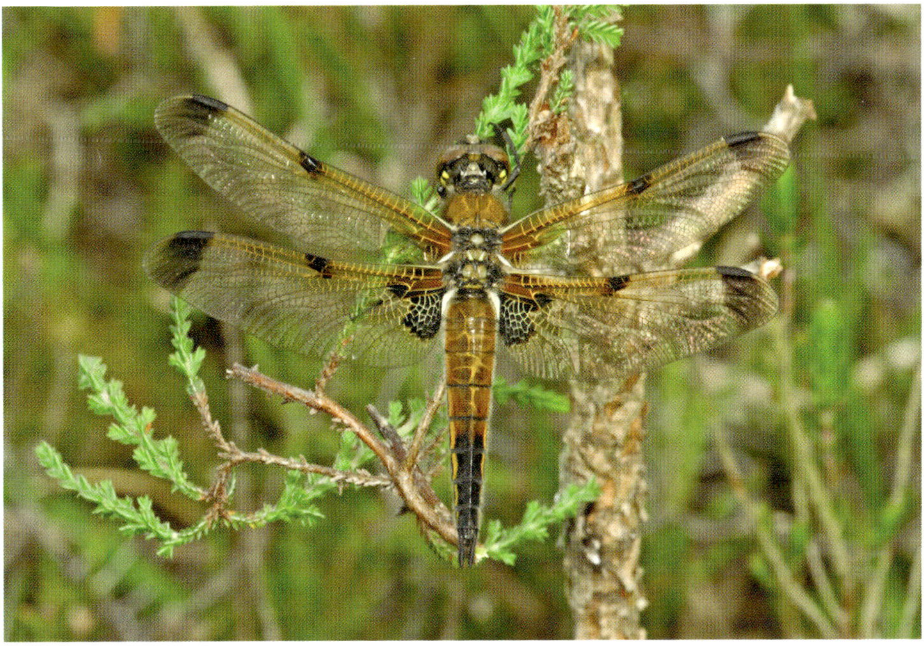

Same shot Four Spotted Chaser taken at F25.

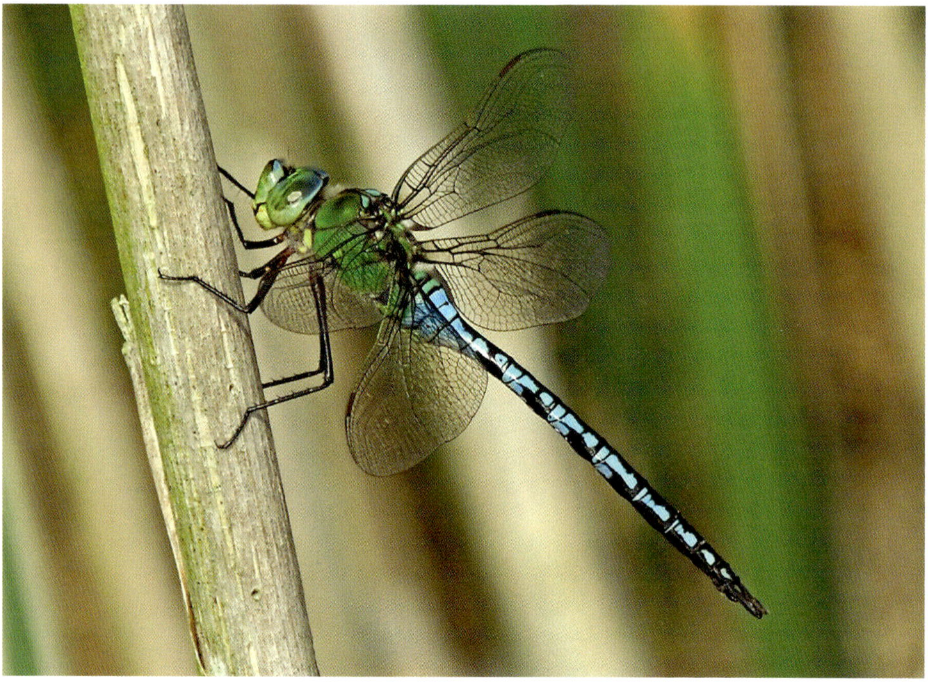

Male Emperor Dragonfly at Wimborne.

The two books that I mentioned are as follows

The Dragonflies of Great Britain and Ireland by C.O.Hammond published by Harley Books ISBN 0-946589-14-3.

Field Guide to the Dragonflies and Damselflies of Great Britain and Ireland by Steve Brooks published by British Wildlife Publishing ISBN 0-953-13990-5

Both the above are absolute "must haves" so do try to get them. Happy hunting and don't get too wet.

Chapter 24

Photographing Grasshoppers And Bush Crickets (Orthoptera)

Whilst this was my own first love it was, nevertheless, many years before I mastered the art of obtaining life size images of something that can not only be as small as half an inch in length but is highly mobile to boot. As with virtually all Wildlife Photography the answers lie in studying the subject. Some grasshopper species are fully winged, some short winged and some have only vestigial wings so that their flying ability varies from species to species. They do, however, have one thing in common and that is the ability to make prodigious leaps. This ability often seems telepathically linked to the forward movement of your shutter release finger! Fortunately, once you are psyched into Grasshopper mode there are many steps you can take to circumvent the disappointment of obtaining perfectly exposed and focussed shots of the perch where a grasshopper "was" when you started to take the shot and "wasn't" by the time that you finished!

Firstly I cannot stress too strongly the importance of separating the subject from its background. The principal role in life of the average grasshopper is to become lunch for one of its many predators. In order to "delay the evil day" as long as possible then, in addition to their acrobatic ability, they have become past masters at the art of camouflage. Most species, particularly those resident in the UK, occur in a variety of colour forms. This characteristic not only hopefully "prolongs their active life" but, inadvertently and coincidentally, makes identifying the various species a nightmare for the newcomer.

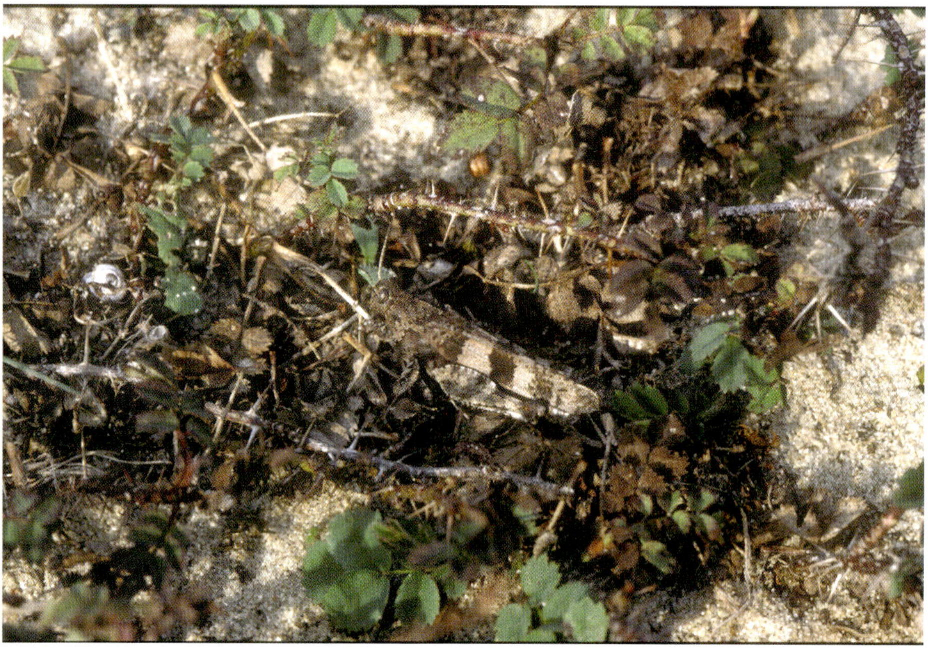

Blue Winged Grashopper showing camouflage effect of body colouring.

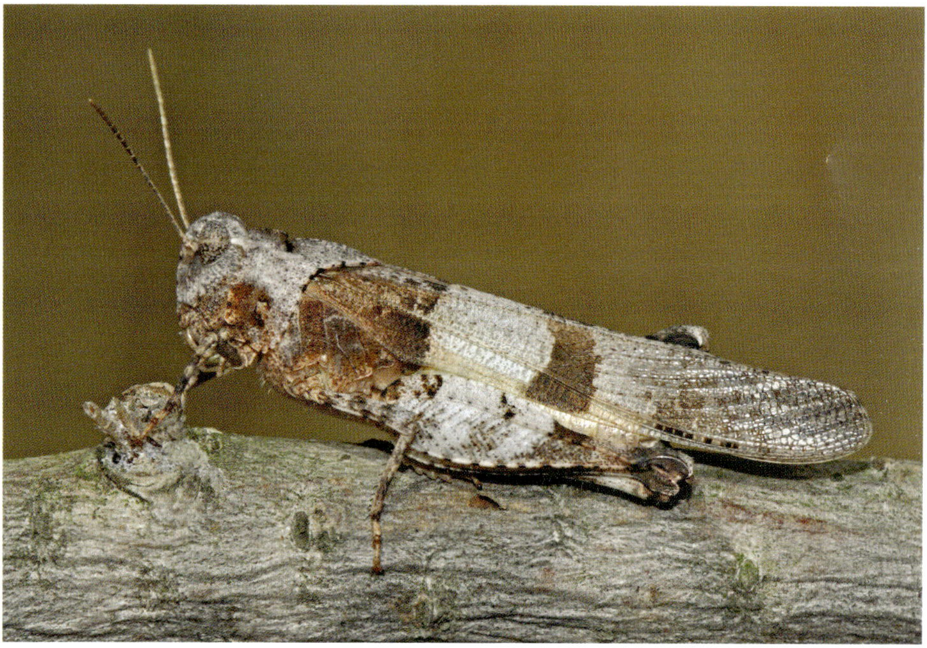

Blue Winged Grasshopper in the field but "set-up" on a twig.

It is uncanny how many times you will find that species such as Meadow or Mottled tend to be green in areas of green vegetation, brown in areas of brown and a mixed combination of the two in those areas where the vegetation is either mixed in colour or occurs in varied patches. To further confuse the issue many of them have purple based colour forms, seemingly in most locations, and occur in dark to even black forms in areas where there has been a recent fire. They do not have the ability to change colour in the way that a Chameleon does, for example, but certainly seem to have the ability to somehow adapt during their life cycle. I have read much theoretical gobbledygook on this subject and, whilst I can believe that someone, somewhere, may have solved the conundrum as to how they achieve it, I have never read a convincing explanation yet. Certainly I have photographed black forms in burnt areas in the same year as the fire in question which would lead one to suppose that the colour change occurs during their current annual life cycle and is not predetermined. It could well be achieved, as has been suggested more than once, by ingesting additional quantities of various minerals or other substances to effect the change. On the other hand it could simply be that they hatch in mixed colours like a packet of Smarties and those that are best matched to the environment are the ones that survive long enough to have their pictures taken. I know not but would be pleased to receive any learned theories.

With this in mind if you try to photograph grasshoppers sitting in, or surrounded by, their natural background then, no matter how much you think they stand out when seen through your view finder, you will find, when you process your shots, that you cannot, so to speak, "see the wood for the trees". The effect of this is that it will quickly become obvious that you have to somehow divorce the subject from its background. This is obviously somewhat easier said than done.

Firstly grasshoppers are far more active on a hot day or in the middle of the day than they are either in cold weather or in the early mornings or late evenings of a nice summer's day. Most of the UK species become adult from late June onwards and most of those that have not become "haute cuisine" in the meantime nevertheless join the ranks of the "dearly departed" sometime in October and certainly by November. By and large they hatch from eggs, laid either underground or into vegetation, from late March through to as late as June depending on species and weather. After hatching the immature grasshopper resembles a mini version of its adult form. It then goes through a succession of instars and ecdysis or "moults" during which it casts its outer layer, or exoskeleton, allowing it to grow larger in its next instar, or stage of development, until becoming adult.

It does not make the best of photographic subjects in its earlier instars, not only because of its diminutive size, but also because, whilst most literature on the subject states that a juvenile closely resembles its adult form, this resemblance must, no doubt, be more discernible to another grasshopper than it is to we photographers. Identification of juveniles or "hoppers" can be a nightmare for even experienced "Orthopterists" as we students of the grasshopper kingdom are known. My advice is to leave well alone until July and August by which time they've "got some meat on 'em".

The common concept of grasshoppers is that they are little green things always hopping about. Both assumptions are wrong. Whilst it is, in fact, true that they do hop they are, on the whole, highly colourful. This hopping, however, seems to be a mechanism primarily for flight and not for locomotion. They normally move around by crawling on their front four legs and are not, generally speaking, in a hurry to get anywhere. Yes they leap about when you walk through the grass but this is mainly to get out of your way. A factor often overlooked is that many of them are only good for two or three hops before the grasshopper version of cramp sets in. A symptom of this is that both the hind legs stick out backwards and can play no further part in their locomotion until time effects a cure. The functionally winged species can still fly of course but the others become "grounded". Grasshoppers should not be hounded to this extent since, not only are they not very photogenic in this state but additionally, as Wildlife Photographers, you have to develop a strict moral code of conduct, one aspect of which is that you should never knowingly cause undue stress to your subject. I state "undue stress" here because most prey species, of which grasshoppers are one, live lives continuously subject to "normal stresses" and I do not believe this has a necessarily deleterious effect on their well being. Certainly those caught after a brief chase and subsequently released show little or no ill effect and are often sunning or eating within seconds of being released or an abortive chase abandoned.

Do not make the mistake of anthropomorphising, or ascribing human thoughts, responses, sentiments and aspirations to your subjects because they do not work that way. Most forms of wildlife fill their lives with two preoccupations – eating and reproducing – and they should be allowed to continue to do both unhampered as befits their rights to life as they know it, and your personal code needs to develop along lines that allows this to happen.

The trick is to get them to accept you as no source of threat. This is actually much easier than it seems. If you go grasshoppering in the cooler periods it is odds on that your body temperature will exceed the ambient temperature of the surroundings. With this in mind if, by fair means, you can

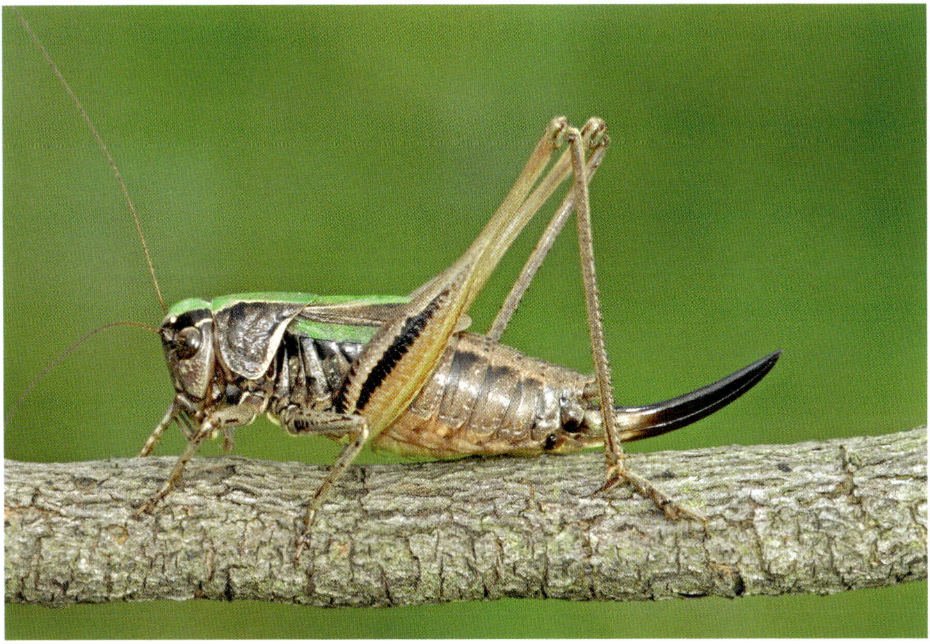

Female Bog Bush Cricket of the green form.

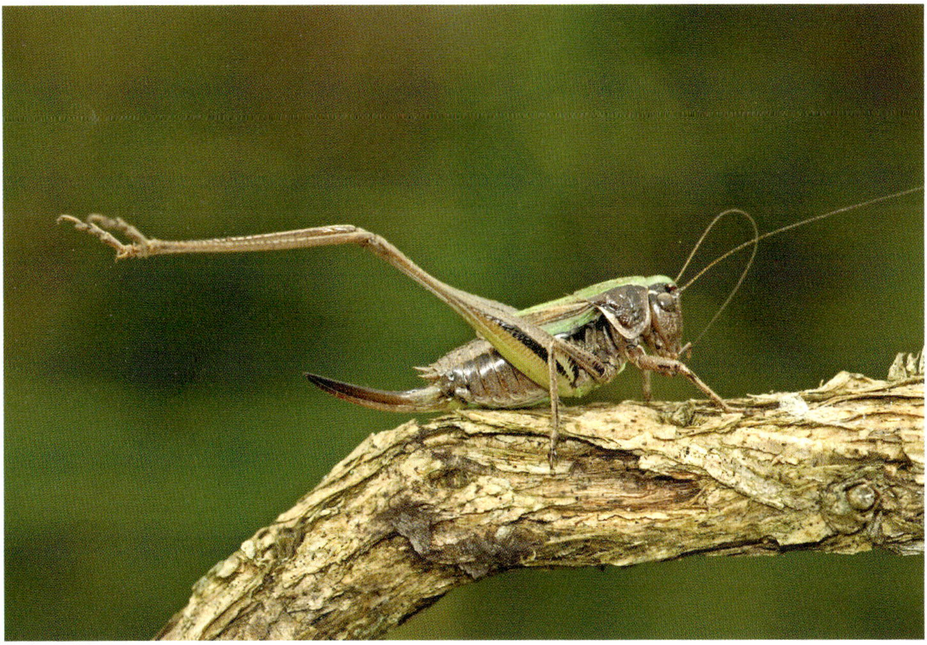

Female Bog Bush Cricket showing effects of "cramp".

get the insect onto your hand and keep it there, (probably best by cupping your hands,) long enough for it realise that you are not, in fact, a threat then you will probably find that it will prefer to stay on your hand, hot and sweaty though it may be, rather than waving around on some windblown grass stem. Often, and the colder it is the better, you will find that if you approach the insect slowly with your finger it will accept it as a heat source rather than a threat and obligingly hop on board. and it is then a straightforward matter to transfer it carefully to a suitable perch where, providing you look sharp, you should have chance to take your photos before it decides to move on.

Failing the above you may need to catch it and this is where the potential controversy begins. However you decide to do it, it must be done quickly to avoid over stressing. You might initially think that a net is the answer but you need to be very careful with these. Grasshoppers tend to be well supplied with "prickly bits", particularly on the back of the legs, and these tend to get caught up in netting. If you have to forcibly disentangle the insect there is always the chance of harming it not to mention the fact that it will subsequently have "the wind up" to such an extent that you are not likely to get much co-operation from it on the photographic front. I have always found that the easiest and least stressful is to use an insect catching pot. This is simply a small clear plastic pot that can be gently placed over the insect almost without it realising. Small glass jars will do but are heavy and fragile to carry. Additionally you are more at risk than normal of falling or tripping over when leaping about enthusiastically in the country and it is not best practice to fall over with your pockets stuffed with glass containers however robust you may feel they are. Some of the proprietary pots that are sold for picnicking and are designed to take small things like salt or mustard or whatever will do. Failing the availability of an economical alternative one of the Scientific Equipment suppliers such as Watkins and Doncaster will be able to fill the bill.

Having got your insect in your pot you then need to get it used to your hand. This is best achieved by replacing the pot lid with your hand and allowing the insect time to come to terms with it. Hold the pot upside down in your hand and allow the insect to slide down the side onto your palm. After an initial couple of instinctive hops inside the pot it will almost invariably settle down and you can then gently remove the pot and place the insect onto a perch. It is a great help if you prepare a suitably photogenic perch in advance so that you do not waste time looking for one when you should be keeping your eye on your subject.

Your choice of a suitable perch is actually quite important if you want to get those world beating shots. I prefer to have my images at an angle of some 30 ish degrees rather than dead horizontal or vertical. Fortunately I have a tripod bush on my 200 mm macro lens, which is my weapon of choice for grasshoppers, and so I can adjust the tilt of the lens to achieve the desired angle with a minimum of effort. For anyone without that advantage it is much easier to position the perch at the correct angle in the first place. This means that your subject will end up perching on top of it. I know you often see grasshoppers, and other insects such as Butterflies, hanging vertically from very slender grass stems but bear in mind that, even for yourself, it is much easier to hang from a thin vertical rope than it is to lie or balance on a horizontal one. Just so for the grasshopper so make sure that you select a twig or stick of sufficient thickness to enable it to perch comfortably or it will "op orf" in double quick time. Try to select one that complements the colour of the insect as it will feel happier to stay put if it is "colour co-ordinated". Choose one without side leaves or branches or invariably, "sod's law" being what it is, then it will be behind one of these that your subject chooses to squat. Something about three feet long should be ideal and enable you to work far enough above ground to avoid having to lie in the mud or "doing your back in".. Stick it in the ground at the required angle about a foot from a suitably coloured background and at right angles to the sun – if there is any about. Remember that to obtain an image of satisfactory size you will be working in close, and at some magnification, so that detail of your background 12ins or more away will become blurred and not intrude into your shot. At right angles to the sun is also important as this is the position a grasshopper will normally assume at rest. When you transfer your quiescent charge to its new "des res" it will normally adopt a rest or sunning position at right angles to whatever source of ambient light there is. This manifests itself by the insect lowering the hind leg nearest the sun to expose its abdomen to the maximum amount of warmth and raising the other back leg above the abdomen so that it, too, can benefit from some "rays". This position actually exposes the absolute maximum amount of body surface to the sun's warmth. Beware! On a sunny day the average grasshopper abdomen could teach a mirror maker something about reflective properties. I must admit that this is a problem to which I have not, as yet, found a satisfactory answer.

Depending on your closeup capability I would always suggest that you try for as frame filling a shot as possible. This will often involve 1:1 size ratio and maybe more. I know that you can, with digital, take a more distant shot and then crop in to suit but you can't beat "the real thing". The problem with relying on a crop to create your "head and shoulder" type close-ups is that your eye, or most people's anyway, is not reliable enough to depend on when taking shots that, in view of subject size, may be relatively distant. You will not be able to be certain that all your relevant points are equally in focus.

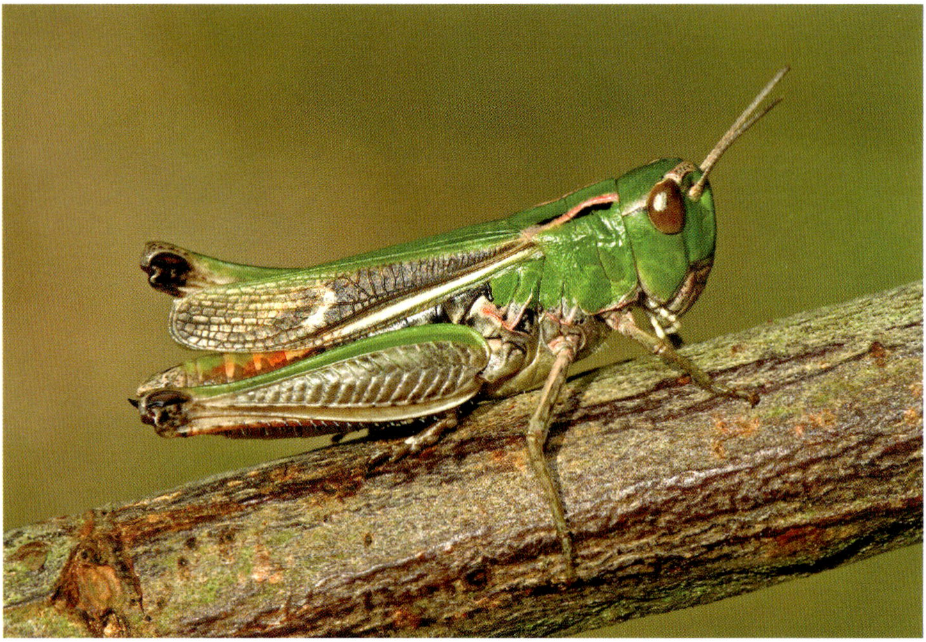

Stripe Winged Grasshopper.

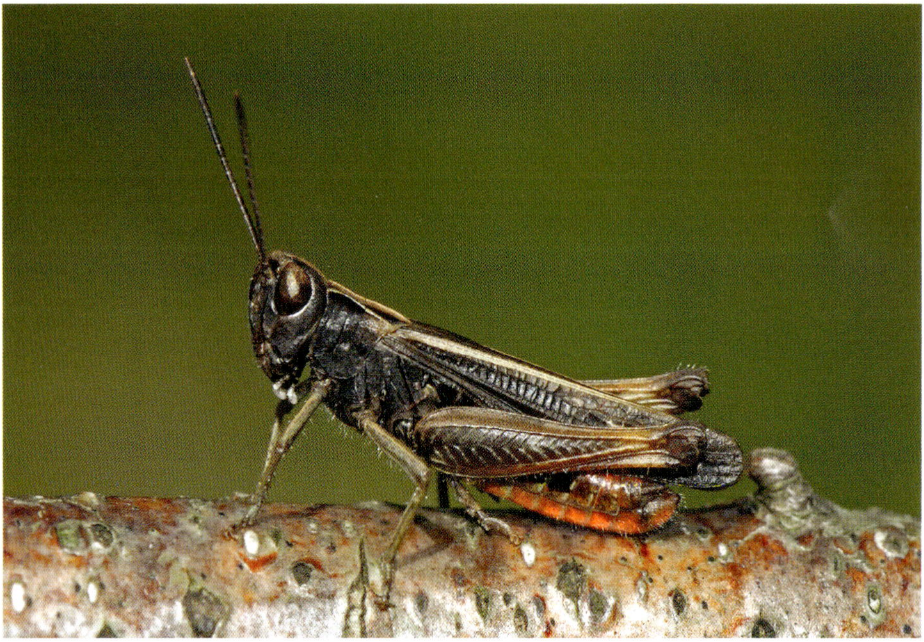

Male Woodland Grasshopper.

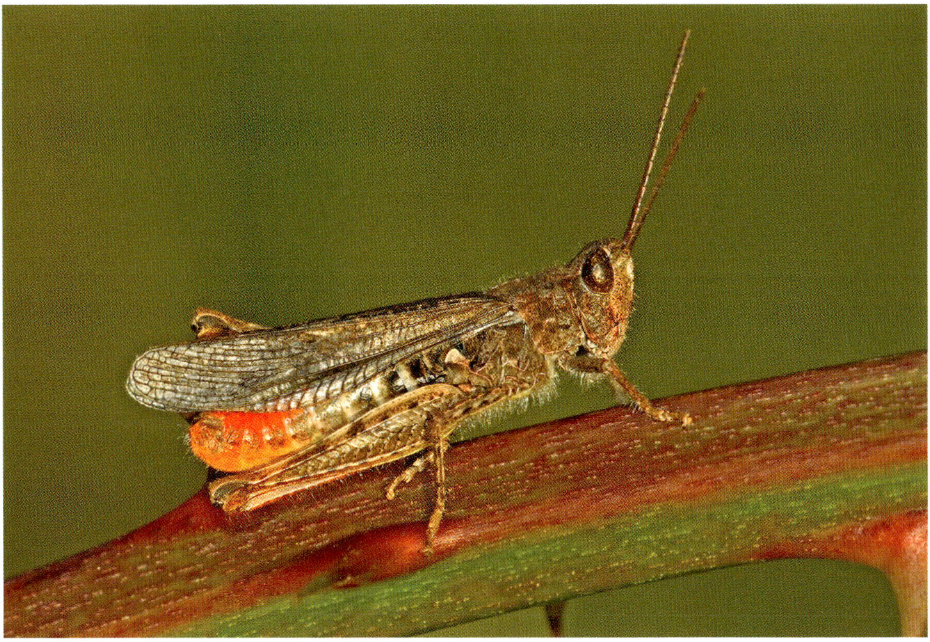

Male Field Grass Hopper showing flare.

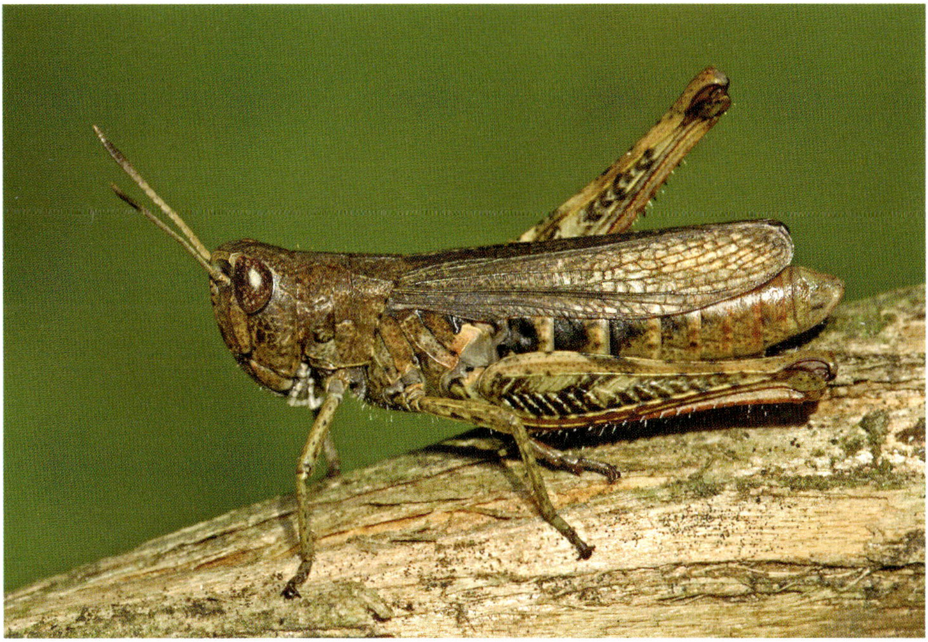

Female Rufous Grass Hopper in typical "sunning" position

Macro photography is a very demanding pursuit and does not suffer fools, or those who think they know best, gladly. Your eye will often mislead you into thinking that all is sharp and well and this delusion will buoy you up until you subsequently apply your mega crop. You only need to be a tad out and the effect of cropping will accentuate every focussing blemish. To get a complete grasshopper's near side fully in focus at life-size is, to all but the best equipment, in any event, near impossible anyway. You will find that, as with most "eyed" wildlife, it is essential, above all else, that the eye be in focus. Unless you are trying for just a front on, or partial sideways, head shot you will need to be square on to your subject. In this position obtaining full focus on the eye is relatively straightforward. I, personally, also prefer to have the abdomen and external genitalia in focus as well. This not only helps in sexual identification but my eye finds it far more pleasing to have the creature fully in focus both "fore and aft". This presents a problem in the form of the nearside hind leg. Working as closely as you will probably have to be, a grasshopper or bush cricket is too thick across its width, where the back leg is positioned, to be able to get eye, abdomen and the nearside of the hind leg all in focus at the same time with most equipment. You will have to compromise and I would suggest bracketing your shots, from a focus point of view, so that you can select the shot that suits you best from amongst several. (My views on bracketing are covered more fully in my article entitled "Modus Operandi".) Species with patterned or textured (ridged patterns are not infrequent) hind legs often demand that greater focussing bias be granted to the legs, especially if the abdomen is pretty bland and uniform, whereas an attractive and coloured abdomen, and especially if you want sharp genitalia, may demand that greater emphasis be placed on those areas. In any event take my advice and take enough shots to give you a choice. Bearing in mind the problems of reflective abdomens, as mentioned in the previous paragraph, bracketing for various exposures will also be to your advantage.

I spend a lot of time photographing in Mediterranean countries where, of course, the sun is not as rare a commodity as it is in the UK. I have tried shading the subject with such as a parasol but you then need some degree of flash to highlight the salient points and this, in turn, creates a reflection of its own. I have tried various filters with which I have seldom obtained good results in closeup. I have also tried crossing my fingers that, despite the evidence being there in the viewfinder, maybe it won't show up, or will be in some way mitigated, when you get the final result. This latter seems to be the most efficacious measure because it at least engenders a feeling of hope, albeit if only until your shots are processed! On a serious note the advent of digital photography and the input of "Mr Adobe" does offer some modern day remedies but make sure that in seeking to dull off the shine you don't end up with an unsightly smudge along an otherwise pristine abdomen!

All the above apart, there are times when grasshoppers are approachable in a natural setting and without any need for work on your part. They live on pretty sorry fare such as grasses and other similarly indigestible and nutrient poor foliage. They, therefore, have to consume an inordinate amount to supply the basic building blocks of life. Following the principle of "what goes up must come down" then, similarly, "what goes in must come out". The consequence of this is that grasshoppers defecate a lot. Not only a lot but it takes them a long time to actually "do it". This is especially true when you are waiting to photograph them without the unsavoury sight of a half emerged foreign object intruding into your composition! Seriously, you may think you can clone this out later, but you will find then that, although you can easily get rid of the evidence itself, you will be left with an unsightly and distended anal area to contend with. In actual fact their abdomens begin to contract quite some time before any visual evidence begins to appear and if you are careful whilst this is going on you will find that you can approach quite closely as they are, naturally, somewhat preoccupied. There will often be a gap between contractions when the abdomen will be still enough to take a shot and, just after completion of the business in hand, and while it is going through the grasshopper equivalent of saying "Phew", you will find that the insect is static and relaxed enough to allow several shots.

Another approachable time is when an insect is "preening" if that be the word when applied to Orthoptera. They spend a fair amount of time cleaning their various moving parts and, whilst preoccupied with this often involved process, you should find that you can approach carefully and get in position for your shot.

Some of my most pleasing shots have been when the subject is "sunning" itself. This has been covered above but when the insect is in this "mode" the position of its limbs does not lend itself to instant flight and a careful approach should get results. Rapid flight or escape is the first unreasoned and purely instinctive reaction of many living things to what could potentially be danger. It works on the basis of "better safe than sorry" and hardly ever involves conscious thought. If you can get beyond the first panic reaction then there is always a chance that, when whatever your subject is has had a chance to collect its thoughts, then it may well accept that you are not, in fact, a threat and, again, a careful approach may well reap rewards.

The above advices apply to practically all the UK Orthoptera with the definite exception of the largest and most attractive of the grasshopper species Stethophema grossum, or the Large Marsh Grasshopper. These were probably used as models when man invented the Harrier Jet! Whilst their flight patterns seem to be directionally random they are quite forceful and can cover 50 to 100 meters in one fell swoop. Add to this the fact that they only seem to inhabit quaking bogs and you will realise that your chances of a productive pursuit are extremely limited. For those not fully conversant with the term "quaking bog" I feel certain that the name must be derived from the feeling that you get in the pit of your stomach as your "welly" disappears through the spaghnum with your leg still in it and no "touching the bottom" in sight.

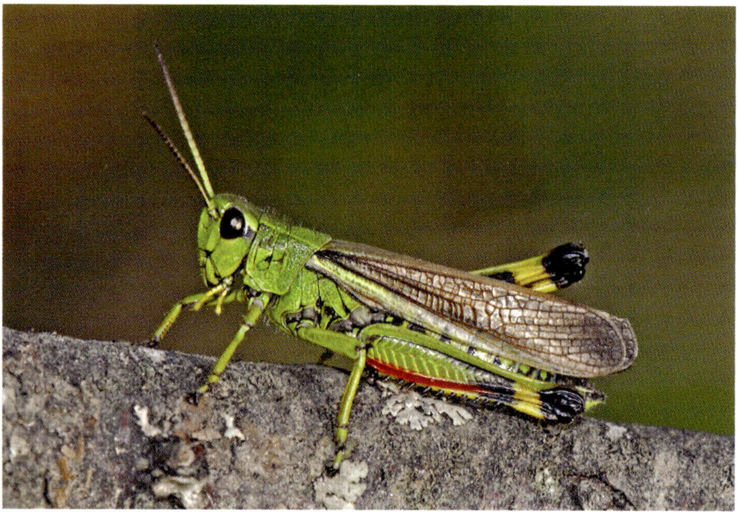

Typical form of male Large Marsh Grasshopper.

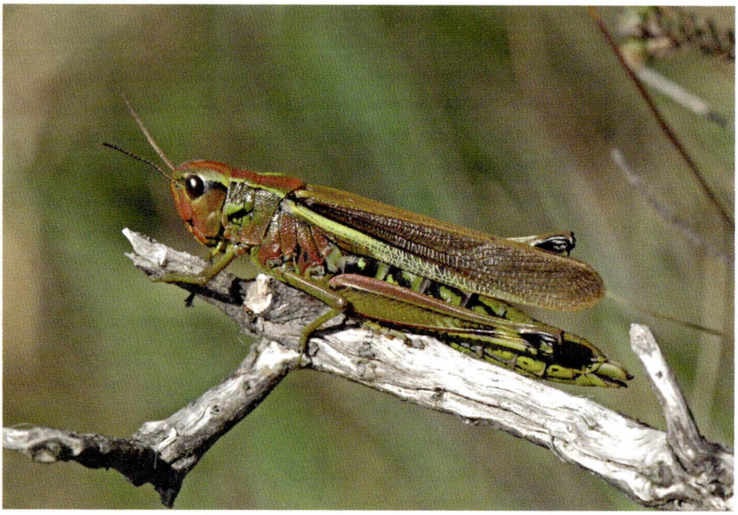

Female Large Marsh Grasshopper.

There are only some twenty odd species of long term resident grasshoppers and bush crickets in the UK and so it is possible, with perseverance, to "bag" them all. However, and this is where Wildlife Awareness and photography need to come together, you will not bump into them all on a convenient street corner. You will really need to do your homework to establish not only identifying features but also preferred habitats and potential sites for those species with a limited distribution. There is little point in spending precious time searching known sites if you are unaware of what the creature looks like. At the same time it is no good being "au fait" with the appearance of, say, the Heath grasshopper if you are going to search for it in Hyde Park since its distribution is so limited that, as far as I am aware, it exists only in East Dorset and West Hants and then only on a very limited number of sites.

You may feel that Orthoptera will be a boring and limited subject that will not demand too large a chunk of your life – but you could be in for a surprise! There may not be that many species, especially in the UK, but those that there are come in a plethora of colour forms. Your target hitlist of shots to be taken can contain headings such as:- Male, Female, Pairs, Juveniles (if you're brave enough to take them on), Mating, Feeding, Preening, "Moulting" and so on. If you aim to cover all, or some, of these headings then you are in for a busy summer and early autumn. Added to which, of course, is that, through a closeup lens, they can be so fascinating and, often, entertaining. Whilst they don't exactly treat you to a "Military Twostep" I do swear some of them definitely seem to wink or wave at you through the lens!!

To those of you who may feel prepared to venture into this realm of really testing Wildlife Photography I would say "Welcome!". To fully equip you for the search your first homework project is to try to obtain copies of the three books that I feel are currently the most helpful on the subject. I am uncertain as to their availability, as one or more may be out of print, but if so then a search via one of the second hand book searching agencies may produce dividends.

These books are:-

Grasshoppers and Allied Insects of Great Britain and Ireland
by Marshall and Hayes.
ISBN 0-946589-36-4 and published by Harley Books.

A Field Guide to the Grasshoppers and Crickets of Britain and
Northern Europe by Heiko Bellman.
ISBN 0-00-219852-5 and published by Collins.

A Photographic Guide to the Grasshoppers and Crickets of Britain and Ireland by Evans and Edmondson.
ISBN 978-0-9549506-1-3
Availability check with www.wildguideuk.com

Your second homework project is to assimilate as much info as possible from these 3 publications and then get out there and try to relate it to those delightful and sadly under recorded species that form the Orthoptera of the UK.

Good hunting!!

Chapter 25

Photographing Reptiles And Amphibians

Fortunately, or unfortunately, depending on your point of view, we are not blessed with too many species under this heading in the UK. Mainland Europe has many more and, of course, some tropical countries are practically awash with them.

Over here we have to settle for two native species of legged lizards, three snakes, a slow-worm or legless lizard and a number of frogs, toads, newts and, more recently, terrapins. Numbers of all these species, but particularly the amphibious ones, can fluctuate as minor introductions from various sources come and go.

The photographing of these species has never been easy, other than on a happenstance basis, unless working with confined subjects. Yes, you can obtain occasional "in habitat" shots with a reasonable zoom lens from practically all of them, but for close-ups it's a different story. Fortunately they all need the sun to warm them up and so early morning forays can turn up semi-torpid specimens eagerly awaiting those beneficial rays. Bear always in mind that, in this country, many wildlife species, including some reptiles, are protected by various laws covering a variety of subjects including handling. Do check the current situation from time to time as headlines in the local rag of "Leading Wildlife Photographer breaks Conservation laws-------" will not serve your reputation too well. (This subject is discussed at greater length towards the end of this chapter).

Keeping clear by two or three metres, after a stealthy approach, will give you the chance to take a succession of shots some of which, if carefully focussed, may be suitable for subsequent cropping in the computer to give you a form of close-up. To achieve any more, however, will require an almost unprecedented amount of stealth in your approach. Your best working altitude will be on hands, knees or belly and, in most cases, it will pay to keep your camera in front of you with something like a beanbag for support. If your stalk is successful you may end up very close to your subject and you will not, then, want to be pulling your equipment out of pockets and back-packs so have it up front and ready for action. Normally tripods and monopods will be out of the question as you will be too low to put them to good use. If you are shooting digital then make sure that there is enough room on your memory card to cover you in case all your dreams come true and you find yourself having gained such a position that an unexpected bonanza of shots is warranted. If you are still using film then make sure that you have as close to a full roll as possible in your camera. You will not want to be changing cards or films if you find yourself eye to eye with a twitchy subject – especially if it is an adder!

I have covered the benefits of fill-in flash elsewhere in this book but feel duty bound to reiterate them here. Reptiles and Amphibians seem to tolerate flash very well and fill-in flash in particular is such a quick, low intensity affair, that you are not likely to scare them off even if using it very close-to. It is a wonderful tool for just lifting the shadows between scales for those species that have them and it emphasises beautifully the often almost sub-cutaneous colours of some of the Amphibians. What it also provides, across the board, is a highlight in the eyes, and this highlight can transform a shot from the merely acceptable to the brilliant. This highlight will often manifest itself as no more than a small white spot in the eye. In this digital age you may feel that you can simulate this with the help of Mr Adobe but I have tried and never really felt that the effect compared with highlights obtained more naturally.

One of the biggest problems with reptiles is the shape of them. By and large they are long and thin and very difficult to fill a frame with. Occasionally you may be lucky enough to find a snake or a slow-worm coiled up which gives you a "lump" as a subject and which should allow reasonably well focussed and frame filling shots. The worst scenario is that your subject may be stretched out, though rarely in a dead straight line, and defying all the laws of lens physics to get both ends and the middle all in focus at the same time. The closer you are, and the more powerful your lens, then the harder it will be. Normally you will have had to select your camera and lens combination before beginning your stalk so you are likely to be stuck with whatever you chose at the outset. My advice is to take a selection of well bracketed shots, from such a distance as to capture the full body length in the frame, on the smallest aperture you can to give you maximum depth of field. Whatever else you do make sure that the eye is sharp and you may then have to leave the rest to chance. This way you will, at least, have some full body shots with varying degrees of success on the sharpness front. As you move in closer you will increase the chances of frightening off your subject but, if the worst comes to the worst and you do so, then at least you will have your insurance shots to fall back on. If the location and angles of the subject are not in your favour then hold your position for as long as the creature will allow you in the hopes that it might move to a better placed situation.

Often it will be possible, if you have managed to get close enough, to get the head and a percentage of the body sharp. Take my word for it, though, that two thirds of a snake or three quarters of a lizard makes a terrible picture. As a general rule of thumb shots of less than 50% of body length will normally prove to be pretty acceptable as they will constitute a "head and shoulders" shot, the dimension ratio of which will satisfy all but the most pedantic of eyes. Anything between 50 and 100%, however, will look quite dreadful as it will be "neither one thing nor the other". Those working digitally can, of course, crop their images down to an aesthetically pleasing length but those still working with film would be well advised to pay particular attention to the body length of their images at point of shoot.

For those of you living within reach of suitable reptile habitat there is another way of gaining access to potential subjects. Firstly try to find an area off the beaten track that seems likely to have reptiles in it. Then see if you can get some pieces of corrugated iron about two feet square. Lay these down in secluded spots (I would suggest placing markers in nearby trees or bushes to make sure that you can find them again), and leave them for a few days. If you can't get corrugated iron then try pieces of plywood, roofing felt or hardboard, though they will not work quite as well since they will not warm up as much. Nevertheless you should still have some degree of success.

You can then periodically check under these "heat pads" for whatever snakes and lizards frequent the area. Make sure that you have your camera set up in advance on a tripod with its flash ready and aperture settings preset (check against surrounding vegetation) since, once you lift the "lid", you will not have very long in which to operate. If you can take a friend along to do the lifting then do so as it will enable you to be poised, eye to view-finder, when the time comes.

In some areas you may come across pieces of tin already laid out for this purpose. They are very likely to be there as part of a herpetological survey. It is probably wishful thinking and highly unlikely that you will be able to resist taking a "quick peep" but if you do, and there is anything there, then leave a note with details of the species, date and time of day under the tin otherwise you may affect the results of the survey by frightening off the reptiles just before the site was due to be checked. Best scenario is to resist the temptation and leave things alone.

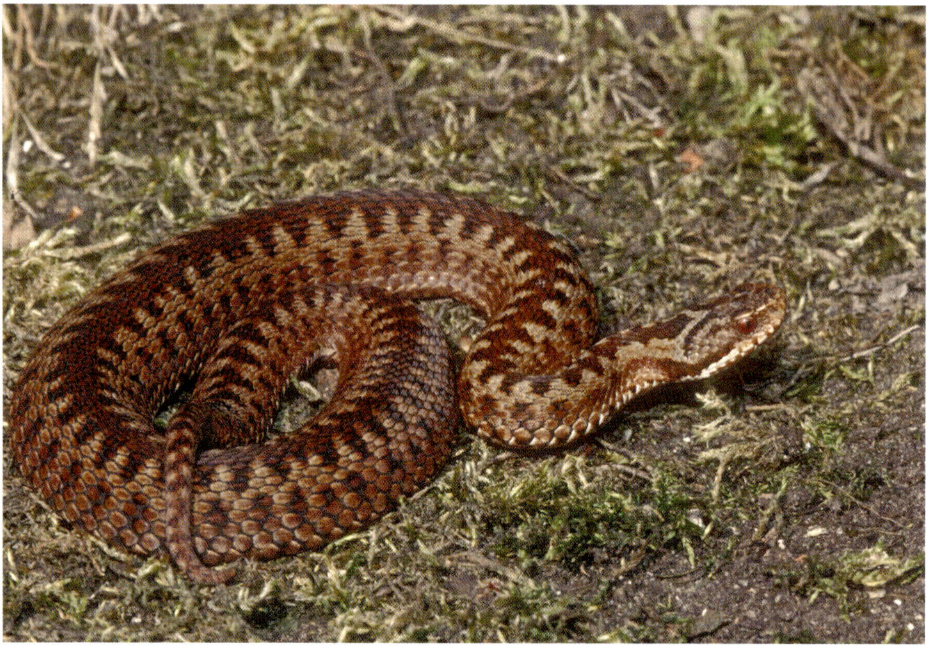

Female Adder of the red colour form.

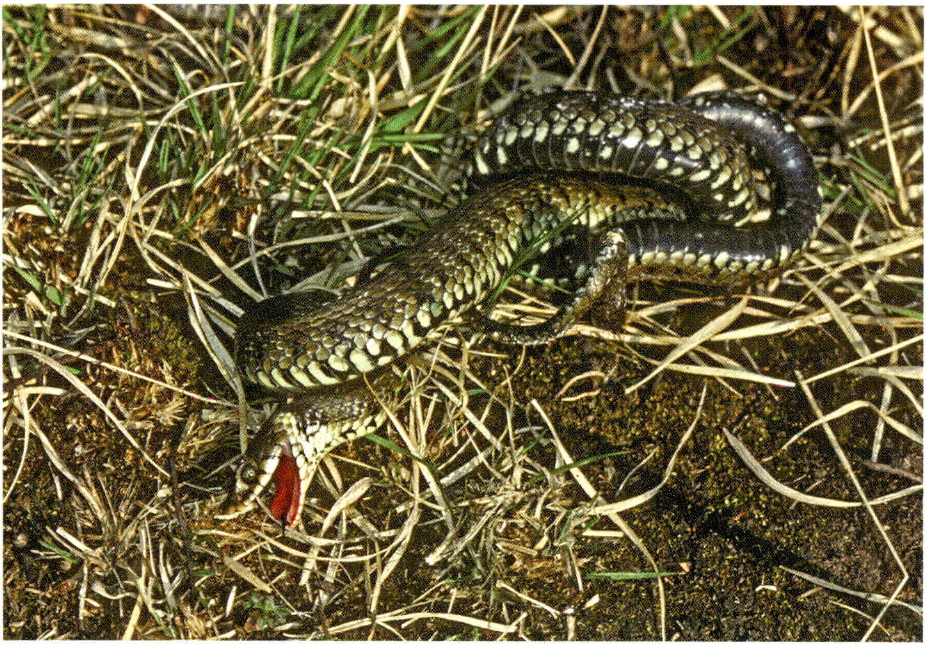

Grass Snake "playing dead".

Do bear in mind the fact that adders are venomous. The good news is that they are not known for actively attacking humans other than as a reflex action if you inadvertently get too close. The easy answer is DO NOT HANDLE SNAKES unless you are a professional herpetologist. If you do get bitten by an adder then do not panic, take things slow and steady and get to a hospital as soon as possible. If you are able to then let someone else do the driving, sit back and don't leap about in your seat even if the bite starts to sting. The further good news is that the vast majority of healthy people bitten by an adder will recover completely in just a few days after varying degrees of, what can even be mild, discomfort. The very frail and very small are most at risk and these should be got to medical attention as soon as possible. The other two snakes that you are likely to encounter are, most commonly, the Grass Snake and, more uncommonly, the Smooth Snake. These two are not venomous but are still likely to bite if handled. Furthermore they have a decidedly anti-social tendency to squirt a foul smelling secretion from their anal glands all over you if you handle them. The noxious nature of this substance is such that should you get any on you then neither your best friend nor your mother will want to know you, let alone allow you indoors. A further somewhat discomforting behaviour trait, particularly with Grass Snakes, is that if the smelly squirt doesn't prompt you to drop them then they enact a simulated death scene and pretend to be dead. This can be quite disconcerting as they twist up into a knot, with their tongue stuck out, looking for all the world as though they have just succumbed to terminal torture. If this happens then place them gently on the ground and stand well back with your camera ready. They may look completely comatose but they will be watching you out of their eye corners and as soon as they think that the coast is clear they will unwind and slither a hasty retreat. I would point out that should this happen to you then you have mucked about with the creature too much and you should suffer a guilty conscience for doing so and the stress you have caused. Furthermore, on a personal note, I hope it got you with its squirt!

If you are fortunate enough to come across a pair of adders courting, or even mating, then they will often be so engrossed with matters of the moment that you may be granted a fairly lengthy photographic session. Two males, vying for the right to "chat up" the local lissom lassie, can make for some interesting shots. They have the habit of rearing up and twisting around one another to establish dominance. Their movements almost constitute a dance and you will need to be working at fast speed settings to capture the action. I have had them dancing round my feet, when I have been too slow to get out of the way, seemingly oblivious to my presence and certainly far too engrossed to pose any kind of threat. Actual mating seems to be a pretty protracted process though frequently takes place in fairly dense vegetation. They do move around a bit though and if you are patient you stand a chance of recording the action. Of the two the male will normally be the smaller and closest to "black and white" in colour. Adult females tend to be more of an "off brownish" colour and a fully adult female can be up to 90 cms in length. Large males can normally be up to around 65/70 cms.

Another situation when you may get prolonged photographic access to a snake is when it is shedding its skin, which it does periodically. Just prior to doing this the old skin tends to take on a milky appearance (even around the eyes, thereby impairing its vision temporarily) and it then tries to scrape it off on sharp vegetation, rather like peeling off a long stocking. The process can take some time and, if you're lucky and unobtrusive, you may be able to photograph the whole performance.

You should avoid handling Lizards and Slow-worms also as they are given to dropping their tails if you grab one. You don't need to grab it actually by the tail for this tail-shedding to take place. Merely a perceived threat can act as a trigger. Most Lizard tails seem to be pre-programmed to be shed at various cut-off points and this can be achieved via voluntary muscular contractions by the tail's owner. It is an escape mechanism as the tail-piece can continue to wriggle for about 20 minutes and often serves to distract a potential predator long enough for the important bit of the lizard to make a get-away. Whilst it is true that these tails will regrow, the new ones, nevertheless, always look like an "add-on" and they will never be their original beautiful selves again. Once more, if this happens as a result of your actions, I can only say "Shame on you"!

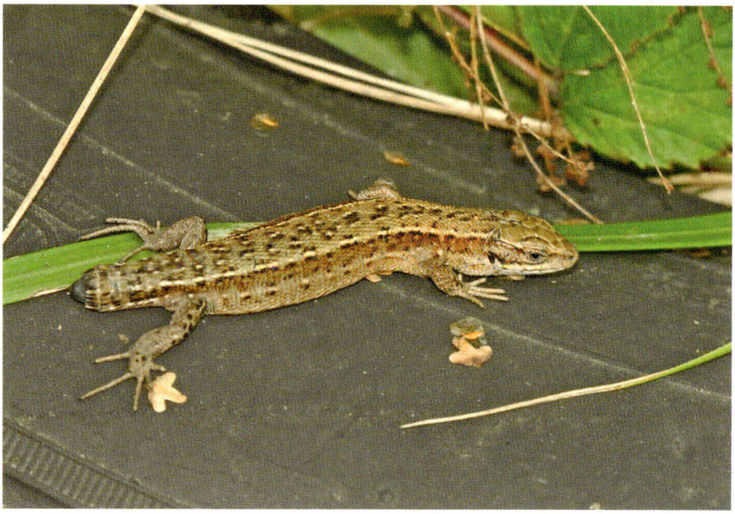

Common Lizard showing tail loss.

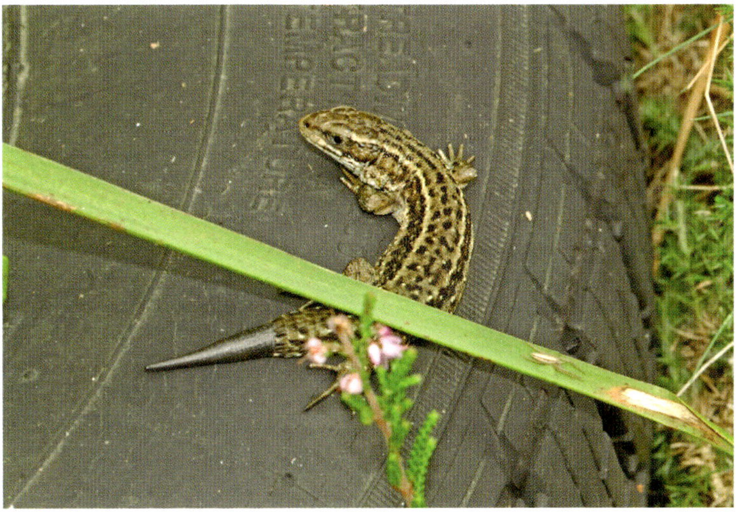

Common Lizard showing new tail "add-on"

Most of the amphibians, except of course the newts, are a different consideration from an image composition point of view as they are nearly as broad as they are long and their physical configuration lends itself to frame filling images. The problem with most of the European frogs, and even many of the toads, is that they top the dietary wishlist of a wide variety of other life forms. A natural consequence of this, of course, is that they are extremely skittish by nature. The most frequently obtained view of many of the marsh frog species is of them airborne, half-way between the bank and the water as they respond all too actively to what you fondly imagined was the world's most stealthy stalk. Once they are in the water, of course, you would need to be a newt to get anywhere close.

In the UK your choice of frogs and toads is not huge. There are many more species in mainland Europe. The common frog, which is essentially brown, though does offer one or two minor colour variations, will be the one that you will most frequently come across. It spends much of its life out of water and can be found in moist places within reasonable reach of standing water. If you come across one in this sort of habitat you may be able to get one or two "grab shots" but they are frequently unsatisfactory aesthetically. If you can persuade it to pose against a suitable background, or set it up in a tank, then you may be luckier. Once you start to handle them, though, they generally "get the wind up" and are tricky to work with.

Located mainly in the Southeast of England there are a number of small colonies of various Marsh type Green Frogs that are probably mostly, if not all, the result of deliberate introductions. As far as I know there are three species to consider. These are the Marsh Frog, the Edible Frog and the Pool Frog. It would seem that the Edible Frog is the Hybrid result of pairings between Marsh and Pool Frogs with a genetically uncanny ability to breed with either parent species and still produce only Edible Frogs. Additionally, unlike many species of hybrid origin, they are able to reproduce amongst themselves and, again, produce only Edible Frogs. These three species are notoriously difficult to differentiate between in the field especially in view of the fact that they can co-exist side by side and all three display a significant range of colour variations. Marsh Frogs tend to be a little larger and more darkly coloured than the other two though this is not always the case.

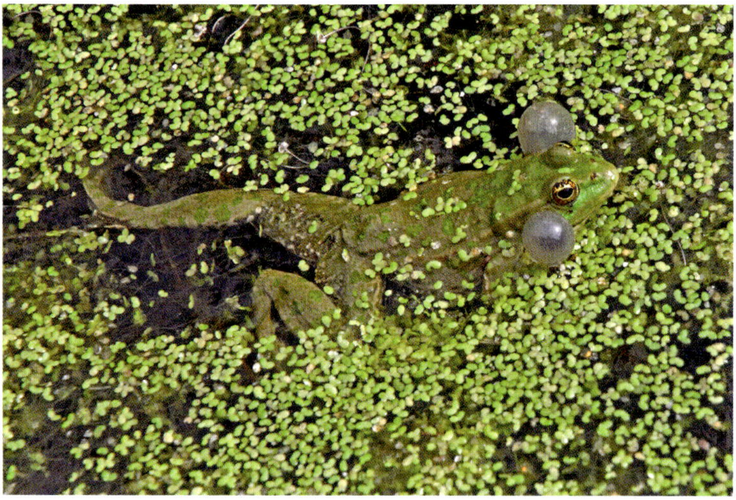

Marsh Frog in full song.

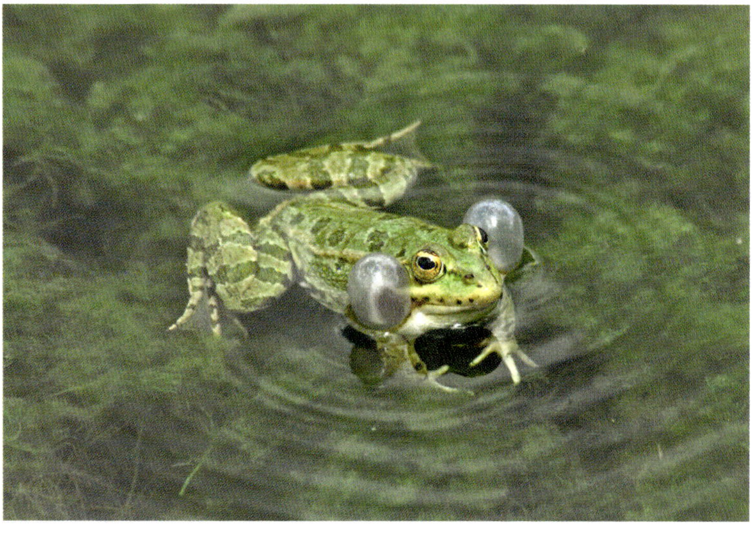

European Marsh Frog.

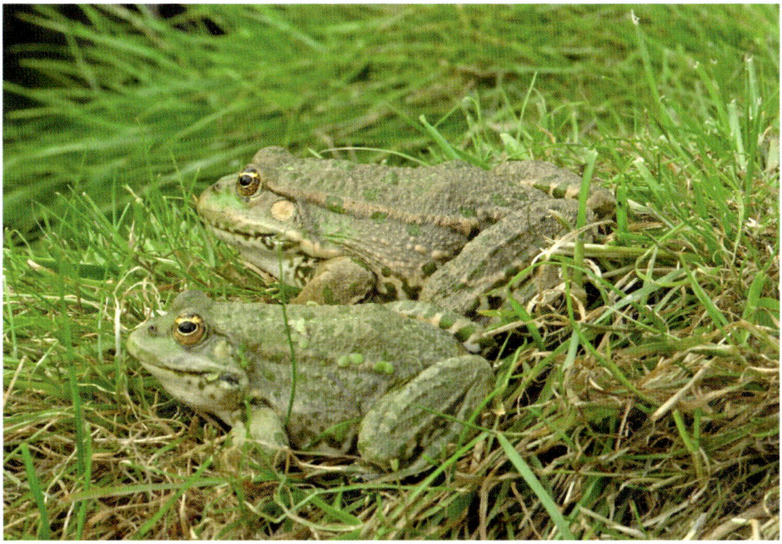

Pair of Marsh Frogs.

Whatever - my advice is, particularly in view of their scarcity, that if you are lucky enough to find Green Frogs in the UK, then thank your lucky stars, take their picture if you can and don't let worrying about their species ruin an otherwise perfect day! If your pictures are good enough you can always seek out knowledgeable help with identification later, and if you can't then you can always rest secure in the knowledge that you found a National Rarity.

Toads here seem to be limited to two species, the Common and the Natterjack. The former can be found most anywhere whilst the latter seem to exist in colonies widely dispersed throughout the country. These latter are a protected rarity and if you are lucky enough to find yourself able to photograph them then pay particular care to depicting the stripe that runs down their backs.

Most frogs, and certainly all the toads that I know of, return to water to breed. At this time they can become somewhat preoccupied with the business at hand and, with care, you should be in with a chance of a variety of shots. Several suitors all claiming simultaneous conjugal rights with the same winsome lass can lead to some boisterous performances and frenetic shutter releasing. Individual pairings off and egg-laying are two of the other options on offer. In the right location you can follow this up in the weeks to come by recording the development and subsequent hatching of the eggs followed by the fairly rapid rate of growth, through various stages, of the ensuing tadpoles.

Newts are somewhat different in that you will probably have to catch them and photograph them in some kind of tank. Don't be put off by the thought of the hassle of it as you can capture some very good images this way. The potential photographic hazard with this is the possibility of reflections from the glass sides of the tank. Of course you can photograph from above but then you have the possible reflections from the water surface to consider. Not only that but most newts have to be viewed from the side to be able to see their salient features and so you will inevitably end up having to photograph through the side of the tank whether you want to or not.

This need not present a major problem and you will find the subject of photographing through glass fully covered in the chapter on "Photographing in Zoos and Safari Parks".

It is not uncommon, these days, to see the odd Terrapin in ponds and slow moving streams. The majority of them will be American Red-eared Terrapins. Most of them, I am sure, are the result of escapes or deliberate release by owners who unexpectedly find that their cute little two inch long "Ninja Turtle" suddenly weighs in at a kilo or more. Whether any are able to survive our winters and have managed to establish themselves by breeding over here I do not know. Suffice to say they are not an uncommon sight and you may well bump into them in your travels. Certainly where I live in Spain there are two native species, the Pond and the Striped Necked, though I am not sure whether the water, in the areas in which they are found, freezes over in winter. If it does then I would suspect that they have the ability to hibernate, which means that they could, presumably, establish over here. Certainly they have the ability to aestivate if their water source dries up, so I would imagine that, in time, they could well become a more regular feature in our landscape.

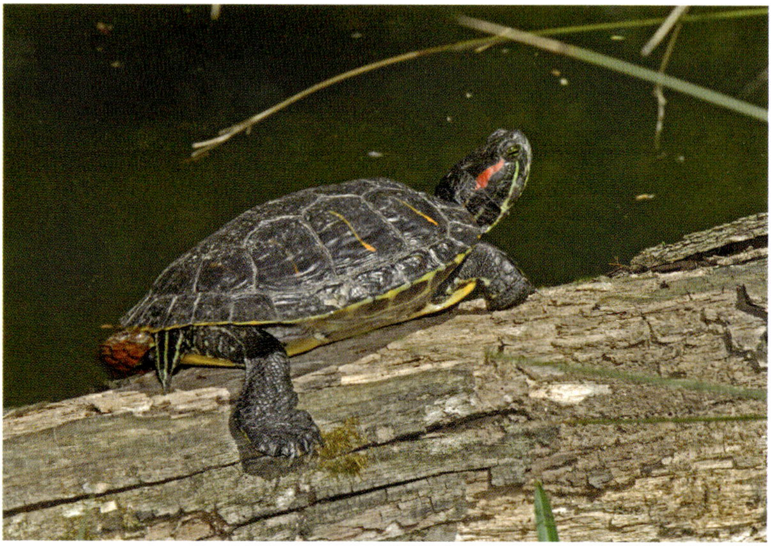

Red Eared Terrapin - a Florida expatriot far from home.

There are a number of Field Guides available on the subject including a very good one by Collins covering the "Reptiles and Amphibians of Britain and Europe". With the limited range of species that we have in the UK you are not likely to get many Guides dealing with the UK only, so don't waste too much time looking for them. Settle for the full European coverage more commonly on offer.

One final word on this section. In keeping with many other Wildlife Groups in the UK there are a number of Laws in existence covering the conservation, protection, handling of and disturbance to, certain species. These Laws have a habit of changing from time to time and rather than advise you of the situation at the moment, which may be out of date before you read this book, I would suggest that you check on the "status quo" of current legislation before embarking in pursuit of your chosen subjects. There is normally quite up to date advice available on the internet and a quick Google could save you having a hard time with the relevant authorities later. In any event quite basically, and even setting legalities aside, most Reptiles and Amphibians do not respond well to being handled and so you should avoid it as far as possible and you will then, coincidentally, keep yourself out of trouble at the same time. Even for those individuals that you may feel will not react adversely you have to remember that their post-handling behaviour patterns will probably not be conducive to meaningful and natural looking picture taking. Far better to be patient and wait in the hopes that the animal will move into position of it's own accord when it will look and act in a relaxed and natural manner. If it doesn't then grin and bear it and try again another day. It's all part of the "name of the game".

ADDENDUM.

I feel that it would be unfair to conclude this chapter without discussing my latest and ongoing project with local Wildlife.

When staying in the UK, Poole in Dorset is my home port. Just locally, along the Poole to Southbourne sea cliffs, we have enjoyed for a number of years the presence of at least two species of supposedly introduced Lizards. I have known of them for some time but it is only recently when, at a loose end one day, I decided to go "have a look-see" for myself. Introduced species are a controversial subject at the best of times and guaranteed to make true conservationists twitch in an alarming manner. There are those who would advocate wiping out alien species willy-nilly on the say-so that they provide a threat to native species. I, personally, take a somewhat more relaxed view and, whilst I would accept that in certain cases they can pose a problem, it is often only temporary since the majority of wild species ultimately learn to adapt to the presence of these "foreigners" and change their lifestyles and/or feeding patterns accordingly. I would stress here that I am not trying to be controversial and have no wish to become embroiled in lengthy correspondence on the issue. Suffice to say that we accept the presence on these shores of many species which have been introduced over the centuries and take them for granted as a normal part of the landscape. I doubt there were many horses in the UK in pre-glacial times and, more recently, I understand that Fallow Deer were only introduced in the 1st Century AD. Their presence today doesn't appear to be particularly contentious. Most of the potential controversy, when it occurs, hinges on whether the introduction was casual or deliberate and whether it subsequently proves to have a deleterious effect on either man or native species. Without casual introduction evolution itself would have been pushed to survive and places like the Galapagos, which is of volcanic origin and never connected to a mainland, would have been Wildlife deserts. Cases of deliberate introduction can, of course, go spectacularly wrong such as in the case of the Cane Toad introduction to Australia and, though normally only with the benefit of hindsight, these are probably to be deplored. There are others though that, as in the case of these Lizards, are from apparently indeterminate origins and, as certain recent schools of thought would hold, may even represent relict populations from days of yore.

Suffice to say I was amazed at what I found. The two species in question are a form of the European Wall Lizard - Podarcis muralis and a European type Green Lizard formerly existing under the banner of Lacerta viridis but more recently, due to the attention of the "herpetological" breed of "species-splitters", supposedly better attributed to the species Western Green Lizard or Lacerta biliniata, though this is apparently not currently certain and, in any event, may revert to its original designation unless proof, such as by DNA testing, establishes something to the contrary!

Anyway --- to cut a long story short there are probably thousands of small Wall Lizards to be found here (about the size of our native Common or Viviparous Lizards) and a much lesser number of the very much larger (up to between 30 and 40cms depending on tail length) Green Lizards. These latter can seem enormous by UK standards and are so strikingly coloured that when you see your first one you could be forgiven for thinking that it is a "joke" rubber Lizard left there for a laugh. The smaller Wall Lizards are much more what we are used to over here though they occur in a vast array of colour forms such as you never see with our true natives. Some, it is true, are very similar to our Common Lizard and you may need a somewhat discerning eye to differentiate between the two particularly in view of the fact that the habitat in question carries populations of both the latter species. Indeed at the Poole end of the cliffs there are also populations of native Sand Lizards as well to further complicate the issue. By and large many of the Wall Lizards come in a range of Yellows and Greens. These latter two colours obviously differentiate them from the Common Lizards but may confuse them with the Sand Lizards, the males of which also show an amount of green, the intensity of which varies throughout the year. As a basic rule of thumb I have found that the Wall Lizards have their strongest colouring along their central back regions whereas the Sand Lizards tend to have their green more on the sides. The Sand Lizards also enjoy a much "chunkier" build.

The advantages with these Wall Lizards from a photographers point of view is that in parts of the habitat, such as where zigzag paths go down from the cliffs to the beach, they have become, especially in summer, so used to a constant stream of trippers that you can approach them very closely. On the main zigzag at Boscombe you will find them all along the path on the stone walls that edge it. It is not uncommon to see 30 or 40 in a single traverse of the path. Funnily enough you will find that you can almost brush past them so long as you keep moving but if you stop then you will have to move a little further away as their "comfort zone" seems to be less tolerant of stationary humans than it is of moving ones. Nevertheless you can certainly get close enough to expect some wonderful images even with basic camera equipment. My lens of choice for lizards is a 200mm macro lens but, in this case, it is often too big to fit the whole lizard into the frame due to the unusual proximity that you can achieve to the subject. My other disadvantage is that with that particular lens there is, of course, no zoom facility. I would recommend that you go equipped with whatever close-up equipment you have settled on for such as Butterfly photography, because you really can, with care, get to within 2 or 3 feet, and a zoom of some 70/80mm to 200/300mm. Nothing fancy is necessary. With the throughput of people associated with the location a tripod can be somewhat anti-social but, nevertheless, well worth the effort because of the proximity, and consequent image size, at which you will be working. In any event, by the time you have conducted a lengthy shoot under those circumstances, and with the "serious photography" defeating antics of many within that traffic stream, your feelings will have become so anti-social that you may be glad of the tripod to wrap around the odd neck or two! After a great many days experience I have found that warm and sunny days are a must since, although some may still come out when it is colder - either fairly early in the morning or on overcast days - nevertheless they are somewhat twitchy, whereas in decent sun and warmth they seem prepared to let you approach much more closely.

There are purportedly more than 20 recorded sites for these Lizards, mostly in the South, and there would appear to be slight colour differences from population to population. I have just recently spent two months in the various mountain ranges of both France and Spain and a great part of the time was given over to photographing the Wall Lizards of the different areas. Whilst I found that many of the individual populations concerned may have displayed a certain overall tendency to their own range of colour patternings nevertheless, in each population, there would always be a number of individuals who could equally well have come from any other of the groups. I therefore feel that local similarities are probably the result of inherited traits from the undoubtedly small numbers of founder members of the group but that the species as a whole has a tendency to multiple colour morphing. I think that it would be virtually impossible to determine an individual's site of origin just from colour alone. There is possibly one exception to this and that is with a population on private land near Poole where they are purported to be almost, or completely black. In this instance, however, this small colony's origins are known to be based on escape from captivity and the original breeder's interest no doubt lay with melanistic animals and that colour form, on that site, has persisted to this day. The spread, and subsequent potential integrating of populations, seems to be limited by habitat characteristics especially in the case of suitable egg laying sites. They lay their eggs under flat stones and it could be that only a small break - maybe no larger than a football pitch - of unsuitable habitat is sufficient to prevent a colony from spreading. That would certainly seem to be the case with the only other colony I have visited, in a disused quarry in Portland, where the site is fairly limited in size but surrounded by grassland devoid of flat stones. Although recorded as being there for a great many years, the colony has never "broken out"

The Green Lizards are something else! Whilst there are one or two to be found in the various patches of vegetation along the length of the Zigzag, the bulk of them seem to be nearer the top of the cliffs and even in and amongst the patches of gorse and bramble on the level ground at the cliff top. Despite their size they are very difficult to see. In large part this is a result of their colouring which, though spectacular in isolation, nevertheless serves to make them all but invisible when lying in, or on the edge of, the shrubbery that they favour. They do not dash about like the wall lizards and so your eye is not drawn by movement and time and time again I have been amazed to find that I have been staring directly at one for some while without seeing it. It's rather like looking at one of those computer generated pictures that just looks like a load of dots until an image suddenly emerges as if by magic.

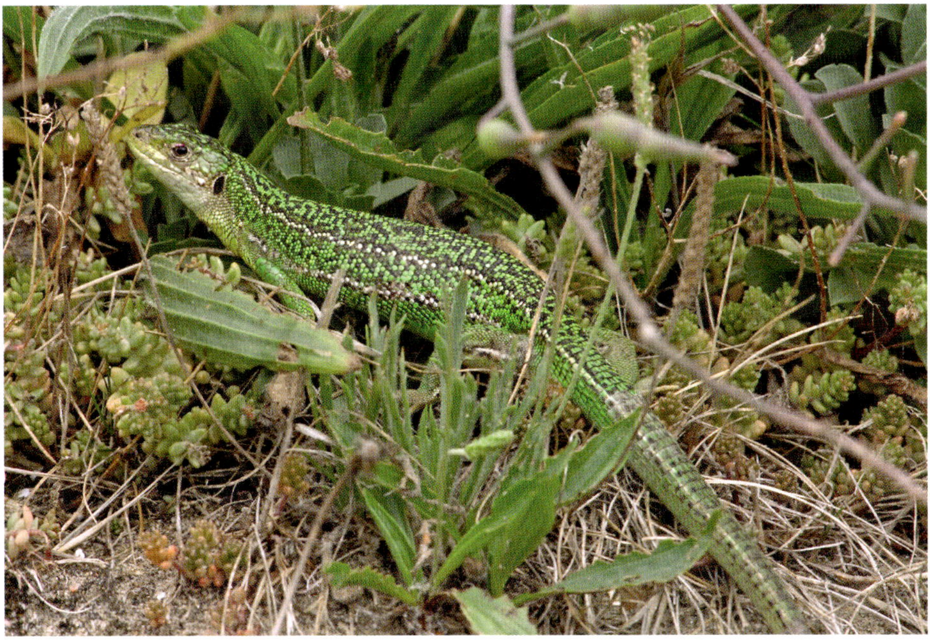

European Green Lizard female at Boscombe.

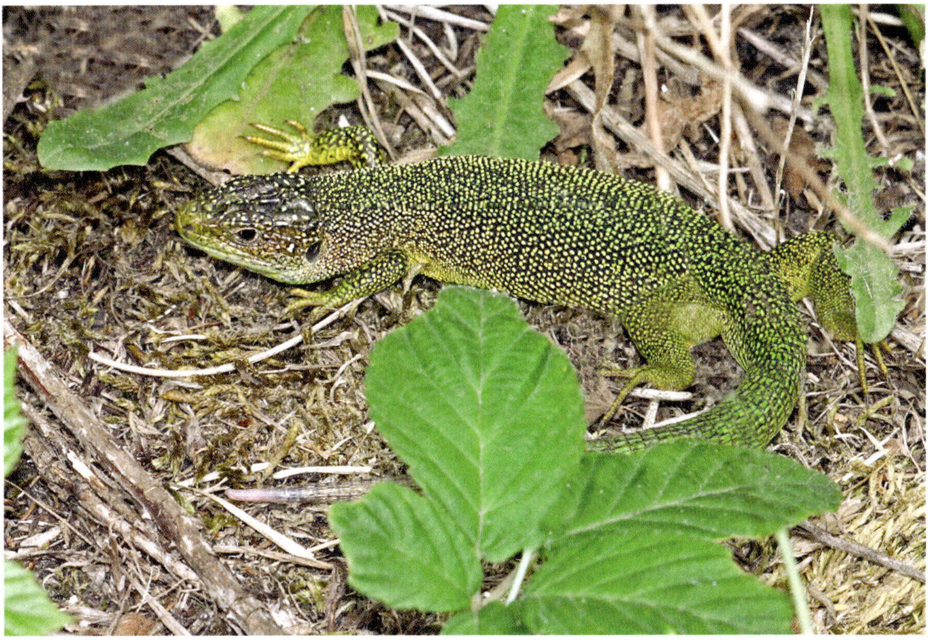

European Green Lizard male at Boscombe.

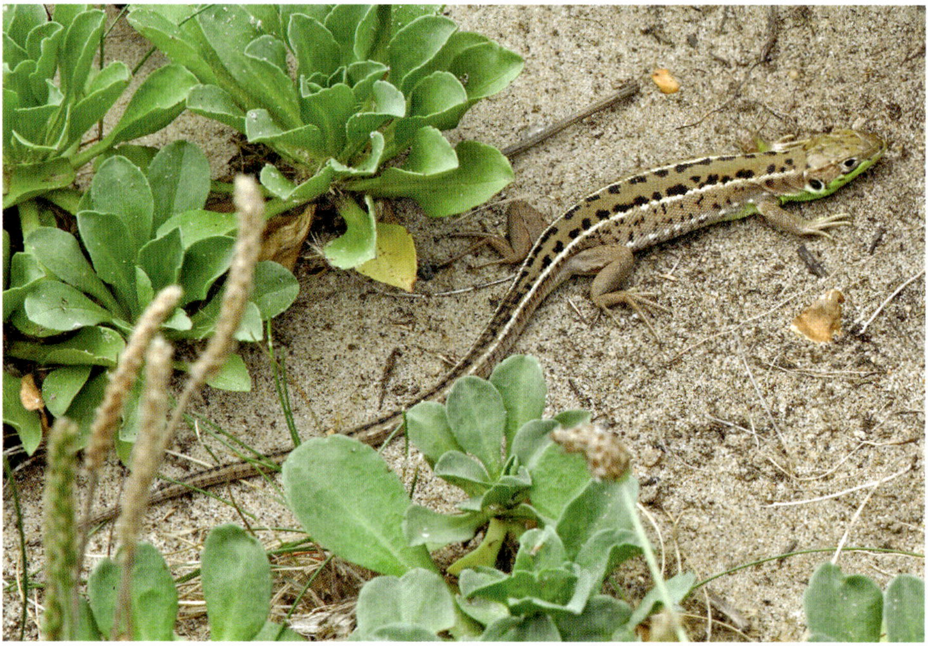

European Green Lizard juvenile at Boscombe.

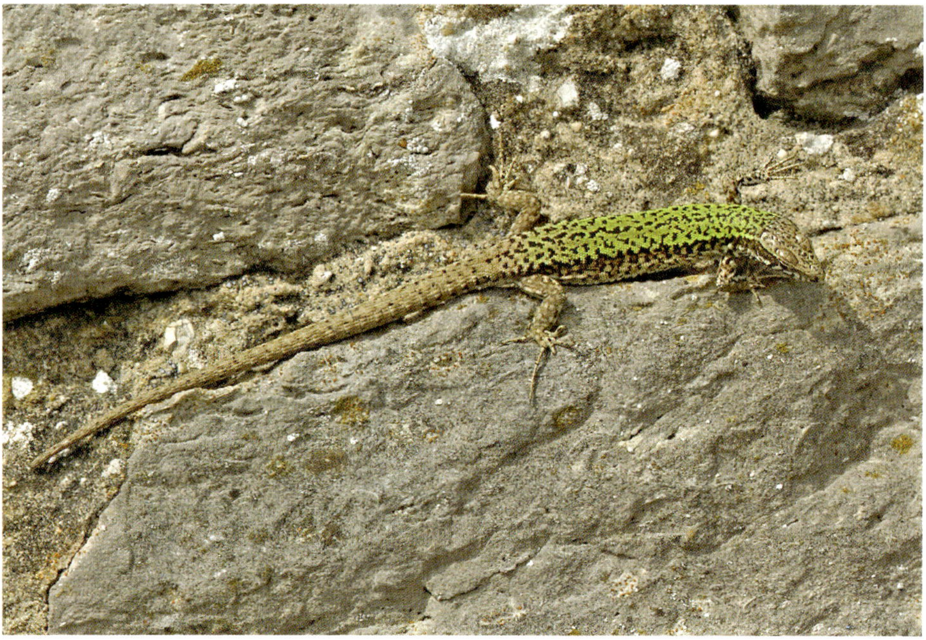

European Wall Lizard at Boscombe.

During my recent montane sojourn I was also fortunate enough to be able to photograph several Schreibers Green Lizards in the Gredos Mountains of central Spain. These are very similar to the Boscombe Greens though the intensity of blue colouring on the heads of the males tends to be far greater.

Whether the various UK populations have been created, or augmented, by deliberate introductions I have no idea and neither, it would seem, has anyone else. No doubt if programmes of DNA analysis are funded in the future then the answer will be forthcoming. In the meantime they are there now and well worth the trouble of searching for wherever they may have come from.

Chapter 26

Photographing On Safari.

Safari! Even just letting the word roll off your tongue engenders a feeling of derring do and adventure in some of the world's deepest and darkest corners.

From its innocuous origins in Arabic and Swahili, where it merely related to a "long journey", its connotations have changed over the years. It now implies a Game Viewing or Hunting experience, normally in Africa. Irrespective of its origins the word is certainly an emotive one in common parlance.

The realities of a modern day safari will probably turn out to be more orchestrated than your imagination would choose to allow but there are a number of ways to maximise the experience from a photographic point of view.

"Safaris" originally were one-off affairs of a lavish nature and really aimed at wealthy hunters and their entourages. Over the years and with the advent of photography, easy access international air transport, and infrastructure and communication advances in the countries concerned, they began to fall within the reach of we "mere mortals". Suitably located Game Lodges began to spring up and suddenly "safari" assumed a different context. Whilst there are still some of the old fashioned hunting safaris taking place with their old fashioned splendour, by far the bulk of safaris these days are conducted primarily on a game viewing only basis. No longer does a "safari" consist of a constantly moving encampment but rather they have evolved into one, or two, centre based affairs, where you can participate on a much tighter timeframe rather than the several months previously required. This, of course, suits current vacation practices and, accordingly, the modern safari experience has expanded exponentially.

Along with this expansion has gone, of necessity, an increase in active Game Management, particularly in the vicinity of the newly established Lodges and on the Reserves. These management regimes, sometimes seemingly ruthless, include organised culling, disease and poaching controls, and frequent relocation programmes.

From a boundary point of view there are two types of reserves throughout Africa at present - fenced and unfenced. The management programmes and photographic opportunities within each will be vastly different.

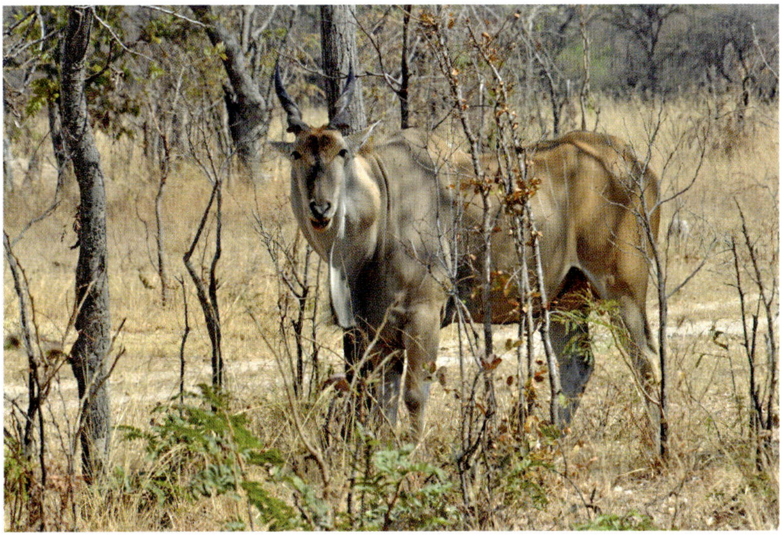

Eland Bull in Selous

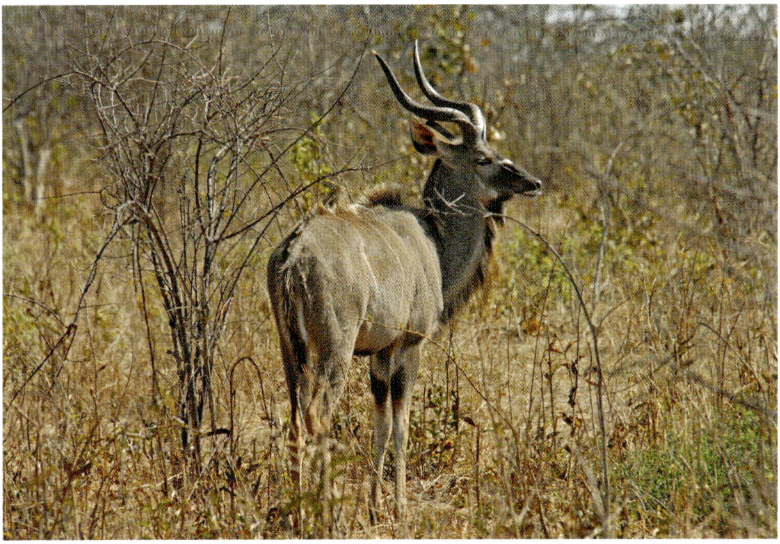

Kudu Bull in Hwange

The fenced ones will have resident populations of wildlife species that will have become accustomed, to a certain extent, to the vehicles, management practices and people throughput of all but the very largest reserves. As a result of this they are likely to be reasonably approachable and you should be able to get some superb, close-up shots. By very dint of the initial price and subsequent maintenance costs of fencing, then most reserves in this category are of a fairly finite size although, by normal European standards, this may be substantial. One of the benefits of this is that, within these reserves, the wildlife will have favourite areas in which they can be found with a degree of certitude, even if those locations change according to the hour of the day, grass burning programmes and the seasons of the year. Game Drives, therefore, with staff who will know these areas, are likely to be highly productive and afford excellent photographic opportunities. The downside is that the species count of the resident mammals within these reserves is likely to be somewhat limited and, in many cases, there will be few, if any, major predators granted free access to the other species. It makes little commercial sense to allow your season's game production to slip down the throats of a resident pride of lions that could easily have been catered for with the constantly available flow of casualties from the surrounding and inevitable farmlands. In some areas, where farms are scarce, certain species, such as Zebras and Giraffes, which are not normally acceptable at the human table, are culled for this specific purpose. Predators such as big cats, therefore, if present, will normally be housed in separate pens or enclosures, albeit of varying sizes and, by UK standards, often enormous. Almost invariably though, these will be "enclosures within enclosures" since, in the localities where these parks occur, they are usually surrounded by farmland and the kind of fencing that is required to constrain big cats is hugely expensive and would normally make fencing the whole park for them out of the question. Within these there will, nevertheless, normally be ample opportunity to photograph these predators in aesthetically pleasing settings that equate to the wild and which will replicate the surrounding "bush" in appearance.

Game management in a fenced, predator free environment often needs to be more hands-on than in the larger unfenced areas, such as the Kruger or the Serengeti. There nature plays a more major role in the management on the basis of survival of the fittest. In effect the enclosed parks are a form of farm, or Safari Park, and someone has to be the Zoo Keeper or Park Manager. Available grazing levels within a reserve will dictate optimum stocking densities and often the management will have to resort to culling or relocating to control this. Culling may be of the "sporting" or hunting kind, or as a form of in-house "cropping" of species that are suitable for the table. Do not react to culling regimes with hand raised horror or emotional outbursts. Within a predator free captive environment it is essential to control not only overall numbers but also to maintain a strict male/female ratio with some species. Some culling will be effected by thc selling of permissions to "trophy" hunters who are normally prepared to pay way above the market value of an animal for what is, to them, the "thrill" of hunting. When judging this activity you must bear in mind that the selling of these permissions can represent a very significant part of the annual income of some reserves and without it they would cease to exist. In addition this is not, normally, a random exercise as only specifically selected animals will be targeted. In many instances those very animals would have had to have been culled by the management anyway for any of a number of different reasons.

It has also become the norm for Game Lodges to include certain of their more prolific species on their menus. I must confess that, personally, I have always found it an anomaly that tourists, spending a fortune to go and view live wild animals, should then be prepared to shovel them down their throats in the evening meal. However, the result of over-crowding is a horrible thing to see and if this culinary demand helps to thin the ranks, balance the books and keep the whole scene going then it certainly gets my support. I fervently believe that eco-tourism is the best long-term chance for the survival of many species in regions approximating to the wild.

Some animals will become troublesome in a predator free environment for a number of different reasons. Wildebeest bulls for instance, past their breeding "sell-by date" and ousted from their herds by up and coming younger males, will be able to live successful solitary lives as outcasts from the herd. In the "wild" their solitary status would normally come to an abrupt end within a very short time of becoming ostracised. They would become prime targets for every predator in the area and, without the protection afforded by membership of a large group, they would quickly succumb. In the absence of predators they become a nuisance animal as they live their lone lives free of threat but become a menace from a management point of view. They will continue to harass the new herd bulls during the breeding season as they probably will not accept that they are "past it". This causes the breeding bulls to exhaust themselves with a much higher than normal succession of challenges leading to an ensuing and deleterious effect on their sperm counts, thus inhibiting their reproductive capabilities. An inadvertent benefit to these outcast bulls is that, as they get older, they frequently develop a heavier "trophy" which, in the case of a wildebeest, is the head. They thus command a higher licence fee if they are placed on the "sport cull" list - at their age they would not be a welcome addition on a dinner plate!

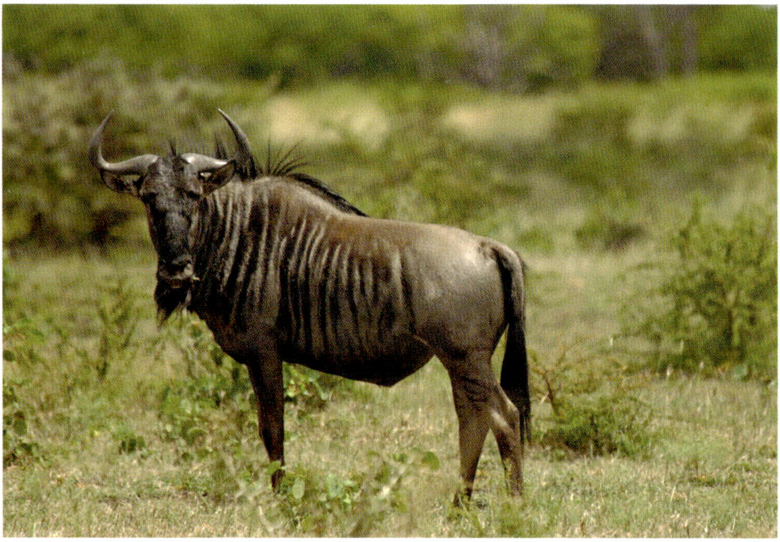

Wildebeest in Selous

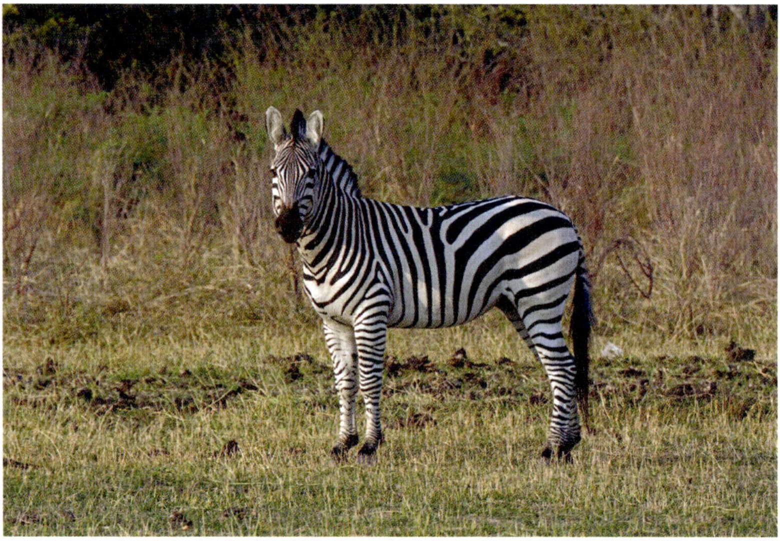

Plains Zebra at Kariba

Zebra stallions also need controlling. Too high a ratio of males leads to continuous struggles to take over the small herds of mares and their young. Even though a lead stallion may individually be the "best of the best", nevertheless, constantly having to fight off an abnormally high succession of new contenders, as well as ex herd leaders, will wear out the sturdiest of breeding males. Apart from affecting their reproductive ability the never ending fights to protect their harems will lead to most herd stallions being deposed just through sheer exhaustion however suitable as breeders they may have been. A new male, on taking over, is prone to promptly kicking all the foals to death in order to bring their dams into season again. Somewhat harsh but the inevitable result if gender ratios are allowed to spiral out of control. In a normal predator/prey environment stallion numbers would have been somewhat controlled and depleted by losses sustained whilst defending the herds against predation. Additionally deposed males, unless they quickly team up with others in a similar situation, would be rapidly taken out of the potential contender equation by a never ending stream of predators and aggressive scavengers.

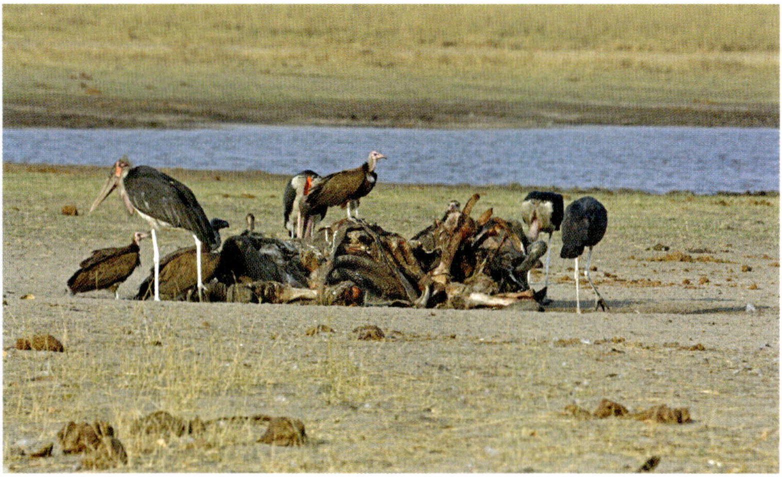

Elephant carcass with scavengers

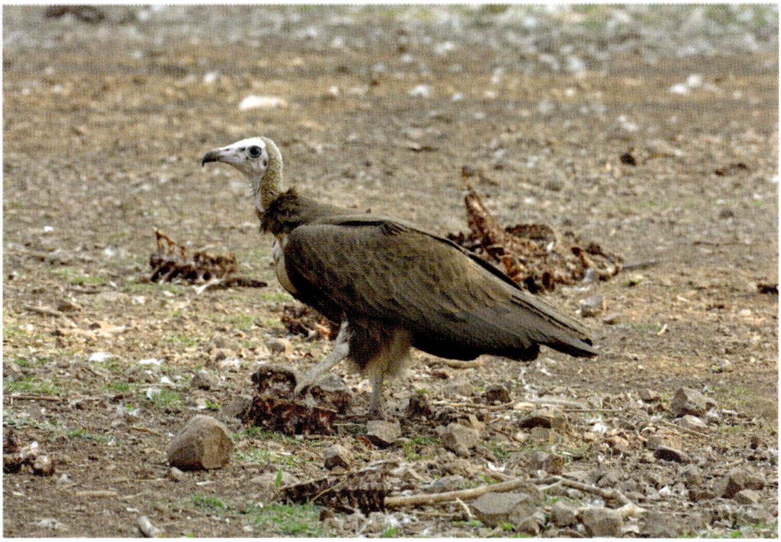

Brown Hooded Vulture

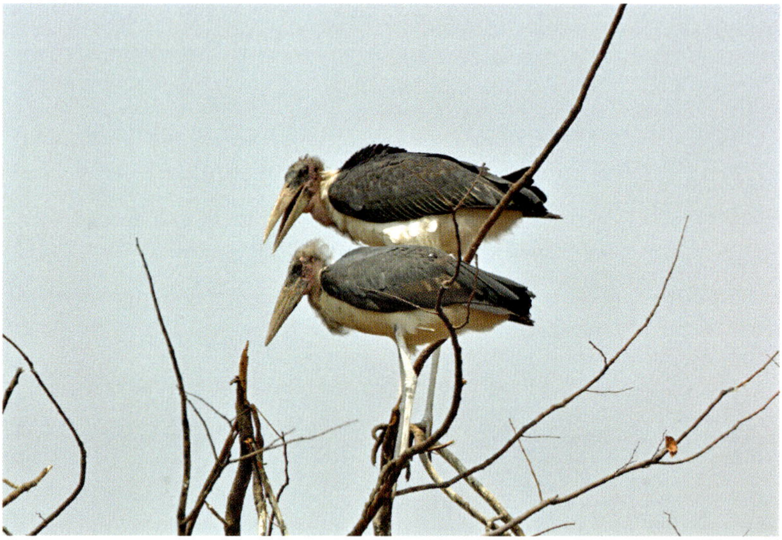

Marabou Storks

Apart from stock levels habitat management is all-important in these reserves. Often there will be a number of waterholes, either natural or man-made, sufficient to ensure an adequate water supply all year round throughout the reserve. Animals dying of thirst in a drought is not, therefore, likely to be a problem, but it is frequently impractical to consider irrigation schemes in such places. In times of low rainfall, therefore, the grazing areas will suffer and supplementary feeding, at great cost to the establishment, may be called for. Natural mineral sources may also become depleted, thus incurring the need for mineral blocks and other supplements.

Controlled burning may also be called for to ensure a constant supply of fresh grazing and also to control potential build-ups of harmful pests such as ticks, mites and flukes. Heavy infestations, particularly of ticks, may call for more direct treatments of the animals themselves. In a large park one to one treatments are impractical due to the sheer scale of the numbers involved. There are, however, various appliances such as Duncan Applicators whose design is such that, whilst licking a mineral block bait, a dab of tick deterrent is administered to the throat or back of an animal's neck as it stretches forward. These applicator units, of course, need constant supervision and replenishing.

Overuse of fertile areas and water sources can lead to exacerbated disease transmission, especially of internal parasites such as worms and flukes, and a separate treatment regime may be called for to combat these.

Fence lines, often electrified, need constant monitoring and attention. The fence of one of the Parks that I was managing was 28 K's long and we had two or three gangs on continuous fence maintenance. My having to constantly check the whole length of this fence line on horseback has left me with a quaver in the voice and a peculiar, John Wayne type, gait! Grass and other vegetation continually grows, often at an alarming rate, up between the wires thus causing an electrical short. Termites seem to love fence posts, even when they have been treated, and the frequent electrical storms result in numerous lightning strikes on the main supporting poles. Warthogs have a habit of tunnelling out under the fence to raid the surrounding shambas and can create fence damage by doing so. Sometimes there is not sufficient depth of soil for them to tunnel and I well remember one location, where the ground was rocky, where they had to actually squeeze under the fence to get out. The problem was that one of the bottom wires was electrified and, due to a warthog's habit of running with its tail stuck straight up in the air, it was impossible for them to get out without incurring an electric shock. Knowing they were going to be nailed they would make a run at the fence to get through as quickly as possible, but would start squealing 50 yards before they got there in anticipation of the shock they knew they were going to receive.

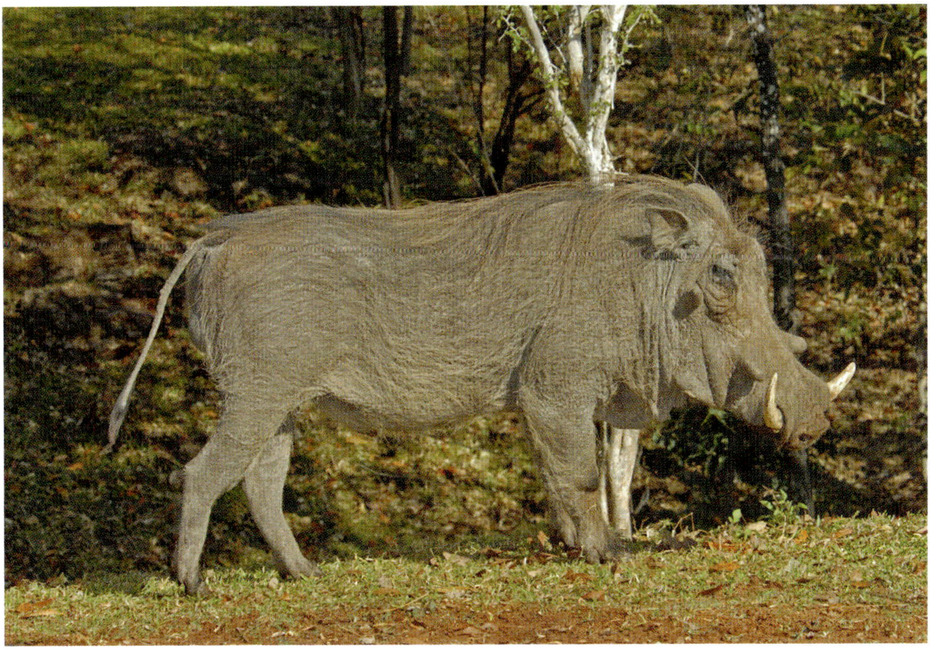

Warthog at Victoria Falls

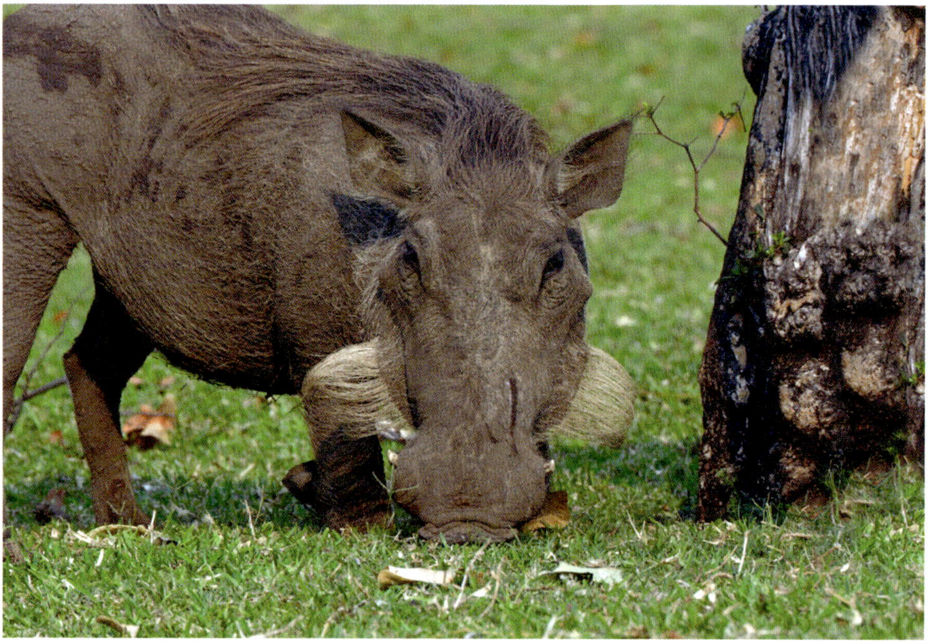

Warthog in Selous

Poaching, of course, is every Game Reserve's nightmare and sod's law is such that there are always going to be more of "them" than there are of you and they will, almost invariably, be better armed. There is something mildly un-nerving in going out at night armed and, of necessity, on foot, least on horseback you make too much noise and offer up too large a target, looking for someone likely to be carrying an automatic weapon and who will think nothing of pulling the trigger to evade capture. With 30 or more rounds in the magazine he doesn't need to be "Dead-eye Dick" - just lucky! We had anti-poaching patrols out constantly. I can remember, over the Xmas and New Year period of the 2000 millennium, having to go out myself practically every night for nearly two months to make up team numbers. It's not quite like strolling down your local High Street I can assure you.

The upshot of all this is that the staffing levels required to successfully manage one of these reserves are far higher than would appear so on the surface. The Park I spent most of my time on had 150 staff, of which only a very small percentage would ever have been seen by the guests. The employing, in Africa, of 150 staff in that sort of location, in practice, means having to provide housing for up to 150 different families as well. This, of course, is one of the reasons why holidays of this nature are not for the financially faint hearted!

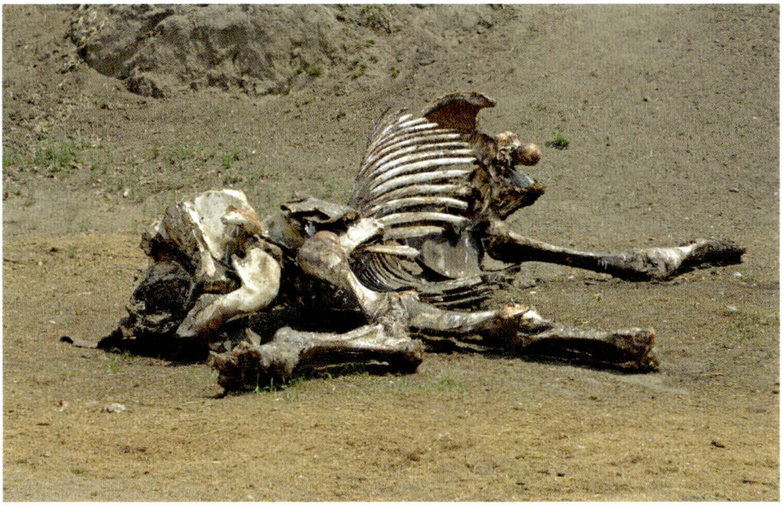

Poached Elephant Carcass - Hwange

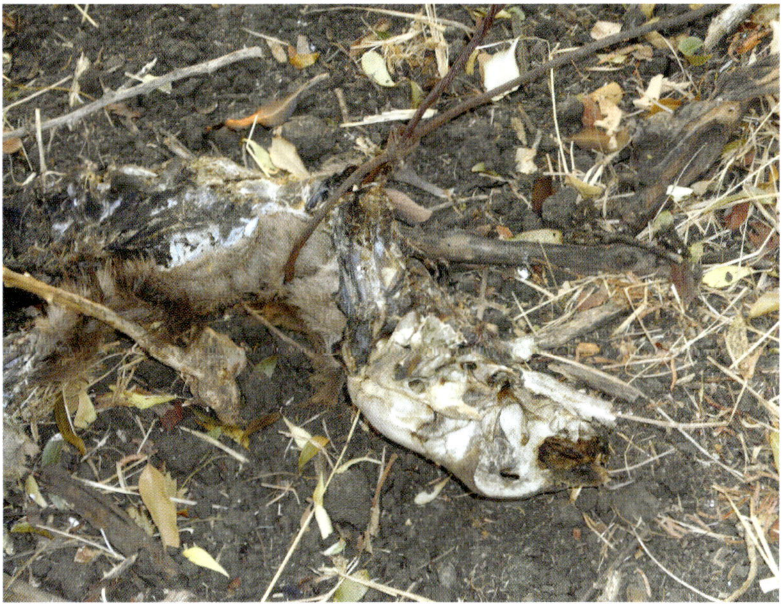

Remains of poached Kudu with snare

The unfenced reserves require a lower level of stock control and habitat management as nature is often the controlling influence. Animals are free to migrate, or at least follow the grazing , even if only over relatively short distances. Predators will normally be present as, without fences, there is no way to keep them out. Indeed they often rank high up on the tourism "wishlist" and so they may actually be specifically encouraged and catered for by deliberate baiting of pre-determined areas. Many of these reserves will be able to boast an almost resident population of predators, such as lions and leopards, as a result of regular feeding. Cheetahs are particularly tractable animals and I have never heard a report of a deliberate and unprovoked attack on a human by a Cheetah, other than in the case of the occasional rabid animal not in control of its own actions. They have a history of being domesticated for centuries and were often trained as hunting animals. They can be kept around the premises, even at liberty, almost as "pets". I can remember, when growing up in Africa in the '50s, that it was quite the norm to see a number of Cheetahs being walked on leads during any visit to town. In those days they could be captured by riding them down on horseback - those phenomenal bursts of speed are of notoriously short duration - and then jumping off and throwing a coat over its head. With its head covered the Cheetah would become quite quiescent and could be restrained accordingly.

On any reserve there will be areas favoured by certain species and these will be known to the Game Drive Guides. Since the size of their potential tip is normally directly related to your degree of satisfaction they will certainly do their best to maximise your Game-viewing experience. In addition many reserves will have spotters out either on foot, horseback, or in vehicles, keeping tabs on any of the "must see" species in the vicinity.

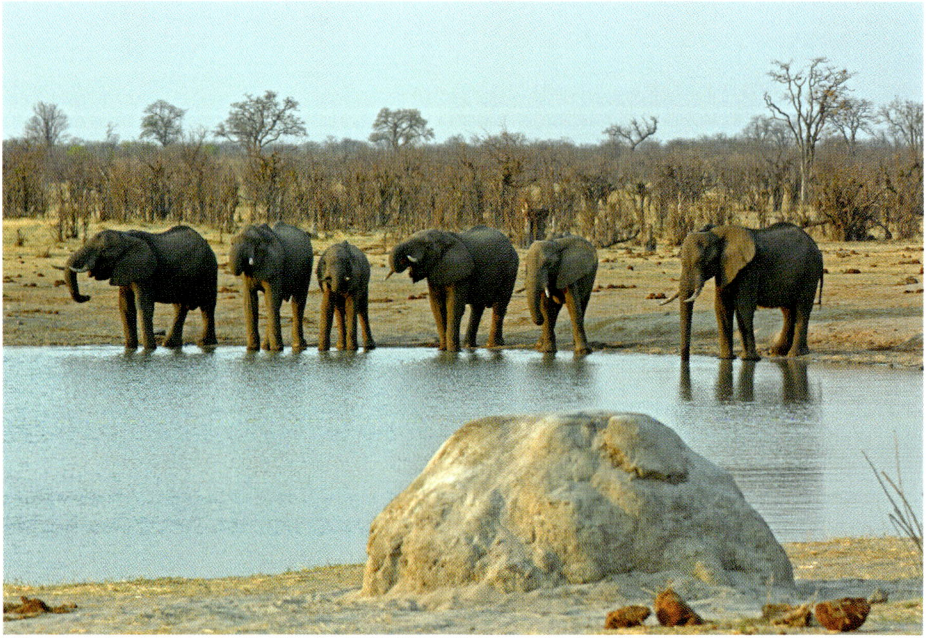

Hwange Waterhole

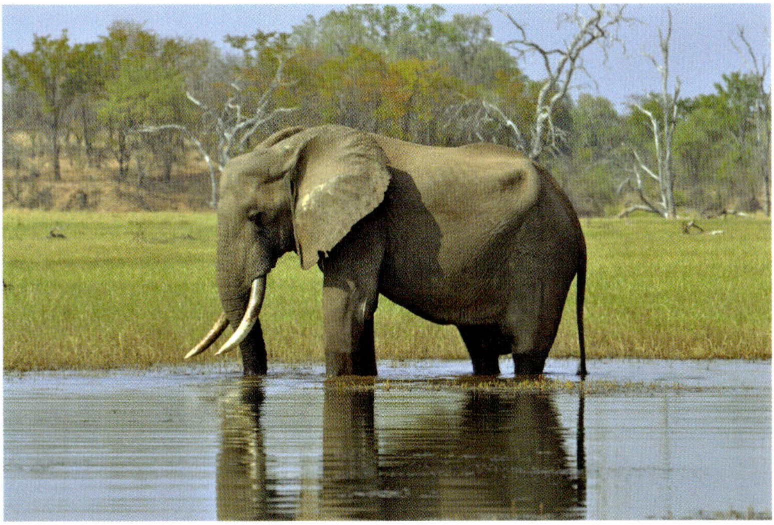

Lone Bull in Kariba

Man-made and borehole fed waterholes are a tremendous attractor of all species and, if adjacent to the Lodge, will often be lit at night when many of the species put in an appearance. Salt licks, mineral blocks and supplementary feeding add to the list of potential attractants and will, invariably, be located in areas designed to maximise the Game-viewing potential.

Both fenced and unfenced reserves will normally offer a range of activities designed to fill your every waking moment and my advice is to try as many as you feel physically competent to tackle. Some of them, such as horse or elephant rides, canoeing, or bush-walking, will afford excellent opportunities photographically. The ones involving animal riding will pose a slight camera-shake problem in that your mount will have to breathe - and I know of no reserves where they have taught them to hold their breath whilst you take your shot! It may not seem like a major problem at first glance but, if you consider the size of an elephants lungs, then you will realise that this results in a somewhat major contraction and expansion with each breath. If you can preset your camera to the fastest shutter speed that conditions will allow and/or increase your ISO setting if your camera allows it, then you should still be OK. Even if your activity falls short in its image taking potential, your participation in it will certainly help fill those memory banks for subsequent recall when you return to the humdrum of normal life. Better to have given it a go and drawn a blank than not to have tried at all.

Sunset in much of Africa hovers between 6.00 and 7-00pm, and dawn between 5.00 and 6-00am. Traditionally the evening meal will take place soon after sunset. Game Drives will probably start just before dawn till mid-morning and again at "teatime" till just after sunset. The middle of the day is normally set aside for lunch and "siesta" as it is the hottest part of the day. If the potential evening socialising with staff and other guests is not what you consider to be an essential part of your safari experience then my advice is to get as much sleep as you can during the hours of darkness and try to forgo the several wasted hours occasioned by taking a siesta. This may not be activity or Game Drive time, and most of the larger species may also be taking their rest but, if you can stay awake, there will be a plethora of other subjects available around the Lodge. Birds and insects will still be on the go and flowering plants will be at their

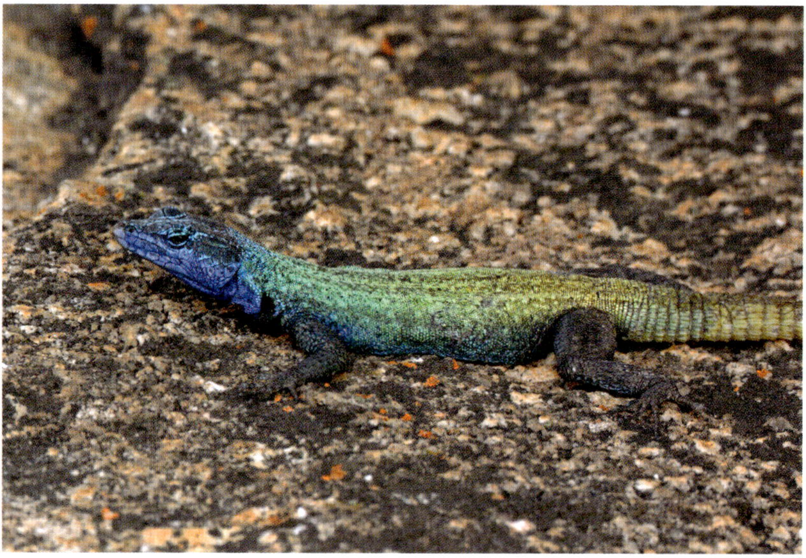

Rainbow Lizard at Rhodes Grave

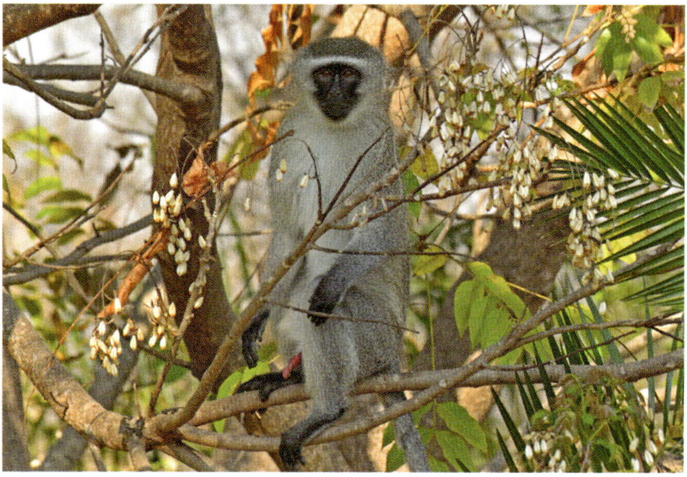

Vervet Monkey in lodge grounds

best. Even many small reptiles such as lizards will be active. Most lodges also seem to have a semi-resident troop of monkeys in the grounds. If you come across a snake and are not used to dealing with them then I would advise you to give them a wide berth. Treat them all as if they are venomous, even if you think that you recognise a harmless variety. That doesn't mean you have to bash them with a stick, just keep out of the way. Very few will chase you unless you are a threat. Even if you think that you recognise a harmless variety just remember that many of the more venomous species are closely resembled by certain of their non-venomous cousins, as the latter have sought protection by mimicking their more harmful relatives and adopting similar colouring and patterning. For the uninitiated this often makes telling similarly marked species apart very difficult. If you are unlucky enough to get one in your room then do not, under any circumstances, attempt to shift it. Shift yourselves - out the door - and get help from the staff. Many people in Africa who get bitten by snakes do so during the process of poking and prodding them with a stick to shift them. Leave it to someone who knows what to do - and is probably being paid to undertake such tasks - and remember that practically all snakes can move far faster than you and a number of them can spit their venom from a considerable distance!!

My advice would be to stay awake during the day - you can catch up on your sleep after you return home! - and, if there are no off-site activities available at that time of day, then just pad about the Lodge grounds and see what you can find. If you only find and photograph 1 extra subject a day then, after a 14 day safari, it will amount to 14 subjects that you would have missed! I would also use this time to take as many shots as possible of the Lodge and its environs. You can never have too many and, even if you bin a lot of them when you get back to Blighty, you will find the extensive coverage that you have obtained will be invaluable when putting together your holiday collection. They will often serve as such a memory trigger, when you go through them, as to almost allow you to experience the whole trip, all over again, from the comfort of your armchair. Even when out and about on Game Drives and other activities do not restrict your picture taking to just the major wildlife subjects. Take as much scenery and "fill-in" shots as you can. Your vehicles, your drivers and other staff, views, trees (there are some very classic African shapes to be had here), skylines, rivers and ravines. All will help to recapture the ambience of the moment when you are looking back in the months to come.

Often you will find yourself on a trip with quite a group of other people and individual exploration may not be feasible. Occasionally, however, you may find yourself in a situation where there are few fellow travellers and small group Game Drives are an option. It may even be possible to arrange something just for you and yours. If this is the case then seize the chance. I would never be so crass as to suggest that bribery should be the order of the day but I think that "lavish tipping", offered as an incentive and promised in advance of the trip against potential results, has a far nicer ring to it and may well open up opportunities. You can be sure that the staff will know the whereabouts of every major species in the area and a little "quid pro quo" (pardon the pun) on your part may just make the difference as to where you are taken.

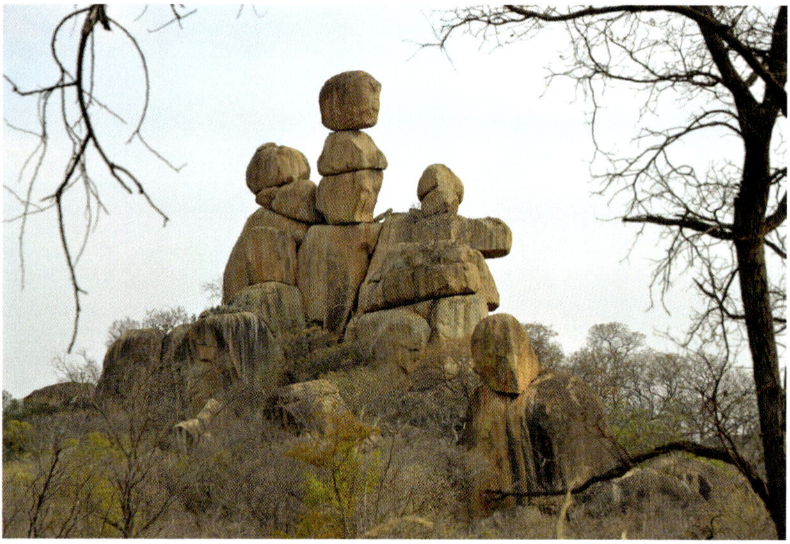

Balancing Rocks - Matopos Hills

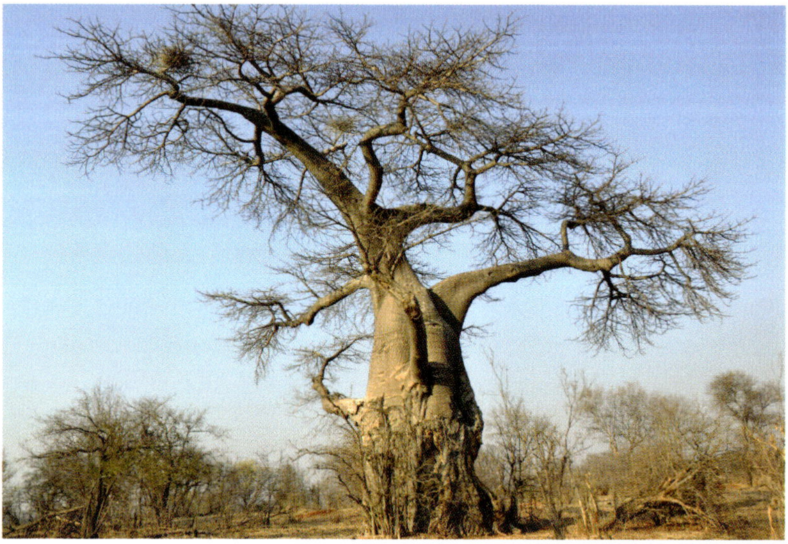

Bao - Bab Tree

By and large Game Drive vehicles will be such that you will either be guaranteed a window seat, or there will be an opening "sun roof" type of arrangement. Two useful accessories come to mind in the form of a window clamp and/or a beanbag, and neither of them is very expensive. Personally I would carry both. The downside to having a window seat is that your picture taking is likely to be limited to that side only of the vehicle and rules out fore and aft and the other side. However, a window clamp will support your camera and what, I imagine, will be your longest lens and allow you to make best use of those opportunities that do arise. The other advantage of a clamp is that, even with it and your gear in place, you can wind the window up most of the way and still operate the camera if the creature outside is of the kind that would like to drag you out for supper. A beanbag tends to be a bit more cumbersome and wobbly on a window's edge although, if that is all that you have, it will be better than nothing. In the case of the open rooftop the beanbag will probably be King. You can buy these from such as Wildlife Watching Supplies (address in the Links section of my website). The bit you buy is just like a pillowcase, or cushion cover, and takes up no more room than that when packed. From a space point of view it will probably have to travel empty and be filled when you arrive at destination. If you can't get a suitable filling such as beans or cereals (both fairly heavy but providing good support), or polystyrene beads or hydroponic pellets (both light but a bit less supporting), then stuff it with your spare laundry or tee-shirts. Even dry grass will be better than nothing. Anything that will afford some support but allow a little "give". The open top vehicles afford a 360degree view depending on how many other heads and shoulders are stuck out of them. Whatever situation you find yourself in do try to support your gear somehow if a tripod is not feasible in the circumstances, as your shots will be so much the better for it. Don't try to emulate the guys you see working unsupported, with huge lenses waving around as though they are conducting an orchestra. They will be working on high ISO's and shutter speeds and probably a very shallow depth of field - that is if they know what they are doing! Often they don't and their fancy gear is more a fashion accessory than a practical setup. Never be tempted to feel like a second class citizen if your gear is not of the huge and expensive kind. Make the most of what you've got and realise that, with it, you will stand a better chance with close-up photographic opportunities than they will with their monster lenses. The enforced restrictions of space within a Game Drive vehicle can also make super sized equipment something of an anti-social impediment. You'll find fellow travellers more prepared to speak to you at dinner if you haven't been knocking them about with your lens end all day!

There may be occasions when you are able to hire, or borrow, a vehicle and drive yourselves. Most of the Parks where this is possible will be reasonably well sign- posted so that you can find your way back afterwards. If they are not, and you have no Park map to guide you, then firstly take note of the direction of the sun relative to the direction that you are taking and, secondly, just jot down any turnings that you take as you come to them (together with any identifying features like "Big tree on the right" or "three rocks on the left"). All being equal, if you don't "come out the other end", then at least you will be able to retrace your steps. Driving in convoy is something that will happen from time to time and it can be a bit of a double edged sword. Having other vehicles in front of you can be very useful from the point of view of the number of eyes available for spotting. There is also, however, the chance that the lead vehicle may spook the animals and only those foremost passengers will get to see them. You will also find that Game Drive vehicles are somewhat like vultures. They seem to communicate by some form of extra sensory perception and can gather in large numbers rapidly and from a seemingly empty "sky". There is nothing more frustrating than to find that what little view of a subject you have managed to get is obscured by either other vehicles or the dust clouds of constant new arrivals. You also need to bear in mind that this African dust, much loved by digital camera sensors - and any other moving parts - is very fine in texture and plentiful in quantity. It can hang in the air for quite a time, especially if there is little or no breeze blowing. The more vehicles in front of you then the thicker it will be. Keep lens changes to a minimum, if at all, and make sure that you take an air puffer with you.

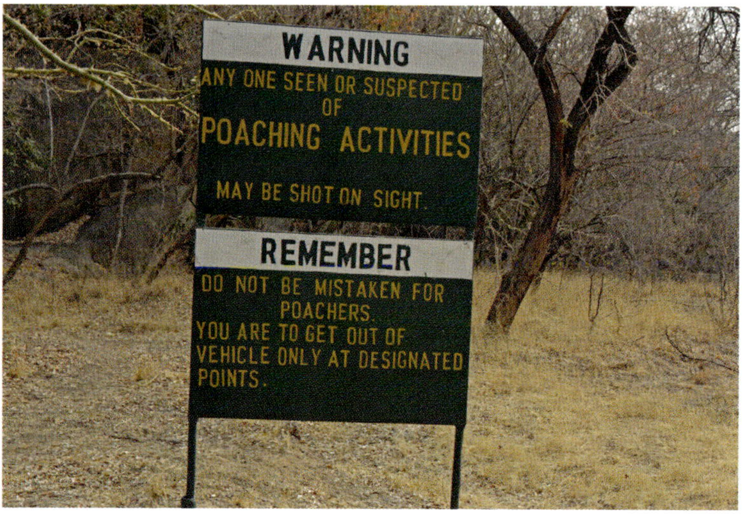

"Don't look like a poacher!!"

Personally I prefer my Game Viewing not to be at the mercy of the presence and behaviour patterns of others and, given the choice, I would prefer to strike out on my own. Admittedly eye numbers will be reduced, but at least if you encounter anything interesting no-one else will spook it for you and, in the absence of others, there will be a much greater chance of jockeying your vehicle into the most favourable position for your photography.

The golden rule in most reserves will be to "Stay in your car at all times", and there will be countless occasions when it will seem unnecessary, and you will be convinced that you would be able to get a much better shot by getting out. Without being there, looking over your shoulder, my advice would be "Do not do it". You may feel, especially in a Reserve where there are no major predators, that there can be no harm in it. You need to bear in mind, however, that while ever you are in the vehicle then most animals will take you to be a part of it and not see you as an independent threat. You will have seen countless documentaries where Big Cats, such as Lions or Tigers, walk right past a Game Drive vehicle, with bits of tourists hanging out all over the place, and spare it hardly a glance. Once you are out and on foot, however, then you become a human and subject to whatever sentiments the wildlife feels towards the human race. You may be the salt of the earth, and a real credit to your old mum, but the animals may not view you that way. Harmless looking creatures like warthogs and antelopes may well perceive you as a threat, or competition, especially if they have young nearby, and treat you accordingly. A warthog up the whoopsy is no laughing matter, especially if it is your whoopsy, and if you fall over during an encounter you could easily be badly gored or even killed. Heaven forbid but you could even be viewed by some of the larger animals as a potential partner. There is nothing more

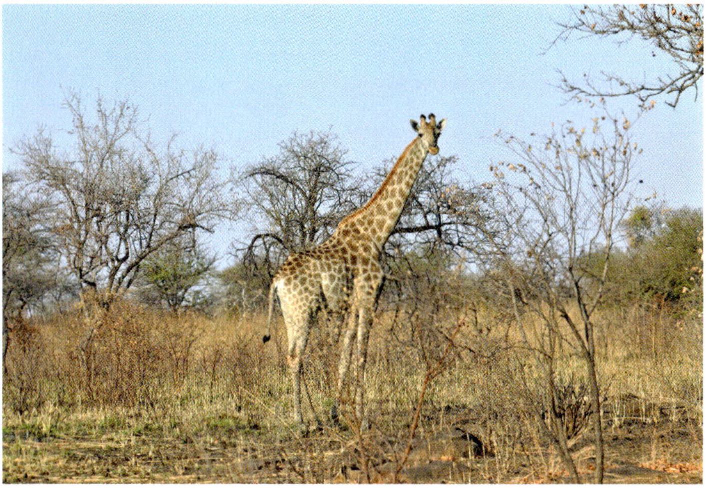

Giraffe at Hwange

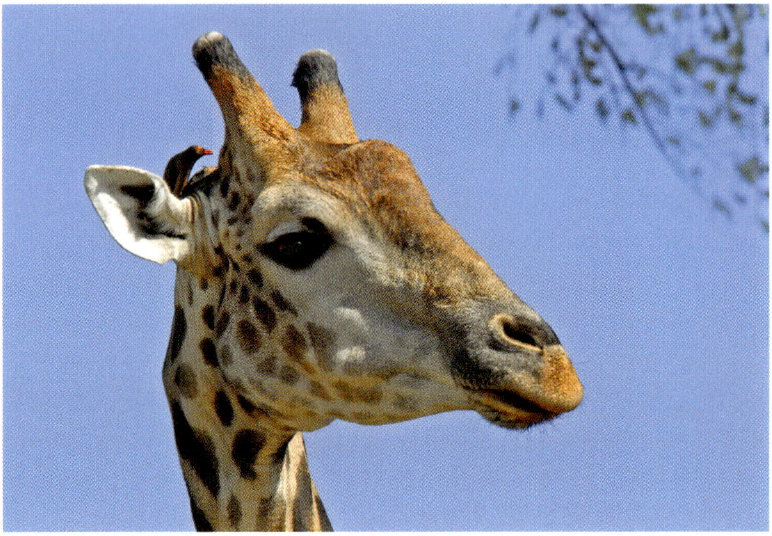

Giraffe with Oxpecker

docile looking than a Giraffe, but I can remember one evening when a colleague and I spent over two hours, crouched against a locked doorway behind a hastily grabbed sunlounger, whilst a rampant male Giraffe called Geoffrey waved and thrust his weapon of choice amorously at us and didn't seem prepared to take the fact that we both had headaches as an answer! Snakes often lie on, or just off, the road because it will have been warmed up by the sun and, if you are not used to dealing with them, they can be difficult to spot. In the reserves where there are predators then getting out of the vehicle can be even more fraught. You may think that the coast is clear, and that there is nowhere for a dangerous animal to hide, but you have to remember, especially in the case of big cats, that's how they earn a living! A stalking lion can flatten itself so close to the ground that it can almost hide behind a clump of grass. You also need to remember that virtually anything that can kill and/or eat you in Africa can certainly run/fly/swim a lot faster than you. Even car door handles can jam just when you need to jump in quick and the shirt that you haven't tucked in because you're on holiday is bound to get caught on the wing mirror as you fly by with all Africa in hot pursuit. Don't risk it. Stay in the vehicle and lean out the window. Your shots will likely be much better and naturally posed anyway, since even the most harmless of subjects will be less wary and at point of flight than they would be if you got out.

Certainly the most efficacious form of camera support when on foot is a tripod, and this is a piece of equipment on which I would not stint. For foreign travel weight can be a consideration and, since the decision was made by the Airlines that tripods represent a deadly weapon within the confines of an aircraft cabin, then you can no longer carry them as hand baggage and their collapsed size will be important as they will probably have to fit in your suitcase. Removing the tripod head for travelling can often shorten the effective length considerably - and reduce your overall baggage weight significantly because you can carry the head in a photographic jacket pocket where it will not be weighed. Modern Carbon-fibre tripods are fairly expensive but very light, and you will find yourself more prepared to carry it with you on your on-foot expeditions if it is not going to leave a nasty dent in your shoulder and an ache in your arm. If you get into the habit of carrying it already extended to eye height, even with the camera already mounted, you will find that you can quickly flick the legs apart and be in action as soon as any opportunity presents itself. Make sure that you set the tripod height such that you can look through your viewfinder whilst stood up straight. You will often spend quite some time waiting for the precise moment to take your shot and if you have to wait stooped over, or with shoulders hunched, then, apart from the discomfort incurred, you will end up with your hand shaking. Unless you are using a remote release (something I would also always advocate), either cable or electronic, then this shake, together with your heartbeat (which may be heightened with the excitement of the moment), will be transferred through to your shutter release and manifest itself as camera shake in your subsequent images.

Some Game Parks in Africa, such as those surrounding Lake Kariba in Zimbabwe or the likes of Chobe in Botswana, will offer waterborne Game Viewing trips in a variety of craft from canoes up to two or three storied Houseboats. Take advantage of these, if you can, as there is often the chance to get very close to a wide range of animals that will not see you as a person - just as part of a boat! Generally speaking smaller boats have the advantage as they can get up the myriad little creeks, inlets and streams that are typical of this type of habitat. The disadvantage of the smaller craft is that they are likely to bob up and down, even when not underway. If this is happening you do have choices. If you have Vibration Reduction, or VR, lenses then engage this option and set your camera speeds and apertures as advised for on horse or elephant back. This should take care of many of the problems and you should be able to hand-hold the camera. If you don't have the VR option then don't worry but still set your camera up for the fastest shutter/aperture combination that you can. If you want to work at lower speeds or ISO's then set up on a tripod, or other support, and wait for the top or bottom of a "bob". If you can get your timing right this should allow you to work at much slower shutter speeds without incurring "camera shake". If you are able to use the tripod option then don't lock your head. Rather just tighten it sufficiently to prevent your camera flopping about and you will then be able to keep a more controlled hold on it and follow through with any necessary re-alignments, necessitated by the boat movements, whilst still retaining the benefits of the tripod's support. If your trip is in a small boat make sure that you are comfortable right from the outset and in such a position as to be ready to take pictures as soon as the opportunity arises. You will quickly learn how not to make friends and influence people if you are constantly shifting around and "rocking the boat" - not to mention the inherent danger of trying to change position in such as a canoe, surrounded by crocs and wallowing hippos!

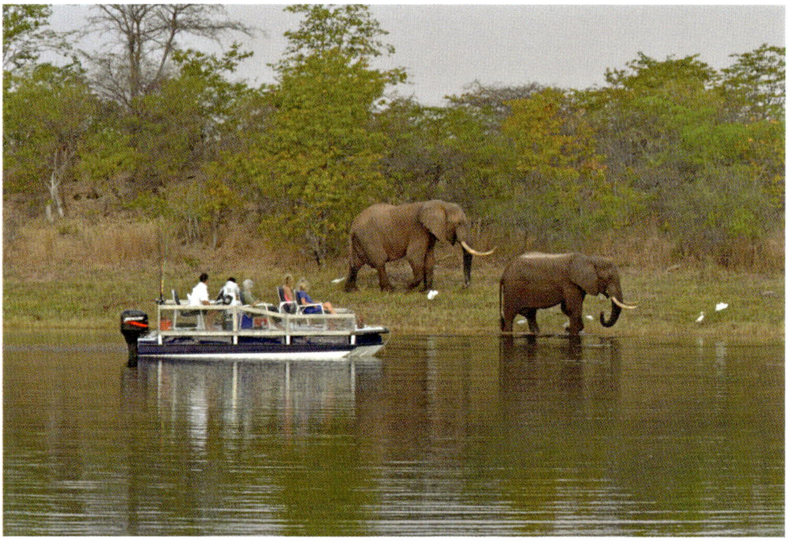

Game viewing trip from the "Karabezi".

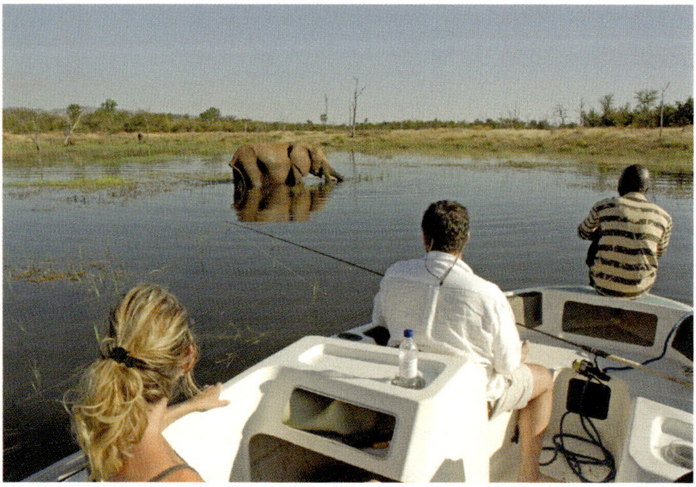

Game viewing on Lake Kariba

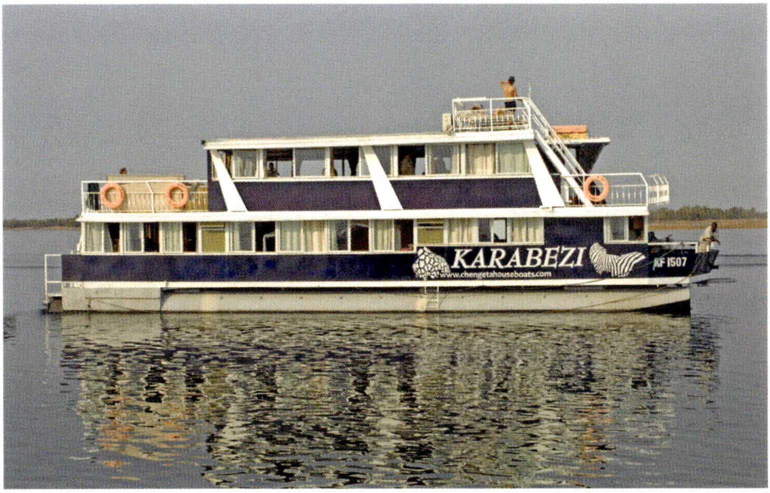

"Karabezi" Houseboat on Kariba.

Finally try not to suffer from tunnel vision. Keep a good look out all round, even when confronted by something spectacular. Elephants, Rhinos and even Lions can often have other species such as Hyenas or Wild Dogs either in association or close by. Keep an eye out in the surrounding bush and background for other potential subjects, as some of them can be just as stunning on the screen as some of the more major players in the game.

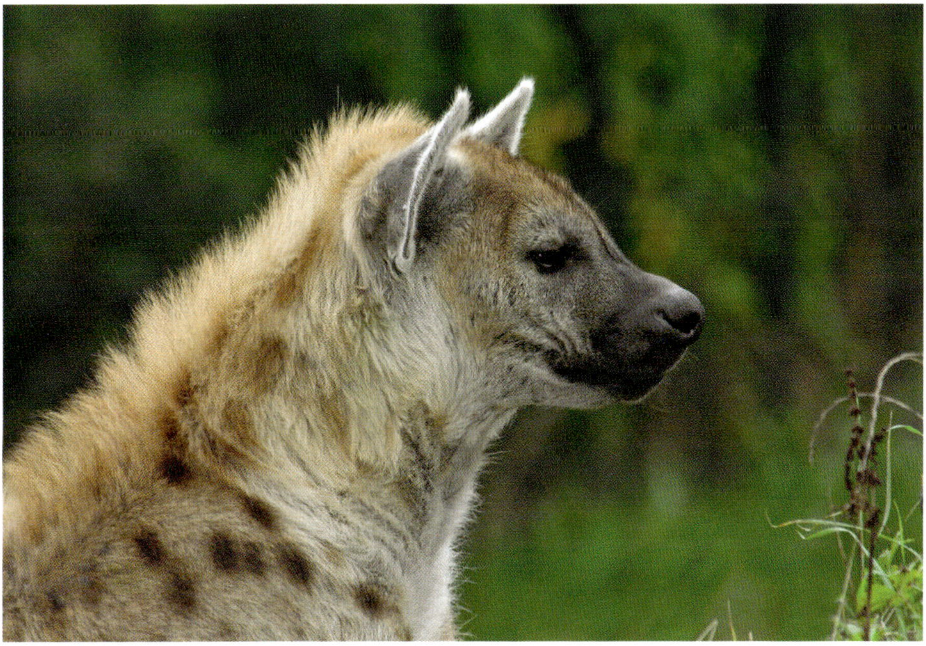

Spotted Hyena

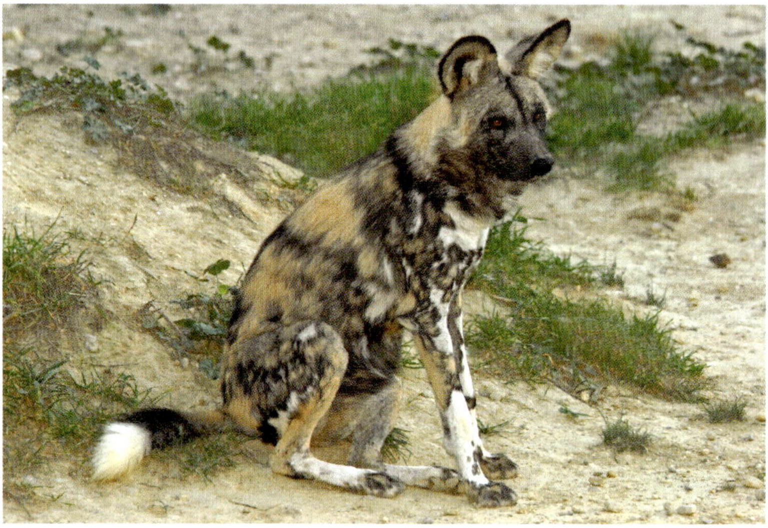

Cape Hunting Dog

There will be many sources of advice regarding your health care available. There will probably be information sheets with your trip booking confirmations and word of mouth from fellow travellers and trip leaders. Let common sense prevail but, at risk of sounding like a Dutch Uncle, be aware that there may not be too many shopping opportunities where you are going. Even if there are, there is no guarantee that there will be any amount of medical supplies in those shops that you can find. The safest bet is to take everything with you. Make sure that you are up to date with your jabs for that area and carry an "inoculation passport" with you showing what jabs you have had and when. Stomach upsets are covered elsewhere in this book (see chapter "To trip or not to trip" for further healthcare advice for situations such as these). Just be aware that, in the tropics, generally speaking, fungal and secondary infections are fairly prevalent. Personal hygiene is all-important and Dettol Soap can help deter insect parasites. Of prime importance is to treat any cuts or grazes immediately with some form of germicidal cream. Even small and innocuous looking ones. I would carry at least a rudimentary first aid kit, including something like Germolene, in your camera bag. Even if you don't have a plaster - get the cream on!

In Africa malaria and bilharzia can be a concern. Malaria is carried by the Anopheles mosquito and, daft though it may sound, the easiest prevention is to make sure that you don't get bitten in the first place. Insect sprays, mosquito nets, long sleeved shirts and full length trousers in the evenings, will all help. Anti-malarial drugs are obtainable in this country before you leave, though you may have to check as to which precise ones are suitable for the region that you plan to visit as some immunities have built up over the years. If you develop flu-like symptoms shortly after returning from your trip then make sure that you inform your doctor as to exactly where you have been. Bilharzia can be another problem, particularly in some parts of Africa. This is a disease carried by water snails and is normally contracted by swimming in infected areas. It is more prevalent in stagnant or slow moving water and in smaller ponds rather than larger lakes, although some of these latter can be a problem as well. Symptoms tend to be a bit of a jaundicey appearance and/or blood in the stool or urine. Again make sure that you remember to tell your doctor where you have been if you need to consult him. As above the easiest prevention is not to swim in infected water, but sometimes in the tropics this is easier said than done. On a piping hot day a cooling lake or river can seem like a great temptation and an invisible disease can be far from your mind. Just think to yourself, when presented with the temptation of taking a dip, how large a crocodile can grow, how far they can travel overland, how fast they can swim, how long they can hold their breath under water, and how they are distributed right throughout Africa, and that should make you head for a shower instead of the swim.

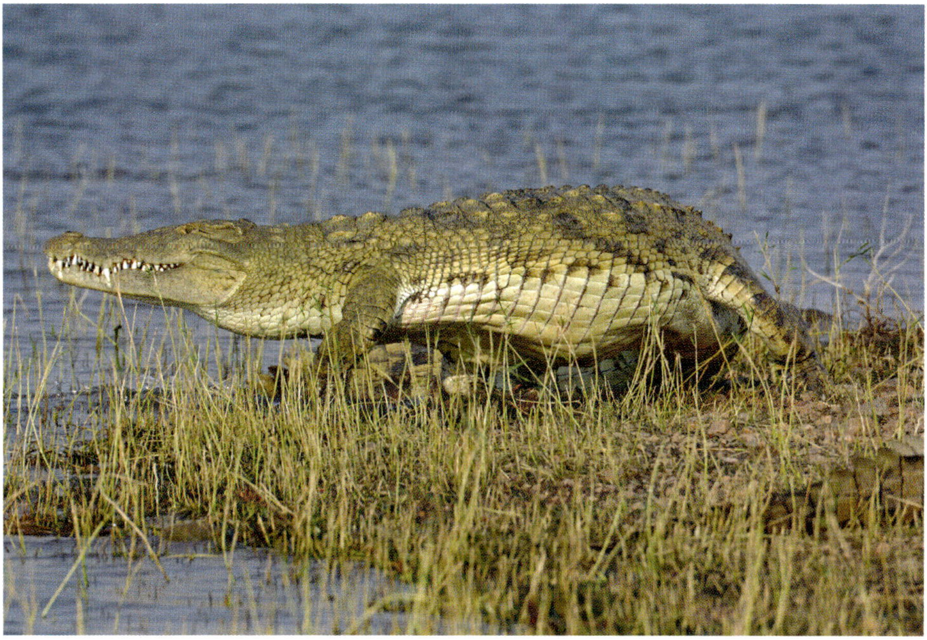

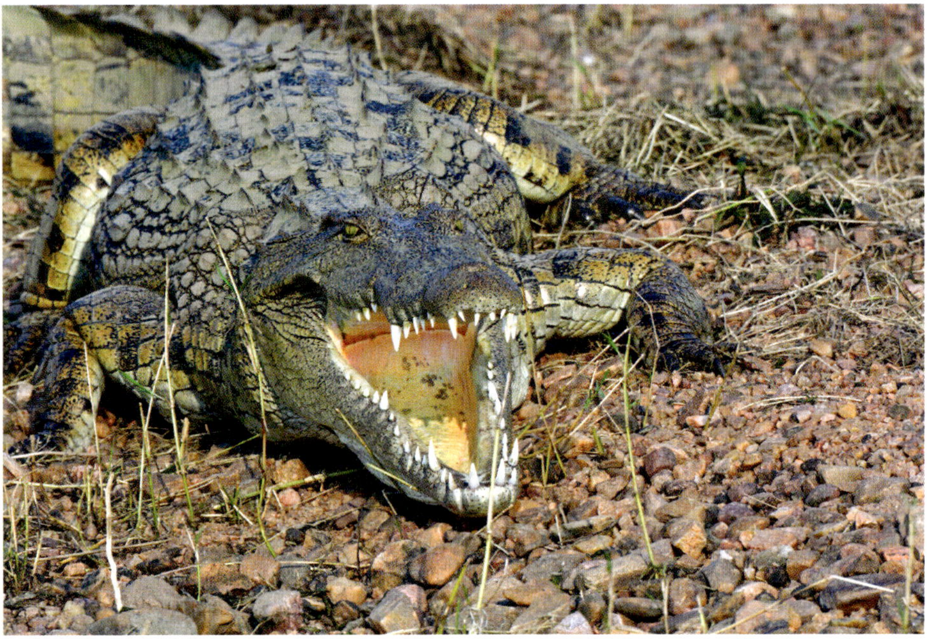

Crocodile Tonsils

To set your minds to rest both the above diseases are normally curable, especially if caught in the early stages. For this reason I would stress that any unusual and unexplained symptoms that follow foreign travel to any part of the world should be reported to your doctor, together with details of where you have been, as soon as they manifest themselves and not left for a few days to see if they go away!

Above all remember that by far the great majority of Safari travellers suffer no ill effects at all and have a truly wonderful time. Just use your common sense and don't leave your brains behind when you get on the plane.

Chapter 27

Going Home

Originally I had intended that this final chapter would cover a number of the more prolific sites that I have visited over the years. When I started putting pen to paper it quickly became obvious that what was intended to be covered by the scope of one chapter could well, in fact, become a book of its own, such was the potential volume of content. The question I was forced to ask myself was that, with a chapter such as this, where to begin? I could not possibly hope to offer a comprehensive guide to sites for everything and I cannot, personally, bring myself to skimp through it and produce a half-hearted effort that would be good for neither you nor I nor man nor beast. Rather, then, I have chosen to highlight just a few stop-offs in the road journey I would typically make to travel back to my home in Spain, on those occasions when time was not of the essence. I would hope that, should readers find themselves travelling in the areas covered, then it may just prove useful for them when deciding that perennial question when you are travelling of "where shall we go tomorrow?".

Rather than attempting to go into finite details of specific sites most of the advices in this chapter will be of a generalised nature and refer to favourite areas where I feel that it may be worth spending some days on a Wildlife Photographic trip though bearing always in mind that the situation in any locality can change dramatically depending on the timing of your visit.

France

To anyone travelling to the continent by road I would offer one or two tips to those who may be travelling via France.

If you are just passing through France on the way to another country, and using motorways, then your journey should be quite straightforward as there will be ample facilities along the way. Motorway travel can, however, be expensive in road tolls and devoid of Wildlife friendly stop-offs. Beware! There are now a number of un-manned motorway exit points where, to escape, you have to feed a machine with money or risk using a card, many of which may not be accepted. Whether or not the machine will give your card back to you if it doesn't work I cannot say as I have never risked it. There are also many more fixed-rate, shorter stretches, where you just pay a certain amount regardless of how far you are going. To avoid the embarrassment of creating a queue of fractious and intolerant Gallic drivers, and getting lessons in how many fingers makes two, at either of these points, carry a decent handful of mixed coinage – in euros – and life will be much easier.

If you are driving in France on non-motorway routes then remember that they run their lives on a different time clock than we do in the UK. Many commercial establishments shut for a sort of siesta period of varying durations in the early afternoons. This can include filling stations as well. Fuel can be a problem. Apart from the fact that in parts of France you can drive distances of up to, and even over, 100ks without passing a filling station, many of the ones that you do find will be un-manned and/or card only. This applies not only in the siesta period but in the evenings, and especially the weekends, as well. The majority of stations on minor road routes seem to shut for the night at any time from 5 or 6 o'clock onwards. Again many cards do not work and you should check with your card issuer, and channel crossing operator, before setting off into the great unknown with no means, other than a card, of paying your way. Personally I always carry a spare fuel can and never let my tank get below half full if I can avoid it.

Unless you can speak French then do take a small travel dictionary as, off the beaten track, many people either won't, or can't, speak English. No reason why they should, really, but too often we Brits assume that the world is under some kind of moral obligation to understand us, especially when the world in question is only a few miles away across the channel!

I will stick my neck out and say that there should be no need to pre-book your accommodation unless you are travelling in August. There are plenty of places to stay and you should have no trouble finding one. Many of these places, however, serve the evening meal at 7 to 7-30 so that if dinner is on your wishlist then it is wise to start looking for somewhere to stay by about 6 o'clock at the latest. If you stay in National chain Hotels such as Campanile or Ibis then you can always pick up a brochure when you pass one and that should contain location details for all their establishments in France.

I, personally, never pre-book, partly because I have never found the need to but mainly because you never know what you are going to come across, and there is nothing worse than having to abandon a prolific wildlife site earlier than you want to just because you are booked in somewhere miles away.

Spain

Spain is a far cry from France. Their body clocks are different but they still operate on the afternoon siesta system. On the whole life seems to be a much more laid-back affair than it is in France.

Siesta in Spain is normally of longer duration than it is in France but this is compensated for by the fact that they tend to work much later in the evenings. Most restaurants don't start to serve the evening meal until around 9 o'clock and it is very rare in Spain to feel pressurised into eating up and moving on. Food seems to be much different than in France as well. Personally I find it very difficult to leave the table in France feeling full but in Spain it is much easier. Both countries are a bit backward at coming forward with any quantity of veg with the main course but there are far more bits and bobs and side dishes to fill up with in Spain.

As in France there are plenty of places to stay, even if relatively off the beaten track. Spain has the added bonus of places called Hostals in which to stay, and even relatively remote villages have at least one. I think the name is off putting to many Brits as it conjures up images of fleapit back-packers Hostels. The difference here is between the "a" and the "e" in the name. A Hostal in Spain is invariably attached to a Spanish Bar and, whilst it is not classed as a Hotel, from inside the rooms you would probably never know. Spain has traditionally always been a country where people such as commercial travellers, work crews and the like move around constantly and over great distances. Hostals have sprung up to cope with this trade and can frequently be found in areas where the potential trade would not support a fully fledged Hotel. Their main business is usually the bar and the inevitable restaurant facility attached, so they can afford to offer accommodation without depending on it for their survival. Rooms normally come with TV and en suite facilities with the added advantage of being far more economical than a formal Hotel. Meals too tend to be much cheaper and you are more or less guaranteed of quality and quantity because they will be used to feeding many of the local workers who expect to leave the table feeling replete. An added bonus is that rates are usually based on a price per head, unlike in France where there is scarcely ever any allowance made for single travellers.

I have never known people to be other than friendly and the lengths to which they will go to help you out if you find yourself in any kind of trouble beggars belief.

Fuel tends to be cheaper than in France, particularly for Diesel, which is subsidised in Spain. Garages stay open quite late even in remote areas and, in any event, their proprietors are not un-used to being knocked up or called out of the bar when they are not in attendance at the pumps.

The Journey Home.

Wildlife diversitywise Europe starts to get interesting as soon as you cross the channel. When rising sea levels destroyed the land bridge across the channel only some 10 to 12,000 years ago the land on both sides enjoyed a similar climate and a similar diversity of species. Whilst the climate similarities still exist the diversity of wildlife on the mainland has increased tremendously, as it has benefited from the expansion in range of many erstwhile southern species, which have moved north as the general climate has warmed up. Until recently the channel has acted as a barrier and effectively prevented the bulk of the non-flying, low mobility, species from reaching and becoming established over here. The recent surge in cross-channel rail and road traffic, especially with the advent of the channel tunnel, and the regular import of fruit and veg from several continental countries, has led to a mini surge in species introductions, many of which are beginning to establish themselves.

In some parts of France every square inch of ground appears to be farmed but they seem to benefit from more copses, woodlands and hedgerows than we do over here and so your search can begin as soon as you are clear of the ports. I have travelled through France a great many times when journeying between the UK and my home in Spain and so I have had the opportunity, over the years, to establish something of a routine. Due to the size of the country I am able to vary my route considerably but, initially, I usually head for the area of La Brenne, which is pretty much central France. I normally catch an overnight ferry from Portsmouth to Caen, which arrives around 7 o'clock in the morning. This enables me to reach La Brenne about 2 o'clock in the afternoon without having to rush too much on the way. Located mid-way between Chatellerault and Chateauroux, La Brenne is a huge area dotted with hundreds of natural and man-made lakes, called etangs, which are managed to suit a number of different purposes. Many of them, together with their surroundings, are maintained for hunting and others either for coarse fishing or fish farming for carp, perch and other species for the table. Whilst many are fenced off, with no public access, many more offer open access and are an obvious magnet for a host of wildlife species of both the plant and animal kingdoms. Once there you can find accommodation in any of the picturesque little villages dotted around and there is a Parc Office with maps and brochures covering a host of activities and places to go.

From La Brenne I then drop down and across country towards the Massif Centrale around and below Clermont-Ferrand. If you avoid the motorways then the route from La Brenne is very rural and passes through some wonderful wild habitats. In spring you will see a host of Orchid species growing on roadside verges along with a profusion of wild spring flowers. They come with an attendant variety of associated insect species and there are many more early flying Butterfly species than you will find in the UK.

There is a toll-free motorway from Clermont to Montpelier and I usually join this just above Clermont itself. Still heading South I take the exit for Mende and thence to Florac which is where I would base my stay whilst in that area. Here you are right in the middle of the French Causse country and it is all a Wildlife Mecca. Monts Lozere and Aigoual are within easy reach but I have experienced fairly heavy snow, right into June, in this region so don't be too early when visiting. Late May is probably plenty early enough and at this time you can expect a variety of Orchids such as to blow the mind, together with Fritillaries, Pasque Flowers, Daffodils – Poeticus and Pseudonarcissus, Birthworts, Irises and Violets, to name but a few. June and early July are bonanza months in this region and the range of Butterflies on the wing has to be seen to be believed.

From here it is only a couple of hours drive down to the Camargue, which is well worth a visit. This is an enormous wetland area of lakes, lagoons and marshes and a plethora of plant and animal species abounds. Many of the towns are well worth a visit too and there is always an excellent range of seafood on offer in the restaurants. This is also the home of the famous "Wild Horses of the Camargue". This is one of those situations where the difference between Wildlife Photographers and Wildlife Artists comes to the fore. Spurred on from seeing various artists' impressions of these wonderful horses galloping through the shallows with their manes flying in the wind, I had always wanted to photograph them but had never been able to visit the Camargue until I first managed it in the early nineties. The reality of it was that the closest I got to my mental ideal was to see a number of very muddy and bedraggled white horses in very muddy and bedraggled barbed wired fields and, occasionally, a string of ready saddled mounts lined up by the road awaiting hire by intrepid(?) tourists wanting to experience a great adventure into the unknown! However, all that apart, it is a wonderful place and I would recommend a visit.

From there I usually cut across and head towards Andorra via Les

Corbieres. This mountain range is not particularly spectacular as far as mountain ranges go, but the wealth of plantlife more than compensates for the lack of stunning scenery. This area seems to benefit more from the proximity of the Mediterranean than do many of the other Mountain Ranges, and so its season seems to begin somewhat earlier than many of the others. The displays of terrestrial Orchids and other bulbous plants can be stunning and, apart from the quantity, there are a number of species, sub-species, forms and varieties that are peculiar to this region alone. Tuchan is a good village for a base and the Hotel in the middle of the village operates an excellent menu that incorporates a "keep on coming back" buffet of splendid variety. This is vineyard country and I must say that the local brew slips down very well at the end of a hard day. Actually it slips down very well at any time of any kind of day!

From the Corbieres I usually cut across to Andorra where the scenery has to be some of the best of the journey. I have covered this area more fully in the chapter based on Narcissus pallidiflorus and would refer you to that for more detail.

From Andorra it is another cross-country route to take me to what is probably my favourite montane region in Europe – The Spanish Pyrenees. The area that really squeaks my pips is the Val d'Aran. My favourite region is the area around the town of Vielha. This whole region is so rich in Wildlife that, despite being a regular visitor for some 20 years now, I can still find plenty to photograph that I have not seen or photographed before. The highlights for me are plants from May through to Sept, Butterflies mainly in June and July, and Grasshoppers and Bush Crickets in Aug and Sept. The local Tourist board is very active in promoting the area and produces a flyer type map of mountain tracks in the area. These can be obtained from any Hotel, most of the shops or any of the Tourist Board kiosks in the area. Do yourselves the favour of a lifetime. Get one of these maps and take the route that is posted to Saut Deth Pish. This track starts at its Southern end near Salardu and its Northern end at Arros just north of Vielha in the direction of France. Whilst it is not for the fainthearted I rate it as OK for a decent car with reasonable ground clearance. Certainly the first half is, when approaching from the northern end, as it is tarmac for the first 10 or so kilometres. When the tarmac runs out at a sort of picnic area you can park-up and walk a few hundred metres to a very photographable cascade. After this you can carry on up the track by car, though from here on it is gravel. This track will then take you right up and over the mountain and drop down towards Salardu on the other side. In between you will be in the nearest thing to Botanical and Invertebrate Paradise as you can get here on earth. If you don't like heights then I would suggest that you give this a miss but I have done it on countless occasions and come through unscathed!

Mammals are about as well, though many of the species that are regularly hunted are hard to find. Various Deer, Ibex, Chamois, Marmots, Foxes, Squirrels, Martens and many more are all likely to cross your path, particularly if you are travelling off the busier tourist routes. Wolves, Bears and Lynx still exist in Spain though you would, indeed, be lucky to see one and even luckier if you managed to photograph it.

All these mountain ranges host a wide variety of birdlife and many species are surprisingly approachable. Probably because there are not enough humans around for mankind to have acquired a predatory reputation, where birds are concerned, in that type of setting. Many areas support resident populations of Griffon Vultures and you can often see the odd Egyptian and Black Vulture flying with them. In the Pyrenees there is always a chance of sighting Lammergeier as well but you need to be lucky to do so. There are a great number of Raptors that are resident in these ranges and, of course, there is a much wider selection that passes through on migration. Assorted Buzzards, Eagles, Kites, Hawks and small Falcons can be seen at more or less any time of the year but Spring and Autumn are probably the most productive periods.

From the Pyrenees I normally drop down through Lleida and then cut inland slightly to reach the Montes Universales around the picturesque towns of Albarracin and Cuenca. Initially the route passes through the Rioja region and I often feel obliged to stop and check that they are maintaining their standards! The scenery in the Universales is stunning though nowhere near as rugged as further north in the Pyrenees. Some fairly impressive forests of lichen covered pines are a regular feature of the landscape and, though there is not much that grows underneath them, they are dispersed enough that there are plenty of areas in between. I usually base myself in a village called Tragacete, where there are a number of places to stay, though I have taken recently to staying in a wonderfully Spanish Hostal, in the village of Frias de Albarracin, which offers excellent value for money. Once again this is a wonderful area for plants though its altitude is such that it can be a late starter in the year. Late May is plenty soon enough and there are a wonderful range of bulbous, and other, plants awaiting you if you get your timing right.

After leaving the Montes Universales I am only about four hours from home and so I usually proceed there without more ado. All is not then over, however, and I feel that I can best describe the joys of the area in which I live, in the words of an article I wrote a few years ago for a local periodical.

"Castell de Castells."

Moving to Castells in the early 80's I was part of a trickle to Spain soon to become a deluge. I cannot recall there being any other "Brits" actually living in the village at the time, though one or two moved in shortly after. English, at that time, was certainly a foreign language and my "Guide to Holiday Spanish" was the next best thing to useless. However waving my arms with a Spanish accent seemed to enable me to communicate sufficiently to be able to buy the staples of life though the range available then, as opposed to now, was somewhat limited to say the least. Those were the days when visitors from the U.K. brought "survival" parcels with them containing all the goodies without which you felt that life was incomplete – Bacon, Cheddar Cheese, Branston Pickle, Worcester Sauce, Teabags and decent Toilet Paper! Then came "Pepe la Sal" supermarket with all its foreign delicacies and independent life began again.

I moved out in an October and quickly realised that no-one had told me that, even in Spain, there is a winter! My old village house was an experience such as I had never encountered before and the tales of my first few weeks are legion. Many of the roads, scenic though they may have been, were such that, whereas you may have attempted them in a hire car, you most certainly would not have tackled them in your own, especially during or after a storm of which we had many more then than now.

However then came Spring and I found myself in a Wild Flower Utopia.

I had spent the bulk of my adult life working with Wildlife both at large and in captivity but, in the U.K., that life had been lived at such a rate, and I was so busy being busy, that I never had time to look around for looking around's sake. Now, with time on my hands for the first time in years, I found myself surrounded by the forebears and counterparts of plants I had long known in cultivation but had never encountered in the wild.

Many people living a sedentary life on the coast will never know the botanical jewels they are missing. The main flowering season up here is a little later than on the coast and extends from late March through June. I will not, here, deal with the ubiquitous species known to all with a floral bent, such as the Antirrhinums, Umbellifers (Cow Parsley type plants such as Fennel, Moon Carrot and a host of others) and other common species but will confine myself to those rarities of the plant world for which many Alpine Gardeners would give their eye teeth.

Amongst the earlier flowering of these are two Narcissi of which one, Narcissus assoanus (who dreams up these names?) otherwise known as Rush Leaved Narcissus, is fairly widely distributed in Spain whilst the other,

Narcissus dubious, is quite rare. The first is a diminutive and highly scented variety and, approaching Castells "the back way" via Tarbena, it can be found, in March, from the ascent to Col de Rates right through to the hills just above the village. This flower is a typical Daffodil Yellow in colour and almost exactly resembles some of those better known garden "trumpet varieties" - but in miniature. Plants are only a few cms high and easily overlooked. The second, N.dubious, enjoys a similar distribution but in only intermittent populations and is never numerous – certainly in this locality. The flowers are the purest white and there are several to a stem. Again it is a diminutive and highly scented plant and easy to miss. During the same flowering period as these latter two species the sharp eyed can find one of the earlier Bee Orchids, Ophrys speculum or Venus' Mirror Orchid, scattered throughout. Bright blue in colour, diminutive in stature and a joy to behold. We are, indeed, fortunate to have several distinctive Bee Orchids around the village and the list makes impressive reading. Sombre Bee, Ophrys fusca, is an early flowerer though not striking in appearance when compared to the slightly later Sawfly, Ophrys tenthredinifera, and Woodcock, Ophrys scolopax. Even these last two are put in the shade by the strident colours of Yellow Bee Orchid, Ophrys lutea, which can be found in a number of localities near the village with a particularly robust colony just above Pla de Alt. Normal Bee Orchid, Ophrys apifera, deserves a mention as, around Castells, it occurs in a variety of striking colour forms with sepals from pristine white to the deepest purple. The most rewarding to find is, for me, the enigmatic Early Spider Orchid, Ophrys sphegodes, which makes up for its lack of colour with a deep black speculum on a maroon coloured labellum surrounded by an almost "bushy" growth of black "hair" looking for all the world like a well groomed beard.

With diligence all these Bee Orchids can be found on the hills overlooking the village and, in addition, several other Orchid species will be bumped into along the way. Early on and hard to overlook is the local form of Early Purple Orchid, here occurring as sub-species Olbiensis, and noted for its variety of striking colour forms and to be found in good numbers on the slopes overlooking the swimming pool and higher up near the Castle. Twice only, in 20 years of searching, I have found the amazing and shocking pink Orchis italica, enjoying the English name of Naked Man Orchid – for reasons which will be immediately obvious to anyone fortunate enough to find one!

For the discerning seeker in April the nodding bells of Fritillaria hispanica can be found in scattered populations though a good eye is needed to pick them out. Many of the rarities such as Burning Bush, Dictamnus, of Biblical Fame and occurring above Pla de Alt, demand a knowing eye to spot them among the massed ranks of Cistus,Vetches, Restharrows, Cranesbills and Geraniums, Flaxes, Sages, Convolvulus in all its myriad of colour forms and that truly lovely plant Meadow Rue, Thalictrum tuberosum, to be found in relative profusion on the Pine covered slopes of the Serellas.

In May the humbler named Man Orchid, Aceras anthropophorum, can be found on El Faro and on the foothills around Pla de Alt with its spike of unassuming but quietly attractive flowers each closely resembling a caricature of a man and giving rise to its name.

Finders of the earlier mentioned Fritillarias would do well to pay attention to the surrounding area since Wild Tulips, Tulipa australis, often grow in similar terrain and are a plant not to be missed, being of a striking Yellow colour to rival even the above mentioned Narc assoanus.

Diminutive Violets and other ground hugging flowers such as Campanulas (also to be found in a variety of erect forms), Helianthemums or Rockroses, in Yellow or Pink, together with a host of taller and more obvious plants clamour for attention. Spanish Rusty Foxglove, Wild Lavender, assorted Alliums, Blue Alkanet, and the hard to miss Blue and Purple flowers of a range of Echiums such as Purple Vipers Bugloss catch the eye with seemingly little effort.

Occasionally, if fortunate, beneath Cistus bushes on hillsides which, in Autumn, are home to a profusion of the beautiful purple Crocus saltzmanii, can be found the unique bright red parasitic plant Cytinus ruber which, in keeping with the wide variety of Broomrapes, Orobanchaceae, that can be found around the village, feeds on the roots of other plants such as Cistus and Restharrow.

There are a considerable number of books and Field Guides available to assist in the identification of flowering plants in the area. Any of those covering Mediterranean Flowers will be of use together with anything on Alpines. For the more dedicated, and if it can still be obtained, is the book that I have found most comprehensive entitled The Flowers of South West Europe by Polunin and Smythies ISBN No 0-19-288178-7 by Oxford University Press. If possible, when choosing your book/s look for those that use photographic plates as opposed to artificially coloured illustrations as the two depictions of the same subject can be worlds apart.

Happy hunting.

Many of the places that I have mentioned seem to be in the context of their plants, and I would not like to give the impression that this is all that is on offer. Obviously where there are plants there is also the associated diversity of other Wildlife species that invariably co-exists with them. I, therefore, crave your indulgence and forgiveness if I have inadvertently given the impression that, in certain places, it is only the plants that are worth a visit. All the areas that I have specifically mentioned enjoy an exceptional selection of Wildlife of all shapes, sizes, colours, kingdoms, families and genera, and all of them would stand alone as a sole destination for a Photographic holiday. There are many other Mountain Ranges in France and Spain too numerous to mention, and they all excel in the diversity of their Wildlife populations. It is my intention, now that I have learnt the lesson of this last chapter, to produce a comprehensive Site Guide to the Mountain Ranges of France, Spain and possibly Italy, and I can only say, in the vernacular, "Watch this space!"

Chapter 28

Conclusion

In conclusion, speaking as one whose sword has always been mightier than his pen, I must confess to a certain relief at now being able to put that pen in a drawer rather than having to put it "to paper" yet again. Even I, positive in outlook though I may be, must admit to having had the odd suspicion that this work would never be done. It was initially intended as a one-off but it seems to have spawned one or two offshoots along the way.

I had always intended to attempt "A Wildlife Photographer's guide to the Bulbous Plants of Europe". That idea has now probably been supplanted by, and partly incorporated into, the much broader scope of "A Wildlife Photographer's guide to the Mountain Regions of Europe". These aspirations probably fall under the caption of "to travel hopefully is better than to arrive" since, having just finished this book I "needs must" address myself to the publishing of it.

If you are reading this in illustrated hard or paperback form then I guess I managed it. If not then there is a place in the bottom of my "Ideas" drawer labelled "and another one bit the dust" where this manuscript will probably see out the rest of its days.

In the meantime I sincerely hope that the foregoing chapters have been of some help to as many as possible of you as you set out on the route to Wildlife Photographic stardom and I most fervently wish that I may have been able to prompt some to move forward who were teetering on the brink and not sure whether to proceed or not.

If you feel that I can assist you in your interests in any way then please get in touch. My email line is always open and, although it sometimes coughs and splutters when it comes to replying, it usually gets there in the end.

Brian Pettit.